Education, Human Rights and Peace in Sustainable Development

Edited by Maigul Nugmanova, Heimo Mikkola, Alexander Rozanov and Valentina Komleva

Published in London, United Kingdom

IntechOpen

Supporting open minds since 2005

Education, Human Rights and Peace in Sustainable Development
http://dx.doi.org/10.5772/intechopen.73483
Edited by Maigul Nugmanova, Heimo Mikkola, Alexander Rozanov and Valentina Komleva

Contributors
Andrew Coggins Jr, C.L. Alexandra Costa, Jorge Aillapán Quinteros, Anton Gertsen, Vladimir Rumyantsev, Solomon Tekle Abegaz, Erika Serfontein, Claudia Chang, Sapir Handelman, Judith Cochran, Hugh Murray, Anthony Luder, Laurent Gabriel Ndijuye, Pambas Basilius Tandika, Alexander Rozanov, Valentina Vycheslavovna Komleva, Alexandra Baranova, Furat Al Mutairi, Maria Ivanchenko, Arkadi Bessonov, Ludmila Ilicheva, Aleksandra Khramova, Maria Ilicheva, Oksana Gryuk, Alina Papsheva, Maigul Nugmanova, Nanche Billa Robert, M Mahruf C Shohel, Gias Uddin, Julian Parker-McLeod, Daniel Silverstone, Elena N. Antonova, Mikhail Smirnov, Olga Belyaeva, Maria Krotovskaya, Tatiana Grabovich, Zaru Utekova, Dmitry Medvedev, Natalya Ogneva, Elvira Shishlo, Amina Surpkelova, Irina Kopachevskaya, Irina Sokurova, Yulia Borisova, Fernando Joao, Artyom Pakulskikh, Polina Chernova, Alexandra Khramova, Jesus Yaniz Gonzalez

First published in London, United Kingdom, 2020 by IntechOpen
IntechOpen is the global imprint of INTECHOPEN LIMITED, registered in England and Wales, registration number: 11086078, 5 Princes Gate Court, London, SW7 2QJ, United Kingdom
Printed in Croatia

British Library Cataloguing-in-Publication Data
A catalogue record for this book is available from the British Library

Additional hard and PDF copies can be obtained from orders@intechopen.com

Education, Human Rights and Peace in Sustainable Development
Edited by Maigul Nugmanova, Heimo Mikkola, Alexander Rozanov and Valentina Komleva
p. cm.
Print ISBN 978-1-83969-041-9
Online ISBN 978-1-83969-042-6
eBook (PDF) ISBN 978-1-83969-043-3

For EU product safety concerns:
IN TECH d.o.o., Prolaz Marije Krucifikse Kozulić 3, 51000 Rijeka, Croatia, info@intechopen.com or visit our website at intechopen.com.

Meet the editors

Maigul Nugmanova graduated from Byelorussian State University with a degree in Political Economy and from Karaganda Economic University with a PhD in Economic Sciences. Her dissertation focused on gender aspects in economic theory. She was a Fulbright Scholar at the American University, Washington, DC, where she focused on gender economics and food security. Currently she is Director of Gender Economics Research Center (GERC), co-financed by Soros Foundation Kazakhstan, at the Narxoz University (Kazakhstan). Dr. Nugmanova was a project leader/researcher of UN Women project on *Women's unpaid labor in Kazakhstan/modeling of the economic impact of care services institutionalization on women's employment and the economy.* Before she started working at GERC, Dr. Nugmanova was a Head of International Office of Kazakh Ablai Khan University of International Relations; Head of International Programs Department of Kazakh National Agrarian University; country coordinator of ERASMUS+ Quality Assurance in Higher Education and SSDS TEMPUS projects; and FAO Extension in Agriculture project coordinator in KazNAU. She was a UNDP national expert for assessment and analysis of the UN/UNDP programs/projects in gender mainstreaming, and elaborated UNDP CO Gender Mainstreaming Strategy. She was a national consultant-researcher on human trafficking in Central Asia with the IOM Technical Cooperation Center in Austria. Dr. Nugmanova was an expert for FIBAA European accreditation agency and Educational Advising Center Director in Astana of Soros Foundation Kazakhstan. She is a fellow of Knowledge Networking and Capacity Building on Gender, Macroeconomics and International Economics Program (USA). She is also a member of Central Eurasian Studies Society.

Heimo Mikkola obtained his PhD from the University of Kuopio, Finland, where he has been teaching before and between his foreign assignments since 1972. Prior to that, he taught for two years at the University of Oulu, Finland, where he obtained his MSc in 1970. In 1988, he became an adjunct professor at the University of Eastern Finland. He has well more than 30 years of experience in development policy and cooperation through working with growing responsibilities in international organizations, including the African Development Bank Group (AfDB), the European Union, UN System, and World Bank. As Resident Representative of FAO and regularly acting Resident Coordinator of the entire UN System, he managed the daily operations and donor coordination in six countries in the period 1989–2007: Mozambique, Swaziland (now Eswatini), Malawi, Gambia, Nigeria, and Uruguay. These regional and country-level activities included education management, food aid and food security, diplomatic representation as Head of the Mission, HIV/AIDS counseling, human rights, peacekeeping, refugee problems, and women in development.

Dr. Alexander S. Rozanov is a specialist in Global Security and a graduate of Lomonosov Moscow State University (Russia). He is the author of more than 60 scientific publications. After graduating, Dr. Rozanov worked in the Russian Ministry of Foreign Affairs and the Russian Government. In 2014 he received his Ph.D. in Politics from Lomonosov Moscow State University. From 2014 to 2017, Dr. Rozanov was invited as a guest lecturer in several well-known universities – University of California, Santa Barbara (USA), Paris-Sorbonne (France), and Wroclaw University (Poland). Dr. Rozanov specializes in the analysis of global and regional conflicts, as well as the global dynamics of world development. He is a member of the European International Studies Association (Great Britain). Dr. Rozanov is an Associate Professor at the Faculty of Regional Studies and International Cooperation at the Russian Academy of National Economy and Public Administration.

Dr. Komleva is a dean of the Faculty of Foreign Regional Studies and Regional Administration, as well as a head of Department of Foreign Studies and International Collaboration (Russian Academy of National Economy and Public Administration, Moscow, Russia). She is a Doctor of Sociology and a general director of the Institute of Political Management. Since 2010, Dr. Komleva has been a member of the Coordination Council under the Chairman of the Council of Federation of the Federal Assembly of the Russian Federation for Interaction with Civil Society Institutions. Dr. Komleva is the author of more than 200 publications.

Contents

Preface

This book has three main topics in the title: Education, Human Rights, and Peace. There is a two- or three-way relationship between these topics: right to education has been recognized as a human right - education has a role in peace-building. All three topics have a significant role in sustainable development. The aim of sustainable development is to balance our economic, environmental and social needs, allowing prosperity for current and future generations [1]. Countries must be allowed to meet their basic needs of employment, food, energy, water and sanitation. Everybody has the right to a healthy, clean and safe environment. The environmentally sustainable economic growth is synonym to the prevalent concept of Sustainable Development, the goal of which is to achieve balance/harmony between environmental sustainability, economic sustainability and socio-political sustainability [1].

Part I. Education and Sustainable Development

The Universal Declaration of Human Rights states that everyone has the right to education, hence the right applies to all individuals, although children are considered as the main beneficiaries [2]. However, International law does not protect the right to pre-primary education and international documents generally omit references to education at this level [3].

Education is the act or process of imparting knowledge, especially at a school, college, or university. Education encourages independent thinking, and it opens doors to new ideas. Independent thinkers tend to try to make sense of the world and draw their own conclusions instead of blindly following the beliefs of others. Independent thinkers may be less likely to join militant groups or be followers and may instead be leaders towards positive change and action [4].

The world surrounding schools have changed essentially since the beginning of the 21st century – the effects of globalization and the challenges of a sustainable future. Skills and competencies required in society and working life have changed so that it is necessary to examine educational contents, pedagogy and schools' working practices. The quality of higher education is an important prerequisite of sustainable social and economic development of society. Global reforms are needed in education management in relation to changes in the operating environment and professional qualification [5]. This book comprises a chapter on the police education in the United Kingdom which is a good example of the changes in competencies required in contemporary society.

Part II. Human Rights and Equality in Sustainable Development

What are Human Rights? They are rights inherent to all human beings, regardless of race, sex, nationality, ethnicity, language, religion, or any other status.

Human rights include the right to life and liberty, freedom from slavery and torture, freedom of opinion and expression, the right to work and education, and many more. The concept of human rights also includes the right to quality food, and one of the most important human rights is gender equality. Everyone is entitled to these rights, without discrimination [6]. It is said to be one of the great achievements of the United Nations that they created a comprehensive body of human rights law – a universal and internationally protected code to which all nations can subscribe, and all people aspire. The United Nations has defined a broad range of internationally accepted rights, including civil, cultural, economic, political and social rights. It has also established mechanisms to promote and protect these rights and to assist states in carrying out their responsibilities. Various chapters in this book demonstrate, unfortunately, that there are still people and nations not respecting the Universal Declaration of Human Rights [7]. Chapters cover topics like civil war, human abuses, the vulnerability of indigenous people, gender inequalities in the economy, abortion, epilepsy, lack of health equities in maternal and child health, and democracy or lack of it.

Part III. Peace

Originally proposed and developed by the United Nations, International Peacekeeping has become an international means of maintaining and establishing peace on behalf of the entire world community under the auspices of the UN [8]. After the end of the Cold War, peacekeeping has firmly entered into the spectrum by means of various regional and sub-regional agreements and organizations.

The main actions within the framework of peacekeeping process have been called "peacekeeping operations", which could be defined as a set of political, diplomatic, military, and other forms and methods of collective efforts to restore international peace and stability in conflict areas through a system of coordinated measures to prevent, reduce, resolve, and eliminate the consequences of international, sub-regional, and local conflicts.

This book intends to provide the reader with a comprehensive overview of the recent peacekeeping activities, as well as the most important international initiatives of peace-building in the world's "hot spots".

The finalization of this book coincided with difficult times for the whole world due to the COVID-19 pandemic, which exacerbated all existing inequalities and contradictions. But at the same time, this universal disaster demonstrated the need for the long-standing concern for the humanization of people and respecting the core values of life, namely freedom, equality and security for everyone.

We sincerely hope that this book will contribute to the desire of humanity to make the world a better place.

We want to thank Author Service Managers Lada Božić, Rebekah Pribetić and Dajana Pemac for their time-consuming efforts to get all the authors to deliver their chapters after corrections. Without their active attitude, some important chapters would have been left out of the book.

Maigul Nugmanova
Gender Economics Research Center,
Narxoz University,
Kazakhstan

Heimo Mikkola
University of Eastern Finland,
Finland

Alexander Rozanov and Valentina Komleva
Russian Academy of National Economy and Public Administration,
Russia

References

[1] Mondal P. What is the Importance of Sustainable Development? Available from: www.sd-commission.org.uk/pages/what-is-sustainable-development.html [Accessed: 25 April 2020]

[2] Wikipedia. Right to Education. Available from: https://en.wikipedia.org/wiki/Right_to_Education [Accessed: 25 April 2020]

[3] Beiter KD. The Protection of the Right to Education by International Law. Martinus Nijhoff Publishers; 2005

[4] Central Asia Institute. Education For Peace: Top 10 Ways Education Promotes Peace. 2017. Available from: https://centralasianinstitute.org/top-10-ways-education-promotes-peace [Accessed: 25 April 2020]

[5] Mikkola H, Nugmanova M. Global Education Management. Bibliographical References, Notes and Comparations. Almaty, Kazakhstan: Kazakh Ablai Khan University of International Relations and World Languages; 2019. 144 p. ISBN 978-601-270-379-5

[6] United Nations. Peace, Dignity and Equality on a Healthy Planet. Available from: https://www.un.org/index.html [Accessed: 25 April 2020]

[7] United Nations. Universal Declaration of Human Rights. Available from: https://www.un.org/universal-declaration-human-rights/index.html [Accessed: 25 April 2020]

[8] Wikipedia. History of United Nations peacekeeping. Available from: https://en.wikipedia.org/wiki/History_of_United_Nations_peackeeping [Accessed: 24 August 2020]

Section 1

Education and Sustainable Development

Chapter 1

Police Education in the United Kingdom: Challenges and Future Directions

M. Mahruf C. Shohel, Gias Uddin, Julian Parker-McLeod and Daniel Silverstone

Abstract

This chapter outlines the historical development of police education in the United Kingdom, more precisely in England and Wales, and highlights new strategies and planning for the professional development of the police. There is a plethora of research carried out regarding professionalism in policing to meet the needs and challenges of the twenty-first century. Considering the recent developments in police education and training, this chapter mainly discusses three newly introduced routes for recruitment and education of police constables under the Policing Education Qualifications Framework (PEQF), namely Police Constable Degree Apprenticeship (PCDA), Degree Holder Entry Programme (DHEP), and Pre-Join Degree (PJD). Higher education institutions (HEIs), in partnership with the police forces, are providing professional qualifications for policing as a graduate level profession. Though they have made remarkable progress in developing police education programmes, they are facing various challenges in implementing the qualification framework. This chapter also explores pedagogical aspects of police education including the effectiveness and contrast between different forms of teaching and learning. While featuring the challenges and prospects of the new police education programmes, this chapter also outlines different aspects of partnership for delivering these professional qualification programmes.

Keywords: police education, Policing Education Qualification Framework (PEQF), Police Constable Degree Apprenticeship (PCDA), Degree Holder Entry Programme (DHEP), Pre-Join Degree (PJD), United Kingdom

1. Introduction

In recent years, professionalisation has become a critical discourse [1–4] for the development of police forces in the United Kingdom. As a result, moving away from traditional training programmes towards more formal higher education programmes has been seen as a way of progress to develop professionalism within the police force [5]. In light of recent development in the field of policing, modernisation became the key concern for workforce development to fulfil the demands of the twenty-first century. The changing nature of policing and the complexity of police work became an integral part of police studies discourse [6, 7]. Recent studies show that having a higher education degree tends to have a more significant impact on police officers' knowledge and appreciation of the values and lifestyles of peoples from different cultures, especially minority groups and immigrants [8, 9]. Therefore, the professional academic education programme has been suggested as a vital tool for the development of police forces in the United Kingdom [10].

In February 2016, the College of Policing, the national professional body for policing in England and Wales, introduced the Policing Education Qualifications Framework (PEQF) for developing academic programmes for the 43 police forces in England and Wales. The PEQF proposed different routes for providing education, namely Police Constable Degree Apprenticeship (PCDA), Degree Holder Entry Programme (DHEP), and Pre-Join Degree (PJD), in professional policing practice [11, 12]. Student officers are recruited by the forces for the PCDA and DHEP routes on a salaried full-time 40 hours per week contract. Within their contract hours, they have to engage 20% of their time for off-the-job learning with a partner university, being students of an enrolled programme [12, 13].

Several police forces have already launched the PCDA programmes in partnership with several universities. On 7 September 2018, Nottinghamshire Police nationally pioneered the PCDA programme with their first cohort in partnership with the University of Derby. This initiative was followed by Derbyshire Police who then ran their first cohort of the PCDA programme with the same university. Then throughout the year in 2019, some other forces such as Leicestershire, Northamptonshire, South Wales, Gwent, Dyfed-Powys, West Midlands, Northumbria, Avon and Somerset, Staffordshire, Merseyside, and Sussex started running the PCDA programme [14]. These programmes, in fact, shifted the nature of police education and training with a particular focus on theoretical knowledge linking with the professional practice of police work with less or no emphasis on physical education. The primary mission for drastically changing police education and training is to make policing a graduate level occupation [14]. It is not only to replace the Initial Police Learning and Development Programme (IPLDP) or give all officers a university degree, but also to make the officers academically and professionally sound for the complex challenges they face in contemporary policing.

It is not an easy task to transform the century-old traditional police training to the university education programmes over a period of 2–3 years. Due to this transition in developing professional qualifications, both the forces and the higher education institutions (HEIs) are facing challenges in tackling different practical and pedagogical issues in implementing new programmes. On the one hand, the police forces are traditionally conservative [15–17] as Reiner ([18], p. 130) claims that the majority of police officers are conservative 'both politically and morally' and the students of these programmes are the trainee officers of a disciplined force [19, 20]. On the other hand, universities are very much student-focused to ensure the best learning experience for every individual student and encourage them to be critical about their learning journey and broaden their horizons. To run an academic programme successfully, HEIs are required to comply with the frameworks of the Institute for Apprenticeships and Technical Education and other funding requirements, for example from the Education and Skills Funding Agency (ESFA) as well as strictly maintaining academic regulations including Quality Assurance (QA) process and satisfy the Office for Students (OfS). Therefore, HEIs have to be in continuous conversations with the partner forces to solve the problems associated with teaching, delivery, and assessment as they arise.

Despite the fact that the Peelian objectives of policing were to ensure safety and security of person and property with the help of the community as well as prevent and detect crime [21], policing around the world became an 'extraordinarily complex endeavour' [22] due to changing demands and new challenges including technological advancement and changing patterns of crimes [23]. Police Officers do not spend a great deal of time in dealing with theft, robbery, and burglary that they did in the earlier days. Nowadays they deal with rapidly evolving crime threats such as terrorism, cybercrime, and serious and organised crime. Yet for the public, their role as citizens in uniform and bobbies on the beat as portrayed in the ever popular BBC series 'Dixon of Dock Green' (1955–1976) has not been lost as they still need to help the people whenever necessary. This is especially the case when austerity has meant a reduction to other public services in the UK leading to increasing demand on the police service, for example assistance with mental health-related incidents [24]. Yet, there was a saying 'if you want to know the time, ask a policeman' ([18], p. 78), people still call the police to help them with non-crime incidents even to buy some groceries for vulnerable residents.

2. Historical development of police education and training

The role of a police constable is one of the oldest professions in Great Britain as its history dates back to 1285 Statute of Winchester, attestation of constables following an Act of Parliament in 1673, Bow Street Runners of 1749, the establishment of the City of Glasgow Police in 1800 and finally the creation of a full-time formal police organisation for London, the Metropolitan Police, in 1829. However, the establishment of the Metropolitan Police, a brainchild of the then Home Secretary Sir Robert Peel, who later served as a British Prime Minister, is seen as the introduction of the 'modern' public policing in the world; as a result, policing became a career that offered status and security at the end of the nineteenth century [25].

It was after 100 years since the establishment of the Metropolitan Police, serious efforts were made to develop police training. The Metropolitan Police College at Hendon was established in 1934 as a military-style institution with the intention to train the serving and newly recruited officers for senior rank. The idea originally came from the Indian Police Service (IPS) that used to recruit officers in senior ranks called probationer Assistant Superintendent of Police. The Assistant Commander of the College was seconded from the IPS. In five intakes, 188 officers were graduated from the college to become inspectors until the institution was closed in September 1939. The college was not re-opened in the same format after the Second World War. Instead, in June 1948, the new National Police College (known as the Police Staff College since 1979) was established at Ryton-on-Dunsmore, near Coventry, to run different training courses for higher ranking officers with potentials to become senior police officers [26]. The college ran residential and non-residential junior, senior, and short courses and also overseas command courses for promising officers, and a scholarship scheme was available [27, 28].

Turning to the London Metropolitan Police 'was the first modern police force in a nation with representative government' ([29], ix) and the British bobbies 'occupy a special place in the history of policing in the world' and was 'a role model of successful policing' ([30], p. 435). The initial recruit training played a great role in turning an ordinary citizen into a uniformed policeman. The Metropolitan Police Training School for constables was established at Peel House in Regency Street, Pimlico in 1907, which was there until 1974, and the Metropolitan Police College in Hendon was rebuilt and opened in 1974, popularly known as the Peel Centre [31].

Historically, initial police training was known as the foundation training or basic police training in the UK, which was followed by police organisations around the world, in particular, in former British colonies. Many national police forces such as the Bangladesh Police still run the same initial police training for the new recruits. After World War II, the specialist cadet college for direct entry senior officers for the Metropolitan Police was turned into a Metropolitan Police Training School for recruit constables. The 17-week initial training was run at Hendon until 2007. However, since the 1960s, intense pressure to change the patterns of recruiting and training for the police force has led to an emphasis on recruiting graduates and since then support for higher education has grown [32, 33].

In addition to Hendon, organisations such as the National Police Training (NPT) (a Home Office unit established in 1993, following the Police Training Council's recognition of problems with the arrangements for managing police training in 1992), the Central Police Training and Development Authority (CENTREX), and the National Policing Improvement Agency (NPIA) were involved in running the initial police training in England and Wales [34, 35]. The NPT aimed at bringing greater coherence to all police training establishments including the Police Staff College, Police Training Centres (PTCs), the Police National Computer School, a centre for the design of training and training of trainers at Harrogate and a centre for the training of surveillance techniques for National Crime Squad officers at Loughborough [36]. CENTREX took over from the NPT in 2002 [37] and ran the Probationer Training Programme at six PTCs in various parts of the country, namely Bruche, Ashford, Durham, Bramshill, Ryton-on-Dunsmore, and Cwmbran. In 2007, the functions of CENTREX were merged with the NPIA, which was dissolved in 2013 and the newly established College of Policing took over some of its responsibilities.

In 2006, the new 26-week IPLDP was introduced and it became the responsibility of the respective police forces to train the newly recruited constables. Since 2010, a level 3 qualification called Diploma in Policing was awarded to the recruits upon successful completion of the IPLDP training, which used to run week by week in four phases, that is induction, community placement, supervised patrol, and independent patrol. The academic qualifications proposed by the PEQF have been gradually replacing IPLDP and it is expected that by 2020 all the forces in England and Wales will run the PEQF programmes[1]. However, the Metropolitan Police is still in the process of implementing the PEQF and it is expected to run the PCDA and DHEP programmes from September 2020.

Following the government White Paper 'Policing A New Century—A Blueprint for Reform' [38], the report of Her Majesty's Inspectorate of Constabulary (HMIC) entitled 'Training Matters' [39] and BBC's the Panorama show entitled 'The Secret Policeman' (2003) that exposed racism in the regional Police Training Centre at Bruche had a significant impact on the long-lasting police training. As a result, the government came forward to reform the initial police training. Charman ([35], p. 73) argues that:

> *'What the HMIC report "Training Matters" (2002) and the 2003 screening of the BBC documentary "The Secret Policeman" revealed was that both the formal and informal training of new police recruits needed a radical overhaul'.*

The creation of the College of Policing in 2012 as well as the Coalition government's approval of the professionalisation agenda of policing and recognition of policing as a graduate level occupation led to the introduction of the PEQF in 2016. It is worth mentioning that as an indirect impact of this new professional body, the world famous Police Staff College, which was relocated to Bramshill in 1960 from Ryton-on-Dunsmore, popularly known as Bramshill, was closed in 2015

[1] It is worth noting here that this initiative was unsuccessfully challenged by the Chief Constable of Lincolnshire Police at the High Court [14].

where many senior police officers from the UK and Commonwealth countries have undergone professional development training since 1948.

In 2017, the Police Minister Brandon Lewis MP while speaking at the PEQF conference identified the successes of the College of Policing in introducing a code of ethics, beginning a culture of continuous professional development (CPD), continually growing the body of professional knowledge, and establishing the final pillar through the PEQF as standards of professional qualification for policing. The Minister identified the implementation of the PEQF in cooperation with HEIs as 'a really big challenge' and justified the argument for professionalisation of policing as he stated that:

> *'... to those who say that policing isn't and shouldn't be a graduate job, I would ask you to just pause for a moment and encourage you to challenge that thought. Because policing needs to be prepared to meet the challenges of the future and the PEQF aims to give officers access to the knowledge and skills they need to succeed in a fast changing environment' ([40], online).*

3. Professionalisation agenda: policing as a graduate level occupation

The notion of the police as a profession is not new [41]. Across different professions, professionalism is changing and being challenged and changed as professionals now increasingly work at scale [42]. However, the policing professionalisation agenda of the College of Policing and the 'Policing Vision 2025' recognise policing as a graduate level occupation similar to those professions requiring specialist degrees in the relevant subjects such as doctor, social worker, and teacher [43]. This 'Policing Vision 2025' has been developed by the Association of Police and Crime Commissioners (APCC) and the National Police Chiefs' Council (NPCC) in consultation with the College of Policing, National Crime Agency, staff associations, and other policing and community partners. Neyroud [44] refers to a new professionalism in policing in England and argues that it focuses on improving and developing effective practice and building partnerships between higher education and police practitioners.

It is imperative that as a professional, police officers must be allowed a high degree of individual autonomy and they should have independence of judgement. The common elements of any profession to serve in a professional manner include a specialist knowledge and ethical practice related to that profession, scope for CPD, and certain standards set out to educate for that profession [45, 46]. But critics argued that knowledge-based policing in practice promotes a concept of knowledge that indirectly threatens the police officers' traditional experience-based knowledge and professional discretion [47].

According to the College of Policing [13], there is a lack of consistency in relation to nationwide educational background or qualifications for all roles or ranks within the police forces, which provide knowledge and skills to meet the current and future challenges. It also says that:

> *'PEQF aims to bring consistent practice in terms of the implementation, assessment and accreditation of initial police training across the 43 forces in England and Wales. This consistency can contribute to the professionalism of the police service and put policing in line with other professions with regard to its formal education standards' ([13]: Online).*

It noted that the PEQF supports the NPCC and APCC's 'Policing Vision 2025' that 'By 2025 policing will be a profession with a more representative workforce that will align the right skills, powers and experience to meet challenging requirements' ([13], online).

After long consultations, the College of Policing introduced the PEQF and three routes to recruit police constables. Before the PEQF, the IPLDP was introduced in 2006 as a level 3 Diploma in Policing [48] that replaced the Foundation Training (still carried out by many police organisations around the world), which is still in use in some forces including the largest force London Metropolitan Police.

For clarity, it is worth mentioning here that Scottish Police runs Police Officer Recruit Training in line with the Police Scotland National Framework for Quality Assurance in Training and Education and therefore they are not part of the PEQF. Police Service of Northern Ireland runs its own foundation training for the recruit constables at the Northern Ireland Police College, which includes a 23-week Student Officer Training Programme that follows attestation ceremony and Probationer Development Programme. Due to the length, discussion about these programmes is beyond the scope of this chapter.

4. Current development

4.1 Policing Vision 2025: graduate level occupation

In 2016, the College of Policing announced that new police officers in England and Wales would have to be educated to degree level from 2020 onwards [49] as the 'Policing Vision 2025' recognises policing as a graduate level occupation. With record numbers of British students attending universities, it would be the best opportunity for preparing the next-generation professional on police studies. A formal possession of specialised knowledge credentials is considered as a key characteristic for the enclosure of a profession [50]. That is why Livingstone and Antonelli ([51], p. 26) argue that 'The most powerful professions have historically used the requirement of a high level of academic education as a primary criterion for entry into the profession'. They also highlight that:

> *'University training programs have been the most pertinent vehicles for providing codified professional knowledge and of testing potential entrants to verify they have obtained a basic grasp of the body of knowledge of the respective professional discipline' ([51], p. 26).*

As an advocate of the professional model, Stone recommends that 'a college or university degree (or comparable educational qualification) to be adopted as the basic educational requirement of a professional police officer' [52]. Providing the Government of the UK learns its lesson from cutting funding in Nursing and ensures sufficient financial support for all new Policing students, HEIs could be able to train 5000 new police officers a year, based on last year's intake into the police force [51]. It is expected that 'By 2025 British policing will have risen effectively to new challenges and will continue to be highly regarded by both the British public and internationally as a model for others' ([52], p. 5).

The recommendations of Neyroud Report (2011) [53] 'represent a fundamental overhaul of existing practices' ([53], p. 67). From these recommendations, Stanislas [54] focuses on four specific recommendations ([53], pp. 47-48) such as 'full professionalisation of the police which in his view is critical to improving its status, clarifying areas of accountability and meeting public expectations'; establishment of a single professional body responsible for important aspects of policing, which will set national standards for entry and progression within the service, in particular a new pre-entry national qualification and a new qualification for police managers;

and finally that 'the police training and education be devolved outside the police training establishment and delivered in partnership with HEIs and specialist police training centres' ([53], p. 67).

4.2 Policing Education Qualifications Framework (PEQF)

In 2012, the College of Policing was established as a national professional body to improve police training in England and Wales drastically. There were arguments from academics and professionals for acknowledging policing as a graduate level occupation similar to doctors, teachers, and social workers who need a relevant degree to be qualified for their job [55–61]. From this realisation, the then Home Secretary, Theresa May, was in favour of this major shift and asked the College of Policing to develop a qualification framework for police officers to get a relevant degree.

David Cameron's coalition government (2010–2015) approved this qualification framework. Wood ([62], p. 1) argued that the development of the PEQF was 'Bolstered by the recommendations of Neyroud [53] and Winsor [63], both of which promoted closer collaboration between policing and academia' in their reports of two government reviews entitled 'Review of Police Leadership and Training' [53] and 'The Independent Review of Police Officer and Staff Remuneration and Conditions' [63].

4.3 Partnership between forces and universities

In building the evidence base in policing, it is very important to ensure that police officers can develop their skills, build their knowledge and expertise about what really works in policing and crime reduction so that they can put it into their practice [64, 65]. Through the partnerships, the police forces will be trained by the experts from a wide range of academic disciplines including policing, criminology, criminal justice, forensics, law, psychology, and cyber security from HEIs [66]. They will be able to learn new skills, understand more about why crimes are committed, the relationship between crime and society, and use that evidence in innovative ways in their policing practice. However, the aim is to establish long-term partnerships between police forces and HEIs to deliver a recognised body of knowledge, evidence, and expertise on policing and crime reduction, and have the potential to meet the needs of the challenging environment through innovative solutions [67, 68].

There are many partnerships across the UK between a police force and a university or a consortium of universities with several forces. Universities or consortiums need to bid to obtain a contract to provide education and training programmes, for example for 5 years with a force to provide their services. A force cannot award the contract to a local university without a competitive bidding process. Several successful procurement processes have already been run. So, for instance, Cumbria Constabulary and Lancashire Constabulary went for a joint tender and the contract was awarded to the University of Central Lancashire. Liverpool John Moores University obtained a partnership contract from Merseyside Police. It established the Liverpool Centre for Advanced Policing Studies (2015) and provides teaching to the trainee officers of their local force. University of West of England received the PEQF contract from Avon and Somerset Constabulary while the University of Northumbria runs similar programmes for Durham Constabulary and Northumbria Police [69, 70].

Some universities individually received contracts with several forces while some HEIs formed consortiums and are in contract with several forces. For example,

Staffordshire University is running the PEQF programmes for four forces in the Midlands, that is Staffordshire, Warwickshire, West Mercia, and West Midlands, and their academic staff travel to the forces' headquarters [71]. The Police Education Consortium has been formed by four universities, namely the University of Middlesex, the University of Cumbria, Canterbury Christ Church University, and the University of Portsmouth, which is in a contract with Surrey and Sussex Police and Hampshire Constabulary to run the PCDA programme and DHEP.

In November 2019, Babcock International, an engineering organisation in the security and defence sector, which also offer recruitment services, received the £309m worth contract valid until 2028 as the learning partner of the London Metropolitan Police [72]. They formed a consortium with four universities namely Brunel University London, the University of West London, the University of East London, and Anglia Ruskin University to teach the newly recruited officers of the largest police service in the UK with 31,746 police officers (as of March 2020) and 25% of the budget for the police in England and Wales [73].

Regarding the current partnerships, one of the interesting observations is that only the post-92 universities came forward to develop police partnerships and run the PCDA programme and DHEP. Most of those involved such as Middlesex, Portsmouth, and Liverpool John Moores University have long-standing reputation for teaching and researching policing, criminology, and criminal justice. However, some HEIs without an established presence in teaching and research in policing, criminology, and criminal justice stepped in for the PCDA programme and DHEP.

This partnership is an opportunity for HEIs to support the police services for professional development of their officers through enhanced education techniques and research-informed teaching utilising an established evidence base. It is one of the main reasons for the universities to develop their partnerships with the police forces to design, develop, and deliver these academic programmes. Undoubtedly as part of these contracts, HEIs will receive a considerable number of students as the police forces are continuously recruiting to meet their recruitment targets. In addition to regular recruitments, the Government promised (publicly known as 'Boris 20,000') to recruit extra 20,000 new police officers [74], which is again an extra boost for both the forces and HEIs. In fact, the partner HEIs will receive several cohorts of student officers throughout the year and they need to be flexible concerning the start date of the cohorts and compromise their traditional term dates to accommodate several intakes in an academic year.

4.3.1 Police Constable Degree Apprenticeship (PCDA) programme

The PCDA is a 3-year apprenticeship degree programme titled BSc (Honours) Professional Policing Practice for someone who has already completed their A levels or BTEC at level 2 and 3 or who are the former members of the Armed Forces. To enrol for this work-based learning programme where the uniformed students will study alongside their operational duties, one needs to join as a police officer first and then pursue the 3-year course as apprentices and will progress from academic level 4 to level 6 (degree level) when student officers need to spend 20% of their contract hours for their academic learning. However, this is a requirement set out by the College of Policing, which is different to the funding rules within the PCDA set by the Education and Skills Funding Agency (ESFA). This 20% protected learning time has been seen very much as an abstraction issue rather than how it is as an 'investment in learning and development'. This 20% has become a significant barrier in the development of some programmes and disproportionately influenced the design of some programmes. This again hampers the opportunity to reach the full potential and development opportunities of these programmes and partnerships.

This is an opportunity for someone who wants to earn £20,880 per annum (varied from force to force) while achieving a professional degree in government's expenses [75]. Entry requirements also vary from force to force. However, within the Derbyshire Constabulary, the entry requirements for policing apprenticeship is Level 2 Qualification in Maths and English (Grade C/4 and above), for example GCSE, Functional Skills and a Level 3 Qualification (A-level or equivalent) equal to 64 UCAS points for anyone aged between 18 and 55 years and the UK, EU, or Commonwealth citizen with no restrictions on leave to remain in the UK [75].

The College of Policing has outlined the National Police Curriculum (NPC) for the three new routes to become a police constable under the PEQF, and HEIs in consultation with their partner force(s) develop their programme and modules in line with the national curriculum for the PCDA, DHEP, and Pre Join degree in Professional Policing Practice and obtain approval from the college [76]. Even officers and police trainers are involved in developing learning materials. However, the name of the modules may not be the same. But the overall programme and modules need to fulfil the requirements of the NPC. Williams et al. ([77], p. 260) are critical about the development of the curriculum that 'on implementation, academia has a responsibility to develop police education in ways that it can achieve this critical feature of the PEQF' and indicate 'a risk of limiting the opportunities provided by the PEQF to deliver a real change to current police training unless the curriculum includes wider forms of knowledge, from the historical research on policing to the evaluative research tantamount to the "what works" agenda'. However, the NPC is very prescriptive about what should be taught and as a result of this prescriptive nature, this could prevent all the benefits of higher education being accessed by the students who undertake these programmes. This is particularly relevant where the PCDA is compared to the DHEP as same content is delivered at different levels.

As prescribed by the NPC, the 3-year programme will be divided into several phases, which is a very traditional approach to delivery. For example, at the beginning of the PCDA student officers will continue 22 weeks of learning that will follow guided practical learning with a one-to-one mentor for 10 weeks. In addition to reflective practice and formative assessment, students' operational progression will be assessed continuously while summative assessments will be done for every module. However, it is very important to move forward from this prescribed delivery approach by adapting a more work-integrated professional practice approach [78].

Programme design and development vary from university to university. Some HEIs run the following modules for their PCDA programmes, which starts gradually some from the beginning, some during the company period when officers will learn more about practical policing with their employer and some modules when they achieve independent patrol status to become operational:

Modules: (Titles of the modules could be different offered by different universities or partnerships. For example, following modules are offered by a university of a partnership).

Year 1 (level 4): 6 modules (6x20= 120 credits): Introduction to Policing, Studying Criminology, Community Policing, Operational Policing, Vulnerability, and Reflective Practice Based Learning.

Year 2 (level 5): 6 modules (6x20= 120 credits): Policing, Operational Policing 2, Community Policing 2, Vulnerability 2, Studying Criminology 2, and Reflective Practice Based Learning 2.

Year 3 (level 6): 3 modules (2 compulsory modules and one specialist module) and a project (2x20+40+40= 120 credits): Coaching and mentoring;

Professional Policing Competence; one specialist module (such as Response policing, Community policing, Roads policing, Information and Intelligence, and Investigation) (This is worth 40 credits); and Professional Policing Practice Project. (This is similar to undergraduate dissertation as the preparation towards the final End Point Assessment (EPA), which will include submission of the project and a presentation to be assessed finally. However, confirmation of permanent employment as a fully operational police constable is subject to successful completion of EPA).

Some other partnership developed the PCDA programme in slightly different way, for example Derbyshire Constabulary adopted the following 3-year programme (**Table 1**).

Currently, faculty members from partnership universities go to police headquarters to teach and tripartite review of the PCDA students in makeshift temporary classrooms. Blended learning approaches are used to provide learning support including delivering little face-to-face master classes, and making all teaching and learning materials available to students via online workbooks and reading lists. Student constables rely upon their handheld devices, that is iPads and laptops connected via Wi-Fi access at force headquarters, police stations where they are attached for their field training and also at their home as the trainee officers stay at home and travel to police headquarters and police stations.

INITIAL PROFESSIONAL DEVELOPMENT
Year 1
Academic Level 4
Operational Deployment
Tutor Patrol Phase
Obtain Independent Patrol Status
CONTINUOUS PROFESSIONAL DEVELOPMENT
Year 2
Academic Level 5
Response Policing
Community Policing
Policing the Roads
Information and Intelligence
Conducting Investigations
ADVANCED PROFESSIONAL DEVELOPMENT
Year 3
Academic Level 6
Specialism from Year 2
Evidence Based Research Project
Academic Assessment
Reflective Presentation and Panel Discussion
Operational Competence Portfolio

Table 1.
Adopted from Derbyshire Constabulary ([75], online).

4.3.2 Degree Holder Entry Programme (DHEP)

The DHEP is a 2-year Graduate Diploma in Professional Policing Practice programme in academic level 6. This programme is for the newly recruited constables who have a university degree in any subject except in policing. They pursue this 2-year course to learn the theoretical knowledge of policing while they in fact apply their knowledge in operational policing. The student officers recruited under the DHEP pursue work-based learning while they work as trainee officers with respective forces in various locations. They can access the online learning materials including audio-visual materials and use them at any time from any location and can engage in their academic learning activities. They earn £24,177 per annum (varied from force to force) as an officer from day one while they pursue on and off-the-job learning through this graduate diploma programme at the expense of the government during their probation period [79].

Some forces post attractive videos as part of their recruitment campaign, which outlines the recruitment process in particular how the candidates will spend half a day at the force's assessment or recruitment centre undertaking a written test, taking part in role-play, and finally being interviewed to become a police officer [80]. Fast track detectives are also recruited under the DHEP and they follow the same syllabus except learning one or two specialist modules and spending a significant period of time at specialist departments such as CID (Criminal Investigation Department). It is understood that the forces received overwhelming response from the potential detectives for the exciting and challenging Fast-Track Detective Development Programme [81]. However, confirmation of permanent employment as a police constable is subject to the successful completion of the course. Structure of this graduate diploma programme is described below:

Modules: Total of 6 modules (may run throughout the course), each module weight 20 credits and requires 20x10= 200 study hours.

Year 1(level 6): 3 modules (3x20 credits): Policing in Context; Communities, Intelligence and Information; Law, Policy and Practice.

Year 2 (level 6): 3 modules (3x20 credits): Ethics and the Policing Professional; Advance Policing Skills; and one policing in practice specialism module from the following Response Policing; Community Policing; Roads Policing; Information and Intelligence; and Investigation. Finally, the completion of a portfolio as an evidence of Full Operational Competence is required to become a fully operational police officer.

4.3.3 Pre-Join Degree (PJD) programme

This PJD programme is a standard 3-year university degree programme entitled BSc (Hons) in Professional Policing. The prospective police officers pursue this course at their own expense and upon successful completion of the degree they can apply to join any police force in England and Wales. They need to learn theoretical knowledge of policing, criminology, and criminal justice as well as various aspects of operational policing over 3 years.

Year 1 (level 4): 6 modules (6x20 credits): Understanding the role of a police constable; Policing, decisions and ethics; Policing vulnerability in contemporary society; Police Legislation; Information and Intelligence; Academic skills and applied social sciences.

Year 2 (level 5): 6 modules (6x20 credits): Operational policing; Professionalism, Values and Standards; Vulnerability and risks; Specialist procedures; Academic research skills; Criminological concepts.

Year 3 (level 6): 6 modules (6x20 credits): Coaching and mentoring; Response policing; Community policing; Specialism—Police investigation; Specialism—Information; and Intelligence; Dissertation.

4.4 Cultural change

The police role was heavily criticised in dealing during Miner's strike (1984-85), Brixton riot (1981), Hillsborough tragedy (1989), and Stephen Lawrence's murder (1993). Reiner [13] noted that despite initial opposition of the establishment of the Metropolitan Police by the London working class, the police achieved legitimacy over 100 years (1856–1959) through 'policing by consent', but he argued that the police again lost public's trust and confidence for its politicisation in 1960. It again deteriorated after the Metropolitan Police was labelled for being institutionally racist by Sir Macpherson in his report [82] on Stephen Lawrence's murder and the Metropolitan Police's total failure in dealing with the investigation was exposed in this unprovoked racial attack in South London.

In the context of strong criticism of police application of unreasonable force against the protesters in the 1960s and 1970s, the Royal Commission on Criminal Procedure in its report (1981) proposed specific legislation and code for police work to ensure its accountability and as a result the Police and Criminal Evidence Act 1984 (PACE) was introduced with specific codes for police conduct. Following the Brixton riots (1981), Lord Scarman Report (1981) identified socio-economic factors for violent protest. Policing became a political agenda when Tony Blair declared during the 1997 election campaign that labour would be 'tough on crime, tough on the causes of crime'. He introduced the 'Crime and Disorder Act 1998' just after the election that included Anti-Social Behaviour Order (ABSO) in section 1 and later brought the 'Police Reform Act 2002'.

In answering the question 'Why degree level education?', the College of Policing justified that the existing recruit training (IPLDP) was not designed to meet the demands of policing to analyse and solve the complex problems where officers have to make difficult decisions and take responsibility for their actions. However, the serving officers mostly learn to do these on the job with additional training. The new academic professional qualifications 'will give probationary officers the best chance of reaching the level of expertise found in serving officers' ([13]: Online). The college further explains the nature of the new programmes:

> *'The empathy, compassion and common sense needed in policing will be supported, not replaced by the new programmes, and will allow officers to get recognition for the complexity of their job' ([13]: Online).*

It is expected that through the higher education programmes, police education and training will make expected changes for developing professionalism with the policing practice and make a cultural shift [83–85].

4.5 Challenges of newly introduced academic programmes

As has been mentioned, the idea of introducing academic qualifications for policing was challenged by the Chief Constable of Lincolnshire in July 2019 arguing that it will put an extra burden on the police forces due to time and resource constraints [86]. The review petition relied on the academic argument of Brown ([8], p. 9) that 'the current body of research evidence is methodologically weak and there remains a gap in the literature for the provision of a convincing, unambiguous empirical case demonstrating the value added by graduates to policing'. The

High Court rejected the application for permission for judicial review of the PEQF in December 2019. However, it is still in a very early stage to determine the success and failure of the three newly introduced routes [87, 88].

Several HEIs started running the College of Policing's approved 3-year Pre-Join degree BSc (Honours) in Professional Policing degree programmes from September 2019. As it is run as a regular academic programme by the universities, licensed by the College of Policing that approve the universities' programmes in line with the syllabus given by them, it will be easier to successfully run the course. But it is difficult for the HEIs to recruit enough university staff with experience of operational policing, and knowledge of policing, criminology, and law to run this degree programme.

There is no alternative for the student police officers to learn both on-the-job and off-the-job as they need to learn the operational aspects, that is the real-life policing as well as theoretical aspects of policing to apply the knowledge to the relevant police work [89]. It is anticipated that there is a division of labour between the HEI and the force, although how this is implemented in practice varies across the country. However, in summary, the force is expected to deliver basic training such as how to handcuff suspects while the HEI is to provide the evidence base and critical arguments concerning their efficacy. It is rather like a driving theory and practical tests that one needs to successfully go through to be allowed to drive vehicles on the road to ensure his/her own safety as well as the safety of the other road users. Therefore, the nature and scope of the PCDA and DHEP courses and learning are characteristically different from regular degree courses as these involve students gaining knowledge, acquiring skills, and developing attitudes and behaviours to prepare themselves to face the challenges of modern-day policing.

As a profession-oriented course, the PEQF programmes are aimed to prepare professional police officers and one of the major challenges the teachers face is in bringing 'the field into the classroom' and 'the classroom to the field' [90]. Incorporation of practice is essential in professional degree courses. It is proven that successful professional courses need to integrate theory and practice to bring the field into the classroom as well as take the classroom into the field [91]—so that student officers can learn theoretical knowledge about crime and policing as well as legislation and procedures in the classroom and return to field learning at their units. Following application of their knowledge in practical policing, students can pursue further learning online and come back to the classroom. According to Wrenn and Wrenn [92], then they share their experience with their tutors or trainers and ask, 'How did you handle that?' Following further discussions the teacher can present more scenarios and ask them, 'What would you do in a case like that?' ([92], p. 259). The trainee officers find this method is really helpful and effective for learning as Boud et al. [93] suggest that when an example from one's own experience is shared learning occurs. Therefore, emphasis on experience is hugely significant rather than mere listening. As a result, 'the theory becomes clearer and more easily applicable to the real cases they face in a practice situation' ([92], p. 259).

Practice needs to be embedded in knowledge only Pre-Join Degree in Professional Policing, however, critical reflective thinking also needs to be embedded in the overall academic programmes based on the PEQF [10]. As degrees in Professional Policing Practice are professional and service-related studies, the main focus is not only to learn theories but also to learn how to apply the theories in practice. Hutchings ([94], p. 1) argues that 'What's at stake is the capacity to perform, to put what one knows into practice' to help students develop as professionals who are able to deal with real-world problems [95]. In learning programmes such as police education, the ability to gain and utilise knowledge from practice [96] and skill building [97] is pivotal as the best learning environment is created when experience and knowledge are integrated within a course such as the DHEP and PCDA.

Experience of police training in various parts of the world shows that the police students prefer on-the-job training to academic studies such as driving police vehicles, shadowing patrol teams, or practising situations for quick and better understanding of practical policing [98]. Therefore, bringing field experience to the classroom of the DHEP and PCDA learners is mandatory as the popularity of reality TV shows proves that people prefer watching other's lives unfold. Enhanced learning models should be applied in police training so that learning can be made relevant, useful, and effective by bringing the real world of policing into the classroom. This will create an opportunity to stimulate the innovative, common sense, and dynamic learners as McCarthy [99] emphasises on educating the 'whole brain' in addition to educating all types of learners. Most importantly, student officers' voices should be heard and their views should be taken into account in planning, designing, and delivering these academic programmes. Their learning expectations should also be considered as the potential police officers consider policing as a job as practical, exercised on the street, close to people, and with hands-on duties rather than sitting behind an office desk [100]. At the same time, it needs to be appreciated that the aim of the newly introduced three routes of police recruitment is to ultimately help to develop police studies as a well-established academic discipline.

Wrenn and Wrenn ([92], p. 258) argued that 'Educators in professional or service-related fields desire their students not only to learn theory and understand why theories are important but also to learn how to apply the theoretical frameworks in practice'. This is absolutely applicable in the case of teaching and learning in Professional Policing Practice degree programmes. Lecturers and police trainers should assist the students to learn how to apply their knowledge and skills in practical policing and help them to develop their attitude and behaviours accordingly. Integration of practice and theory is the central consideration of all learning [93] and students learn by doing and solving problems in real-life contexts [101, 102]. Rief ([103], p. 53) noted that students retain '10% of what they read, 20% of what they hear, 30% of what they see, 50% of what they see and hear, 70% of what they say and 90% of what they say and do'. A study by Kramer et al. [104] found that students taught by a practising faculty member scored higher as Good and Schubert [105] argue that they are able to relate theory to practice effectively. Genuine knowledge, understanding, and skills derive not from abstract thoughts, but rather by integrating thinking and practical application of the same.

Undoubtedly an active learning environment enhances the integration of practice and theory in the classroom involving students [106]. However, a substantial amount of materials provided for these academic programmes is self-learning materials access through Virtual Learning Environment (VLE). It is, therefore, essential to make the online learning materials more interactive as most of the time the trainee officers have to engage with their online materials. These also need to be presented in an organised way so that student officers from diverse academic backgrounds find the provided materials user-friendly and to help them to bridge their knowledge and skill gaps to provide a comfortable and enjoyable learning experience.

Because of the nature and structure of these programmes, different blending learning approaches are useful as the students can access their learning materials at any time from anywhere [107]. Apart from online live sessions, all electronic course materials could be downloaded in their devices and used offline. However, for online access they would require internet connection whether they are at their homes or workplaces (police headquarters or police stations). In practice, some may struggle to have uninterrupted broadband access and some of them struggle to obtain proper connections at police premises due to existing restrictions.

In Australia, Charles Sturt University works with the NSW Police Academy where university lecturers and experienced police trainers teach and run university courses and officers are awarded a degree by the university. Police trainers need to involve students in the classroom and keep in mind that an active learning environment enhances the integration of practice and theory in the classroom by engaging students. As part of online learning and face-to-face master classes, students need to be involved in various activities as activities allow students to clarify, question, consolidate, and appropriate new knowledge [108]. However, although experience may be the foundation of learning, it does not automatically lead to it [93] and experiences alone is not enough for learning to take place and it requires a theoretical base.

Unlike previous contents for police training, the modules developed for the PEQF programmes highlight vulnerability, legitimacy, equality, diversity, and ethical issues along with the National Decision Model [109]. These are the changes that highlight transformation of police education, in particular to prepare the newly recruited officers with necessary knowledge and skills to fulfil demands of time as well as to develop their skills, attitudes, and behaviours to bring them outside the traditional rank and file mindset and police culture.

5. Major challenges

5.1 Leadership of the partnership

One of the key issues about the nature of partnership related to the leadership could be a challenge. There could be debates whether this academic and professional partnership should be led by HEIs or the police forces. In most cases, these are HEIs which lead the partnerships so that they can comply with the national Apprenticeship Standard for the PCDA programme [110]. Some forces may choose co-delivery approach and some may decide for their programme to be the police force led where they will develop course materials in line with the NPC and will be approved by the partner HEIs. In those cases, the main workload will be on the partner forces to implement the programme. Questions may be raised about the quality assurance and student learning experience of this type of programme. Within the HEIs, there are discussions whether the PCDA, DHEP, and Pre-Join degree programmes should be led by a pure academic or a practitioner-turned-academic as they are involved in curriculum design, development of course materials, coordinating modules and assessments, and running the overall programme. However, they need to decide on the availability of people with relevant knowledge, skills, and experience. The differing partnerships may also raise issues in regards to the uniformity of delivery across the country.

5.2 University faculty recruitment

There has been a reduction in the number of police officers, trainers, and training facilities [111, 112]. To address the shortage of police officers, when the Prime Minister Boris Johnson announced in 2019 to recruit 20000 new officers for the police forces across the country, neither the police forces, nor the HEIs were prepared although some universities in the UK have a long-standing working relationship with the police service as they helped the forces in developing their training programmes ([54], pp. 62-63). Though the College of Policing welcome the policing pledge to address the shortage of police officers by recruiting 20,000 new officers, but warned of 'logistical challenges' at the time to achieve the goal, following the closure of police stations across the country as well as concerns over the lack of training instructors [113]. In particular it is argued here that there is a scarcity of academics in policing and practitioners-turned-academics into policing as there is a shortage of suitable teaching staff. Against the advertisement for recruiting faculty members, the response rate is very low. HEIs need a good number of staff to run the PCDA programme and DHEP.

As part of the role, the academic staff, that is programme leader, module leaders, and work-based tutors and assessors need to travel to the police forces' premises. Therefore, it is a mandatory requirement for them to go through level 2 Non-Police Personnel Vetting (NPPV) or Disclosure and Barring Services (DBS) process by the relevant forces. Some academics may not be necessarily willing to go through the process, which will ultimately limit their access and contribution to the police headquarters, police stations as well as specialised software such as Aptem as access is strictly maintained by the forces. Students will have access to the College of Policing's Managed Learning Environment (MLE) for further reading such as Authorised Professional Practice (APP) in addition to HEI's VLE, for example BlackBoard, Canvas, or Moodle for online learning materials.

Some HEIs are in favour of recruiting former police officers and in some cases officers from the same force they are in a contract with as they know the force well. While other HEIs are in favour of recruiting pure academics and practitioner-turned-academics to lead the programme and modules by ensuring academic standards. They argue that police trainers are enough to teach the practical aspects of policing and, therefore, ex-cops are not necessarily important to link theory into practice. In the context of police education in the USA, Sherman [114, 115] recommends based on a 2-year national study that full-time faculty members with PhD should be employed, not to make prior criminal justice experience as one of the essential criteria for recruiting faculties to run the academic programmes. However, there is a set of factors, as we are discussing in this chapter, for understanding the processes linking demands for further development in police education and practices [54].

As an example, Babcock International recruited lecturers and tutors, a mixture of former police officers and traditional academics, to run the PEQF programmes in conjunction with the consortium universities in London. Some universities are still in the process of recruiting programme leaders and module leaders and are facing difficulties due to lack of suitable candidates. Moreover, other universities also recruit teaching and research staff with similar backgrounds to run their existing programmes in criminology, policing, and criminal justice as this is a rapidly expanding subject area. Jones ([116], p. 232) noted that 'in 2015, the Universities and Colleges Admissions Service (UCAS) identifies 48 higher education institutions (HEIs) in England and Wales offering undergraduate policing degree programmes'. HEIs also need to recruit work based tutor and assessor to help the module leaders and police trainers in particular to do tripartite reviews of the PCDA and DHEP students and to provide them pastoral support.

5.3 Tripartite engagement and collaboration

Pursuing an effective tripartite review involving three parties, namely the student officer, university, and the police force (employer) is a major challenge for the successful continuation of the PCDA. Although there is no such mandatory requirement for the DHEP, it will use the best practice of the PCDA to pursue tripartite review. Academic staff and work-based tutor-assessors face practical difficulty to travel to various locations of police units in the force area, where the student officers are attached, to run face-to-face tripartite review. Throughout the tripartite engagement and collaboration, the complex process of quality assurance to satisfy both HEI regulations and College of Policing requirements is a real challenge in addition to meeting the requirements of the Institute for Apprenticeships and Technical Education that approved the PCDA programme for delivery in March 2018 and Office for Students [117]. The effective relationship between university staff (i.e. lecturers, module coordinators, or programme leaders) and police trainers is very important for this tripartite engagement and collaboration.

5.4 Diversity and recruitment

Since Macpherson's report published in 1999, there is still significant challenge for the police service to diversify its profile. The expectation of the NPCC is that by 2025 policing will be a profession with a more diverse workforce which mirrors the UK's population. While there has been a large increase in the numbers of female officers over time, there are still ongoing issues in regards to the recruitment of BAME staff and in particular black police officers. For example, in London, the Met head of recruitment, Clare Davies [118] commented, "If we continue even with the great progress we've made it would take over 100 years to be representative" of London. Currently, 58.4% of black people live in London, a population of between 1.1 and 1.2 million. Black people make up 15.6% of London's population whereas they number only 3.3% of metropolitan police officers. The PEQF routes should be an excellent opportunity for this community as for black Londoners, on average in 2016, 8% of first-year undergraduates across the UK were black. In the same year, London has the highest proportion of black students, making up 17% of students overall [119]. However, initial impressions from recruitment outside of London are not positive as the initial cohorts do not reflect this aspiration for diversity.

Although, the Macpherson's report recommended the recruitment of more black officers and this has been followed by further diversity initiatives, it is still the case that either members of the BAME community are not able to satisfy the criteria and successfully go through the selection process or more likely, are not willing to serve in the force. Nevertheless, forces are still encouraging application from under-represented black and ethnic minority candidates to apply to become a police constable [79]. Apart from diversity in recruitment, interestingly some forces received a tremendous response for fast track detective roles [120].

5.5 Higher education sector-wide engagement

According to the Guardian's list of top universities, no university in the top 20 applied to deliver the PEQF programmes. In London, all the top-ranking universities did not show any interest to be involved in running PEQF courses although London School of Economics and Political Science (LSE), Kings' College London, and the University College London (UCL) lead policing and criminology research globally. Only HEIs such as the University of East London, the University of Law, the University of Cumbria (London Campus), and Coventry University (CU London) offer pre-join degrees in policing.

5.6 Academic contact hours and blended learning approach

While designing learning materials for police studies to teach student officers, the 'diverse range of operational challenges' identified by Reiner and Newburn need to be considered [121]. In designing, developing, and delivering the academic programmes, the 'peculiar features of late-modern society' [10] need to be underscored for ensuring equity and social justice as 'one-size-fits-all' blueprints are not applicable in the changing world of policing. Emerging communication technologies and media indeed brought changes and complexity in police work [122].

In practice, academics and students may find it insufficient to spend only 20% of working hours towards the academic degree while students in regular university programmes are required to study and learn throughout the week. Although it is appreciated that the PCDA and DHEP are perfect examples of blended learning, the syllabus given by the College of Policing is vast and students need to work more and more to learn the course materials, given the fact that most of the materials are online and that involves self-study, although they can contact their module coordinators or trainers at any time for further understanding or clarifications. Moreover, the PCDA programme and DHEP, as technology enhanced blended learning programmes, face significant challenges as there are no PEQF-specific textbooks available although Bryant and Bryant [123] suggest that Blackstone's Handbook for Policing Students 2020 'Covers the learning requirements of all major entry routes into the police service, including pre-join degree courses and degree apprenticeships'.

In particular, the students may struggle to understand legislation and interact more in workshops. It should be considered that the PCDA and DHEP students are not learning to pass their assessments or to obtain university degrees, they will need this knowledge throughout their policing career as the constables are independent decision-makers who attend crime scene, instantly gather information and intelligence, and analyse and make decisions on their next steps to tackle the situation. In doing that, they need to continuously consider the National Decision Model (NDM) as well as National Intelligence Model (NIM) with an emphasis of ethics at the core of the decision-making process as the officers are accountable for their actions and may be liable for any wrongdoings or mistakes for which they may face departmental proceedings or even lose their jobs. Therefore, they need to properly understand the legislation, policy, and guidance such as Police and Criminal Evidence Act 1984 (PACE) and its codes that outline clear guidelines for various police work.

5.7 Multidisciplinary professional understanding

Officers need to understand the paradigm shift of applying their own judgement, common law fairness, and Wednesbury reasonableness to specific legislations such as the Human Rights Act 1998, which makes it mandatory to be considered in any police actions with a minor exception in cases related to counterterrorism actions. Savage [124] argues that the 1998 human rights legislation that incorporated the European Convention on Human Rights has significance for all institutions in the UK but particularly for the police. Officers are required to understand the English Legal System and procedures in the criminal justice system such as how the Magistrates Court and Crown Court operate and what role the defence and prosecution play to ensure justice. Students of Law degrees study the laws and legal procedures throughout their programmes. However, the student police officers will have limited time to cover relevant laws, policies, and guidance from few classroom-based lessons.

6. Future of police education

6.1 Progress made so far

One of the major achievements of the PEQF is to shift the main focus of the initial policing training from rigorous physical training to developing knowledge, skills, attitude, and behaviours in addition to the empathy, compassion, and common sense that the British police officers already have. Through the academic programmes, personal and professional development of an individual officer will continuously focus on ethics at the centre of their learning and preparation for their professional career. As a result, police practice will be able to put in first place mandatory consideration of human rights and respect for equality to maintain the pride for democracy and the rule of law in the diverse British society. It is appreciated that police officers, as the law enforcers, need to be physically and mentally fit to perform their challenging duties efficiently. They necessarily need to learn drills, first aid, and law; however, the PEQF will put less emphasis on quasi-military style drill and parade. Rather they will go through essential Officer Safety Training (OST) before they become operational.

The police forces should afford a residential accommodation for the trainee officers in a purpose-built campus with technology-facilitated master classrooms, small classrooms for seminars and group discussions, and assessment centre with required facilities for student officers who need additional support. This is also essential to have the facilities for physical training, arms training, safety training as well as gym, sports centre, and hydra simulation suit to facilitate immersive learning. Should the students reside in the police education premises, they could have time and space for protected learning and they could access library facilities in addition to existing access to the HEI's library and online resources.

To fulfil the demands of the twenty-first century, successful implementation of the PEQF will assist the society in achieving sustainable development goals (SDGs) related to peace and prosperity through reasonable policing by graduate officers who will be able to make informed decisions by applying their cognitive, affective, and psychomotor skills. As the UK historically led the development of professional policing, if the academic professional qualification programmes based on the PEQF are successfully implemented (as the first PCDA cohort is expected to be qualified in 2021 and the first Pre-Join Degree students will be graduated in 2022), this model of ultimate police education will be followed in other parts of the world especially where countries are seeking effective police reform to overcome the crises of legitimacy and efficacy. However, this model of new policing will bring a significant change in police occupational culture, which has been blamed for many decades for lack of police legitimacy. Savage [123] describes policing as a performing art and its paradigm shift as a process of reform.

Despite the Government of Australia has not recognised policing as a graduate level occupation, the NSW Police Force (NSWPF) has developed a unique programme in partnership with Charles Sturt University (CSU) where the prospective candidates first need to complete the University Certificate in Workforce Essentials (UCWE), a foundation level programme [125]. Then they go through the recruitment process to be offered a police recruit position and enrolment for the CSU-run Associate Degree in Policing Practice (ADPP) at the NSW Police Academy. CSU's School of Policing Studies is located at the NSW Police Academy to jointly run this course where student officers need to reside at the Academy throughout the week [126]. This 2-year programme also includes a field observation placement in Year 1 that will follow attestation and then the students will pursue the Year 2 studies as probationary constables. However, their employment as police constables will be subject to successful completion of the Year 2 [127].

The Bangladesh Police Academy, Sardah, which was established in 1912 in British-ruled Bengal, still runs the fully residential basic police training [128] with significant emphasis on physical training such as early morning exercise, morning parade, afternoon parade, horse training (for the probationer Assistant Superintendents who join through the national civil service) and less focus on academic learning, arms training, safety training, and driving lessons. However, since 2008 probationer Assistant Superintendents of Police receive a Masters of Police Science degree from the University of Rajshahi upon successful completion of this police-led training. The UNDP-DFID sponsored Police Reform Programme in Bangladesh failed to bring a paradigm shift in police training and culture due to constant opposition of civil bureaucracy and lack of a strong political will as the policy-makers want to keep their strong control over the force [129]. Similarly, many police organisations in the developed and developing world have their own police academies, police training centres such as Louisiana State Police Training Academy, USA that has a residential academy in Baton Rouge with a massive training area including Joint Emergency Services Training Center [130].

The physical learning environment is also crucial for an enjoyable learning experience. In practice, it is argued here that the lack of adequately equipped on-site residential facilities for the uniformed PCDA and DHEP students may have a negative impact in their learning as well as their team spirit as the members of a disciplined force. In this aspect, more could be learnt from the other professional qualifications offered by the universities and should be adapted for these programmes.

6.2 Leadership development

Developing Police Leadership is one of the crucial priorities for the twenty-first century's policing across the globe including the UK [131]. The apprentice-turned-graduates under the PCDA programme, officers with a graduate diploma under the DHEP, and policing graduates-turned-officers are qualified enough to be promoted in leadership roles in 43 forces in England and Wales in the days to come. Although there are five entry routes into policing, namely constable, police staff, Fast Track to Inspector, Direct Entry at Superintendent, and Direct Entry at Chief Constable (for eligible overseas chief officers), most of the senior officers begin as a constable and follow the traditional route to be promoted to lead the forces. Undoubtedly the Fast Track for both new candidates and experienced officers as well as Police Now, which runs the National Graduate Leadership Programme and the National Detective Programme, will play a pivotal role in creating future leaders. However, the question for debate is 'will the NPC really allow this level of development, or do these programmes set the foundations on which to build leadership more strongly than current training provision?' which is beyond the scope of this chapter.

According to Bergan and Damian ([132], p. 8), '[e]ducation is about acquiring skills but also about acquiring values and attitudes' which are essential characteristics for leadership in an ethically and economically diverse society' that also needs a 'diverse student body' ([132], p. 9). In the same vein, Bok ([133], p. 19), a former President of Harvard University, emphasises that 'Our institutions are now the leading sources of all three of the most important ingredients for progress and prosperity in modern societies: new discoveries, expert knowledge and highly trained people'. He further argues that 'universities are the essential institutions for preparing leaders throughout society. Every politician, every civil servant, every judge, doctor, priest and virtually every top business executive will attend our universities. Although this often goes unnoticed, more and more of these leaders are also returning to universities in mid-career for further education'.

Therefore, university education will help the forces to have more prudent police leaders who can bring diversity of thought and perspective into policing. They should pursue continuing professional development courses throughout their career to obtain up-to-date knowledge and prepare them to lead the forces and achieve legitimacy and set examples for the world. The College of Policing's Leadership Review ([134], p. 31) recommended to 'Create a new model of leadership and management training and development which is accessible to all within policing'. It has also echoed the Peelian principles of 1829, which are still relevant for public approval of police work as it states:

> *'From the origins of British policing in the 19th century, an emphasis on preventing crime was established as the most important duty of the police, along with the notion that securing public approval and cooperation are fundamental to achieving police objectives' ([134], p. 15).*

Leadership is the one of the keys for an organisation to be efficient, effective, and successful in managing people and achieving goals. Bowling et al. ([135], p. 28) argue that 'The police are supposedly a "totalizing institution" with a "chain of command"'. Therefore, this is very important for the police forces to develop well-prepared future leadership so that they can lead their respective forces. According to the College of Policing ([134], p. 6),

> *'The ideal police leader is driven by the core values of policing, seeks out challenge and is quick to adapt. ... This is a leader who empowers, trusts and supports every individual to succeed among their peers, within their teams and across their organisations; who copes with the challenges of emerging crime and public safety issues; who values difference and diversity; and who readily accepts personal accountability while retaining the trust of communities'.*

6.3 Pedagogical aspects

Generally, police education has been based on a top-down, instructor-led form of teaching by focusing on a student officer's technical competencies [5]. These approaches are contrasted with the mainstream higher education pedagogies, that is learner-led participatory teaching and learning where critical thinking and innovative ideas are the keys to success [2]. However, very little has been known from research regarding the pedagogical impact of different educational and training pathways into policing [136]. In this light, we are hoping to see wider discussion on the relationship between the NPC and higher education elsewhere between academics and practitioners [136–139].

In the professional contexts, the police officers' learning must be followed by reflective thought and internal processing that links the experience with previous learning as learning takes place within a cycle of action, reflection, and application [140]. A study on graduates from a professional graduate programme of Social Work found that class work had not adequately prepared them for real-world practice [91]. Failure to incorporate knowledge in a relevant and meaningful way creates a barrier for effective learning. Practical examples help the learners to understand and apply theories from the textbook to real situations, which enhanced their learning experiences. Similar views were expressed in The Relation of Theory to Practice in Education [141] that content knowledge should not be remote from practical issues. In the initial stage of academic police education programmes, learning may be found difficult by fresh students due to the lack of experiences.

However, examples from their earlier life could be created and delivered through a virtual learning environment to assist the trainees in understanding the contexts and link with the theories. They should be given the opportunity to deal with real-life scenarios as student police officers who are too afraid to test their abilities will probably be worried police officers, which is not expected at all.

6.4 Interpersonal communication and critical thinking

As a professional course, interpersonal communication skills including critical thinking are very important in police education [142]. The nine Peelian principles of policing are the main mantra of policing, which suggests police officers are citizens in uniform and they cannot succeed without the support and approval from the community [143]. Throughout the curriculum of the professional education programmes, there should be an effective structure for teaching essential interpersonal skills so that student officers get a solid foundation, which enables them to remove some of the barriers between the police force and the public. Initial training through academic programmes builds an essential foundation for new officers because they need to master communication skills before they execute tactical and legal tasks in practice.

Effective policing occurs when police officers and members of the public become partners to create safe and crime-free communities. This partnership requires well-prepared police officers who display not only strong technical capabilities but also interpersonal skills. Therefore, police forces as the law enforcement agencies must train their officers on how to interact effectively with the public and work with them. In the professional setting, technical and interpersonal skills help the offers to perform their police work well.

Police officers face unique challenges and critical discourse as part of their role and they need to constantly reflect on their learning and experience to overcome the situations successfully. It is therefore a key focus of the PCDA and DHEP to make the officers critical reflective thinkers and students reflect and write their reflective journals throughout these work-based learning. There is a pressing need to incorporate the practice into degree programmes for effective learning and developing skills as Hornyak et al. [144] suggest that people learn best from direct experience with guided reflection and analysis. It is also essential for the best student learning experience and to develop necessary knowledge, behaviours, and skills for the student officers to become fully operationally competent police constables.

According to a recent study [145], students who are studying police studies at HEIs quickly assimilated a police identity, which affected their attitudes and behaviour. For fulfilling the potential of the PEQF, police services need to embrace, promote, and enable their police officers to become reflective practitioners through critical thinking and policing must be a reflective practice in the fullest sense [62]. If the recently developed academic police studies programmes are able to provide interpersonal communication skills and critical thinking, only then HEIs will be able to provide radically transformed and well-equipped policing degrees for the better future.

6.5 Policing in emergencies

In times of crises or emergencies, there are more constraints imposed on the police forces, for instance, the recent COVID-19 pandemic restricted individuals' movements and mass gatherings. As a result, education and training programmes have to be put on hold advised by the College of Policing as the situation demanded the forces to deploy more officers to support the operations throughout the country, to such an extent that the Metropolitan Police Service requested the retired officers to come back on a paid or unpaid role and the officers who are approaching their retirement age to not leave the force [146]. Again, due to the emergency situation and imposed restrictions, student officers have been grappling with different problems, for example, staying at home and even looking after some family members, having less time to engage with their ongoing courses. In some cases, they have been struggling to connect with stable internet connections to access the virtual learning environments, in particular during their assessment day to participate in exams or submitting their work on time. In the changed circumstances, they have to sit for online examinations, in some cases for a fixed 2-hour assessment in a 24-hour window. There were concerns about these exams' compatibility, credibility, and integrity as there was no physical surveillance and learning materials might be available to them during these exams. Although the PCDA student officers were at the very beginning of their academic learning, still there was a pressure on the forces due to the crisis to deploy them operationally after completing their safety training and public order training.

7. Conclusion

Incorporating practice into professional learning is essential as Clapton and Cree [91] suggest to integrate theory and practice to bring the experiences of the field into the classroom as well as take the classroom into the field. It is commonly accepted that experience is a great teacher; however, it cannot replace a classroom, for example for learning law and legal procedure, and vice versa. To find a balance between theory and experience, similarly in between classroom and practice, the professional policing practice needs to be embedded in its entirety in the Pre-Join degree, PCDA programme, and DHEP. Policing is a life-long learning process; indeed it is a part of the professionalisation agenda, and to ensure this life-long learning to happen the police should be a learning organisation [147–151].

Recently introduced, these three academic professional programmes are still under experiment as HEIs are running the programmes for the first time in partnerships with the police forces. HEIs and police forces need to learn from their partnerships through different approaches and efforts of 'trial and error' to find better ways to prepare future police workforce and they must work out their ways to develop effective partnerships to learn from each other to be successful in achieving the goals of the 'Policing Vision 2025'. Then this model of partnership for providing police education can be a beacon for other police organisations around the world as the Leadership Review ([134], p. 5) suggests that many around the world envy the British police service and respect it 'for its strength of purpose and public service ethos'. Especially Commonwealth countries such as Bangladesh, India, Pakistan, Malaysia, and Nigeria, where those countries still are continuing their colonial legacy may be able to reform the recruitment process and education and training programmes of their forces to make a graduate level occupation through academic professional qualifications.

Although the newly introduced police education programmes are at the very early stage of their implementation as none of the three programmes has completed its cycle for its first cohort since introduction, continuous careful consideration is required to understand the challenges and overcome them in due course. This ongoing learning by doing effort is like 'trying to build an airplane while you are flying it' as the Chief US Training Officer for the Iraqi National Police Force said while expressing his experience of police capacity building in Iraq [152]. Indeed the recent developments 'offer new and potentially unprecedented opportunities for HEIs to play a major role in the education of police officers at all levels' ([54], p. 67). The success of the academic professional qualification programmes based on the PEQF will depend on how stakeholders provide the opportunities to the HEIs to experiment their innovative administrative and pedagogical approaches and assist them to run the programmes as smoothly and flexibly as possible bearing in mind that 'the politics of the police and policing is complicated' ([135], p. 20).

Author details

M. Mahruf C. Shohel[1]*, Gias Uddin[2], Julian Parker-McLeod[2] and Daniel Silverstone[3]

1 Institute of Development Studies, University of Sussex, Brighton, United Kingdom

2 Institute of Criminal Justice Studies, University of Portsmouth, Portsmouth, United Kingdom

3 School of Justice Studies, Liverpool John Moores University, Liverpool, United Kingdom

*Address all correspondence to: m.m.c.shohel@alumni.manchester.ac.uk; mahruf.shohel@yahoo.co.uk

References

[1] Tong S, Hallenberg KM. Education and the police professionalisation agenda: A perspective from England and Wales. In: Rogers C, Frevel B, editors. Higher Police Education: An International View. Palgrave Macmillan; 2017. pp. 17-34

[2] Simmill-Binning C, Towers J. Education, training and learning in policing in England and Wales. In: N8 Policing Research Partnership. Lancaster: Lancaster University; 2017

[3] Green T, Gates A. Understanding the process of professionalisation in the police organisation. Police Journal: Theory, Practice and Principles. 2014;**87**:75-91

[4] Martin D, Wooff A. Treading the front-line: Tartanisation and police academic partnerships. Policing: A Journal of Policy and Practice. 2020;**14**(2):325-336. DOI: 10.1093/police/pay065

[5] Paterson C. Adding value? A review of the international literature on the role of higher education in police training and education. Police Practice and Research. 2011;**12**(4):286-297

[6] Ramshaw P, Soppitt S. Educating the recruited and recruiting the educated: Can the new police education qualifications framework in England and Wales succeed where others have faltered. International Journal of Police Science and Management. 2018;**20**(4):243-250

[7] Cordner G, Shain C. The changing landscape of police education and training. Police Practice and Research. 2011;**12**(4):281

[8] Brown J. Do graduate police officers make a difference to policing? Results of an integrative literature review. Policing. 2018;**14**(1):9-30

[9] Paterson C. Higher education, police training, and police reform: A review of police-academic educational collaborations. In: Kratcoski PC, Edelbacher M, editors. Collaborative Policing: Police, Academics, Professionals, and Communities Working Together for Education, Training, and Program Implementation. London, UK: CRC Press; 2016. pp. 119-136

[10] Christopher S. The police service can be a critical reflective practice ... if it wants. Policing: A Journal of Policy and Practice. 2015;**9**(4):326-339

[11] Strong J. Policing education qualifications framework (PEQF) implementation: Frequently asked questions. In: Research and Policy Support Briefing Paper. Bedford, UK: Police Federation; 2019

[12] College of Policing. Police education qualifications framework: Police constable entry programmes. 2018. Available from: http://www.college.police.uk/What-we-do/Learning/Policing-Education-Qualifications-Framework/Pages/Policing-Education-Qualifications-Framework.aspx [Accessed: 20 April 2020]

[13] College of Policing. Legal challenge around training for new officers rejected. 2019. Available from: https://www.college.police.uk/News/College-news/Pages/PEQF-Judicial-Review-Outcome-December-2019.aspx [Accessed: 19 April 2020]

[14] College of Policing. Entry routes for police constables. 2020. Available from: https://www.college.police.uk/What-we-do/Learning/Policing-Education-Qualifications-Framework/Entry-routes-for-police-constables/Pages/Entry-routes-for-police-constables.aspx [Accessed: 16 April 2020]

[15] Farrell A. Crime, Class and Corruption: The Politics of the Police. London, UK: Bookmarks; 1993

[16] Skolnick JH. Justice without Trial: Law Enforcement in Democratic Society. 3rd ed. London, UK: Wiley; 1994

[17] Cockcroft T. Police Culture: Themes and Concepts. London, UK: Routledge; 2013

[18] Reiner R. The Politics of the Police. 4th ed. Oxford, UK: Oxford University Press; 2010

[19] Halsey P. Police officer professional standards. Metropolitan Police. 2011. Available from: http://www.met.police.uk/msctraining/documents/police_officer_professional_standards.pdf [Accessed: 15 April 2020]

[20] Stone DC. The control and the discipline of police forces. The Annals of the American Academy of Political and Social Science. 1929;**146**:63-73

[21] Hilton J. Instructions to the new police. The Police Journal: Theory, Practice and Principles. 1977;**50**(1):23-28

[22] Goldstein H. Problem-Oriented Policing. New York, USA: McGraw Hill; 1990. Cited in Marks M, Sklansky D, editors. Police Reform the Bottom Up: Officers and their Unions as Agents of Change. London, UK: Routledge; 2012

[23] Parliament UK. Commons Select Committee: Policing for the future inquiry launched. 2017. Available from: https://www.parliament.uk/business/committees/committees-a-z/commons-select/home-affairs-committee/news-parliament-2015/170111-new-inquiry-policing-future/ [Accessed: 16 April 2020]

[24] College of Policing. College of policing analysis: Estimating demand on the police service. 2015. Available from: https://www.college.police.uk/News/College-news/Documents/Demand%20Report%2023_1_15_noBleed.pdf [Accessed: 18 April 2020]

[25] Emsley C. The English Police: A Political and Social History. London, UK: Longman; 1996

[26] Martin JP, Gail Wilson G. Police: A Study in Manpower. London, UK: Heinemann; 1969

[27] Williams CA. British police training in the 1940s and 1950s: the inculcation of skills and class. n.d. Available from: https://www.academia.edu/7075837/British_Police_Training_in_the_1940s_and_1950s_the_Inculcation_of_Skills_and_Class [Accessed: 30 April 2020]

[28] Watt I. Police Higher Education and Training in the United Kingdom. Chicago, USA: University of Illinois at Chicago; 1988

[29] Miller W. Cops and Bobbies. Chicago: University of Chicago Press; 1977

[30] Reiner R. Police research in the United Kingdom: A critical review. Crime and Justice. 1992;**15**:435-508

[31] Open University. Policeman as a Worker. 2009. Available from: http://www.open.ac.uk/Arts/history-from-police-archives/Met6Kt/PoliceWorker/pwTrain.html [Accessed: 29 April 2020]

[32] Lee M, Punch M. Policing by degrees: Police officers' experience of university education. Policing and Society. 2004;**14**(3):233-249

[33] Shernock SK. The effects of college education on professional attitudes among police. Journal of Criminal Justice Education. 1992;**3**(1):71-92

[34] Select Committee on Home Affairs. Appendices to the Minutes

of Evidence. Annex A. 1999. Available from: https://publications.parliament.uk/pa/cm199899/cmselect/cmhaff/81/81ap35.htm [Accessed: 01 May 2020]

[35] Charman S. Police Socialisation, Identity and Culture: Becoming Blue. London, UK: Palgrave Macmillan; 2017

[36] Select Committee on Home Affairs. Appendices to the Minutes of Evidence. Appendix 10. 1999. Available from: https://publications.parliament.uk/pa/cm199899/cmselect/cmhaff/81/81ap34.htm [Accessed: 01 May 2020]

[37] HMIC. Central Police Training and Development Authority 2003 Inspection. 2003. Available from: http://library.college.police.uk/docs/hmic/centrex03.pdf [Accessed: 27 April 2020]

[38] Government UK. Policing a new century—A blueprint for reform. 2001. Available from: https://www.gov.uk/government/publications/policing-a-new-century-a-blueprint-for-reform [Accessed: 17 April 2020]

[39] Her Majesty's Inspectorate of Constabulary (HMIC). Training Matters. London, UK: Her Majesty's Inspectorate of Constabulary; 2002

[40] Government UK. Speech to the Police Education Qualification Framework Conference: Minister addresses the conference on the topic of police professionalism. 2017. Available from: https://www.gov.uk/government/speeches/speech-to-the-police-education-qualification-framework-conference [Accessed: 16 April 2020]

[41] Holdaway S. The re-professionalization of the police in England and Wales. Criminology and Criminal Justice. 2017;**17**(5):588-604

[42] Evetts J. The new professionalism? Challenges and opportunities. Current Sociology. 2011;**59**(4):406-422

[43] National Police Chief's Council (NPCC). Policing Vision 2025. 2016. Available from: https://www.npcc.police.uk/documents/Policing%20Vision.pdf [Accessed: 19 April 2020]

[44] Neyroud P. Leading policing in the 21st century: Leadership, democracy, deficit and the new professionalism. Public Money and Management. 2011;**31**(5):347-355

[45] Clapton G, Cree VE, Allan M, Edwards R, Forbes R, Irwin M, et al. Thinking 'outside the box': A new approach to integration of learning for practice. Social Work Education. 2008;**27**(3):334-340

[46] Stout B. Professional ethics and academic integrity in police education. Policing: A Journal of Policy and Practice. 2011;**4**(4):300-309

[47] Gundhus HI. Experience or knowledge? Perspectives on new knowledge regimes and control of police professionalism. Policing. 2012;**7**(2):178-194

[48] National Policing Improvement Agency (NPIA). A Guide to the Diploma in Policing—The New National Minimum Qualification for Student Police Officers. London: National Policing Improvement Agency; 2008

[49] Bekhradnia B, Beech D. Demand for Higher Education to 2030. Oxford, UK: Higher Education Policy Institute; 2018

[50] Derber C, Schwartz WA, Magrass Y. Power in the Highest Degree: Professionals and the Rise of a New Mandarin Order. New York: Oxford University Press; 1990

[51] Livingstone DW, Antonelli F. Teachers and other professionals: A comparison of professionals' occupational requirements, class positions and workplace power. In: Clark R, Livingstone DW, Smaller H,

editors. Teacher Learning and Power in the Knowledge Society. Rotterdam, Netherlands: Sense Publishers; 2012

[52] Stone R. The Stephen Lawrence review: An independent commentary to mark the 10th anniversary of the Stephen Lawrence Inquiry. London: Uniting Britain Trust; 2009

[53] Neyroud P. Review of Police Leadership and Training: Volume 1. Home Office: The Government of the United Kingdom; 2011. Available from: https://www.gov.uk/government/uploads/system/uploads/attachment_data/file/118227/report.pdf [Accessed: 16 April 2020]

[54] Stanislas P, editor. International Perspectives on Police Education and Training. London, UK: Routledge; 2014

[55] Hough M, Stanko B. Developing an Evidence-based Police Degree-holder Entry Programme: Final Report. London, UK: Office for Policing and Crime, Mayor of London; 2018. Available from: https://www.london.gov.uk/sites/default/files/debpdhp_pages_5.6.18.pdf [Accessed: 29 April 2020]

[56] Tong S, Wood D. Graduate police officers: Releasing the potential for pre-employment university programmes for aspiring officers. The Police Journal. 2011;**84**:69-74

[57] Dominey J, Hill A. The higher education contribution to police and probation training: Essential, desirable or an indulgence? The British Journal of Community Justice. 2010;**8**(2):5-16

[58] Hallenberg K. Scholarly Detectives: Police Professionalisation via Academic Education [unpublished doctoral thesis]. School of Law, The University of Manchester; 2012

[59] Hallenberg K, Cockcroft T. Police and Higher Education. Canterbury Christ Church University; 2014

[60] Hallenberg K, Cockcroft T. From indifference to hostility: Police officers, organizational responses and the symbolic value of 'in-service' higher education in policing. Policing. 2017;**11**(3):273-288

[61] Heath L. Preparing new police officers for their careers: In-house training or university education? Widening Participation and Lifelong Learning. 2011;**12**(2):105-123

[62] Wood DA. Embedding learning and assessment within police practice: The opportunities and challenges arising from the introduction of the PEQF in England and Wales. Policing: A Journal of Policy and Practice. 2020;**14**(2): 374-382. DOI: 10.1093/police/pay087

[63] Winsor T. The Independent Review of Police Officer and Staff Remuneration and Conditions. Home Office; 2012. Available from: https://webarchive.nationalarchives.gov.uk/20130312170837/http://review.police.uk/publications/part-2-report/ [Accessed: 16 April 2020]

[64] Blakemore B, Simpson K. A comparison of the effectiveness of pre- and post-employment modes of higher education for student police officers. Police Journal. 2010;**83**(1):29-41

[65] Bryant R, Cockcroft T, Tong S, Wood D. Police training and education: past, present and future. In: Brown J, editor. The Future of Policing. London, UK: Routledge; 2014. pp. 383-397

[66] Tilley N, Laycock G. Engineering a safer society. Public Safety Leadership: Research Focus. 2016;**4**(2):1-6

[67] Fleming J. Learning to work together: police and academics. Policing; A Journal of Policy and Practice. 2010;**4**(2):139-145

[68] Goode J, Lumsden K. The McDonaldization of police-academic

partnerships: Organisational and cultural barriers encountered. Policing and Society. 2016;**28**(1):75-89

[69] Durham Constabulary. Major recruitment drive launched by Durham Constabulary. 2019. Available from: https://www.durham.police.uk/news-and-events/Pages/News%20Articles/Major-recruitment-drive-launched-by-Durham-Constabulary.aspx [Accessed: 17 April 2020]

[70] Northumbria University. Partners in detecting and preventing crime: university and police join forces. 2019. Available from: https://www.northumbria.ac.uk/about-us/news-events/news/police-partnership/ [Accessed: 17 April 2020]

[71] Staffordshire University. All new West Midlands police recruits will 'earn and learn' to gain a Staffordshire University award. 2019. Available from: https://www.staffs.ac.uk/news/2019/04/all-new-west-midlands-police-recruits-will-earn-and-learn-to-gain-a-staffordshire-university-award [Accessed: 18 April 2020]

[72] Babcock. Babcock awarded contract to provide services to London's Police. 2019. Available from: https://www.babcockinternational.com/news/babcock-awarded-contract-to-provide-services-to-londons-police/ [Accessed: 20 April 2020]

[73] Metropolitan Police. The structure of the Met. 2020. Available from: https://www.met.police.uk/police-forces/metropolitan-police/areas/about-us/about-the-met/structure/ [Accessed: 20 April 2020]

[74] Government UK. National campaign to recruit 20,000 police officers launches today. 2019. Available from: https://www.gov.uk/government/news/national-campaign-to-recruit-20000-police-officers-launches-today [Accessed: 16 April 2020]

[75] Derbyshire Constabulary. The opportunity to obtain a fully-funded degree while working and earning a salary. 2020. Available from: https://careers.derbyshire.police.uk/what-you-could-be-doing/police-officers/police-constable-degree-apprenticeship [Accessed: 15 April 2020]

[76] College of Policing. Policing education qualifications framework. 2016. Available from: https://www.college.police.uk/What-we-do/Learning/Policing-Education-Qualifications-Framework/Pages/Policing-Education-Qualifications-Framework.aspx [Accessed: 15 April 2020]

[77] Williams E, Norman J, Rowe M. The police education qualification framework: A professional agenda or building professionals? Police Practice and Research. 2019;**20**(3):259-272

[78] Copley S. Reflective Practice for Policing Students. Exeter, UK: Learning Matters Ltd.; 2011

[79] Surrey Police. Police Constable degree holder entry programme (DHEP). 2020. Available from: https://www.lumesse-engage.com/policejobssurreyandsussex/jobs/police-constable-degree-holder-entry-programme-dhep--sysx-unfm00027 [Accessed: 20 April 2020]

[80] Hampshire Constabulary. Police officers recruiting now. 2020. Available from: https://www.hampshire.police.uk/police-forces/hampshire-constabulary/areas/careers/careers/police-officers/ [Accessed: 20 April 2020]

[81] Sussex Police. Fast-track detective development programme. 2020. Available from: https://www.sussex.police.uk/police-forces/sussex-police/areas/careers/jobs/fast-track-detective-development-programme/ [Accessed: 20 April 2020]

[82] Macpherson W. The Stephen Lawrence Inquiry. London, UK: Home Office; 1999. Available from: https://assets.publishing.service.gov.uk/government/uploads/system/uploads/attachment_data/file/277111/4262.pdf [Accessed: 28 April 2020]

[83] Jones T, Newburn T, Smith DJ. Democracy and Policing. London: Policy Studies Institute; 1994

[84] Paterson C, Pollock E, Robinson A, Senior P. Developments in police education in England and Wales: Values, culture and 'common-sense' policing. In: Cowburn M, Duggan M, editors. Values in Criminology and Community Justice. Bristol, UK: Policy Press; 2015. pp. 187-206

[85] Reiner R. The Politics of the Police. Oxford: Oxford University press; 2000

[86] Lincolnshire Police. PEQF—Judicial Review Action Launched. 2019. Available from: https://www.lincs.police.uk/news-campaigns/news/2019/peqf-judicial-review-action-launched/ [Accessed: 16 April 2020]

[87] Charman S. Changing landscapes, challenging identities—Policing in England and Wales. In: Wankhde P, McCann L, Murphy P, editors. Critical Perspectives on the Management and Organization of Emergency Services. Oxon, UK: Routledge; 2019

[88] Moeberg RJ, Pettersson O. Different educations—Different police recruits? In: Paper presented at the European Conference of Criminology; 22 September 2016

[89] White D, Heslop R. Educating, legitimising or accessorising? Alternative conceptions of professional training in UK higher education: A comparative study of teacher, nurse and police officer educators. Police Practice and Research. 2012;**13**(4):342-356

[90] Payne BK, Sumter M, Sun I. Bringing the field into the criminal justice classroom: Field trips, ride-alongs, and guest speakers. Journal of Criminal Justice Education. 2003;**14**(2):327-344

[91] Clapton G, Cree V. Integration of Learning for Practice: Literature Review. Edinburgh, UK: Scottish Institute for Excellence in Social Work Education; 2004

[92] Wrenn J, Wrenn B. Enhancing learning by integrating theory and practice. International Journal of Teaching and Learning in Higher Education. 2009;**21**(2):258-265

[93] Boud D, Cohen R, Walker D. Introduction: Understanding learning from experience. In: Boud D, Cohen R, Walker D, editors. Using Experience for Learning. Bristol, UK: Society for Research into Higher Education; 1993. pp. 1-17

[94] Hutchings P. Assessment and the Way it Works: Closing Plenary Address. Washington, DC: Association of Higher Education Conference on Assessment; 1990

[95] Choi I, Lee K. A case-based learning environment design for real-world classroom management problem solving. TechTrends. 2008;**52**(3):26-31

[96] Dorfman RA. Clinical Social Work: Definition, Practice and Vision. New York, USA: Brunner/Mazel; 1996

[97] Kramer BJ. Preparing social workers for the inevitable: A preliminary investigation of a course on death, grief, and loss. Journal of Social Work Education. 1998;**34**(2):211-227

[98] Lauritz LE, Astrom E, Nyman C, Klingvall M. Police students' learning preferences, suitable responses from the learning environment. Policing. 2012;**7**:195-203

[99] McCarthy B. About Learning. Barrington, IL: Excel Inc.; 1996

[100] Lauritz LE. Police identities: A study of student police officers and new police officers' professional identity [doctoral dissertation]. Umeå: Umea School of Business, Umeå University; 2009

[101] Knowles MS, Elwood R, Holton R, Swanson A. The Adult Learner: The Definitive Classic in Adult Education and Human Resource Development. 5th ed. New York, USA: Heinemann; 1998

[102] McMillan J, Forsyth D. What theories of motivation say about why learners learn. New Directions for Teaching and Learning. 1991;**1991**(45):39-52

[103] Rief S. How to Reach and Teach ADD/ADHD Children. New York: The Centre for Applied Research in Education; 1993

[104] Kramer M, Polifroni C, Organek N. Effects of faculty practice on students learning outcomes. Journal of Professional Nursing. 1986;**2**:289-301

[105] Good DM, Schubert CR. Faculty practice: How it enhances teaching. Journal of Nursing Education. 2001;**10**(9):389-396

[106] Sheridan BJ. Police learning in the university context: Student perceptions of the classroom environment on a police foundation degree course [unpublished doctoral thesis]. Institute of Criminal Justice Studies, University of Portsmouth; 2014

[107] Shohel MMC, Cann R, Atherton S. Enhancing student engagement using a blended learning approach: Case studies of first-year undergraduate students. International Journal of Mobile and Blended Learning. 2020;**12**(4):article 4

[108] Meyers C, Jones TB. Promoting Active Learning: Strategies for the College Classroom. San Francisco, USA: Jossey-Bass Inc.; 1993

[109] College of Policing. National Decision Model. 2013. Available from: https://www.app.college.police.uk/app-content/national-decision-model/the-national-decision-model/ [Accessed: 19 April 2020]

[110] Universities UK. The future growth of degree apprenticeships. 2016. Available from: https://www.universitiesuk.ac.uk/policy-and-analysis/reports/downloads/FutureGrowthDegreeApprenticeships.pdf [Accessed: 19 April 2020]

[111] Institute for Government. Performance tracker 2019: Police. 2019. Available from: https://www.instituteforgovernment.org.uk/publication/performance-tracker-2019/police [Accessed: 28 April 2020]

[112] Neyroud P, Loader I, Brown J, Muir R. Policing for a Better Britain: Report of the Independent Police Commission. 2016. p. 25

[113] BBC. Recruitment of 20,000 new police officers to begin 'within weeks'. 2019. Available from: https://www.bbc.co.uk/news/uk-49123319 [Accessed: 29 April 2020]

[114] Sherman LW. The Quality of Police Education: A Critical Review with Recommendations for improving Programs in Higher Education. San Francisco, USA: Jossey-Bass; 1978

[115] Sherman LW. College education for police: The reform that failed. Police Studies: The International Review of Police Development. 1978;**1**(4):32-38

[116] Jones M. Creating the 'thinking police officer': Exploring motivations and professional impact of part-time higher education. Policing. 2015;**10**(3):232-240

[117] Institute for Apprenticeships and Technical Education. 2017. Available from: https://www.instituteforapprenticeships.org/apprenticeship-standards/police-constable-degree/ [Accessed: 27 April 2020]

[118] Davis C. The Telegraph. It could take 100-years to make Met Police representative of London, the force admits. 2019. Available from: https://www.telegraph.co.uk/news/2019/02/19/could-take-100-years-make-met-police-representative-london-force/ [Accessed: 15 April 2020]

[119] BBC. Five charts that tell the story of diversity in UK universities. 2018. Available from: https://www.bbc.co.uk/news/education-44226434 [Accessed: 28 April 2020]

[120] James A, Silverstone D, Carr R, Kelly T, Karecha J. A report for the National Police Chiefs Council (NPCC) on innovative programmes for the recruitment and training of investigators. In: Currently in Operation in Police Forces in England & Wales. 2019. pp. 1-91

[121] Reiner R, Newburn T. Policing and the police. In: Maguire M, Morgan R, Reiner R, editors. The Oxford Handbook of Criminology. Oxford, UK: Oxford University Press; 2007. pp. 910-952

[122] Phillips WE, Burrell DN. Decision-making skills that encompass a critical thinking orientation for law enforcement professionals. International Journal of Police Science & Management. 2009;**11**(2):141-149

[123] Bryant R, Bryant S. Blackstone's Handbook for Policing Students. Oxford, UK: Oxford University Press; 2019

[124] Savage SP. Police Reform: Forces for Change. Oxford, UK: Oxford University Press; 2007

[125] Wimshurst K, Ransley J. Police education and the university sector: Contrasting models from the Australian experience. Journal of Criminal Justice Education. 2007;**18**(1):106-122

[126] NSW Police. NSW Police Recruitment. 2020. Available from: https://www.police.nsw.gov.au/recruitment/the_training/associate_degree_in_policing_practice/accommodationmeals_for_students [Accessed: 16 April 2020]

[127] Green T, Woolston R. Police training and education and university collaboration in Australia. In: Stanislas P, editor. International Perspectives on Police Education and Training. London, UK: Routledge; 2014. pp. 42-56

[128] Bangladesh Police. Training. 2020. Available from: https://www.police.gov.bd/en/training [Accessed: 10 April 2020]

[129] Uddin G. The Politics of Police Reform in Bangladesh. Saarbrücken (Germany): Lambert Academic Publishing; 2011

[130] Louisiana State Police. Joint Emergency Services Training Center (JESTC). 2016. Available from: http://www.jestc.org/index.html [Accessed: 18 April 2020]

[131] Hoggett J, Redford P, Toher D, White P. Challenges for police leadership: Identity, experience, legitimacy and direct entry. Journal of Police and Criminal Psychology. 2019;**34**:145-155

[132] Bergan S, Damian R. A word from the editors. In: Bergan S, Damian R, editors. Higher Education for Modern Societies—Competences and Values. Strasbourg Cedex: Council of Europe Publishing; 2010

[133] Bok D. Converging for diversity and democracy: A higher education. In:

Bergan S, Damian R, editors. Higher Education for Modern Societies—Competences and Values. Strasbourg Cedex: Council of Europe Publishing; 2010

[134] College of Policing. Leadership Review. 2015. Available from: https://www.college.police.uk/What-we-do/Development/Promotion/the-leadership-review/Documents/Leadership_Review_Final_June-2015.pdf [Accessed: 18 April 2020]

[135] Bowling B, Reiner R, Sheptycki J. The Politics of the Police. 5th ed. Oxford, UK: Oxford University Press; 2019

[136] Wheller L, Morris J. Evidence Reviews: What Works in Training, Behaviour Change and Implementing Guidance? London: National Policing Improvement Agency (NPIA); 2010. Available from: https://whatworks.college.police.uk/Research/Documents/What_Works_in_Training_and_Behaviour_change_REA.pdf [Accessed: 18 April 2020]

[137] Heslop R. Reproducing police culture in a British university: Findings from an exploratory case study of police foundation degrees. Police Practice and Research. 2011;**12**(4):298-312

[138] Loftus B, Skinns L, Munk T, Rice L. Police partnerships: Evidence review. N8 Policing Research Partnership. 2015. Available from: https://www.n8research.org.uk/media/PolicingPartnerships_EvidenceReview.pdf [Accessed: 19 April 2020]

[139] Macvean A, Cox C. Police education in a university setting: Emerging cultures and attitudes. Policing: A Journal of Policy and Practice. 2012;**5**(1):16-25

[140] Norman J, Williams E. Putting learning into practice: Self-reflections from cops. European Police Science and Research Bulletin. 2017;**3**:197-203

[141] Dewey J. The relation of theory to practice in education. In: McMurry CA, editor. The Third Yearbook of the National Society for the Scientific Study of Education, Part I. Chicago, USA: The University of Chicago Press; 1904. pp. 9-30

[142] Clare R. Global citizenship and critical thinking in higher education curricula and police education: A socially critical vocational perspective. Journal of Pedagogic Development. 2017;7(2):46-57

[143] Neyroud P, Loader I, Brown J, Muir R. Policing for a Better Britain: Report of the Independent Police Commission. 2016

[144] Hornyak M, Green SG, Heppard KA. Implementing experiential learning. In: Reynolds M, Vince R, editors. The Handbook of Experiential Learning and Management Education. New York, NY: Oxford University Press; 2007. pp. 137-152

[145] Cox C, Kirby S. Can higher education reduce the negative consequences of police occupational culture amongst new recruits? Policing: An International Journal of Police Strategies and Management. 2018;**41**(5):550-562

[146] Metropolitan Police. Call to retired officers to return to the Met. 2020. Available from: http://news.met.police.uk/news/call-to-retired-officers-to-return-to-the-met-398385 [Accessed: 15 April 2020]

[147] Wood D, Tong S. The future of initial police training: A university perspective. International Journal of Police Science and Management. 2009;**11**(3):294-305

[148] Jasper M. Professional Development, Reflection and Decision-Making. Oxford: Blackwell; 2006

[149] Marquardt MJ. Building the Learning Organisation. New York: McGraw-Hill; 1996

[150] Watkins KE, Marsick VJ. Sculpting the Learning Organisation: Lessons in the Art and Science of Systematic Change. San Francisco: Jossey-Bass; 1993

[151] Senge PM. The Fifth Discipline: The Art and Practice of the Learning Organization. New York, USA: Doubleday; 1990

[152] Hinton MS, Newburn T. Introduction: Policing developing democracies. In: Hinton MS, Newburn T, editors. Policing Developing Democracies. Oxon: Routledge; 2009. pp. 1-27

Chapter 2

Enhancing Quality of Higher Education and Employability in Kazakhstan: Gender Aspects

Maigul Nugmanova

Abstract

How can the higher education system of Kazakhstan be improved so that graduates are in demand in the labor market and are prepared for the challenges of a changing world? This chapter provides an analysis of the quality assurance (hereinafter the QA) systems of European universities, national QA system analysis of Kazakhstan, Belgium, France, and Sweden; and survey of internal QA systems in Kazakhstani Universities. This chapter examines the possibilities and acceptability of applying the best European practices in Kazakhstani Universities and argues that educational reforms successful in Europe may be ineffective in Kazakhstan due to the different starting conditions to reform. This chapter agrees that improvement of the internal standards of the QA and the quality culture contribute to improving the education quality and graduates employability, provided that all other areas such as economy, business, and living standards shall comply with international standards. The main aspects of this research deal with the interrelation between quality of education and employability of graduates, interconnection between gender discrimination and restricted employment opportunities of women. The chapter argues that the quality of higher education and training of highly qualified and employable specialists are the important prerequisites of sustainable social and economic development of society.

Keywords: external and internal quality assurance system, quality of higher education, employability of graduates, gender discrimination

1. Introduction

Quality of higher education and training of highly qualified and employable graduates are the important prerequisites of sustainable social and economic development of society [1]. Training of graduates in line with international standards can positively impact population's well-being in the long-term period. Nowadays, the HEIs must provide the high-quality student-centered learning and the ongoing adaptation of study programs and teaching methods to diverse expectations of labor market.

QA in higher education assumes, on the one hand, the process of creating conditions to promote the education quality, and, on the other hand, focus on an objective evaluation of the quality of learning outcomes and the professional competencies of students and graduates [2]. The education quality is one of the important components in the reproduction of the labor force, which contributes to the quality of the labor force and through it to the increase of the country's social and economic growth. Currently, the quality of higher education is an important issue for Kazakhstan, as the country needs highly qualified personnel capable of adapting to the changing realities of the labor market and solving complex issues to ensure sustainable social and economic development of the country. Having joined the Bologna Process in 2010, Kazakhstan introduced reform of the quality assurance system aimed at further improvement of the education system, its quality, and efficiency. As a guideline, the Bologna Declaration standards [2] were chosen. In 2011, a new version of the Kazakhstan Law "On Education" was adopted [3]. It aimed at the creation of a national quality assurance system in Kazakhstan, development of an internal quality assurance system in the HEIs, increase of the capacity of national quality assurance agencies, establishment of a network of independent local quality assurance agencies, and provision for procedures of the HEIs' accreditation. In 2012, the "Register 1" of independent accreditation agencies was worked out.

However, at the moment, there're no effective internal quality control systems in Kazakhstani HEIs [4]. There are no clearly defined internal standards to ensure the quality of education to evaluate the educational programs and the graduates' training level [4]. The HEIs manage in accordance with outdated internal standards and quality assurance tools that aren't adapted to modern conditions and national practices [4]. Normally, the quality assurance issues are limited to documentation and document workflow. The modern education system still encounters problems of centralized management [4]. The education reform came across with evident contradictions such as outdated laws and regulations governing the educational system. The new law "On Education" dated July 4, 2018, which is the so-called Law on the Autonomy of the Higher Educational Institutions provides innovations designed to resolve the contradictions between the efforts to reform education and the old management and the rules and regulations [5]. This paper analyzes the possibility and acceptability of the European best practices to be applied in Kazakhstani HEIs considering country's local contexts and how educational reforms successful in European countries are effective in Kazakhstan. The paper provides an analysis of the QA systems of three European universities (University de Liege, Royal Institute of Technology KTH, University de Lorraine), visited in the framework of international project experts training on QA in higher education; national quality assurance system analysis of Kazakhstan, Belgium, France, and Sweden; and survey of internal QA system in three Kazakhstani universities (University of International Relations, National Agrarian University, and University of Economics, Finance and Trade). This research uses data from a survey of Kazakhstani students, faculty, and staff between March and April 2018 as one of the methods to assess the education quality. However, often the HEIs aren't interested in an objective assessment of their effectiveness [1, 4]. In this regard, in order to get more objective assessment of the education quality, an additional survey was done to determine the more real picture of the University of International Relations graduates' employability. Employability would be one of the indicators of the competitiveness and demand for graduates in the labor market and proof of the high quality of education in the HEI they have graduated. This research was also aimed at the identification of the nature of employment to analyze its gender aspects.

Now, there is a clear gap between the labor market, the market needs, and the education system. The labor market is managed by employers who dictate the labor force demand and specify the demand for HEI graduates on the labor market. In this regard, this research analyzes the actual situation with the employment of the University of International Relations graduates in order to assess how competitive our graduates are in the labor market and assess the quality of their training, conduct a gender analysis of the opportunities and conditions of graduates' employment in the labor market, and analyze the role of the university-employer partnership to ensure the education quality and enhance the graduates' employability.

2. Methods

Analysis of the internal QA system of Kazakhstani universities is based on a survey conducted with the staff of the Quality Assurance units and observation of three Kazakhstani universities, as well as on their self-evaluation reports provided to the accreditation commission. In all these universities, the author was engaged in the accreditation process either as an expert of the accreditation commission or as an employee who participated in the preparation of a self-evaluation report to be accredited. For the purpose of survey, the questionnaire was used to cover questions on the institutional QA, namely, whether there is a specific structure/unit in charge of the QA or major directions of the QA strategy. Is there a specific official document on a QA strategy or is it an integral part of the university's overall strategy? Describe the QA mechanisms such as commissions, indicators, and assessment procedures. What are the internal and external stakeholders involved in the QA? Describe how they participate. Check the list to set the Standards and Guidelines for Quality Assurance in the European Higher Education Area (hereinafter ESG). Describe activities to confirm this standard implementation.

Analysis of the national and the institutional QA systems of European universities such as University de Liege (Belgium), Royal Institute of Technology KTH (Sweden), and University de Lorrain (France), which were visited under the international project training for QA experts in higher education, was done in terms of the possibilities and acceptability of application of the best European practices in Kazakhstani universities. Information provided at trainings by national QA agencies in Belgium, Agency for Quality Assurance in Higher Education (AEQES); in France, Commission des Titres d'Ingénieur (CTI) and High Council for the Evaluation of Research and Higher Education (HCERES); and in Sweden, The Swedish Higher Education Authority (UKÄ), was used in this paper.

One of the methods of internal evaluation of the University of International Relations effectiveness is monitoring and analysis of the quality of the educational services provided. In March–April 2018, the anonymous survey "Faculty Through the Eyes of Students" among the students and the questionnaire of faculty members "The social well-being of the academic staff" were conducted. Questionnaires "Faculty Through the Eyes of Students" had 10 questions regarding the faculty teaching competence in the following areas: the student-oriented approach, interaction with students including ethical behavior, the relevance of the material provided to students to the latest science achievements, the information relevance, and the use of innovative teaching methods and technologies. The students filled in 12,036 questionnaires about 404 faculty members, while the survey coverage was 90% of the entire teaching staff. According to the survey results, 96% of students were satisfied with the teaching quality. The average score was 4.8 points out of 5 possible. Thus, according to this internal assessment, the University of International Relations has a high education quality.

Under the questionnaire "The Social Wellbeing of the Faculty Members," 413 questionnaires or 92% of the total staff were filled in by the faculty. A respondent might choose several answers from the set list of questions. A survey of respondents showed that 73% of the faculty members are satisfied with their work at the University of International Relations while 23% aren't. 51% of them are in favor of improving the psychological climate, and 49% think that it is necessary to improve working conditions, reduce unnecessary paperwork, provide more time for scientific creative work, computerize all processes, increase the Internet speed, and improve automated processes. In general, based on the results of both surveys, the University of International Relations has a high grade of the faculty effectiveness and the entire educational process. However, just the opinions of students and faculty do not provide an objective assessment of the education quality. A more fundamental indicator of the University of International Relations effectiveness would be the graduates' employability. "Employability is an aggregate of competencies, skills, understanding, and personal characteristics that provide graduates with career prospects that contribute to the development of the economy and society" [6]. A high indicator of the graduates' employment proves the relevance of demand for graduates and their specialty. It would be a proof of recognition of the competences received and the education quality in this HEI.

Under this research, 1261 graduates of 2017 from 1323 of the University of International Relations were interviewed. Sixty-two graduates were foreign citizens and were not interviewed. To confirm data received under this survey, information was requested from the Interdepartmental Settlement Center for Social Payments (hereinafter Center for Social Payments) on the pension contributions made by our graduates. The 2017 database of graduates with information on respondents including passport data and the University of International Relations name was provided to the Center for Social Payments. It was done to track respondents in the tax base and to get data on their social payments. The social payments of a respondent would confirm his/her official paid employment.

Open questions with an open-ended choice of answers were used. The survey was done in the form of a telephone interview with pre-prepared questions in February to March 2018, that is, the 8th–9th months after the graduation.

3. Data analysis, results, and discussion

3.1 Analysis of the national and the institutional quality assurance systems

In 2010, in an effort to integrate into the global educational space, Kazakhstan has signed the Bologna Process. Most Kazakhstani HEIs have signed the "Magna Carta of Universities," which is the fundamental of the "Bologna Declaration." The Lisbon Convention "On the recognition of qualifications on higher education in the European region" and the Sorbonne Declaration "On the harmonization of the architecture of the European higher education system" were signed, while the declaration "Zone of European higher education" was adopted. Having signed these documents, Kazakhstan demonstrated its will for democratization, improvement of the education quality, and the establishment of the autonomy of HEIs [7]. Kazakhstan has chosen to modernize the education system and comply with international standards. All the HEIs nationwide have transferred to a three-level system of education including the undergraduate, graduate, and doctoral (PhD.) The educational process was reorganized into a credit training system based on comparability with the ECTS credit transfer system. The HEIs all by themselves have started to develop and approve the procedure to transfer credits according to the ECTS type and regulate its application. "The Rules to organize the educational process under the credit technology" and "Classifier of specialties of higher and postgraduate education of the Republic Kazakhstan" with enlarged groups of specialties were approved nationwide [8].

A critical issue of modernization is the creation of a National QA system, which would not just control over the education quality but also the development of the system to ensure the quality of education. The ESG were applied as the basis for the QA system in Kazakhstan. Accreditation of the HEI and study programs is the external quality assurance mechanism. The national accreditation model is independent and voluntary. Accreditation shall be implemented by accreditation agencies included in the Register 1, which is the list of accreditation agencies in the field of education, which are the National Register of Accreditation Bodies of the Republic of Kazakhstan (hereinafter the RoK) Ministry of Education and Science. The RoK Ministry of Education and Science recognizes all European accreditation agencies listed in the European QA Register (EQAR). However, in order to be able to accredit Kazakhstani HEIs, they shall be registered in Kazakhstan and join the Register 1. Currently, 11 accreditation agencies are listed in Register 1, among them are 6 Kazakhstani organizations, Kazakhstan Agency for Quality Assurance in Education (IKAQAE), Independent Agency of Accreditation and Ratings (IAAR), Kazakhstan Association for Engineering Education (KAZSEE), Agency for Recognition and Quality Assurance in Education (ARQA), Eurasian Center for Accreditation and QA (ECAQA), and Independent Accreditation Center (IKAC), and 5 international ones—FIBAA (German), ASIIN (German), MusiQue (Belgium), ACQUIN (German), and ACBSP (USA).

Since 2017, national agencies IAAR and IKAQAE became the international ones and joined the European Association for the Quality Assurance in Higher Education (ENQA). In addition, they were listed in the European Register for Quality Assurance (EQAR) [9]. According to the report of the Center for the Bologna Process, the listing of Kazakhstani agencies into the European Register "demonstrated the recognition of procedures and processes at the European level the whole Kazakhstani education" [9]. The RoK National agencies accredit under the QA standards they have developed, in accordance with national education standards and the ESG. "Special standards analogous to the ESG in the field of the QA are not developed in Kazakhstan yet" [9]. Conceivably, the IAAR and the IKAQAE are the independent agencies and do not depend on public finance. However, the HEIs pay the agencies for accreditation and choose an accreditation agency by themselves. Eventually, these factors affect the assessment fairness, by taking into account the low level of quality culture. For example, the French High Council for Evaluation of Research and Higher Education (HCÉRES) is an independent national QA in higher education agency, which does not depend on state funding and of HEI. The HCÉRES is funded by the parliamentary vote.

Despite the fact that accreditation is voluntary for the HEIs, all of them are interested in it. First of all, the non-accredited HEIs shall not train the state-funded grantees. The status of an accredited university is critical for a HEI. Such status would confirm the compliance of a university and its educational programs with international standards. This status provides an HEI with a chance to be recognizable in Europe and to develop joint educational programs and academic mobility. However, the ambitions of Kazakhstani HEIs to be accredited shortly and the competition for being top in the ratings often resulted in an unreliable self-assessment reports and colored truth. But it is just the transparent, objective, reliable results of the internal assessment and audit of a HEI and the quality of its educational programs that are done by its staff at the institutional level could help to identify weaknesses and ways to address them. The accreditation procedure as such presupposes to pass a final verdict upon the completion of the assessment. The "F" would entail no access to many of the above benefits. It might be advisable to use the experience of the French agency HCÉRES and first provide Kazakhstani HEIs with an independent evaluation. Such an evaluation does not imply placing a HEI in the ranking, but is done in order to identify weaknesses and provide an opportunity to improve a HEI management.

One of the impediments to improve the education quality would be the non-transparent and inaccurate statistics. All the HEIs of the country on an ongoing basis upload their data to the ESU-VO, Unified Management System of Higher Education. This is a multilevel information system that includes all the HEIs, the RoK Ministry of Education and Science, and other government structures and agencies involved in the education development. Quite often, the data uploaded by universities in ESU-VO differ from those provided by them in self-assessment reports and from the real situation at a HEI. HEIs are not interested in creating a transparent statistical database. For example, data on the number of students and their socioeconomic status are overestimated, since the amount of funding from the Ministry of Education and Science depends on this. The decrease in the number of students, specifically the students from low-income families, as a result has a decrease in funding from the Ministry of Education and Science. Efforts by the Ministry of Education and Science to introduce the "Platonus" electronic system have not gained traction in numerous HEIs. Specifically, at the University of Liege, a statistic list has been created on the university's website in the public domain. All the university's statistics is placed there. This is the automated data processing. This list is ongoingly updated. Each university unit has access to a statistical database. The use of this French experience could reduce the time spent by employees of Kazakhstani HEIs to collect and process data to be provided to accountable bodies and make university statistics transparent.

The survey of Kazakhstani universities found that all the HEIs have the developed QA system (according to their responses) with a separate unit in charge, the QA policy, mechanisms, and procedures that comply with the European QA Framework and ESG. The QA procedures include surveys of students and employers. The major standards and parameters of the Bologna Process were proclaimed in Kazakhstan at the national and institutional levels as "adopted and implemented." However, their real implementation is yet an issue. Challenges arise since the HEIs' employees have no skills to develop educational programs which shall comply with the qualification framework and in the regulation and evaluation of the HEIs' activities, and they have no responsibility for learning outcomes. Universities encounter the overcentralized management and outdated internal QA tools. The institutional QA systems are limited to a quality management system that complies with the ISO 9001. The academic integrity, rating methods, the teaching quality, and the development of a "culture of quality and trust" [4] remain problematic. The development of a quality culture implies that each unit and each staffer shall be responsible and aware of their involvement in the final result, namely, in the qualitative training of specialists, and participate in the continual improvement of the education quality.

Most HEIs in France, Belgium, and Sweden are public; however, all of them have academic and financial independence. Currently, higher education in Kazakhstan transits from the centralized administration by the RoK Ministry of Education and Science to the HEIs' autonomy. Unfortunately, very often autonomy is considered by the HEIs barely as financial self-sufficiency and independent distribution of financial and material resources. In an effort to reduce the expenditure side of the university budget, the administration often downsizes the number of faculty and staff, increasing the workload of those remaining. In the HEIs, there is still a practice to finance in-service training of faculty on a residual basis. There are contradictions between the outdated methods of education management and efforts to modernize the education system. The reforms undertaken do not yet provide full academic and financial freedom to the HEIs. Reform of the higher education system and the will to provide greater autonomy to the HEIs are restrained by outdated laws and regulations in all areas of a HEI's development. For example, the transition to credit training technologies implies for students the independent choice of subjects for study, that is, have freedom of choice. However, the strategy of public financing of the HEIs is still based on the state education standards and compulsory model curricula, which means no alternatives to choose [10]. This contradiction limits the academic autonomy of the HEIs. Overcentralization prevents the HEIs from consideration of local needs.

The HEIs' right to develop a corporate governance designed to fulfill not only an advisory, but also a controlling role, and to ensure interrelation and consideration of the national interests, business, and society was limited to the creation of the regents of the universities and the supervisory board at a HEI, which do not have any legal force and exist just on paper. The lack of appropriate laws and regulations restrains the expansion of the HEIs' autonomy. Most HEIs operate as national state-owned enterprises on the basis of the right of economic management. The law "On State Property" governing these HEIs conflicts with the main strategies to develop academic and financial independence [11, 4].

To further promote the HEIs' autonomy, a new RoK Law "On Amendments and Additions to Certain Legislative Acts of the Republic of Kazakhstan on the Expansion of the Academic and Administrative Independence of Higher Education Institutions" of July 4, 2018, was adopted, and over 70 regulatory legal acts were elaborated [5]. This law provides the state enterprises for possible transformation of the legal form into nonprofit joint-stock companies. Such transformation would be another step to autonomy, since the nonprofit form of organization makes it possible for HEIs to maintain corporate standards in management and ensure the efficient redistribution of income for its development. This law shall entitle the HEIs to legally pursue commercial activities. The reform also affected the methods to finance the HEIs and provides for the transition to credit financing without reference to the period of study [5]. The new law also provides the development of a new Classifier on the training areas. In accordance with this Classifier, the HEIs shall independently develop the new educational programs. The new Classifier will replace the old one with numerous specialties which have not been in demand in the labor market for a while [12].

The institutional autonomy is not a goal in itself. The main argument to expand the HEIs' autonomy would be an effective QA system, which implies the HEIs' institutional responsibility for the education quality and social responsibility for the population's well-being in the end. "Autonomy shall be implemented under a national framework that balances institutional freedom with various social goals" [13, 14]. The HEIs' overcommercialization, increased tuition fees, and the current methods of the RoK Ministry of Education and Science to distribute educational grants have resulted in limited access to education for the disadvantaged population. Educational grants are primarily awarded based on academic merit. School graduates from low-income families and applicants from rural areas, where poverty is 2.7 times higher than in the urban ones and the instruction level and material security of schools is lower than in the cities [15], were on a back foot. Granting autonomy to the HEIs would not mean taking away responsibility of the state to support them and the vulnerable groups. Given the low level of socioeconomic development of the country (compared to European countries), Kazakhstan needs the Government support for the HEIs at this stage of transition to academic and managerial independence.

In Europe, the transformation period in the education system to create the common education space and the labor market has more than 50 years. The national and domestic QA systems of the HEIs in France, Belgium, Romania, Sweden, and Bulgaria are guided by the ESG standards aimed at improving the education quality and developing a quality culture in higher education, bolstering the role of students and employers in the QA processes. The national QA agencies evaluate the HEIs' activities and intend, per their recommendations provided, to promote them providing quality services and increase the graduates' employability as the main indicator of the education quality. However, the policy to ensure the quality of each country has its own specifics, adapts to local terms, and considers the conditions for the development of the local labor market and the living standard of the population.

At the end of the last century, France and Belgium already had a developed quality assessment system. In the early 2000s, in order to ensure comparability of educational programs, create a common educational space, and promote student mobility, the European HEIs begin to transit to accreditation as the final stage of assessment to confirm that a HEI complies with the ESG standards. Currently, Belgium develops a new methodology for an external QA system. It focuses on support of HEIs and promotion of their quality approaches, the internal QA system, and strengthening autonomy and responsibility for the QA in a HEI and transfers from just a summative assessment to an effective formative assessment which involves monitoring in order to provide its results to the HEIs to improve teaching and learning.

All the analyzed European HEIs are independently responsible for the education quality while keeping their traditions and specifics that took years. The QA system of all European HEIs gives priority to their self-evaluation, assessment of learning outcomes, increased autonomy, and the level and nature of the graduates' employment. For example, the University de Lorraine Quality Management Unit has been monitoring graduates for employment for several years. The survey key questions are set by the Ministry of Education, but the HEIs can freely add any questions of their interest. The statistics received under the survey are available on the universities' website and used to evaluate their activities. They are also provided to the Ministry of Education to create a centralized database of all universities. At the national level, the survey results are processed, and databases are compiled at different levels, in different subjects, for each university, and at the national level.

The Swedish QA system under the requirements of the Bologna Process was formed with the already high-quality education in the country. The Swedish Higher Education Authority (UKÄ) is a state agency controlled by the State. The major focus of this agency is to ensure that the assessment conducted by the agency helps to improve the education quality at the university. Sweden has developed a new QA system implemented since 2017 and made up four separate assessments: an institutional assessment of the QA process, an assessment of educational programs, an assessment of degree applications, and thematic assessments. Thematic assessment would mean evaluation of the entire educational system, comparison of the achievements of the HEIs in areas important to the country, and ensuring quality in higher education by topics such as internationalization or gender equality. "Sustainable development in education" was determined for a thematic assessment in 2017. The Swedish QA system is characterized by ongoing monitoring and periodic evaluation of educational programs; a university has a close relationship with the business sector and with employers and is strongly orientated to the labor market. In Sweden, a government agency, working on labor market research, works effectively to determine the skills and competencies that will be in future demand in a country and regions.

The Swedish experience in the study of the labor market could be a good guide for Kazakhstani students when choosing subjects, for the HEIs and employers to develop educational programs, and for the Ministry of Education and Science to determine state education standards, working out strategies and programs for education development. The RoK Ministry of Labor and Social Protection of the

Population in cooperation with the RoK Ministry of Education and Science forecast specialties that will be in demand on the labor market. According to the forecasts, a state educational order is formed. According to the latest forecast data, the most on-fire specialties are the industrial and the technical ones [16]. However, there is practically no more national industrial sector, and therefore there will be no demand for graduates in these subjects in the labor market. The Soviet experience of the development of vocational education which had strong relationship with the industrial sector was completely ignored since there is no industrial sector anymore. Since applicants are not interested to enroll on these specialties, it would be advisable to provide them with incentives to stimulate their choice of specialties strategically important for the country's future.

The European HEIs are financially independent, yet the state provides them with financial support. According to the latest available data from UNESCO, in 2015 government expenditures on education in Kazakhstan amounted to 2.79% of GDP, which is way below than in European countries (**Figure 1**). Herewith, in Kazakhstan the share of expenditures on tertiary in total expenditures on education is lower (**Figure 1**). Likewise, the share of expenditures on tertiary in total expenditures for education in Kazakhstan tends to decrease and amounted to 15.26% in 2015, 11.64% in 2016, and 10.56% in 2017 [17].

Currently, Kazakhstani HEIs encounter financial difficulties such as provision of a decent salary for employees, renovation of material-technical basis of HEI, promotion of academic mobility, and in-service faculty training. An unreasonable increase of tuition fees (compared to the financial capacities of local households) results in a loss of students due to the general low level of the population's well-being. Consequently, the public finance of Kazakhstani HEIs is needed and should be a priority for the state as support to the economy and business. For the internal QA system of Kazakhstani HEIs, it would be advisable to adopt the experience of European HEIs to create mechanisms for continuous, comprehensive, and transparent assessment. On this basis further improvement of the education quality would be developed. The current practice to conduct an accelerated and chaotic assessment under the preparation for accreditation creates stress for all the HEI employees and suspends all its activities. All European countries under consideration are characterized by a high life quality and a high level of economic development, the industrial sector, the SME, the popular employment in nongovernmental organizations due to decent salaries there, and the social environment. All this creates a wide labor

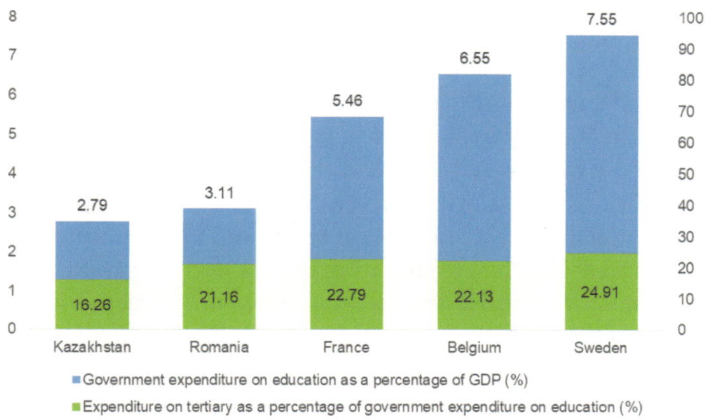

Figure 1.
Government expenditure on education as a percentage of GDP (%). Expenditure on tertiary as a percentage of government expenditure on education (%). Source: based on UNESCO data (http://data.uis.unesco.org/), accessed on August 2019.

market and hence a greater demand for graduates. To ensure the effective modernization and reform in Kazakhstan, the government support of education also should comply with international standards; the level of the populations' well-being and the country's socio-economic development would allow students to choose a university that provides sound academic background and they would be able to pay for quality education and later find a decent work and fair salary.

3.2 Quality of higher education and employability in Kazakhstan: gender aspects

According to the graduates' survey results, out of a total number of respondents 1261 (100%), 929 (74%) of the University of International Relations graduates have found a job and are currently employed, of which 18 persons have started a business and are registered as individual entrepreneurs. Of a total number of respondents, 178 (14%) graduates have continued their education, while 154 (12%) persons had no job at the survey time. However, the Center for Social Payments confirmed official data for any payments only for 771 graduates out of the 929 graduates who answered they were employed. This means that only 771 graduates had a paid employment while the remaining 158 (12.5% of all respondents) were informally employed (**Figure 2**).

Seventy percent (992 persons) of all University of International Relations graduates (1323 persons) are women, while 30% (331 people) are men. Of a total number of interviewed (1261) graduates, 75% (945 persons) were women and 25% (316) men. Evidently, among those who received higher education in the University of International Relations, women are in majority. Similar situation is nationwide. In Kazakhstan, the education level of the employed population is high: 39% of the employed population have higher education, 37.5% specialized secondary education, and 17% general secondary one. At the same time, the education level among women is higher than that of men. 43.8% of employed women have higher education; this number among men is 34.5%. According to the survey, the percentage of female graduates with a high GPA (3.2–4.0 out of 4.0 possible) is 46% (out of all female graduates of 2017). Of a total number of male graduates, 42% of male graduates have a high GPA. However, whereas there're no gender differences in the cognitive abilities of women and men, there're gender inequalities in the labor market, namely, in hiring, in access to highly paid and prestigious jobs.

According to the graduates' survey results, 74% of the University of International Relations female graduates surveyed have found jobs (701 persons), and out of 316 of the interviewed male graduates, 72% (228 persons) were employed. Thus, the percentage of the University of International Relations female and male graduates' employability is almost the same. However, there is a significant difference in the employment nature. Namely, there're gender differences in the spheres chosen by women and men and the positions offered by employers, in employment conditions and salaries. On the surface, there's no gender discrimination as a phenomenon in Kazakhstan. Equal rights and opportunities for men and women are legislated at the state level. But in reality, there is gender discrimination in the labor market such as professional segregation, which, namely, is evident as the feminization of low-paid jobs and in the representation of women mainly at the lower levels of the economic hierarchy. A simple comparison of the average monthly wages of men and women shows the existence of gender differences when women's labor is paid lower than men's one, and women's wages are 69.6% of men's wages [18]. According to the RoK Statistic Agency, the wages of men in major groups of positions and professions are approximately 1.1–2.2 times more than the average wages of women on similar positions (**Figure 3**).

Women have limited access to prestigious work, since it is assumed their labor has a low return. According to the survey results, almost 70% of employed female graduates work in schools and colleges as teachers. In turn, the majority of male graduates (about 60%) work in prestigious companies, where wages are higher. The education sphere in Kazakhstan is one of the lowest paid with majority of women employed, since the men aren't interested in such employment and do not compete with women here. Female graduates do not sustain competition with the males for well-paid jobs, where they shall work overtime and ongoingly upgrade qualifications. Even if a woman is unmarried at the time of hiring, employers prefer the man since a woman's employment is sort of risky, namely, in terms of her future marriage and maternity leave. It is known that in future women will devote all their off-hours to the family and practically will have no opportunity to upgrade their skills and work overtime. Incompatibility of biological reproduction and economic production is "a fundamental source of dynamic allocative inefficiency and a basic cause of women's inequality" [19].

Currently, paid work outside the home and unpaid chores and women's time for childcare, especially in young low-income families, are almost incompatible.

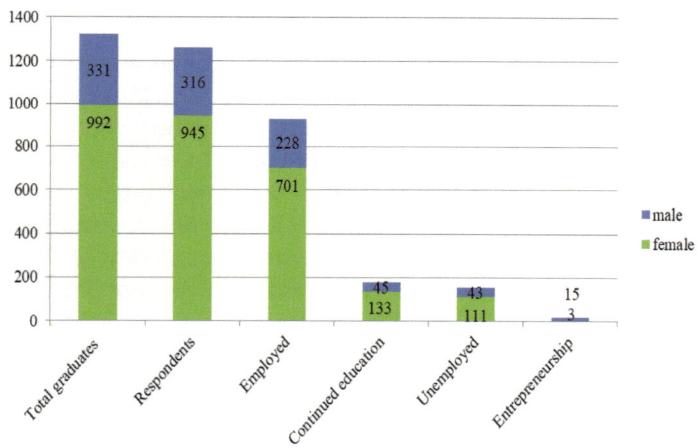

Figure 2.
Survey of 2017 University of International Relations graduates employability. Source: based on survey results.

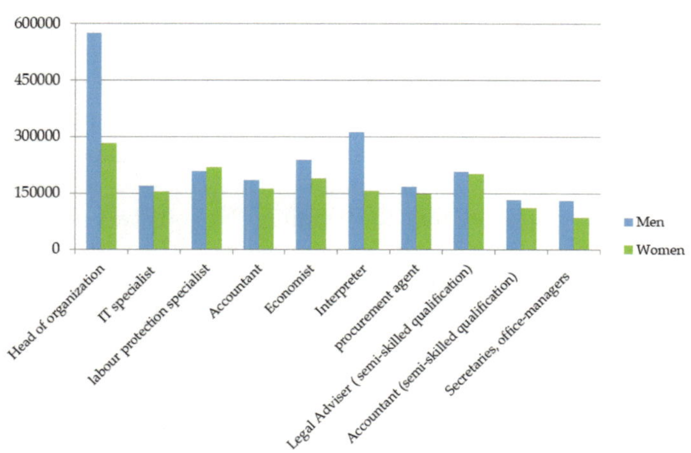

Figure 3.
Average monthly nominal wage of men and women for selected occupations and functions (for all observed forms of economic activity). Source: the RoK Statistic Agency, 2018.

Low-income families cannot afford to automate their chores, hire a babysitter, and pay for preschool education. The lower the level of a household welfare, the higher the women's workload in the household, and the less is her ability to get paid work outside the home [20]. This situation is exacerbated by inadequate social support by the Government and the lack of social infrastructure accessible to the needy families. "The lack of social policy measures and supports for unpaid family responsibilities hits poor and vulnerable families the hardest, as they have the weakest economic capacity to purchase goods (processed foods, labor saving devices) or services (private childcare, domestic help) that can free up their time for paid work. They are often forced to choose between employment and care or to combine them—choices which require painful sacrifices in terms of quality of employment and/or quality of care. These choices also have longer-term welfare and economic consequences" [21]. The functions of a mother and housewife are very critical for a Kazakhstani woman who sincerely believes that it is her mission to be the guardians of the hearth. However, in order to support our national traditions, we need to create proper social economic conditions for women to provide reasonable conjunction of mother's responsibility and homework with paid work. Moreover it should be a woman's choice either to stay at home or to work outside for salary.

Nationwide, in 2017, the share of the paid-employed was 77% or 6.5 million and self-employed 23% or 2 million persons [18]. At the same time, women make up 62% of all self-employed. Informally employed in the country make up 16% of the total number of employed or almost 1.4 million individuals, and almost half of them are women. Informally employed in the country do not have access to social security, are not eligible for loans, and do not have stable incomes and pension savings. According to a survey at the University of International Relations, it was revealed that 12.5% (158 individuals) of all respondents are employed in the informal sector. 57% (90 individuals) of them are women. Most of them responded that they work as interpreters/translators, but since they do not pay taxes and social contributions, they apparently work as freelancers in informal sector. This means that the work of 158 unemployed graduates is not protected by law and is normally characterized by worse working conditions. Informally employed women are more vulnerable in the labor market due to the fact that they are more dependent on social benefits, sick leave, and maternity leave.

All respondents noted that it is very difficult to find jobs in national and private companies, where wages are higher than in public sector, without any support and patronage. Employers require work experience in a certain field, which is mostly unacceptable for the HEIs' graduates. All respondents said the majority of job ads require 1–3 years of work experience in the relevant field. Also, respondents noted that if any work experience wasn't required, such job did not require higher education and had low wages (50,000KZT/month ($135)). Employers aren't interested in additional on-the-job training for newcomers. One of the respondents said he lost his first job because the employer would need employees who already know everything and would not waste time for training. "Nobody was eager to share information I didn't know," the respondent complained. The HEIs' graduates are the least competitive in the labor market due to a lack of work experience and relevant skills. The situation with female graduates is exacerbated due to gender stereotypes about hiring. State-support programs for the HEIs' graduates to encourage employers to hire graduates could assist newcomers to avoid stress, depression, and disappointment.

According to official statistics, the unemployment rate in the RoK among youngsters is 38% of the total number of unemployed nationwide, and most of them are the HEIs' graduates [18, 15]. In this case, it is more difficult for female graduates to find job than for males. The level of woman's unemployment nationwide among the youth is about 8%, while the man's unemployment rate is 6% [18]. Women are the majority among the unemployed. Female graduates face great difficulties in the labor market while getting more prestigious job. Employers secretly prefer to hire men, because they assume that women would marry sooner and go on maternity leave and could not work overtime due to their family obligations. Several female respondents noted that employers asked them on job interviews whether they intend to marry or have children sooner. Such questions shall violate women's rights.

One hundred fifty-four persons out of all the respondents did not get a job. 61% of all unemployed respondents are women while 39% are men. Some unemployed respondents have valid reasons, among them are the army service for men and the maternity leave for women who have to perform only unpaid chores and childcare. Unemployed female graduates with children at the survey time responded they cannot get paid work since they devote all their time to childcare and chores, due to the fact that they cannot afford the babysitting services. Women's unpaid work in the reproductive sector including childcare and education of future generation is important to reproduce the labor force and the future national economic growth [22]. The state support of young families and the improvement of social infrastructure would be cost-effective both for the families and for society as a whole.

Women are in minority among those who start business in the country. At the same time, most women entrepreneurs have small businesses. Only 15% of large companies in the country are headed by women [18]. Women choose small businesses since it does not require high costs and resources, as well as special knowledge and skills to manage financial documents and reports [23]. The University of International Relations graduates both females and males are in equally difficult positions when in open business, due to lack of financial resources and entrepreneurial skills. According to the survey results, only 1.9% of employed graduates were able to start business. Herewith, among the respondents who started business only 16% are women, while 84% are men. Obviously, the HEIs' graduates need the state support to start and run the business, in the form of preferential taxation, access to loans, etc. In addition, the HEIs could pre-train students for business through the integration in the curricula of courses on the basics of entrepreneurial skills, business management, and project management.

The most important aspect to ensure the education quality is the development of partnerships with real sector of economy. All the universities surveyed have entered into partnerships with business and public sectors where students had internships. For students, it is a good opportunity to test their knowledge and skills in real conditions, and for employers it is possible to assess the competencies of potential employees. According to the survey at the University of International Relations, 37% of employed graduates found jobs through the university in entities which are the university's strong partners and mainly in the organizations where they'd internships. The university-employer cooperation is also implemented through business and public sector representatives teaching at the university, development of educational programs, assessment of students, and job fairs. Employers' survey on their satisfaction with the quality of training of the HEIs' graduates is one of the methods to assess the conformity of knowledge, skills, and competencies gained with the needs of the labor market. The question remains. How to ensure the objectivity of the assessment? How to process the comparability of the assessment results on the training quality in different universities? How to consider the different specializations of the HEIs, differences by region, between urban and rural areas and cultural and national aspects?

The further strengthening of the University-Business network and the more systematic involvement of employers in the development of educational programs would facilitate the adaptation of program content to the needs of the labor market and the elimination of the gap between the labor market and education.

To be competitive, the HEIs' graduates currently should be able to solve issues in different fields of expertise. In this regard, interdisciplinary education is relevant for the HEIs. Educational programs including interdisciplinary courses in the field of entrepreneurship or project management can develop business and projects' development skills. Interdisciplinary courses in the gender economics can increase awareness of socioeconomic processes in society, instill a culture of equality, and develop critical thinking.

4. Conclusions

The primary standards and parameters of the Bologna Process adopted at the national and the institutional levels in Kazakhstan encounter a problem of their real implementation. First of all, the reformation should consider the level of socio-economic development of the country, the conditions to develop the local labor market, and the living standard of the population. It may take some time to change the mindset, develop skills, and teach the universities' staff to be responsible in developing educational programs that comply with international standards and in regulating and evaluating the HEIs' activities.

The internal QA system of Kazakhstani HEIs should focus on the adoption of the experience of European HEIs to create mechanisms for continuous, comprehensive, and transparent assessment. The current practice to conduct an accelerated and chaotic assessment under the preparation for accreditation creates stress for all the HEI employees and suspends all its activities. An analysis of the QA systems of European universities has revealed that using the best practices of the European national and institutional QA systems can be a solution to the education quality in Kazakhstan. In the meantime, it should be borne in mind that Kazakhstan has completely different starting conditions for modernization than European countries. This paper argues that educational reforms successful in European countries are still ineffective in Kazakhstan due to the lower level of socioeconomic development of the country, a quality culture and quality of life, and insufficient budget expenditures to finance education.

Currently, Kazakhstani HEIs need the support of the state and the QA agencies to create a mechanism of an ongoing, comprehensive, and transparent self-evaluation that helps to improve the university and educational programs and does not imply a race for a place in ratings, in creation incentives for an effective and objective internal evaluation.

For the successful implementation of the best European practices in Kazakhstan, it is necessary that government expenditures on education, the welfare level of the population, and the life quality and socioeconomic development of the country also comply with international standards, so that Kazakhstanis can choose a HEI that provides quality education, be able to pay for quality education, and get a decent work.

Based on the survey results, the University of International Relations has a high percentage of graduates' employability and trains competitive graduates. Despite the fact that there're no gender differences in the cognitive abilities of male and female graduates and the employability percentage is almost the same for both women and men, women are more vulnerable, cannot compete in the labor market, and are employed in less paid sectors. Women are fewer among those who start and run their business. The low competitiveness of the female labor force in the labor market is primarily associated with their childcare and chore obligations, which require more women's time the lower the well-being is in the household. Woman's labor in the reproductive sector is not paid for but is important in shaping human capital and the labor force quality. Thus, the gender aspect is an essential factor that can impact future wages, employment opportunities, and skills development and retraining. State social support for young families and incentives for employers to hire female and male graduates will ultimately bring economic benefits to society as a whole. Employability is a common issue that should be solved jointly by a student himself and with the support of the HEIs, business, and the state.

The employers' survey on the assessment of the graduates' competences could provide a more realistic picture of the demand for graduates in the labor market, as well as their professions, and most importantly, on the quality of their training in the HEIs. It would also be rational to have an additional survey of the same 2017 graduates a few years later, to track/analyze considering the gender aspects—whether they were able to retain their jobs or find opportunities to retrain in order to get new skills that meet the modern demands of the labor market, who of them was able to be promoted, and whether women after maternity leave could brush up and compete in the labor market.

Acknowledgements

I would like to express my special thanks to adjunct professor of University of Eastern Finland Heimo Mikkola for the scientific guidance, technical assistance, and moral support. I am very grateful to Erasmus+ program and European team of the project "Implementation of Education Quality Assurance System via Cooperation of University-Business-Government in Higher Education Institutions" for the great opportunity to go through experts training on QA in higher education.

Author details

Maigul Nugmanova
Gender Economics Research Center, Narxoz University, Almaty, Kazakhstan

*Address all correspondence to: maigulnugmanova@yahoo.com

References

[1] The State Program of Education Development of the Republic of Kazakhstan for 2011-2020. 2010. Available from: http://control.edu.gov.kz/ru/gosudarstvennaya-programma-razvitiya-obrazovaniya-na-2011-2020-gody

[2] ESG-Standards and Guidelines for Quality Assurance in the European Higher Education Area. 2015. Available from: http://www.ehea.info/cid105593/esg.html

[3] The Law "On Education" of the Republic of Kazakhstan. 2011. Available from: www.zakon.kz/141156-zakon-respubliki-kazakhstan-ot-27.html

[4] OECD. Reviews of National Policies for Education–Higher Education in Kazakhstan. 2017. Available from: http://www.oecd.org/publications/higher-education-in-kazakhstan-2017-9789264268531-en.htm

[5] The Law of the Republic of Kazakhstan "On Amendments and Additions to Some Legislative Acts of the Republic of Kazakhstan on the Expansion of the Academic and Management Independence of Higher Education Institutions". No. 171-VI dated July 4, 2018. Available from: http://adilet.zan.kz/rus/docs/Z1800000171

[6] The Enhancing Student Employability Coordination Team–(ESECT). Employability in the context of the bologna process. General conclusions and recommendations. In: Bled. 2004. pp. 196-198

[7] Sorbonne Declaration/Center for the Bologna Process and Academic Mobility under the RoK Ministry of Education and Science. Available from: //http://enic-kazakhstan.kz/ru/bolonskiy-process/dokumentatsiya

[8] On the approval of the Rules to organize the educational process under the credit technology. Order No 152, dated April 20, 2011 of the RoK Minister of Education and Science. Available from: http://adilet.zan.kz/rus/docs/V1100006976

[9] Analytical Report on the Implementation of the Bologna Process Principles in the Republic of Kazakhstan. Astana: Center for the Bologna Process and Academic Mobility under the RoK Ministry of Education and Science; 2018. 64p. Аналитический отчет по реализации принципов Болонского процесса в Республике Казахстан, 2018 год. – Астана: Центр Болонского процесса и академической мобильности МОН РК, 2018. 64 с

[10] Omirbaev S. Methodological approaches to choose a model to finance Higher Educational Institutions. KazKKA Khabarshysy. 2010;**4**(65):187

[11] The RoK law "On State Property" No 413-IV, dated March 1, 2011. Available from: http://adilet.zan.kz/rus/docs/Z1100000413

[12] The RoK HEIs will receive academic freedom. Available from: https://www.zakon.kz

[13] From Bologna to Bergen: A Mid-Term Re- view from the Academics Point of View. Bo- logna Conference. Policy Statement on the Bo- logna Process in the 'Bergen' Round (EI), Brussels, February 12, 2005. Available from: https://download.ei-ie.org/Docs/WebDepot/(2005)%20Policy%20Statement%20on%20the%20Bologna%20Process%20in%20the%20Bergen%20Round%20en.pdf

[14] The Bologna Process 2020 – The European Higher Education Area in the new decade. Communiqué of the Conference of European Ministers Responsible for Higher Education, Leuven and Louvain-la-Neuve,

28-29 April 2009. Available from: http://www.ehea.info/media.ehea.info/file/20090223-Ostend/54/2/BFUG_Board_CZ_19_4_draft_communique_200209_594542.pdf

[15] OECD. 2018. Education Policy Outlook: Kazakhstan. Available from: http://www.oecd.org/education/Education-Policy-Outlook-Country-Profile-Kazakhstan-2018-RU.pdf

[16] Electronic resource "Electronic government: The most demanded professions". Available from: https://egov.kz/cms/ru/articles/job_search/02207joblist, accessed August 2019

[17] Electronic resource: http://data.uis.unesco.org/, accessed on August 2019. Statistic Agency of Kazakhstan, 2018. http://stat.gov.kz/

[18] Statistic Agency of Kazakhstan. 2018. Available from: http://stat.gov.kz/

[19] Corner L. Women, Men and Economics: the Gender-Differentiated Impact of Macroeconomics (with special reference to Asia and Pacific). New York, NY: United Nations Development Fund for Women (UNIFEM) Asia-Pacific Regional Office; 1996

[20] Floro M. Women's well-being, poverty, and work intensity. Feminist Economics. 1995;**1**(3):1-25

[21] Maria F, Meurs M. Global Trends in Women's Access to Decent Work. Dialogue on Globalization Occasional Papers. Geneva: Friedrich Ebert Stiftung and International Labor Organization; 2009. No 43. May. Available from: http://lastradainternational.org/lsidocs/06399.pdf

[22] Cagatay N, Elson D, Grown C. Introduction. World Development. 1995;**23**(11)

[23] Tambunan T. 2009. Women Entrepreneurship in Asian Developing Countries: Their Main Constraints and Personal Reasons, Policy Discussion Paper Series Center for Industry, SME & Business Competition Studies Trisakti University, No. 7/08/09. Available from: http://www.online.fe.trisakti.ac.id/pusatstudi_industri/index4.html

Chapter 3

Towards Global Peace and Sustainability: Role of Education in Peace-Building in the Great Lakes Region of Sub-Saharan Africa

Laurent Gabriel Ndijuye and Pambas Basil Tandika

Abstract

The Great Lakes Region of sub-Saharan Africa is well known for being volatile and turbulent in terms of peace and stability. For over 60 years, almost all countries in the region have experienced some kind of political and social turmoil such as civil war, coup de tat, and genocides. In 1960, the first democratically elected Congolese prime minister was assassinated. There were unprecedented social and political havoc in a nearby "other Congo" characterized by power struggle between various political and ethnic factions in the post-independence Congo Brazzaville. In Burundi and Rwanda, ethnic tensions between the Tutsi and Hutu engulfed the developmental dreams of nationalist freedom fighters until 2015. Though arguably stable, Tanzania has experienced its own share of socio-political messy including the 1998 Mwembechai and 2001 Pemba massacres. Efforts to build a sense of sustainable peace and development based on mutual understanding and socio-political harmony has brought limited success. In all these countries, the missing link in building sustainable peace and security has been a lack of education. The chapter intends to fill this gap by critically analyzing the potential role of basic education, especially pre-primary and early grades education, in sustainable peace-building in the sub-Saharan context.

Keywords: Great Lake region, Burundi, D.R. Congo, Tanzania, Rwanda, Uganda, education, peace-building

1. Introduction

Great Lake Region (GLR) constituted of United Republic of Tanzania (URT), Uganda, Democratic Republic of Congo (DRC), Rwanda and Burundi [1] have made different and remarkable developments in the improvement of services it offers to her citizens. Education is among such development that has been recorded to contribute into several dividends to the GLR citizens. The available economic data [1] indicates its member states have been impacted by the civil wars that have lowered their progress. For instance, before the eruption of the civil war in Burundi in 1965, the gross domestic product (GDP) was United States Dollar (USD) 286 and after the war it dropped to an estimation of USD170. Similar trend of the impact of the war is vivid in the DRC as its 71% of people live in extreme poverty and nearly two thirds of the active populations (especially young people) are unemployed. Rwanda is the most densely populated country in Africa with over 11 million habitants, and it abolished school fees in 2003/2004 as from primary (which takes 6 years) to lower secondary (offered for 3 years). In Tanzania basic education (pre-primary to lower secondary) has been compulsory and fee free since 2001. Uganda is one of the pioneers in Sub-Saharan Africa in terms of setting the goal to achieve universal access to basic education and it introduced Universal Primary Education (UPE) since 1997.

2. Education objectives of basic education systems in Great Lake Regions

GLR countries (**Figure 1**) have at different times taken basic education (from pre-primary to lower secondary) as a basic need to their citizens, hence made it fee-free. Basic education (comprising of primary 1 to primary 6 and an additional of senior 3; and the secondary education) in Rwanda was made compulsory and fee-free since the 2010 election campaign of President Paul Kagame re-election and it is now guaranteed in the Rwanda Constitution. Therefore, it has been the duty of the State to take measures to ensure it is inclusive [2]. The objectives of the education in Rwanda are to improve and increase: (1) access to education for all, (2) quality education at all levels, (3) equity in education at all levels, (4) effective and efficient education system, (5) science and technology and ICT in education, and (6) promotion of positive values, critical thinking, Rwandan culture, peace,

Figure 1.
Africa Great Lake Regions. Source: https://reliefweb.int/map/cameroon/africa-great-lakes-region-refugees-and-displaced-populations-8-dec-1997.

unity and reconciliation. In the DRC [3] the education provision is structured by three strategic objectives: (1) developing access and ensuring equity aiming to ensure the free primary education policy is effectively put in place for all children and implemented by increasing and rationalizing school constructions, and registration and payment of all teachers by 2020, (2) improving the quality of learning by improving quality assurance and monitoring as well as the learning environment across the system, and (3) improving governance and oversight of the system by strengthening the education system through implementing transparent norms and mechanisms for managing resources, and improving management at all levels.

3. Enrollment trends and literacy rate in basic education

Enrolment trends of pupils particularly in primary schools in the GLR are varied. Importantly, the region sadly contributes high in number of children who are out of schooling. For instance; while it is estimated that 54.6 million African children in Sub-Saharan Africa-SSA of primary- and lower secondary school age (averaging 24% of this age group) were out of school in 2015, accounting for 45% of the global out-of-school population, 3.2 million of the out of school children in the region were from the DRC [4]. Burundi is among the six countries in sub-Saharan region countries with success in increasing number of children enrolled in primary school for the period between 1999 and 2008 [5]. On literacy and numeracy performances, Burundi is ahead of other Francophone African countries as its performance internationally indicates to have lowest proportion of non-readers among African countries (A maximum of 20.4% of non-readers in grade 2 cannot read a word aloud) [6]. In addition, it has been reported that early grade children in Burundi show good learning outcome as in their assessment they observed that over 60% of second-grade pupils could read more than 20 letters per minute with only 3% of them failing to read even a word, hence scored zero [4]. On numeracy, pupils in Burundi had during the assessment attained sufficiency competency in mathematics as 63% of assessed children in the country demonstrated good skills in oral counting and like children in DRC, 60% of them could solve a one-digit addition problem.

Various reasons are associated with Burundi doing well in literacy and numeracy than other countries in the GLR. It is almost linguistically homogeneous with 98% of the population speaking a single language [4]. Kirundi has been the language of instruction from first through fourth grade since 1973 and it is phonetically coded using the Latin script and has stronger written traditions than many African languages. Consistent use of the education policy that has favored a "structured pedagogy" approach is another factor for Burundi doing better in literacy and numeracy than other countries in the region. The structured approach has caused that:

- Teaching-learning is facilitated using aids produced in Kirundi that makes it easy to transfer of knowledge and skills of children in reading and mathematics concepts. Introduction of oral French in grade one builds a foundation for performance in reading and mathematics in later grades.

- Ensured government support in school infrastructure by concentrating on financing teachers and teaching-learning materials, also in the schools that are run by religious organizations.

- Pre-service and in-service training of urban and rural teachers in all contexts to undertake teaching and learning activities efficiently.

- Use of appropriate pedagogical practices and resources in the classroom with participative approach to teach reading and writing in first and second grades. Accommodates use of the whole-word method, posters and play for learning and teaching reading and writing in an active manner, and

- Continued coaching from district supervisors, use of radio programs and distance-learning interventions and substitute teachers to support effective learning to children.

Comparatively, educational management of the GLR countries observes and recognizes contribution and participation of non-state organs including parents and community members, and civil society organizations (CSOs) [3]. The difference exists on the extent of the non-state organs in managing the education provision. For example, in DRC, though parents and community participate in school management and CSOs in education issues, they lack voice and the later seldom meaningfully represent parents' interests. Administratively, fee-free education policy is common in almost all GLR countries. However, in DRC parents contribute some 2000 CFs (equivalent to United States Dollar-USD 2.05) and other illegal and informal fees are collected at the school for support the implementation of the fee-free education policy. Obviously, some collected funds disappear into someone's pocket leaving primary education inadequately financed [3]. Further, the GLR countries have recorded doubling of the net enrolment of the primary school students from 5.5 million in 2001/2002 to about 13.5 million in 2013/14 which is an increase of the gross enrollment ratio (GER) from 62% in the respective years to 107% [3].

DRC has recorded good completion rate of the primary school pupils despite decline of the same with lower secondary students and worse for advanced secondary school students [7]. The DRC education system for primary and secondary schools can be classified into two: (i) public schools consisting of schools directly managed by the government and the schools managed by religious institutions, and (ii) private recognized schools which receive no government funding [8]. The privately organized schools receive funds from different funders and from different sources and they continue to expand at all levels, albeit slowly and with major oscillations. However, due to prevalence of nearly a decade of conflict, there is no sustained progress towards the goal of universal primary completion as large proportion of young children are not attending the primary school compared to 15 years ago.

Regardless of the different schools in the DRC education system, there has been some improvement in enrollment and completion rates [9]. However, learning achievements by students have remained weak as indicated by various indicators. It has been reported that up to 2018:

- More years (appropriately 9 years) of schooling are needed for students to be sufficiently literate. It has been described by authors that at 15 years of age the number of literate youths raises only to 47.3% placing the DRC lower than other countries in GLR.

- That initial grades from pre-primary to grade one, children are inadequately prepared for formal learning (primary schooling) as 26% of students have difficulties with their learning in grade 2 (PASEC scores)

- The Early Grade Reading Assessment (EGRA) tests showed that 52% of pupils in fourth grade were incapable of reading a single word. In addition, there are variations within the country regarding mathematics and reading.

For example, half of grade 2 pupils in Katanga have learning difficulties and 65% of children in grade 5 while in Bandundu only 18% have learning difficulties in grade 2, and 42% in grade 5.

Uganda is one of the pioneers in Sub-Saharan Africa in terms of setting the goal to achieve universal access to basic education and it introduced Universal Primary Education (UPE) since 1997 characterized of abolishment of primary school tuition, Parents and Teachers Association fees, and the textbook fees for up to four children per family [10]. Following the abolishment of fees, primary school enrolment increased from 2.5 million pupils in 1996 to 8.3 million in 2015 and the primary GER increased to 118% in 2011 before it stabilized at 111% in 2017. Uganda has progressive GDP growth from 6% in the financial year 2017/2018 to 6.4% in 2018/2019.

However, Uganda invests less in the future productivity of its citizens mainly children and has had low levels of learning achievement compared to Burundi as measured through the Human Capital Index-HCI [10]. The low levels of learning achievement of children in Uganda were also revealed by the measure of the Southern and Eastern Africa Consortium for Monitoring Education Quality (SACMEQ) assessment administered in 2013 with 70% of grade 6 students achieved the minimum competence level in reading, and only 40% of those tested reached that same competence level in Mathematics. In addition, EGRA evidenced that only 28% of children were able to read 20 words per minute in the third grade of primary (P3).

Rwanda has its Vision of 2020 and Economic Development and Poverty Reduction Strategy aiming at moving from an agriculture-based economy to 'a knowledge-based hub for business and information technology' by 2020 [11]. As education has been used by countries as an instrument in attaining its development goals, the government of Rwanda abolished school fees in 2003/2004 as from primary (which takes 6 years) to lower secondary (which is offered for 3 years) hence ensuring equitable access to education and high-quality education enabling its citizen with the skills and knowledge required for the socioeconomic development of the country [12]. In addition, abolishment of school fees was used to increase enrolment, retention and completion rates for basic education, especially for vulnerable children [13]. Consequently, the GER for primary education improved steadily as in 2013 it reached 97% (98% of the enrolled were girls) though primary education completion rate was still down at 69% (64% for boys and 74% for girls) [12, 14]. The Ministry of Education achieved enrolment targets due to abolishment of school fees, hence managing to make preprimary, primary and secondary levels with gender parity [15].

Despite the achievement made by the Republic of Rwanda observes some pupils failing to attain the curricular expectations (for example through the measure of quality standards and assurance program of education, the Learning Achievement in Rwandan Schools-LARS) as 37% failed in literacy and 46% in numeracy compared to 55% of students who managed to meet the expectations in literacy and 27% in numeracy [13]. Geographical positioning affected numeracy results as results indicated significant difference between provinces and between districts. That implied that being in rural areas is a disadvantage as pupils in rural areas largely failed to meet curricular standards compared with their peers in urban areas with achievement distribution in both literacy and numeracy being relatively equal for girls and boys [13].

While the number of primary and the above levels of education are well recorded in Rwanda, pre-primary education (nursery education as they call it) started to be documented only in 2016 [16]. The number of nursery schools increased from 2757 in 2016 to 3186 in 2017; and students from 185,666 in 2016 to 220,435 in 2017 indicating a Gross and Net Enrolment Rate increase from 23.8% (in 2016) to 24.1% and 17.5% (in 2016) to 20.6%, but the rates are still very low compared to the SDG target of 100% by 2030 [16].

In Tanzania, just as it has been in other GLR countries, basic education (pre-primary to lower secondary) has been compulsory and fee-free since 2001 when the Primary Education Development Program (PEDP) was introduced and it has continued to be fully State-funded through the Tanzania Education and Training Policy of 2014 [17]. Regarding the objectives of the education, the government tells that the general objective of the education is *Kuwa na Watanzania walioelimika na wenye maarifa na ujuzi kuweza kuchangia kwa haraka katika maendeleo ya Taifa na kuhimili ushindani* translated as "to have Tanzanians who are educated with knowledge and skills for contributing effectively and timely for national development that can sustain competition" [18]. On enrolment, the net enrolment for pre-primary education is among the highest in Sub-Saharan Africa as it reached 44.6% in 2017 while primary education gross enrolment rate has almost become universal with net enrolment of 84% and more than 70% of the primary school leavers transit to secondary education [19]. Another report indicates that pupils' completion rate in Tanzania was 80% while in Rwanda it was close to 55% [7].

The gross enrolment rate in Tanzania is close to universal in primary education, but the government reports that a large number (close to one in every four pupils in primary and more than two in every five lower secondary students) were found be out of school [20]. Such report on Global Initiative on Out-of-School Children, Tanzania Country Report summarizes that about 2 million primary-school-age children and 1.5 million lower-secondary-school-age children were out of school in Tanzania by the time of the profiling. This number is huge and gives a lesson to the achievements of the SDG 4 and global vision of no one should be left behind.

4. The concept of peace-building and its relationship with education

The word 'peace-building' was first coined and famously used by Galtung [21] in his publication 'Three Approaches to Peace: Peacekeeping, peacemaking, and peace-building'. He developed the most of the popular core concepts that continue to be used in defining peace-building today, including negative peace, positive peace, structural violence, root causes of conflict, and sustainable peace [21]. Accordingly, peace-building involves addressing and removing the root causes of violence. These may include the structural and the cultural violence which is considered to feeds into and enables direct violence. The primary goal of peace-building is to establish positive, sustainable peace in societies once beleaguered by any form of violence. In Galtung's words:

> *"... structures must be found that remove causes of wars and offer alternatives to war in situations where wars might occur" (1976: 297).*

To build and achieve peace and tranquility, there is a need to emphasize the importance of local knowledge, ownership and participation in whole process of peace-building. For example, the work of John Paul Lederach has systematically documented the gradual evolvement of the definitions of peace-building. Accordingly, peace-building are processes which are dynamic and social and involve transforming relationships of various groups and powerful individuals in the communities.

5. The role of education in peace-building in the great lakes region of sub-Saharan Africa

Available education and economic evidences indicates that violence and conflicts are some of the biggest barriers and challenges to development in most of the world's poorest countries [22]. Of the 40 poorest countries in the world, 24 are either in the midst of armed conflict or have only recently emerged from it [23]. Empirical evidences and life experiences have consistently indicated that education is the most important tool for improving human development and to eradicate poverty. For generations, it has been used as a means by which to develop the values, knowledge and skills for the personal health, safety, and for future economic and social development. Perhaps, this may help to explain why the MDGs and SDGs places so much emphasis through Education for All (EFA) on achieving universal, free and compulsory basic education.

However, in the sub-Saharan region, there are many impediments to the achievement of EFA. In the Great Lakes Region, these impediments are said to include lack of priority to education on the part of national governments. In this context, lack of priority include misallocation and insufficient spending as a percentage of GNP, inequitable distribution of funding and resources across and within provinces or regions and districts within the countries, and sometimes limited or totally no commitment and/or effective action in the use of development assistance on the part of the international community. Even within individual countries in the GLR, barriers to the enrolment of children in school include the existence of armed conflicts and displacement, child-labor, poverty, distance from school, gender biases, and cultural factors.

Evidence from empirical and gray sources indicates that the number of out-of-school primary-age children in the world has fallen in recent years, and the situation in conflict-affected countries has seen very little improvement. While conflict-affected countries are home to only 13% of the world's population, yet half of all the children out of school (37 million out of 72 million children) live there. More disturbing fact is that these countries receive less than one-fifth of education aid from the international community [24].

One of the available the most recent estimates by the EFA Global Monitoring Report [5, 25] is that 28 million children live in conflict-affected countries (42% of the world total of children out of school). A huge segment of them (46%) live in the sub-Saharan region especially in the GLR of the African continent [26]. This section provides a brief summary of three ways in which the international community and aids agencies may think about the role of education in conflict-affected situations. Broadly, the noted agencies represent areas that have gained greater attention in the last three decades in international development discourses. It is important to note that background and scope this discourse can be traced back to the Second World War (1939–1945). Although each discourse seems to represent a slightly different perspective arising from a common concern, however, all are about the way that conflict affects the lives of school children, their families and their right to access quality education.

The first discourse is concerned with protection of children and a better way to respond to the negative impacts of violent conflicts on their education and psychological wellbeing. To some extent, this approach is primarily of humanitarian motivation. The second discourse focuses on the fact that education is provided in a way that 'does no harm' to anybody including children. Some scholars have termed it as a conflict-sensitive education. That is, it is sensitive to sources of conflict in the society in which it is situated, and is provided in a way that does not worsen the existing antagonisms or animosities. In other words, in this discourse education can 'do some good' to individuals and societies. The most cited argument is by contributing to transformations within conflict-affected societies and individuals that might make peace possible and more likely to sustain and endure. In other words, the focus is on education that contributes to peace-building efforts. It is important to note that overlapping elements of these discourses have emerged and sometimes, co-existed throughout a considerable period of time. However, at times one perspective may have gained more prominence than another. Although in most cases the discourses do interact, separate development has been more common than their integration. This has been reflected in the emergence of distinct communities of practices across academia and conflict-affected contexts.

6. Education as a humanitarian response

Globally, experiences indicate that education systems face various exceptional challenges before, during and after times of violent conflict. While during conflict international humanitarian laws have particular importance, there are no laws to guide education systems before and during violent conflicts. However, the Geneva Conventions make specific references to protections related to education at times of war or violent conflicts. These include that:

- Involved parties to ensure that children under 15, orphaned or separated from their families, have access to quality and appropriate education;

- Occupying parts and/or powers should facilitate the maintenance of education;

- Education should be provided for incarcerated children and young people including those who were once child-soldiers;

- And education should be provided throughout non-international conflicts.

A noticeable limitation of the above provisions which has received some critiques from both academia and practitioners, is that the Geneva Conventions were developed and adjusted after the Second World War when state and ultimatums of wars had been declared among nations and alliances. It was recently that UN declarations, resolutions and protocols have tried to update and accept rules of engagements during conflicts and wars to accommodate the increasingly more complex nature of modern conflicts. Close observations of this matter seem to suggest that it is challenging to implement the Geneva Convention resolutions in the current situation in which armed-conflicts are often waged by groups within countries. In most cases these within countries armed groups have no sense of accountability to international authority. This results into more complex problem of disregarding the values and norms represented by the Geneva Conventions [27].

7. Impacts of conflicts and wars on education

Scholars began to pay serious attention on the impact of violent conflicts and wars on children during the 1990s. It was first comprehensively documented in a study commissioned by the UN Secretary-General [28]. The report identified a number of important implications for the education sector, including arrangements for the education of refugees and displaced persons [29], strategies to prevent the use of child soldiers, protection for girls against sex crimes, landmine education and trauma counseling. This report provided the basis for a number of initiatives and interventions which shaped later aid policies and practices. Most of the issues identified by the report have become specialized areas of international development. It was from this report that arguments had been developed and made that education should be an integral part of humanitarian responses to any calamity including wars and violent conflicts [29, 30]. This argument is rooted on the fact that education is a fundamental right as articulated in the Universal Declaration on Human Rights (1948) and the Convention on the Rights of the Child (1981).

A well-established fact is that children should not lose this fundamental right to education simply because they are caught in the midst of a conflict or war-torn areas. Further, during violent conflict or after the war, education is regarded as an integral part in the physical, psychosocial and cognitive protection of children. Some of the benefits of education include provision of a sense of normalcy and stability, lessening the psycho-social impact of violent conflict or traumatic experiences of war. Experiences has consistently shown that a safe learning environment may shield children from the everyday physical violence of a conflict, protect them from being recruited as child-soldiers. Further, education is an important channel in conveying life-saving information on how to protect oneself from danger. In the GLR, these dangers include sexual attack, child recruitment as combatants, and child-labor in landmines. It further provides cognitive protection by supporting intellectual development through the teaching of literacy and numeracy and, in some cases, conflict resolution and peace-building skills. However, given the severity and notoriety of the warring factions in the GLR, there remains considerable and of course very fierce debate among educational stakeholders about the necessity to include education in frontline humanitarian aid responses in war-torn areas.

A significant and notable danger is related to a fragmented and highly uncoordinated immediate responses and efforts from longer-term development plans for the education sector in the GLR. In most cases, the international agencies involved in immediate responses are different from those involved in longer-term planning of the development aid for education. Further, the disturbing fact is that sometimes education sector personnel and experts with experiences and understanding of the local education setting and authorities are not involved in the early stages. However, it is worth noting the a significant developments made since the World Education Forum in 2000 and its resulting Dakar Framework for Action which focuses on including an explicit call for donor support to the field, commonly known as 'education in emergencies' [31].

While this field is not defined exclusively in terms of conflict, the disruption of education due to conflict is certainly one set of circumstances that come within the definition of an emergency [32]. The most important initiative so far which has been made is the formation of the Inter-Agency Network on Education in Emergencies (INEE). The network includes Norwegian Refugee Council, CARE International, Save the Children Alliance, UNESCO, UNHCR and UNICEF. The primary role and responsibility of the INEE is to define minimum standards for education in emergencies which until recently is being used in all GLR countries. While in the GLR the INEE does not implement nor coordinate responses during crises, it is known to have enabled members to share information and encourage collaboration [33].

Despite these achievements, available evidence suggests that those working within other sector still need to be convinced about the inclusion of education in frontline humanitarian responses. This is indicated by the fact that despite a decade of advocacy, education still receives only 2% of humanitarian aid. Further, compared with food, health, shelter, water and sanitation, it receives the lowest response to funds requested [3]. This is perhaps because education is still perceived as part of longer-term development, rather than as an immediate humanitarian response. Part of the problem may be based on the fact most of the field workers use to justify more funding for education during the humanitarian phase are more about the need for earlier engagement instead of longer-term issues. These issues may include collection of accurate data, assessing whether and how to reform education, and developing better capacity. In most cases, concerns of the funders are that rebuilding the education system during the emergency response period may reproduce old problems. And the most cited problems include unequal access that may leave legacies that are more difficult to redress in later development phases.

It is important to note that the inclusion of conflict-affected contexts within the broader concept of 'education and emergencies' has not been helpful from a peace-building perspective in the GLR. This is because while it's understandable that conflicts undoubtedly create crises and situations similar to other emergencies, it is conceptually confusing to suggest that understanding the role of an education system during or after conflict is the same as responding to humanitarian or natural disasters. This necessitates and suggests that any analysis needs to be context-and conflict-specific.

8. Conflict-sensitive education in the GLR

For several past decades, various studies have increasingly highlighted aspects of education that have implications for violent conflict and peace-building [34–36]. These studies suggest a number of reasons why we should be cautious about how education is provided [35]. Firstly, education may be perceived politically as a powerful tool for ideological development as it has been in some countries which have experienced coup de tat and genocides [36]. This can take many forms, ranging from the use of education in the development of liberal ideas, to nation building and, in extreme cases, political indoctrination as it was witnessed before and during the 1994 Rwanda genocide. Secondly, education may be perceived as an instrument for providing the knowledge and skills necessary for economic development and societal mobility [37]. However, this may or may not be include equity concerns, thus further excluding certain groups from economic and social benefits that education can provide. The exclusion of some groups in accessing quality education may further divide the society and bring it closer to escalation of violent conflicts as it has been the case in post-independence Burundi. Thirdly, education can be used as a means by which social and cultural values are transmitted from generation to generation. This may depend on the values concerned for it may convey negative stereotypes or encourage attitudes that explicitly or implicitly condone violence or generate conflict as it is the case in South Sudan [38, 39].

This necessitates the need to thorough analyses of education systems from a conflict perspective for it is one of the underdeveloped areas in education research. This is extremely relevant to educational practitioners such as policymakers, education administrators, teachers, parents, and other development workers. There are many entry points to the various levels of an education system in developing conflict-sensitive education systems. It may include critical analyses of the political ideology driving a system, and sometimes it may require legislative, structural and administrative features. The efforts may have significant implications for the development of non-discrimination and equal access to education policies and practices. However, the most contentious challenge for the international development agencies is to find a way of raising critical questions about the form and content of education and its implications for relations between peoples, groups and nations. The difficulty will be in finding ways for this to be accepted internationally as a legitimate concern and as part of improving the quality of education in emergencies.

In the GLR, the extent to which education can be regarded and used as a tool for political and/or ideological tool can be evidenced by political and ideological involvements in daily operational issues, such as appointments of educational officers, deployment and allocation of teachers and the determination of the content of the curriculum. In many circumstances, political and social elites have consistently indicated their desire to see and use education for their own ends and purposes. Although evidences and experiences had shown that decentralization of education systems carry the potential to increase participation and ownership, however, it may also leave education open to manipulation as part of local politics. This has been observed in Kenya after the 2007 violence and the 2010 constitution. This highlights the need for critical and broad analyses that identifies the political and economic influences operating on and within the education system in post-conflict environments. The starting point could be the capacity building and training for those in public service. This may therefore be a necessary prerequisite for the success of the overall education sector plan which targets to take into account the concept of conflict and peace-building education. At all levels of the education system, governance is a crucial issue [40]. The arrangements that are in place for representation and participation in consultation [34, 41], decision-making and governance may be potential sources of conflict, or they may be opportunities for inclusion and the resolution of grievances [42]. This necessitates the arrangements for accountability and transparency to be reflected in an education system's capacity to accept and address inequalities that might otherwise become sources of future conflict.

Broadly, the way in which education provision is implemented may compound inequalities and erode confidence in government's capacity to provide basic services [43]. In such a situation, grievances are likely to become increasingly politicized, making it easier to mobilize support for violent conflict [44]. For example, education may become a source of conflict depending on whether it promotes conformity to a single set of dominant values (assimilation) [22], permits the development of identity-based institutions (separate development) or encourages shared institutions (integration) [45]. The extent to which any of these approaches make conflict more or less likely will be highly context-dependent. This is what happened in the pre-genocide Rwanda whereby the Hutu ruling elites and their government side-lined the Tutsi minorities.

At the practical level, there are many aspects of curriculum that have a bearing on conflict or can be used to promote future escalation of conflict [46]. When a narrow view of curriculum aims as the transmission of knowledge, attitudes and skills from one generation to the next, it may be used as an extremely powerful tool to promote particular political, cultural ideologies or religious practices as it happened in Tanzania where the quota system in accessing secondary education was used to promote and forge a sense of national-hood. The contemporary trend in many countries in the GLR is to 'modernize' the curriculum so that it is defined in terms of 'learning outcomes'. In their contexts, learning outcomes refer to skills, attitudes and values as well as factual knowledge. This may include the development of 'generic skills' such as communication skills, the ability to crosscheck facts from multiple sources of information, evaluate conflicting evidence, the development of media literacy, critical thinking and moral development [25]. In the GLR settings, there is a particular emphasis on 'life skills' as a means of providing child protections, social and health education (id21, 2004). The rationale for this argument is that, these are the type of skills that are essential in peace-building efforts [47].

Additionally, in terms of 'content', every area of the curriculum carries values with the potential to communicate implicit and explicit political messages. However, close observations of curriculums in the GLR will show that many of these involve specialized areas of study in a form of subject contents. For example, the UNESCO position paper on language of instruction highlights the importance of sensitivity to majority and minority languages. It further distinguishes between 'national' and 'official' languages by saying that:

> *The choice of language in the educational system confers a power and prestige through its use in formal instruction. Not only is there a symbolic aspect, referring to status and visibility, but also a conceptual aspect referring to shared values and worldview expressed through and in that language [25].*

The question of what should be official and national language has been a center of controversy and "educational politics" in the GLR than anything else in the curriculum. While Tanzania successfully used Kiswahili language as a national-unifying factor and medium of instruction, D.R. Congo is until now much divided along various ethnic groups and against or for French. Though Burundi and Rwanda almost everyone speak, write and communicate in Kirundi and Kinyarwanda respectively, having common languages have not helped these countries achieve national unity and build sustainable peace and tranquility. Recently, Rwanda has shifted from Kinyarwanda-French to Kinyarwanda-English with Kiswahili as an alternative language.

Another area of curriculum controversy is the teaching of history and the extent to which history education may become a vehicle for promoting particular versions of history, revising historical events or confronting the past in a critical way. Given the political turmoil experienced by all countries—with the exception of Tanzania, in the GLR, history taught in schools are too fluid and twisted depending on who is in power by then. For example, in Rwanda the official history taught seems to ignore the critical role played by previous Hutu governments before the current regime. Political dimensions in the way that geography is taught and the lexicon it uses for disputed territories can be problematic and the content of teaching material for areas such as culture, art, music and religious education often get drawn into controversy [27, 48]. Such areas are sometimes referred to as 'national subjects', in many instances tightly controlled by governments and regarded as essential tools for nation building as it is the case in Tanzania and Rwanda.

In the GLR, another area of curriculum controversy which requires specialized concerns is the values represented in official textbooks and other learning resources. For example, the operation of a single textbook policy in Tanzania offered a Ministry of Education a way of guaranteeing a 'minimum entitlement' for all pupils to basic learning resources. This is particularly important and very effective approach in low-income GLR countries where equal access to education needs to be clearly demonstrated. However, questions arise about who controls and benefits from the production of textbooks; who decides their contents, and under which circumstances. In contested and highly diverse societies as it is the case in D.R. Congo, arguments related to content of textbooks has been a source of cultural and ideological battlegrounds. In the GLR textbooks review processes have a long history. For example, there were joint initiatives on French-Kinyarwanda textbooks during the 1990s; French-Kirundi cooperation following the end of the 1990s wars; and a Congo-Brazaville - D.R. Congo textbook project in the 1980s [9]. They raise sensitive issues about what might be considered offensive and by/to whom. Examples include concerns raised by Rwanda about the treatment of the 1994 genocide in the textbooks and a critique of international assistance for the replacement of textbooks [49].

An interesting observation has been a concern that an emphasis on conflict analyses, conflict resolution skills and peace-building strategies potentially highlights negative aspects of provision of education. Practically, some international aid organizations and workers seem to suggest that this makes it more difficult to persuade donors to provide fund to invest in education in conflict-affected GLR countries. Some go as far as to claim that this makes it difficult to maintain a positive and practical relationship with local education authorities and officials hence, underplaying the important contribution that education can make to 'peace-building' efforts in this region.

9. Education for reconstruction, reconciliation and peace-building

A report on 'Education for Reconstruction' [45] distinguishes between 'physical' reconstruction of school buildings (including emergency repair strategies, the needs of refugee education and landmine safety issues); 'ideological' reconstruction that refers, for example, to democratization of an education system or retraining of teachers; and 'psychological' reconstruction that responds to issues of demoralization, loss of confidence and health-related issues of stress and depression. This contrasts significantly with a report on the World Bank's experience with post-conflict reconstruction, which suggests that the main priority during the 1990s was on the reconstruction of physical infrastructure [50].

The main recommendations of the report illustrate how the World Bank's position was to maintain a watching brief, but stop short of providing development assistance while conflict is underway. However, a later publication from the World Bank Conflict Prevention and Reconstruction Unit acknowledges the need for a shift in position from an emphasis on post-conflict reconstruction to 'a sensitivity to conflict' [51]. This is also reflected in a study undertaken by the World Bank on Education and Post-conflict Reconstruction [38]. The main objective of the noted study was to review experience of education system reconstruction in post-conflict countries and identify lessons that may assist in the achievement of EFA goals. These reports reflect a move away from the notion of thinking about conflict in discrete stages, to an appreciation that the analysis of conflict and 'conflict sensitivity' needs to be built into routine thinking as part of mainstream operations. Further, there is also a growing appreciation that reconstruction is not simply about replacing the physical infrastructure of schools, but needs to include opportunities for rebuilding human relations and inclusive education systems.

The concept of reconciliation has received attention across a range of international contexts, but each conflict is quantitatively different in terms of the level of violence and number of casualties, and qualitatively different in terms of the social context and the nature of atrocities that may have taken place. These factors mean that those affected by conflict have different perspectives on what is reasonable or realistic in terms of reconciliation attempts. This makes it extremely difficult to consider reconciliation as a generic concept with the same implications for different conflicts. For example, the concept of reconciliation in Rwanda means a fresh start and forgetting the atrocities committed. The gravest part of the assertion is that in Rwanda, the official version of the genocide indicates that only Tutsis were killed by the Hutu extremists. It is against the law to question this official claim.

The concept of 'reconciliation' is also problematic in terms of the difficult and controversial issues it raises. The term embodies positive connotations about healing past conflicts [52]. Despite research into the role of education in relation to truth and reconciliation processes in contexts such as Burundi and Rwanda [31, 46, 53] deeper understanding of the role of education in contributing to reconciliation processes has yet to be developed. Reconciliation may be necessary at many levels (between individuals, between groups in conflict, between peoples or nations at war). There are implications for education in terms of facilitating reconciliation by addressing the legacies of conflict. These include the impact on the bereaved and injured, remembrance and commemoration; debates about forgiveness, expressions of regret, apology and symbolic events; understanding the role of amnesties, prisoner releases, alongside concepts of restorative and transitional justice. These are challenging, long-term tasks that link reconstruction programs into the mainstream education sector and the longer-term goal of conflict prevention. Education for reconciliation may therefore be seen as a contribution to peace-building, concerned with conflict transformation within societies. In Rwanda, the *gacaca* courts as efforts for reconciliation created more hatred and rage than peace and tranquility. This necessitated the government to use force and specific educational policies to suppress anger in the communities.

While it has got its own share of socio-political violence, Tanzania adopted a rather pragmatic approach to building sustainable peace and harmony by instilling to children a sense of tolerance and understanding. In 1998 following the Muslim assault of a Catholic parish priest of Mburahati - Dar es Salaam, and the "question of pork eating" violence, the government of Tanzania ordered its police force to storm and quash the Muslims rebellion at Mwembechai area killing at least four people. To build sustainable peace and tranquility, one of the strategies adopted by the Ministry of Education was to include in the existing curriculum the question of patriotism and social understanding and civic education. In 2001 the police shoot 22 Civic United Front—*Chama cha Wananchi* (CUF) members in Pemba, Zanzibar—Tanzania [54]. CUF, the opposition party in Tanzania was predominant in Pemba. It establishes itself there due to some genuine social, political and economic grievances among common people—*wananchi wanyonge.* Apart from union grievances, one of the main and very serious concern was sidelining of Pembas in accessing quality education in a larger Zanzibar context. To restore order and harmony in Pemba, after signing of the peace and harmony agreement commonly known as *Mwafaka II,* the existing regime in Zanzibar devised a quota system across five regions of Zanzibar and introduced peace-building education in the curriculum. However, concerns remains with the current political willingness to implement the curriculum.

The concept of 'peace-building' received renewed attention following the UN Secretary General's call for the establishment of the Peace-building Commission (PBC), the Peace-building Support Office (PBSO) and the Peace-building Fund (PBF) in 2006. So far, all these structures emerged as a result of concerns to prevent relapses in the aftermath of conflict. The initiatives provide support to immediate post-conflict countries through funding of political, governance, security and macroeconomic reforms. However, some scholars recommend that:

> *"focusing on social policies such as education and healthcare, as opposed to macroeconomic reforms, is especially important for preserving peace in countries that have emerged from civil conflict" [23, 55].*

Also others highlight the limitations and sometimes negative effects of peace-building that focuses exclusively on electoral and economic reforms [55]. The PBF has funds of US$360 million and is supporting more than 150 projects in 18 countries, but social programming, such as education, has received less than 14% of its funds (PBF status as of November, 2017).

Renewed interest in peace building may also be due to the greater priority that is being given to security as a consequence of global events during the past decades.

This is evidenced by the focus of the most recent World Development Report (2018) [56] on Conflict, Security and Development. It is also reflected in the EFA Global Monitoring Report [57] in two main ways. Firstly, the GMR reports on an increasing number of attacks on education that use political and military violence against education staff, students, teachers' unions, government officials and institutions. UNESCO has also produced a report on 'Protecting Education from Attack' that explores possible motives, responses and prevention strategies including armed protection, community defense, and strengthening international monitoring systems and humanitarian law [58]. Secondly, the report highlights concerns about links between aid and security. It identifies 21 developing countries (all countries in the GLR included) that are spending more on arms and the military than on primary schools, and presents evidence that the amount of aid to certain countries may be driven more by global security concerns rather than poverty. The merging of national security concerns and international development policies is a significant challenge for those in both the development and peace building fields. It highlights the use of education to 'win hearts and minds' as part of counter-insurgency strategy in D.R. Congo, Congo-Brazaville and Burundi. This raises concerns about the confusion of roles between military and aid personnel [34, 58].

The change in security context in the GLR during the past decade also creates new challenges for aid agencies and development organizations. There are two main dimensions to this. Firstly, there is growing awareness among donors that a purely technical approach to programming is insufficient in the political environments present in situations of conflict in the GLR. This has led to more emphasis on the need for political economy analysis of the education sector. There is increasing recognition that blockages for effective reform at the sectoral level (including for delivery, planning and procurement) can be political and that technical solutions alone may not be enough. Governance of a sector and the way in which politics and institutions interact within that sector, will in practice have a critical impact on sector policies and services [59, 60]. A number of donors have developed tools and approaches to political economy analysis [61, 62] and these have been reviewed by various stakeholders. These build on early work by DFID on 'drivers of change' and approaches such as the Government of the Netherlands, Strategic Governance and Corruption Analysis (SCAGA) [63]. However, there are very few examples in the literature of these being applied to the education sector or in post-conflict environments, although the European Commission is currently reviewing how political economy analysis can inform its programming in education.

Secondly, the changing context and increased emphasis on the global security agenda will require aid agencies to make more explicit choices about how they position themselves and their work. Humanitarian interventions suggest time-limited emergency responses to humanitarian crises and natural disasters, some of which will be caused by conflict. Development assistance that adopts a 'conflict-sensitive' approach has been encouraged by both the Paris Declaration on Aid Effectiveness (2005) and the OECD DAC Principles for Good International Engagement in Fragile States (2007), and suggests only a degree of intervention that 'does no harm'. The noted agencies are the major donors in the GLR, hence key players. However, if agencies accept that 'conflict transformation' is the distinguishing feature of a peace-building approach, then this is likely to require a more interventionist stance. Development informed by political analysis inevitably means making decisions based on judgments about what is best from a peace-building perspective education, and these may not always be consistent with the views of national governments or the Paris principles.

In terms of linkages between education and peace-building, the role of education is often stereotyped as 'peace education', perceived to involve working with children and youth on peace education programs for personal development, inter-group contact and conflict resolution techniques [64]. However, there have been a number of more recent initiatives that have reviewed research in this area [52, 55, 65].

10. Recommended way forward

Escalation of conflicts and wars are significant impediment to achievement of Education for All goals. Currently more than half of all children are out-of-school in conflict-affected and fragile states. Available data indicate that about 39 million children (54.2%) lived in conflict-affected or fragile countries, out of a total of 72 million children who were not in school [66]. The GLR has its fair share of out of school children—about 9 millions. This impedes achievement of Sustainable Development Goals, especially SDG number 4 which targets to ensuring inclusive and equitable quality education for all including children in conflict affected areas such as those in the GLR.

For long time, the education in conflict-affected and fragile states is under-funded. Education for children in conflict-affected and fragile states receives less than one-fifth of education aid despite representing more than half of the world's population of out of school children. Further, children in conflict-affected areas in low-income GLR countries receive less than 5% of all the education aids supplied globally. Particular attention is drawn to the fact that education as a response to emergency or conflicts, receives between little more than 1–4% of funding from humanitarian appeals [67]. Given this fact, it is beyond doubts that funds allocated for pre-primary and early grades as part of emergency response package in conflict-affected countries in the GLR is extremely low. Given its critical role in sustainable peace-building efforts, this level of education cannot be ignored.

There is deliberate lack of attention to education as an important subsector following signing of peace agreements. The analyses of the 17 full peace agreements in the GLR signed between 1989 and 2015 that are publicly available, 11 make no mention of education at all. Even in those that do, include education, there is great variation in the way it is perceived and addressed in terms of security, protection, economic development or socio-political issues' [67]. The report highlighted research that documented attacks on education and suggested that investment in education has a potential 'peace dividend' following peace agreements so long as it is developed in ways that are inclusive and accessible; safe and protective; relevant and appropriate; and accountable. Given the critical role of education in peace-building, the subsector should be part and parcel of any future signed peace agreements. This will be critical in the developing GLR states where literacy rates are still low and there are some mushrooming rebel groups.

Increase educational opportunity for the poorest and most disadvantaged, particularly through early childhood education, social protection, and flexible and alternative education such as accelerated learning programs. It is important to note ECE has the potential to level the play field between children from advantaged and disadvantaged backgrounds [47, 67]. Evidence indicates that children from disadvantaged conflict and violent backgrounds benefits much from early childhood interventions [28, 36]. As such, it will be an important move to increase access to education by all children in the GLR region.

There is an urgent need to focus on teachers and teaching quality, particularly through clearly stated strategies for recruitment, training and professional development. Further, given geographical and urbanicity variations, educational stakeholders may need to offer sufficient remuneration and incentives to work in the poorest and most remote areas. Very unfortunate, in the humanitarian responses

DOI: http://dx.doi.org/10.5772/intechopen.92417

in conflict-affected areas, humanitarian workers and aid for education accounts to 4.2% only [47]. In the GLR, this should go hand in hand with increasing relevance and purposefulness of education through relevant curricula which are sensitive to diversity and promote values that support sustainable peace-building efforts.

There is a need to increase the financing of education in conflict-affected and fragile GLR states. This can be done by ensuring allocation of at least 20% of national budgets to education, broaden access to free education, and allowing involvements of civil-societies in monitoring of educational budgets, increasing international aid to meet the annual financing requirement for basic education needs in the low-income GLR countries. This will allow attainments of pre-set educational goals, especially those related to sustainable peace-building efforts. Finally, success of all of the suggested strategies will solely depend on the level of community involvements, and political willingness of existing governments in the GLR and their development partners.

Author details

Laurent Gabriel Ndijuye* and Pambas Basil Tandika
The University of Dodoma, Tanzania

*Address all correspondence to: buritojr1980@yahoo.com

References

[1] UNDP. Building Peace and Advancing Development in the Great Lakes Region. New York, USA: Regional Bureau for Africa United Nations Plaza; 2012

[2] Japan International Cooperation Agency (JICA). Basic Education Sector Analysis Report—Rwanda. Kigali: International Development Center of Japan Inc. (IDCJ); 2012

[3] Groleau G. Improved Management and Accountability: Conditions for Better Access and Quality of Primary Education in the Democratic Republic of Congo? Policy & Practice Discussion Paper. New York, USA: International Rescue Committee; 2017

[4] Bashir S, Lockheed M, Ninan E, Tan JP. Facing forward: Schooling for learning in Africa. In: Africa Development Forum Series. Washington, DC: World Bank; 2018

[5] UNESCO. The Hidden Crisis: Armed Conflict and Education. EFA Global Monitoring Report. Paris: UNESCO; 2011

[6] Verly P, Mazunya M. Report on the Quality of Education in Burundi. Bujumbura: The Government of Burundi; 2018

[7] Sefa-Nyarko C, Kyei P, Mwambari D. Transitions from Primary to Lower Secondary School: A Focus on Equity as Part of the Secondary Education in Africa: Preparing Youth for the Future of Work Series (SEA) of MasterCard Foundation. Participatory Development Associates Ltd. 2018. Available from: https://mastercardfdn.org/wp-content/uploads/2019/07/Transitions-from-Primary-to-Lower-Secondary-School-A-Focus-on-Equity.pdf [Accessed: 25 February 2020]

[8] World Bank. Education in the Democratic Republic of Congo: Priorities and Options for Regeneration. Washington, DC: The International Bank for Reconstruction and Development/World Bank; 2005

[9] Visser M, Fenning C. GPE 2020 Country-Level Prospective Evaluations: First Annual Report. 2020. Available from: https://www.globalpartnership.org/sites/default/files/2019-03-gpe-drc-cle-report.pdf [Accessed: 27 February 2020]

[10] Walker R, Stucka T, Ezzine M, Vasiliev K, Sebudde R, Juzon J, et al. Economic development & human capital in Uganda: A case for investing more in education. In: Uganda Economic Update. 13th ed. Washington: The World Bank; 2019

[11] UNICEF. Improving Quality Education and Children's Learning Outcomes and Effective Practices in the Eastern and Southern Africa Region: Rwanda Country Case Study. 2016. Available from: https://www.unicef.org/esaro/UNICEF-ACER(2016)QualityofEducation-Rwanda-CS.pdf on [Accessed: 27 February 2020]

[12] Ministry of Education (MINEDUC). Curricula for Secondary Schools. 2014. Available from: http://www.reb.rw/Secondary.html [Accessed: 28 February 2020]

[13] Rwanda Education Board (REB). Curricula for Primary Schools. 2012. Available from: http://www.reb.rw/Primary.html [Accessed: 28 February 2020]

[14] MINEDUC. Education Statistical Yearbook. Kigali: Republic of Rwanda. 2016. Available from: https://mineduc.gov.rw/fileadmin/user_upload/pdf_files/2016_Education_Statistical_Yearbook.pdf [Accessed: 27 February 2020]

[15] MINEDUC. Education Sector Strategic Plan 2018/19 to 2023/24.

Republic of Rwanda: Government of Rwanda Press; 2018

[16] MINEDUC. 2017 Education Statistics. Kigali: Republic of Rwanda; 2018

[17] TWAWEZA. Citizens' Views on New Developments in Education. Brief No. 30. Dar Es Salaam: Twaweza; 2016

[18] Jamhuri ya Muungano wa Tanzania. Sera ya Elimu na Mafunzo. Dar es Salaam: Wizara ya Elimu na Mafunzo ya Ufundi; 2014

[19] United Republic of Tanzania. Global Initiative on out-of-School Children: Tanzania Country Report. Dar es Salaam: Ministry of Education, Science and Technology and UNICEF; 2018

[20] United Republic of Tanzania. Education Sector Development Plan (2016/17-2020/21): Tanzania Mainland. Dar es Salaam: Ministry of Education, Science and Technology; 2018

[21] Galtung J. Three approaches to peace: Peacekeeping, peacemaking and peacebuilding. In: Galtung J, editor. Peace, War and Defence: Essays in Peace Research. Vol. 2. Copenhagen: Christian Ejlers; 1976. pp. 282-304

[22] Ahonen S. Politics of identity through history curriculum: Narratives of the past for social exclusion—Or inclusion? Journal of Curriculum Studies. 2001;**33**(2):179-194

[23] Collier P, Hoeffler A. Aid, policy and growth in post-conflict societies. European Economic Review. 2004;**48**:1125-1145

[24] Save the Children Alliance. Rewrite the Future: Education for Children in Conflict-Affected Countries. London: International Save the Children Alliance; 2006

[25] Paulson J. The educational recommendations of truth and reconciliation commissions: Potential and practice in Sierra Leone. Research in Comparative and International Education. 2006;**1**(4):335-350

[26] UNHCR. The State of the World Refugees' Annual Report. Washington: UNHCR Publications; 2015

[27] Tawil S. International humanitarian law and basic education. International Review of the Red Cross. 2000;**82**(839):581-600

[28] Lombard J. Towards Nurturing Care: Advancing Early Childhood Development in 2018. Early Childhood Matters. 2018. Available from: https://resourcecentre.savethechildren.net/sites/default/files/documents/ecm18_eng.pdf#page=6

[29] Crisp J, Talbot C, Cipollone D. Learning for a Future: Refugee Education in Developing Countries. Geneva: Office of the United Nations High Commissioner for Refugees; 2001

[30] Retamal G, Aedo-Richmond R, editors. Education as a Humanitarian Response. London: Cassell; 1998

[31] Johnson D, van Kalmthout E. Forced Migration Review, Supplement: Education and Conflict—Research, Policy and Practice. Geneva: UNHCR Publishing; 2006

[32] Paulson J. Education and Reconciliation, Continuum (ed). London, New York: Sage Publishing; 2010

[33] Anderson A, Mendenhall M. Inter-agency network for education in emergencies. In: Forced Migration Review Supplement: Education and Conflict: Research, Policy and Practice. New York: UNHCR Publishing; 2006

[34] Bush K, Salterelli D. The Two Faces of Education in Ethnic Conflict.

Florence: UNICEF Innocenti Research Centre; 2000

[35] Burde D, Linden LL. The Effect of Proximity on School Enrollment: Evidence from a Randomized Controlled Trial in Afghanistan. 2009. Available from: http://sticerd.lse.ac.uk/seminarpapers/dg11052009.pdf

[36] Davies L. Educating against Extremism. Trentham: Stroke-on-Trent; 2008

[37] Murphy KM, Yoshikawa H, Wuermli AJ. Implementation research for early childhood development programming in humanitarian contexts. Annals of the New York Academy of Sciences. 2018;**1419**:90-101

[38] Smith A, Vaux T. Education, Conflict, and International Development. London: Department of International Development; 2003

[39] Buckland P. Reshaping the Future: Education and Post Conflict Reconstruction. Washington, D.C.: World Bank; 2004

[40] Davies L. Education and Conflict: Complexity and Chaos. New York: Routledge; 2004

[41] UNESCO. Education for All: The Dakar Framework for Action. Dakar, Senegal. 2000. Retrieved from: http://www.unesco.org/education/efa/ed-forall/ framework.shtml

[42] Lindblad S, Johannesson IA. Education governance in transition: An introduction. Scandinavian Journal of Educational Research. 2002;**46**(3):25-43

[43] Burde D. Weak State, Strong Community? Promoting Community Participation in Postconflict Countries. New York: Teachers College, Columbia University; 2004

[44] Pherali T, Smith A, Vaux T. A Political Economy Analysis of Education in Nepal. London: Department for International Development; 2011

[45] Spinner-Halev J. Education, reconciliation and nested identities. Theory and Research in Education. 2003;**1**(1):51-71

[46] Phillips R. History Teaching, Nationhood and the State: A Study in Educational Politics. London: Cassell; 1998

[47] UNESCO. EFA Global Education Monitoring Report: Education for People and Planet - Creating Sustainable Futures for all. Paris: UNESCO Publishing; 2017. Retrieved from: http://unesdoc.unesco.org/images/0024/002457/245752e.pdf

[48] UNICEF. A Year of Progress and Promise, with New Responsibilities to Deliver Results for Children. Washington, DC: UNICEF Publishing; 2015. Retrieved from: https://www.unicef.org/publications/files/UNICEF_Annual_Report_2013_web_26_June_2014.pdf

[49] Hoepken W. History-Textbooks and Reconciliation: Preconditions and Experiences in a Comparative Perspective. Washington, DC: World Bank Meeting; 2004

[50] Spink J. Education and politics in Afghanistan: The importance of an education system in peacebuilding and reconstruction. The Journal of Peasant Studies. 2005;**4**(2):20-35

[51] World Bank. The World Bank Experience with Post Conflict Reconstruction. Washington, D.C.: World Bank Publishing; 1998

[52] World Bank. The Role of the World Bank in Conflict and Development. Washington, D.C.: World Bank Publishing; 2004

[53] Dupuy KE. Education in peace agreements: 1989-2005.

Conflict Resolution Quarterly. 2008;**26**(2):149-166

[54] UNICEF. Improving Quality Education and Children's Learning Outcomes and Effective Practices in the Eastern and Southern Africa Region: Rwanda Country Case Study. 2016. Available from: https://www.unicef.org/esaro/UNICEF-ACER(2016)QualityofEducation-Rwanda-CS.pdf [Accessed: 27 February 2020]

[55] Mkapa BW. My Life, My Purpose: A Tanzanian President Remembers. Dar Es Salaam: Mkuki na Nyota Publishers Ltd; 2019

[56] UNESCO. EFA Global Monitoring Report. Education for All 2000-2015: Achievements and Challenges. 2015. Retrieved from: http://unesdoc.unesco.org/images/0023/002322/232205e.pdf

[57] UNESCO. Protecting Education from Attack. EFA Global Monitoring Report. Paris: UNESCO; 2010

[58] Machel G. UN Study on the Impact of Armed Conflict on Children. New York: UNICEF Publishing; 1996

[59] Foresti M, Wild L. Analysing Governance and Political Economy in Sectors: Joint Donor Workshop Report. London: Overseas Development Institute; 2009

[60] Organisation for Economic Co-operation and Development/Development Assistance Committee. Guidance on Evaluating Conflict Prevention and Peacebuilding Activities: Working Draft for Application Period. Paris: OECD; 2008

[61] World Bank. The Political Economy of Policy Reform: Issues and Implications for Policy Dialogue and Development Operations. Washington, D.C.: World Bank Publishing; 2008

[62] Department for International Development. Political Economy Analysis: A Practice Paper. London: DFID; 2009

[63] Ndijuye LG. Developing conflict resolution skills among pre-primary children: Views and practices of parents and teachers in Tanzania. Global Studies of Childhood. 2019. DOI: 10.1177/2043610619832895 [Online First]

[64] Save the Children Alliance. Rewrite the Future: Global Evaluation. London: Save the Children Alliance. 2010

[65] Save the Children Alliance. Rewrite the Future: Education for Children in Conflict-Affected Countries'. London: International Save the Children Alliance; 2016

[66] Save the Children Alliance. Rewrite the Future: Education for Children in Conflict-Affected Countries. London: International Save the Children Alliance; 2018

[67] Ndijuye LG. Early childhood educational policy, children's learning outcomes, and home learning environments in Tanzania: Comparisons between naturalized refugees and local majority groups [Thesis]. Pokfulam, Hong Kong SAR: University of Hong Kong; 2017

Chapter 4

Will Saudi Arabia Move toward Democracy as Socialism Falters?

Judith Cochran and Hugh V. Murray

Abstract

Saudi Arabia's Global Goals stated in Vision 2030 are faltering under its current socialistic system. The military, the civil servants, and 35,000 royals with income assured, they have little incentive to want to work or to obtain education. However, in order to employ their citizens, the Saudi government is forcing businesses to hire 70% Saudi citizens to replace the expats who are being expelled under a mandated quota system. Their education system, which has prepared citizens to be loyal to the monarchy and Islam, has neglected secular, market place skills. Citizens continue to want to be paid in the socialistic manner of the past. Now technology skilled citizens and problems solvers are needed, as the monarchy builds two technology-based cities: NOME and Economic City to meet some of its 2030 Vision goals. Another Vision 2030 global goal is to advance Saudi Arabia as the Islamic and Arab Cultural leader of the world. To accomplish this ambition, Saudi Arabia must educate a workforce that wants to work and can help solve its problems and achieve its goals. As the number of citizens increases in order to obtain greater family stipends, the monarchy is moving its religious and mostly socialistic economy toward techno-economy. The prognosis for religious, socialistic country against a techno-economic future will be problematic.

Keywords: socialist, Islamic, 2030 vision, education, techno-economic, Saudi Arabia

1. Introduction

Saudi Arabia's future can be predicted by examining Vision 2030 presented in 2018. The primary goal is to reduce the country's dependency on oil and establish it as a global economic, industrial, cultural and religious center. Much in Saudi Arabia's current environment supports this vision with an authoritarian King and Crown Prince and unknown oil and gas resources at their disposal. However, there are a few external and internal challenges of urbanization, tourism, education and a unique economy. Starting with the economy, 35,000 members of the royal family along with military and civil servants expect a living stipend from the government. Human capital too is at risk. With their income assured, there is little incentive for Saudi citizens seek or maintain employment or to get a degree of any kind. While attempting to change, education leaders agree that in the past the Saudi education has not prepared students with secular, technical or marketplace skills. Still, the Crown Prince has moved forward in requiring businesses to hire 70% of its employees in positions formerly held by ex-pats. Another goal of Vision 2030 is to make Saudi Arabia the recognized religious and Arab cultural leader of the world. Saudi Arabia is well on its way to achieving this expectation with over 19 million haj and umrah pilgrims arriving yearly to visit the major mosques and other significant religious sites located in the country. Businesses and an extensive tourist industry exist to serve these visitors. Saudi Arabia is opening entertainment areas, concert venues and building independent city-states with new technology for these pilgrims, tourists and hopefully other visitors. The internal and external challenges to Vision 2030 can be discussed. The manpower needed to address these goals rests on the shoulders of the over 50% Saudi citizens who are now under 25 and will either accept or reject the work involved in achieving the 2030 goals.

2. Key factors to consider: key factors that bare on Saudi Arabia's intermediate and long term future

Because of its great oil wealth, Saudi Arabia has been able to make cash grants to those who have served in the military or civil service and particularly large grants to those who are members of King Saud's tribe. Particularly large grants have gone to King Saud's fellow tribesmen. These grants have created a large number of indigenous Saudi's who do not see themselves as needing to get much education or to enter the workforce to support themselves. King Salman and the new Crown Price have published a new plan, Vision 2030, which envisions society's move from socialism to market based labor markets without social disruption. Fortunately this transition will be occurring under a highly centralized authoritarian government that currently does not need to cope with participatory democracy, except a highly constrained democracy at the local level.

Love for and appreciation of education is generally learned from one's parents, friends, relatives, and early teachers. This is true of both vocationally useful education (e.g. computer programming, carpentry, etc.) and education for self-improvement (e.g. history, philosophy, etc.). The Saudi Arabians have hurdles to overcome here: (1) their religion encourages believers to suspect knowledge from outside their Islamic religious framework, a framework that was set down with great specificity in the seventh and eighth century in both the Qu'ran and early Hadiths. (2) They have been somewhat sheltered from the massive training requirements that most of the world's population has dealt with because Saudi Arabia has been able to hire outsiders to provide the specialized skills needed to extract oil and run a modern infrastructure. (3) Saudi Arabia has been a leader in establishing Islamic Wahhabi madrassas, supporting over 150,000 such schools worldwide; naturally Saudi education follows this model at home [1].

Vision 2030 recognizes educated Saudi citizens must acquire needed marketplace skills so they can hold at least 70% of all jobs in the kingdom within 10 years. The question then is how does one insert a love of education into a pampered population that has been living directly or indirectly off of the nation's oil wealth?

Vision 2030 envisions Saudi Arabia as the hub for three very important activities: (1) it will continue as the global center of the Islamic religious world with its possession of the holy sites, Mecca and Medina. The country will lead the globe with its formal political/religious understanding between the Saudi governmental aristocracy and the Wahhabi Islamic purest who by agreement always serve in government. Furthermore, the religious sites foster Islamic tourism from all over the world. (2) The Saudi wealth and geographic location makes it a natural meeting point for a variety of elites, traders, meeting organizers, and business leaders from South Asia, Africa and Europe. However, the former group and the latter group aren't exactly compatible. The former group wants to visit a place with strict adherence to Islamic rules (e.g. no alcohol, no nightlife, etc.) while the latter group is coming to their "meeting hub" to meet and greet but also to enjoy themselves. (3) By leveraging its wealth and the sale of ARAMCO stock and oil, the country will become the financial center of the region. So how does the country serve as a meeting hub for these antithetical groups of religious and financial, business leaders?

In addition to refocusing education and emphasizing Islamic Sunni leadership, there is a human capital issue within the country. Historically, there has been considerable inbreeding (i.e. cousin marriage) within the Saudi native families and tribes. There is hard evidence in Saudi medical journals that there has been significant genetic deterioration in these groups. For instance, Saudi military recruiters have had some trouble finding native Saudi men who can differentiate among yellow, red, and green. At the urging of medical experts, the Crown Prince has required premarital genetic screenings so couples can at least be forewarned of the genetic problems their children will experience. It is estimated that 135,000 marriages were canceled after the couples received their results [2]. Nevertheless, great family wealth tends to encourage inbreeding to keep the wealth in the family. The question then is how does one discourage inbreeding when there is so much wealth about and the Prophet's own behavior sanctions cousin marriages?

Thus far, in order to keep the modern Saudi society operating, 12 million immigrants have been imported. Many of these people are well educated and have brought badly needed specialized skills to the country. All immigrants, regardless of educational attainment, brought a willingness to work. Not surprisingly, nearly all are Muslim. Of all the immigrants in the country only about 150,000 are Christians. While Muslims may be granted "permanent immigrant status"; Christians can only receive "temporary immigrant status". Since all women in the country have to follow strict Islamic dress and behavior codes, Muslim immigrants are more likely to bring their wives with them in contrast to non-Muslim immigrants. These Muslim immigrants comprise roughly 1/3 of the country's population. In the coming years, will these Muslim immigrants be accepted as citizens?

Another problem, although not frequently mentioned, is that fresh water supplies in this largely desert country are tenuous. Generally a modern society uses about 370 l/person/day. Saudi Arabia has 34,000,000 people and uses only 225 l/person/day. This means the country is already operating under tight water conditions. Of course, a wealthy country, like Saudi Arabia, can increase its water supply by using expensive alternatives like desalination of sea water. Will Saudi Arabia be able to maintain its current and growing tourist and citizen population given its tenuous water supply? [3].

The desire of Saudi leaders is to create independent tech center cities and economic zones within the country is laudatory. However, two hurdles exist: (1) most local people lack the education in science, engineering and business to implement such ideas; of course such people might be brought in, but their presence might aggravate other problems. (2) The government seems inclined to separate such activities from the large Saudi cities in the south. For example, the current Saudi plan is to build another new tech oriented city, tentatively called NOME, in the northwestern corner of the country near Jordan, the Palestinian West Bank, and Israel. This area is not far from the Saudi city of Tabuk (Pop. 900,000) and has two fairly good sized non-Saudi population centers nearby, Aqaba, Jordan (pop. 150,000) and Eilet, Israel (pop. 50,000). This part of the country is nearly 800 miles away from the country's southern population centers (e.g. Riyadh and Jeddah). Will a wealthy, conservative, deeply religious country be able to establish a successful independent technological city state starting from nothing?

In order to implement Vision 2030, the Crown Prince has demonstrated a willingness to use state power to crush opposition. In Yemen, Saudi involvement on the side of Sunni Arabs in a civil war has precluded a settlement which might have allowed healing from the conflict to occur quickly [4]. After helping the Sunni faction to extend the war, the death tolls have risen and healing will likely take generations. In Turkey, the Crown Prince is suspected of authorizing the assassination of a Saudi journalist, Jamal Khashoggi, who had published unflattering information about the Crown Prince [5]. Does such behavior on the part of a young leader facing 10 years of major societal change indicate the needed flexibility to achieve success?

The Saudi government is counting on raising $100 billion for their Vision 2030 projects by selling a 5% stake the Saudi government's oil monopoly (Aramco) to European and American investors. The problem is most oil analysts are not inclined to give Aramco the required $2 Trillion valuation needed to justify the $100 billion sale.

The problems are several:

1. Aramco's expenses are higher than analysts expected; this is now being explained by the fact that several royal families have been secretly charging family expenses to Aramco.

2. The world selling price for oil has been lower than the $65 per barrel number used to justify the $2 trillion amount; this is not likely to change as the US has become an exporter of crude oil rather than an importer, and Russia continues its oil export,

3. Aramco insists on being paid in US dollars which bothers the likes of China that would like their currency to be acceptable particularly right now because of the trade disputes with the US and because the dollar is so high at this time.

In addition, to the valuation problem mentioned above, there are other questions with this 5% offering of Aramco stock. These questions include: (1) what "on going" reporting to all shareholders will be provided, (2) will the subordination of the company's interest to the needs of the Saudi government continue, (3) what would be the consequence if the bulk of this 5% stake ends up in the hands of the Russian or Chinese, (4) will the company stop being used by certain Saudi royals as their personal piggy bank, and (5) what legal processes will be available to disgruntled shareholders if they see maladministration or misuse of corporate funds. All these questions should be addressed before the offering is completed. Is the Crown Price likely to go forward with Vision 2030 if he has trouble raising the money?

The final and most important thing to consider is the kind of governmental and cultural system that might evolve in this expansive, wealthy country in the coming decades. Social scientists have shown us that change is always occurring in every society. Some societies move toward more participation and/or greater freedom for its residences (e.g. United States of America). Some societies move the other way (e.g. Venezuela). The Saudi Kingdom maintains a social police force that compliments Sharia approved public behavior and punishes deviations. The Kingdom has shown little interest moving toward democracy or toward dropping the restriction on political behavior that they place on their citizens. However, in the area of social control the Crown Prince has shown some flexibility. Women are now allowed to drive cars, engage in sports, serve on local leadership councils, and attend public entertainment events (e.g. concerts, sporting events, etc.) [6]. However, suggestions from the international human right groups demand that women should be freed from the Saudi requirement of having a male guardian to direct her affairs. Additionally political gatherings, even peaceful gatherings, are punishable by imprisonment and possible beheading. The Shi'a minority, 15% of the population, remains under very tight control. Will the authoritarian religious and political leadership give up some of its power and control? Is democracy and religious accommodation in Saudi Arabia's future?

3. The next 10 years: the effect of vision 2030 of Saudi Arabia's future

The Crown Prince is heavily invested in his Vision 2030 project that will bring both new physical facilities and social changes. While the facilities are visible, the social changes are likely to be more consequential.

A look at a few of the larger projects, is impressive: A completely new Red Sea resort encompassing both shoreline and off shore island development, a complete refurbishment of Jeddah's downtown with the addition on a civic entertainment area on a nearby offshore island, a major push on renewable energy development, a new high tech and business center in northwestern Saudi Arabia called NEOM, and perhaps the completion of the technological cities begun under previous Kings. All this development will cost more than the $100 billion likely to be raised by the sale of 5% of ARAMCO.

The original plan called for considerable outside investment of both direct dollars and international joint venture involvement. The war in Yemen but also the royal involvement in the killing of Jamal Khashoggi in Turkey have cause international partners to pull back. The most notable was Richard Branson, the CEO of Virgin Atlantic airline, who has withdrawn from his major role promoting the new Red Sea resort. However, some of the international investors have begun to return to the fold not wanting to miss a promising opportunity [7]. The Crown Prince had hoped that Saudi Arabia would become the "Davos of the Middle East," a Saudi financial conference held in 2018, but several companies withdrew their initial support. These included to executive from: Google, KKR, Ford, J.P. Morgan Chase, BlackRock, Uber, and the Blackstone Group.

All this does not mean the entire Vision 2030 program is dead, but it indicates it may be harder to implement than originally thought. Probably Crown Prince Mohammed bin Salman will have to give up more social controls so that projects like the Red Sea resort, the city of NEOM, and the "Davos of the Middle East" ideas can become realities. But it is in loosening of the social control that the Crown Prince might be subsequently forced to relinquish controls in other areas of life.

The questions raised in this investigation have not been answered. They identify the tension in the country between the Crown Prince's desire to refurbish modernize and update the Saudi economy and his desire to retain the Saud's family control of the country. The longer term future of Saudi Arabia has several possibilities.

4. The longer term future of Saudi Arabia

Given the level of change in the broader world it is almost certain the Kingdom will change significantly. So what are the kinds of possibilities?

One possibility is it will revert from currently being only the fifth most authoritarian regime in the world and return to its former status as the most authoritarian regime in the world. As modern ideas creep into the kingdom, the number of beheadings will probably increase. The talented Saudis will seek to leave. Most of the positive accomplishments in Vision 2030 mentioned above will be lost. The country will experience difficulty finding partners to support and participate in its major projects: NEOM, the Red Sea Resorts, the "Davos of the Middle East" ideas, etc. The religious leaders may resist moves toward liberalization: democratic councils at the local level, women's sports teams, etc. The Shi'a who live around the oil fields might find themselves even more tightly controlled. Women will still have men control their movement, dress and acceptable occupations ... if they work.

Another possibility is the Saud family would turn on the country's religious leaders and openly push them out of the government to demonstrate their bonafides as a worthy member of the community of nations. This would probably trigger a civil war, marked by terrorist attacks led by religious leaders who are currently being sheltered and funded by true Saudi believers across the countryside. The government would be hard pressed to control the Shi'a in the East who would likely rise in rebellion, fight the religious terrorists, and discipline the now secretive reformers likely to demand more civil rights. The internet which was used effectively to organize the Arab Spring in Cairo would be shut down or be tightly controlled. Tourist traffic to the holy sites of Mecca and Medina would remain steady unless there were safety concerns. Tourism to the Red Sea resorts would decline. Non-Saudis in NEOM and other advanced learning and research sites would likely leave. Even the country's enormous oil revenues could hardly sustain such disruption. Which group would win is impossible to predict. The only thing very likely to happen (without US intervention) would be Shi'a success in taking many of the oil fields away from the Saudis, probably with the help of the Iranians. It is unlikely they would become a province of Iran, but they could operate their own small country, like Kuwait.

A final possibility would be to continue gradual liberalizations. This would require forgoing dramatic killings (e.g. Jamal Khashoggi) and winding down the war in Yemen. There should be a program that allows the non-citizen Muslims to become citizens of Saudi Arabia. Perhaps granting birthright citizenship would make the process of merger between the two groups gradual. To solve the cousin marriage problem, a bonus program might be established wherein a marriage contracted by an immigrant family member and a Saudi family member would earn a $100,000 bonus. The money flowing to the descendants of King Saud could be curtailed significantly perhaps by the total of the $100,000 bonuses paid above. Perhaps the Crown Prince might set up an elected national advisory council with 10 advisories from each million population. Electing these advisors might get the people used to debating the qualifications of candidates and to the idea of going to the polls regularly to vote. The Kingdom might very gradually evolve into the structure found in England with a figurehead monarch and an "advisory council/ parliament" eventually holding the real power.

5. Conclusion

The role of the Islamic religion is the major variable in this situation because conservative religious leaders do not like being forced to simply advise or urge people to do what their religion promotes and proscribes. Such leaders like the state to assist them in gaining compliance. In Western Europe there was a bloody war fought for 30 years when the Lutherans of Northern Germany wanted to be free of Catholic proscriptions. It will require a firm leadership style to liberalize Saudi Arabia without causing the religious leaders to go into open revolt and take their conservative followers with them. It should be noted that neither Catholics nor Lutherans could find an authority for the Catholic demands and proscriptions in their holy book, the Bible. However, in Saudi Arabia both the progressives and the religious conservatives acknowledge their Holy Book, the Quran, contains the demands and proscriptions that the religious leaders advocate. In addition, the Catholics of Europe had a method for revising their many "questionable" requirements (e.g. Councils of the Church, statements by the Pope, etc.) whereas the Islamic world has no definitive way or process to revise the rules found in the Qu'ran. It is very difficult to "modify" the exact words of God as revealed to the Prophet Mohammed. Such modifications are unlikely to occur. Who is man to reinterpret the word of God?

So which path is likely to emerge in Saudi Arabia? The gradual liberalization path seems the most likely to continue going forward. The only questions are the tempo of change and the degree of change. The central question is will the change include some democracy at the national level? The Crown Prince seems to be a very proud, strong willed, self-confident man who is not afraid of enacting violence. He has one wife and four children. This speaks to the respect he has for his wife who is also a member of his tribe. Today he is relatively young and he has the confidence of his failing father, King Salman. In the present with the King living and supporting him, Mohammed bin Salman is continuing to move quickly to embrace change. With this in mind, the changes are likely to continue, but they are more likely to be focused on social areas and avoid governmental structures. There will be push back from the religious leaders. As the Crown Prince grows older, these two forces of social and governmental structures are likely to slow the tempo of change and to be less dramatic. Will the other interested groups be generating counter forces to keep the progressive changes coming? It is not likely but possible. There are three such counter force groups: the Shi'a, the Muslim immigrants, and the important new arrivals with special skills that Vision 2030 will bring to the country in the coming decades. These will represent perhaps 50% of the people present in the land, but they will have few effective ways to communicate with each other or existing forums through which they might be heard such as Rotary, political parties or the Chamber of Commerce.

A warning is needed should some national level democracy develop. A participatory democracy requires such things as the education of voters in government, civics, and the history of democratic successes and failures. This sort of education is completely lacking in Saudi Arabia today. Any democratic change should be implemented slowly so the educational component can be infused into the schools completely. The failure to educate the common men and women will lead to a credulous electorate that can be easily misled by propaganda and unrealistic political promises.

A few concluding thoughts on perhaps the most intractable problems described above:

1. To move from authoritarian (kingdom) government to democratic government (particularly a fully participatory democracy) requires not only the historical and civics education of the people, but at an even more basic level, there must be at least a general feeling of mutual self-respect for "the other", a basic feeling of equality among all people (e.g. of the Sunni for the Shi'a, of men for women, of the Crown Prince for Jamal Khasogghi, of the rich Muslim student for her visiting Christian teacher, etc.). Islam, as a world force, achieved its greatest success in the seventh through the sixteenth centuries by actualizing an opposite sense (i.e. of Muslims over non-Muslims, of men over women, etc.). The current educational system reinforces loyalty to the King, Islam and tribal superiority. Equality is not fostered in the government, religion, social or educational systems.

2. To reduce the increase of physical and mental abnormalities within the nation's gene pool, the nation will have to instigate a major push to get citizens to at least think about marrying people that their parents would never consider appropriate. This "push" could take the form of stipends or social status. Because Islam sanctions cousin marriage, the religious leaders will have to be involved.

3. Will Saudi Arabia move toward democracy as socialism falters? The interaction of lower oil prices and growing number of Saudi's receiving stipends is sustainable in

> the near future. However, the social and Islamic religious structures argue against a participatory democracy. Socialism may falter but a turn toward democracy would threaten the power of the King, Crown Prince Mohammed bin Salman and the religious leaders.

And finally, the authors of this chapter come to their task with internal "frames of reference" that have been heavily influenced by the enlightenment and western Christianity. They have attempted to understand the Saudi Arabian mind set through study and interpersonal contacts both in America and, in the case of the lead author, in the Middle East as well. However, they know they can never fully predict the impact of the culture, the religion, and the effect of extended family relationships which have been internalized by the people of Saudi Arabia. These factors will, in the long run, have the greatest impact on Saudi Arabia's future.

Author details

Judith Cochran[1,2,3] and Hugh V. Murray*†

1 University of Missouri - St. Louis, USA

2 AIN Sham University in Cairo, Egypt

3 Turkish Air Force School in Istanbul, Turkey

*Address all correspondence to: hvm@aol.com

† Editor of three different monthly stock research bulletins for three brokerage firms over 20 years.

References

[1] Bin Issa AM. Saudi plans to overhaul poorly performing Education. Yidan Prize Summit, Hong Kong, December 11, 2017. Young Vision: The Youth Educational Magazine. The Emirates Publication; 2017

[2] Alsaeed ES et al. Distribution of hemoglobinoplathy disorders based upon data from premarital screening and genetic counseling programs 2011-2015. Journal of Epidemiology and Global Health. December 2018;7(1):S41-S47

[3] Saudi Arabia launches program for a drastic reduction in water use. World Water Magazine; May 2019. p. 21

[4] Middle East moves from bad to worse. Mediterranean Dialogues; Beyond Terrorism to Positive Agreement News Conference, Rome Information Office. The Peninsula Qatar News. 24 November 2018

[5] Silicon Valley Saudi ties faces fresh scrutiny in wake of Khashoggi affair. The Guardian World; 20 October 2018

[6] A changing future: The economic role of women in Saudi Arabia. The Abdul Latif Jameel Organization's Publication–Perspectives; 31 January 2018. Available from: https://www.alj.com/en/media-center/perspectives/changing-future-economic

[7] Saudi Arabia: US companies return to the Kingdom. The Week. 13 November 2019. p. 34

Chapter 5

Archaeological Sites, Cultural Heritage, and Sustainable Development in the Republic of Kazakhstan

Claudia Chang

Abstract

This paper addresses the problem of protecting and preserving archaeological sites from the Bronze Age through the Medieval Period (ca. 2500 BC–1500 CE) as part of sustainable development that includes such economic and social benefits as (1) promoting national status; (2) integrating archaeological sites into the Silk Route narrative; (3) developing tourism related to historic and cultural heritage; and (4) creating a citizenry that values its cultural and historic resources in the face of rapid economic development and changing natural and cultural landscapes. Two UNESCO World Heritage sites will be discussed briefly: Otrar and the surrounding oasis, a medieval complex of sites along the Great Silk Route, and Tamgaly, a petroglyph and archaeological reserve. These two UNESCO World Heritage archaeological sites or preserves will be contrasted with the Talgar Iron Age sites (400 BC–100 CE) situated in a rapidly changing landscape due to economic development and infrastructure (pipelines, railways, roads, and housing) about 12–15 km east of the major city of Almaty. The goal of this article is to discuss the complexity of the entangled sectors of cultural and historic preservation, economic development, tourism, and global transnational heritage within the framework of sustainability.

Keywords: archaeology, UNESCO World Heritage sites, preservation, cultural properties

1. Introduction

The goal of this paper is to examine global, national, and regional policies and practices of cultural heritage and preservation of important archaeological sites, monuments, and landscapes in the Republic of Kazakhstan. The global and national importance of the Republic of Kazakhstan's rich cultural and historical heritage is apparent in the UNESCO World Heritage inscriptions of three archaeological and/or historic sites and two natural areas from 2003 to 2016. Thirteen additional nominations dating from 1996 to 2016 have been added to the tentative list for inscription to the World Heritage List. In 2014 the UNESCO has granted World Heritage status to 34 places along the Silk Route that includes the nations of China, Kazakhstan, and Kyrgyzstan and with funding and support from Norway, Japan, and South Korea [1]. The "One Belt, One

Road" initiative launched by the Chinese government is a set of economic and political alliances meant to strengthen trading, cooperation financial integration, and people-to-people bonds. From 2013 to 2017, the Republic of Kazakhstan has been one of the 21 states who serve on the nominating committee for cultural and historical properties for the UNESCO (usually a 4-year term) (personal communication Yuri M. Peshkov). The UNESCO World Heritage inscriptions in the Republic of Kazakhstan, along with the tentative list for World Heritage inscriptions, have reinforced the necessity for Kazakhstani diplomats, politicians, government officials, and the local citizenry to include archaeological sites, monuments, and cultural properties as part of sustainability efforts. In the case of places such as the archaeological sites of Otrar placed on the tentative list of UNESCO World Heritage sites in 1998, Kazakhstani archaeologists have since worked toward linking archaeological protection and conservation with increased local and international tourism [2]. At the archaeological landscape of Tamgaly, an important petroglyph reserve already nominated as a World Heritage place in 2004, there have been efforts to document the over 5000 rock carvings in the Bronze through Medieval and Contemporary sites, and an area of about 900 hectares has been under state jurisdiction and placed under the 1992 Law on the Protection and Use of Historical and Cultural Heritage (UNESCO World Heritage List Kazakhstan website) [3].

The archaeological community, both as part of government organizations under the Kazakhstan Republic's Ministry of Sciences and Higher Education and the Ministry of Culture, has been directly involved in policies for the protection and preservation of archaeological sites and monuments since independence in 1991. Before, under Soviet rule, there were strict mandates and codes for the protection and restoration of archaeological sites and monuments. Thus, the legal status for protecting, restoring, and preserving archaeological and historical sites has indeed had a long and venerable history in both Soviet and post-Soviet periods. Of interest, however, is how recent infrastructure development (road building, railways, pipelines, gas and oil, mineral development, and housing) has impacted archaeological sites and monuments. Sustainable development also is the larger umbrella for the consideration of important natural, cultural, and historic landscapes and places. This paper will address these issues at different scales: the local and regional, the national, and the international and global levels by using several case studies in the Talgar region near the major city of Almaty, in the Otrar basin including the UNESCO World Heritage medieval site of Otrar, and at the petroglyph complex of Tamgaly. All these places are in southern Kazakhstan or the Zhetysu Region (Seven-Rivers area). By no means, they are necessarily the most important regions for cultural heritage, but they serve as important examples for other places in the Republic of Kazakhstan either designated as World Heritage places or as tentative listings on the World Heritage inscription list or known as archaeological sites that should be protected as part of the nation's cultural and historic heritage while still obtaining the goals of sustainability in a rapidly developing nation.

My sources come from Russian, Kazakh, and English reports, anecdotal data, and informal discussions with my Kazakhstani colleagues since the mid-1990s. Also I address changes in land property from collective landholdings to privatization of landholdings, especially in areas where archaeological sites have been found, inventoried, and listed under Svod Pamyatnikov or the official national archives of registered archaeological sites and monuments for the major provinces of the Republic of Kazakhstan. Much of this inventorying, built upon the earlier task of the Archeologische Karta (or the Archaeological Map of Kazakhstan) published in 1960, has been conducted by the Kazakhstan Office for the Preservation and Restoration of Sites and Historic Monuments under the direction of the Kazakhstan Republic's Ministry of Culture.

2. Local and regional considerations of cultural heritage and historic monuments

In the early 1990s just after the breakup of the Soviet Union, the state organizations for archaeological research and preservation of artifacts, sites, and monuments were often at the brink of transition, lacking both necessary structural guidelines once in place during Soviet rule and sufficient government funding. The permit system remained the same as in Soviet times and was known as the Akrites List, or Open List, by which archaeologists from the institutes such as the Academy of Sciences, Institute of Archaeology, universities, museums, and other government-sponsored entities could apply for permits to survey, excavate, and research archaeological sites for scientific purposes. These permits or permissions were obtained through the appropriate bureaucratic entities in the name of qualified archaeologists. The government offices along with the individual archaeologist, to whom the permit was granted, were responsible for reaching all criteria including submitting a final or interim report annually on the methods and results of the research. There were further stipulations that the Ministry of Culture required such as complying with rules of where artifacts and archival information would be placed after the completion of research and study. For international researchers, we were bound to deposit all scientific materials, including ancient objects, to government institutions or museums in the Republic of Kazakhstan. In order to obtain permission through the Open List, international archaeologists work collaboratively with the local archaeologists. Foreign researchers, such as myself, are required annually to sign a scientific protocol and agreement or memorandum of agreement that indicates (1) scientific exchange through sharing of books, articles, and other printed material; (2) listing of all personnel to be included in a project; (3) the funding of the project (usually the responsibility of the international archaeologists through grants); (4) curation of collections (artifacts and reports) which are to remain in the Republic of Kazakhstan; and (5) responsibilities for publishing articles in Russian, Kazakh, and English.

Local mayors (akims) and other officials of the oblasts (provinces) also play an important role in supporting archaeological research in their regions. Often these bureaucrats have funds from their local or regional coffers to aid in costly research work, protection of collections, and furthering museum collections. For example, the "Two Thousand-Year Jubilee Celebration" of important cities along the southern Silk Route in the 2001 such as Taraz and Almaty resulted in funds given for local archaeologists to excavate new sections of urban medieval sites, initiate new restoration and conservation projects, and to mount important exhibitions in local museums and cultural centers.

The importance of scientific archaeological research in the service of providing national and ethnic identities was understood in the 1920s as a way to integrate the far distant republics of the USSR into one nation. In a republic such as Kazakhstan, where the indigenous population of Kazakhs comprised a considerable proportion of the populace, it was also important to highlight important ethnic heroes such as the last nineteenth-century poet, composer, and philosopher Abai Qunanbaiuly. By the time rapid collectivization took place in 1929–1930, the Kazakhs suffered famine and starvation [4–6]. The land was now held under the state apparatus.

2.1 The Talgar case: land privatization, infrastructure development, and UNESCO World Heritage inscription

In 1997–1998 when the Kazakh-American Archaeological Expedition (KAAE) sponsored by A. Kh. Margulan Institute of Archaeology and American archaeologists conducted surveys across a 550 sq. km area of the Talgar alluvial fan, an area about

25 km to the east of the city of Almaty, much of the land we surveyed were open agricultural fields held by state collective farms. It was possible to walk in uncultivated agricultural fields in order to find inventory archaeological sites, usually apparent from scatters of animal bone, ancient ceramic fragments, and grinding stones. By the early 2000s, much of the collective lands were now held by private owners and therefore became fenced, enclosed, and closed to archaeologists and others who wished to conduct scientific research. Private owners of the land once designated as collective lands that previously had been surveyed and even excavated by archaeologists under the proper official channels were now subject to judicial actions and potential lawsuits. Therefore, it became a point of contention as to whether private owners had the right to control and use their land in any way they desired versus the protection and preservation of archaeological sites once found on collective lands.

This kind of acrimony and conflict between stakeholders would continue in the Talgar area from 2008 through 2016 when a private archaeological firm was investigated for destroying cultural properties within the designated borders of medieval Talgar, a 9 h town, occupied from the ninth to the eleventh centuries AD and inscribed as one of the eight sites in the Republic of Kazakhstan found along the Chang'an-Tianshan Corridor of the Silk Route in 2014. The resolution of the dispute between the private archaeological firm, the construction work that built a bridge across the Talgar River, A. Kh. Margulan Institute of Archaeology, and the Republic of Kazakhstan's Ministry of Culture led to a unilateral government mandate that halted all construction work on the bridge and salvage archaeology along the proposed bridge corridor on November 21, 2016 [7].

3. Kazakh nationalism and historical tradition

Kazakhstan became independent from the USSR in 1991, at the point where the republic's population had <50% ethnic Kazakhs; the other predominant ethnic group was Russians along with many other ethnic groups. The move toward erasing ethnic Russians as the "elder brothers" to colonizers was achieved by removing Russians from the public sector, business, banking, and the law [8]. In fact President Nazarbayev made moves to create a Kazakh homeland by moving the capital to Astana in 1998–1999. He also declared 1998 "the year of national unity and national history." During this year, specifically in 1998 major archaeological campaigns were carried out at the medieval city of Otrar, and the Saka period frozen tomb burials in Berel, in the Altai region, were excavated by a French-Kazakh team, and many other state-funded archaeological projects were conducted.

Elsewhere I have written about the role of nationalism in archaeological investigations in the Republic of Kazakhstan [9]. The desire to establish the origins of the Kazakh Khanate in the sixteenth century CE also aided in the creation of a Kazakh homeland. Ancient Saka warriors of the Iron Age (ca. 800–200 BCE) such as the Golden Warrior, a 17-year-old youth discovered in the Issyk burial kurgan 40 km east of Almaty (the main city) in 1969, already established an historical connection between Saka Indo-Europeans and Kazakh nomadic culture.

A relatively young nation independently requires a historic tradition, in this case, one that extolls the nomadic past of the major component of the Republic of Kazakhstan's populace, the Kazakhs. As a breakaway from the Russian Imperial rule in the eighteenth century and Soviet rule in the twentieth century, the Kazakh ethnic identity must be promoted as root of the nation while still including the hundred other nationalities or ethnic groups. The adoption of the Kazakh language as the state language where all official documents must be in Kazakh language appears to be a major step toward Kazakhization of the nation and proclaiming one state language [10].

From the very beginning of Kazakhstan's independence from the former USSR, President Nazarbayev initiated the cultural and political ideology of Kazakhization on December 10, 1991, by referring to Ablai Khan who already in the eighteenth century revitalized Kazakh statehood from "the brink of collapse" [11]. The history of Kazakhstan, and especially its deep history regarding the connections of Kazakhs to the ancient Turks. Karin and Chebotarev [11] quote fragments of official speeches from President Nazarbayev from 1996 to 1997 that specifically name the Paleolithic sites in southern Kazakhstan at Shoktas and Koshkurgan established the antiquity of human occupation on the territory of Kazakhstan that could establish the antiquity of human history to 100,000 years or more. Of importance is an underlying concept of ethnogenesis, or the idea that the "ethnos" or the national people originated from a very ancient heritage that established this territory as specifically Eurasian in origin.

4. Transnational and global heritage and the Republic of Kazakhstan

In 2014, 33 sites along the Silk Routes of the Network of the Chang'an-Tianshan Corridor were inscribed as UNESCO World Heritage sites; 8 of these sites are located in the Zhetysu Corridor of the Republic of Kazakhstan and 3 are located in the Tian Shan Mountains in the Republic of Kyrgyzstan [12]. The entire Silk Routes of the Networks of the Chang'an-Tianshan Corridor consist of a 5000 km section from Chang'an/Louyang capital of the Han and Tang Dynasties in China to the Zhetysu Corridor of Central Asia along the Tian Shan Mountain Corridor into the desert oases of Central Asia and dating from about the second century BCE to the first century CE and then lasting until the sixteenth century CE. In particular the Ili, Chuy, and Talas Valleys of Central Asia and these archaeological sites were important for the transfer of Zoroastrian and Manichaeism religions. As previously mentioned, Talgar, a medieval site, was adversely impacted by potential bridge building and the salvage archaeology associated with that proposed construction in 2016 [7]. This, therefore, is an excellent case by which local and regional conflicts between rapid infrastructural development and national and international interests underscored by the UNESCO inscription of archaeological sites along a corridor become visible to the general public and citizenry of the Republic of Kazakhstan. Should a new nation exercise its ability to undertake large infrastructural development at the expense of its rich cultural and historical heritage? Do local stakeholders have any say? Or are the larger issues of national pride and international relations able to override a local, municipal government's desire to introduce modernization in the form of roadways and bridges to its territory? Here the answers lie in the nature of political process whereby cultural and historic heritage sometimes comes at the cost of infrastructure development. The stakeholders may not have even concerned themselves with the larger macroscale processes of transnational cooperation in the form of the designation of a Silk Route Corridor. When the right hand does not know what the left hand is doing, this suggests a failure on the part of all stakeholders to participate in the process of negotiating between the heritage community, the public, and the national and international arenas [13, 14].

This transnational set of historic linkages between the nations of China, Kazakhstan, and Kyrgyzstan also mirrors the geopolitical push made by China in the "One Belt, One Road" initiative which has the objectives of increasing unimpeded trade; infrastructure connections such as railways, pipelines, and road; and financial integration [1]. The Chang'an-Tianshan Corridor is the example of "soft diplomacy" coupled with hard economic integration and colonization of periphery areas to the Chinese core. As Winters [1] puts it so eloquently:

> *"For many in the region, the Silk Road is a story of peaceful trade, and a rich history of religious and harmonious cultural exchange. The Belt and Road seeks to directly build on this legacy. It rest up a historical narrative that connectivity—both cultural and economic—reduces suspicion and promotes common prosperity...." [1]*

For developing nations such as Kazakhstan and Kyrgyzstan, the invitation to join the Chang'an-Tianshan Corridor Silk Route initiative gives these nations status, recognition, and also a stake in the "One Belt, One Road" economic initiatives of the core state of China. World Heritage status of archaeological sites often brings cultural, scientific, and financial backers into a nation. For example, the UNESCO-backed restoration of the medieval city of Otrar, a main city along the southern Silk Route, was for the most part financed by Japan. Petroglyph research and the training of local archaeologists and museum personnel at Tamgaly, the major archaeological rock art and landscape reserve in southern Kazakhstan near the Karatau Mountains, were supported in part by Norway. For local archaeologists in Kazakhstan, these World Heritage nominations attract more tourism and boost employment and research opportunities. Government grants through the Kazakh National Institute of Science and Technology have been awarded to archaeologists pursuing the excavation, survey, and research into significant archaeological sites; both are included in World Heritage site nominations and on the tentative list of cultural properties to be protected.

5. Conclusions

In the Republic of Kazakhstan, cultural and historic heritage of archaeological sites and monuments arises out of the previous Soviet system for the protection and restoration of important archaeological sites and historic monuments. This tradition of heritage management continues to this day but has been influenced now by rapid infrastructural development and national and global mandates under the UNESCO system of inscribing World Heritage sites and natural landscapes. This new level of transnational and global heritage has both positive and negative impacts on the stakeholders of Kazakh history and culture and the citizens themselves. Nationalism, especially with regard to the early evolution of prehistory on the territory of the Republic of Kazakhstan, as mentioned by former President Nazarbayev in 1997–1998, builds among its citizenry a sense of pride and belonging to a greater Eurasian past. The linkage between the contemporary Kazakh culture, whose historic roots can be traced to the sixteenth century AD, and earlier nomadic steppe traditions such as the ancient Saka (eastern variants of the Scythians), although perhaps historically inaccurate, does instill a national pride in the dominant ethnic group, the Kazakhs. Under Soviet rule, indigenous nomadic peoples were often seen as the "little brothers" to the dominant Russian cultural and historic traditions. Former President Nazarbayev since independence in 1991 has been able to weave a national identity that is both multiethnic and multireligious within the territory of the nation-state while asserting the political dominance of the Kazakhs through language reform and the Kazakhization of the national culture [8, 10, 11]. In spite of rapid infrastructural development from vast oil and gas reserves, it is also of great importance to the politicians and diplomats as well as the professional archaeologists and historians to promote the role of cultural and historical heritage in the Republic of Kazakhstan. There will still, however, be tensions in these competing national and global narratives as long as sustainable development appears to be separate from the management of heritage policies.

Acknowledgements

I wish to thank Yuri Peshkov, former cultural officer of the Almaty cluster office of the UNESCO. Boris A. Zheleznyakov provided reports and other information about the World Heritage listing of Tamgaly Reserve Park for which I am grateful.

Author details

Claudia Chang
Sweet Briar College, Sweet Briar, VA, USA

*Address all correspondence to: cchang@sbc.edu

References

[1] Winter T. One belt, one road, one heritage: Cultural diplomacy and the silk route. The Diplomat. 2016;**29**:1-5. Available from: http://thediplomat.com/2016/one-belt-one-road-one-heritage-cultural-diplomacy-and-the-silk-road/

[2] Voyakin D, Baipakov K. Monument in its setting, case study Akrytas and Otar Archaeological projects. ICOMOS Open Archive: Section II: Vulnerabilities within the settings of monuments and sites: understanding the threats and defining appropriate responses. In: 15th ICOMOS General Assembly and International Symposium: 'Monuments and sites in their setting-conserving cultural heritage in changing townscapes and landscapes' 17-21 October 2005; Xi'an, China: [Conference or Workshop Item]; Available from: http://openarchive.icomos.org/id/eprint/351

[3] World Heritage Site UNESCO. Available from: http://whc.unesco.org/en/statesparties/kz [Accessed: 20 April 2019]

[4] Olcott M. The Kazakhs. 2nd ed. Stanford, CA: Stanford University: Hoover Institution Press; 2005. 388 p. ISBN-13: 978-0817993528

[5] Cameron S. The Hungry Steppe; Famine, Violence, and the Making of Soviet Kazakhstan. Ithaca: Cornell University Press; 2018. 294 p. ISBN-13: 978-1501730436

[6] Kindler R. Stalin's Nomads: Power and Famine in Kazakhstan. Pittsburgh: University of Pittsburgh Press; 2018. 328 p. ISBN-13: 978-0822965435

[7] Medieval Ancient Settlement Talgar will not be removed from UNESCO list of world heritage sites. 2016. KazTAG. Available from: https://kaztag.kz/en/news/medieval-ancient-settlement-talgar-will-not-be-removed-from-unesco-list-of-world-heritage [Accessed: 20 May 2019]

[8] Kuzio T. History, memory, and nation building in the post-soviet colonial space. Nationalities Papers. 2002;**30**(2):241-264. DOI: 10.1080/0090599022014064 9

[9] Chang C. Rethinking Central Asian Prehistory: Farmers, Shepherds, and Nomads. London: Routledge Press; 2018. 160 p. ISBN-13: 978-1138737082

[10] Aksholakova A, Ismailova N. The language policy of Kazakhstan and the state language in government service. Procedia-Social and Behavioral Sciences. 2013;**93**:1580-1586. DOI: 10.1016/j.sbspro.2013.10.085

[11] Karin E, Chebotarev A. The policy of Kazakhization in state and government institutions in Kazakhstan. In: The Nationalities Question in Post-Soviet Kazakhstan. Institute for Developing Economies, Japan External Trade Organization; March 2002. Available from: www.ide.go.jp/English/Publish/Dowload/Mes/51.html [Accessed: 20 May 2019]

[12] World Heritage Committee. UNESCO. Available from: https://whc.unesco.org/en.list/1442 [Accessed: 20 April 2019]

[13] Meskell L. States of conservation: Protection, politics, and pacting within UNESCO's World Heritage committee. Anthropological Quarterly. 2014;**87**(1):217-243. ISSN: 0003-5491

[14] Willems WJH. The future of World Heritage and the emergence of transnational Heritage Regimes. Heritage and Society. 2014;**7**(2):105-120. DOI: 10.1179/2159032X14Z.00000000029

Section 2

Human Rights and Equality in Sustainable Development

Chapter 6

A Human Rights-Based Approach to Maternal and Child Health in Ethiopia: Does it Matter to Promote Health Equities?

Solomon Tekle Abegaz

Abstract

A rights-based approach to health helps to address health equity gaps. While several aspects of health as a human right exist, this chapter highlights particular indicators relevant to shaping a human rights approach to maternal and child health in Ethiopia. These indicators include recognition of the right to health; national health plan; accessible and acceptable health-care services; accountability; and a civil society that draws on the agency of vulnerable groups. Probing the extent to which the Ethiopian health system includes these features, this chapter identifies that the Federal Constitution does not adequately recognize maternal and child health as a human right. While identifying the positive developments of increased access to women's and children's health-care services in Ethiopia, the chapter also charts problems that limit further improvement, including health workers' inability from making the right health-care decisions; extreme gaps in ensuring accountability; and a restrictive law that restrains social mobilization for a proper health rights movement. The chapter concludes by providing recommendations to the government of Ethiopia that addressing these problems using a rights-based approach offers an alternative pathway for the progressive realization of the right to health of women and children, and it thereby improves health inequities in the country.

Keywords: a rights-based approach, health, maternal, child, Ethiopia

1. Introduction

It is at present 40 years since the Alma-Ata Declaration on primary health care [1]. Grounded in certain human-rights norms and public-health principles, the declaration urged governments and other actors to ensure the attainment of maternal and child health-care through primary health care by the year 2000. However, despite the significant reductions, women and children are still dying of inadequate health-care services, particularly in vulnerable communities. In our world, the majority of deaths occur in relation to maternal and under-five child mortality. Needlessly, the causes for most of the deaths are both treatable and preventable. It is likewise discovered that increases in maternal and child health are not shared equitably and that between and within countries, health inequities or gaps have widened [2].

In order for governments to scale up primary health care and thereby to narrow health inequities, among other things, the declaration indicates the importance of universal health coverage, national health plans, and a health workforce that includes community health workers [2].

Following Alma-Ata various attempts have been constructed to delineate some of the right-to-health features of health systems. Acutely aware of the centrality of a human rights-based approach (HRBA) to health to the creation of equitable health systems, Gunilla et al., for instance, have attempted to identify some of these to include legal recognition, standards, participation, comprehensive national planning, accountability, equity, equality and nondiscrimination, and respect for cultural difference and quality and proposed 72 indicators that reflect some of these features [3].

Maternal and child health is equally a central challenge of the Ethiopian health system, and health gain disparities concerning these categories of persons exist within the various parts of the country. This chapter examines the degree to which the Ethiopian health system (1) promotes awareness of the complementary relation between the Ethiopian health system and the right to maternal and child health; (2) selects a manageable set of indicators to assess the degree to which a health system includes some of the right-to-health features; (3) increases accountability in relation to the Ethiopian health system and the right to maternal and child health; and (4) deepens the understanding of the important role of indicators in relation to the progressive realization of the right to maternal and child health.

For the discussion on the human-rights features of maternal and child health and measuring Ethiopian compliance of its obligation to the right to health, this chapter relies mainly on current literature, General Comment 14, the Alma-Ata Declaration, and elements of the World Health Organization (WHO) building blocks of a good health system, the Convention of the Right of the Child, General Comments 3 and 4 of the Committee on the Rights of the Child, and the requirement that health facilities and services are available, accessible, and culturally appropriate—respectful of the culture of those concerned— and of good quality [4–11]. Further, it draws an examination of relevant Ethiopian laws, polices, plans and institutional mechanisms. Before discussing these features, the chapter attempts to highlight the conceptual framework of a HRBA.

2. Understanding a HRBA in the maternal and child health

Although conceptually rigorous, much has been written on the relevance of a HRBA to development and in particular to women and children's health care. There is consensus that the international community has lately achieved a full understanding that maternal and under-five mortality is no longer simply an issue of public health but a human rights concern [12]. This concern over a rights framework to maternal and child health grows due to the fact that a significant portion of maternal and under-five mortality is from preventable causes—an indication that avoidable maternal and child fatalities are potential violations of human rights constituting social injustice [13]. Essentially, a HRBA to maternal and child health aims to realize the right to the highest attainable standard of health (or "right to health") and other health-related complementary rights of vulnerable women and children.

Various features can be used as useful indicators to measure compliance of state obligations to the right of health care of their population: (1) legal recognition of the right to health; (2) availability, accessibility, acceptability, and quality of health-care facilities and services; (3) participation; (4) equality and nondiscrimination; (5) national health plans; (6) well-trained and motivated health workers; (7) and monitoring and accountability. This chapter analyzes how the Ethiopian health system deals with some of these features, in the section 'Access to maternal and child health care in Ethiopia'.

2.1 Legal recognition of the right

Similar to many other rights, recognition of the right to health takes different levels. In the main are the global and domestic dimensions, where the former is expressed through ratification of human rights treaties and the latter deals with the recognition of the right to health in the national constitution or other statutes. Legal recognition requires acknowledgment of the range of binding human rights obligations in the national legal and policy framework, and the jurisprudence and other pronouncements elaborating upon treaty provisions over the past decades [14]. This feature further requires avoiding euphemisms and rather urges to employ the language of human rights law in adoption of development laws and policies which laws and policies may include in the area of health-care [15]. This means, for example, that words such as "needs", "equity", "good governance" to identify things that are human rights or "citizens' rights" are employed in a manner that avoids reference to employ human rights standards and are reckoned to constitute euphemisms. The latter is distinguished as an "effort to depoliticize development discourse" whether they relate to issues of health care or education [14, 15]. But, why unambiguous recognition of rights is central?

Legal recognition is significant as it increases stakeholders' accountability and gives attention to ways of empowering marginalized children and women or their representatives to be aware of and claim their rights [16]. It can too cause the authorities accountable before courts, contributing to tangible improvements in maternal and child health care services. However, the realization of the right to maternal and child health can mean a commitment towards the recognition of the right, this does not necessarily warrant the actual operation or success of implementation [3]. China's law on Maternal and Infant Care, which specifically targets the health of mothers and young children, is a notable exception and is thought to possess a positive effect on child survival rates. Similarly, Vietnam's Child Protection, Care and Education law provides free health care for children under six. As well, in some jurisdictions, recognition has generated judicial decisions and non-judicial mechanisms of accountability that have improved the delivery of wellness-related services [17].

2.2 National health plans and health workers

The realization of women and children's right to health may be pursued through numerous approaches of which the adoption of national health plans that embraces health workers is one. General Comment 14 requires States parties to the International Covenant on Economic, Social and Cultural Rights (ICESCR) to develop a comprehensive home health plan encompassing human resources with a sentiment to assist them to realize their obligation of access to quality of health care to their population [18]. Adoption of national public health plan is a core obligation. But, what must a comprehensive national health plan, which incorporates health workers, exhibit?

First, health workers in preventive, curative, and rehabilitative health, encompassing physical and mental health must be available. Second, health workers must have appropriate preparation. Third, incentives must be in place to encourage the appointment, and retention, of health workers in underserved areas to better access, especially of marginal communities and populations. Fourth, human rights, including respect for cultural diversity and treating patients with courtesy, should be a compulsory part of the training for all health workers. Fifth, health workers must receive domestically competitive salaries and other reasonable terms and conditions of employment.

2.3 Availability, accessibility, acceptability, and quality (AAAQ) of health-care

General Comment 14 provides an in-depth articulation of the four interrelated and essential AAAQ elements, which can equally be applied to women's or children's right to health. *Availability* implies that structures, goods and services necessary for women and children's health are made available for the whole of the population within a state (this includes hospitals, clinics and other health-related buildings, medical and professional personnel, drugs and other equipment). Nevertheless, the handiness of such commodities and services depends on the physical and financial accessibility to those women and kids in need of them. Structures, goods and services have to be accessible to all women and children without discrimination —addressing discriminatory laws, policies, practices and gender inequalities in health care and in society that prevent children from accessing good quality services [18]. Accessibility has four dimensions: nondiscrimination, physical, economic, and information accessibility. *Acceptability* implies that structures, goods, and services are to be respectful of medical ethics and culturally appropriate [18]. *Quality* signifies structures, goods, and services must be scientifically and medically appropriate and of good quality [18].

2.4 Accountability

Accountability is fundamental to a HRBA. Paul Hunt notes "human rights can become no more than window-dressing without accountability" [19]. When accountability operates in a system, duty-bearers are answerable for their human actions or omissions in relation to their responsibilities. As a procedure, "accountability provides right-holders with an opportunity to understand how duty-bearers have discharged, or failed to discharge, their obligations, and it also provides duty-bearers with an opportunity to explain their conduct" [20]. Accountability does not necessarily imply punishment or blaming but constitutes elements of responsiveness, monitoring, independent review, answerability, and remedial action.

Different international and national accountability mechanisms can be envisaged within and outside the health systems that aim to hold all actors responsible, identify gaps and failures of institutions and programs, and provide remedy and redress for those (such as children) whose rights have been violated. According to the UN Office of High Commissioner for Human Rights (UNOHCHR), four broad categories of accountability mechanisms are identified: judicial, quasi-judicial, administrative, and political [21]. Helen Potts identifies a fifth case of accountability mechanism, social [19].

This chapter will only concentrate on the part of judicial accountability. This is mainly because litigation is increasingly used to seek accountability and redress for violation of constitutional and international human rights law dealing with the right to maternal and child health [22]. Yet, for litigation to be in force, certain conditions must exist.

First, there must be a direct entrenchment of the justiciable right to health in the national law/s of a given country that presents a specific right to health accountability mechanisms, which in turn can provide access to the courts to enable rights-holders to challenge government legislation and policy through litigation. Fitting in with Leslie London's view, constitutional recognition of "human rights standards can and do inform more powerful methods to establish accountability for realizing basic human needs" [23]. Furthermore, the stipulation of the international human right to maternal and child health has significantly contributed as an interpretive role to establish state obligations to ensure access to health care towards their population. Today each country is a state party to at least one of the international human rights instruments incorporating the right to health care [24]. Clearly, subscribing to these instruments raises an obligation upon state parties to guarantee accessibility of a detailed implementation program and comply with the AAAQ.

Second, due to their incapacity and vulnerability caused by biases and inequalities, women and children need an efficient legal representation to seek remedy before judicial bodies for systemic violation of their right to health [25]. Civil society organizations (CSOs) or human rights non-governmental organizations (NGOs) play a substantial role in this regard as discussed in the subsection below.

Despite the recent evolutions in the judicialization of maternal and children's rights which has increased access to health-care services in nations such as India, South Africa, and Columbia, accountability in many health systems remains extremely light. In some states, the same body provides and regulates health services, as well as having those responsible to account [3].

2.5 Social mobilization

Civil society organizations' contribution in litigating constitutional matters concerning health rights is of paramount importance. London underscores that active agency by those vulnerable to human rights violations is an aspect of health as a right relevant to shaping a HRBA to health [23]. Civil society action has an emancipatory or transformative potential to challenge state neglect or omission of health rights of children and women. A good example is post-apartheid South Africa, where CSOs have litigated most, if not all, major constitutional human rights cases, inclusive of the right to health care affecting women and children [25].

The extent of the actual significance of CSOs in women and children's rights advocacy and representation depends on the sociopolitical and legal environment in which they function. In emerging democracies, such as South Africa and Brazil, CSOs tend to sustain a relatively relaxed operational environment, and there is room for a mushrooming of vibrant human rights NGOs, whereas in restrictive settings—as in many African countries where laws are promulgated that constrain the natural processes and operational space of CSOs—they are regarded as obstructive by their governments [26]. In the latter case, the restriction on CSOs is manifested, for instance, in the content and implementation of legal instruments that are meant to govern their formation and operation. The next section analyzes the challenges presented to civil society in engaging human rights advocacy concerning women's and children's health care rights in Ethiopia.

3. Access to maternal and child health care in Ethiopia

3.1 The legal framework of maternal and child health in Ethiopia

With a population of above 100 million people, Ethiopia is the second most inhabited country in Africa and is one of the few countries in the globe with a high population of maternal and child deaths [27, 28]. There are legal, policy, and institutional mechanisms that respond to this challenge. The Federal Democratic Republic of Ethiopia (FDRE) Constitution (1995) along with the nine regional states constitutions dedicate a specific provision entirely dealing with the rights of women due to their vulnerability [29]. It states that women have the right "to prevent harm arising from pregnancy and childbirth and in order to safeguard their health, women have the right of access to family planning education, information and capacity" [29]. Similarly, the constitution guarantees the right to equality of women with men and further provides for the obligations of the state to eliminate the influences of harmful customs, laws, customs, and practices that oppress or cause bodily or mental harm to women [29]. However, none of these provisions adequately mention women's right to access to health care and the underlining determinants of health other than the ones mentioned under Article 35(9) of the FDRE Constitution. This particular sub-article provides for women's right of access to family planning, education, information, and capacity.

With respect to minors, the FDRE Constitution equally incorporates a specific article exclusively governing on children's rights but does not, nevertheless, take an express provision of children's right to health or the underlining determinants of health, such as admission to food, safe drinking water, sanitation, and living accommodations. Although Ethiopia has acceded to international instruments of children's rights the Convention on the Rights of the Child (CRC) in 1991; the International Convention on Economic, Social, and Cultural Rights (ICESCR) in 1993; as well as regional instruments such as the African Charter on the Rights and Welfare of the Child (ACRWC) in 2002, the constitution (article 36) fails to entrench children's right of access to health care and their other socioeconomic rights explicitly [29].

However, children's right to life and the best interests of the child are recognized in the constitution. Besides, women and children have the same rights as all other persons under the constitution, such as the right to life, information, equality, and nondiscrimination. However again, none of these provisions adequately incorporate children's right to access to health care and the underlining determinants of health. The Backman et al. study also indicates the right to health not to have been explicitly recognized in Ethiopia [3]. Overall, this manifests lack of compatibility between the domestic law with the relevant provisions of the ICESCR and ACRWC in the area of health care. As clearly highlighted in the decision of the African Commission in the case of *Purohit and Moore* V *Gambia* (2003), when a state's legislation in the area of health care does not meet human rights treaties that such state has ratified or acceded, then the state is required to repeal its existing laws and replace it with a new legislative regime to ensure compatibility [30]. While the author maintains the importance of explicit legal recognition of the right to health and proposes amendment of Article 35 and 36 of the constitution, in the absence of explicit and women's and children's right to health care and their other socioeconomic rights, the provisions dealing with the right to life and others should be invoked to realize health rights of women and children by way of temporal solution.

3.2 Analyzing the Ethiopian health care plan and health workers

Ethiopia restructured its health system in 1993, in the same year the national health policy was issued. Under the umbrella of the health policy, the Ethiopian health sector adopts a seemingly innovative and rolling health program, namely, the Ethiopian Health Sector Development Program (HSDP) [31]. The HSDP has been introduced in recognition of the failure of essential health such as in terms of the challenges of reaching health care services and goods to the people at grassroots level, in particular to the underserved rural population. It was projected based on the concept and principles of comprehensive primary health care, which essentially includes maternal and child health [32]. Its target has been the expansion of essential health system inputs towards the achievement of the Millennium Development Goals (MDGs)—an indication that its focus has not complied with the human rights obligations to health [33].

After evaluation of the second HSDP in 2002/2003, it was revealed that constraints existed in terms of availability of trained, high-level professionals, and essential services to reach the people at the grassroots level. In response to this challenge, in 2003 the Ethiopian Federal Ministry of Health launched a new health-care plan, the "Accelerated Expansion of Primary Health Coverage," through a comprehensive health extension program (HEP). The HEP is designed to shift health-care resources from predominantly urban to rural areas and rests on the rapid vocational training and deployment of health extension workers (HEWs) starting in 2003. Ethiopia is one country unable to provide a skilled health workforce to the majority of its population, and the question arises: Is there any evidence that the Ethiopian health plan, which incorporates HEWs, will improve women and children's prospects of survival and their well-being?

Health extension workers are expected to perform a wide range of functions—from preventive and promotive engagements to case management. HEWs' engagement in these functions has brought about marked achievements. It has improved access to maternal and child health services to the rural poor, and after the introduction of the HEW program, the proportion of households with access to improved sanitation reached 76% in the intervention villages from 39% at baseline [34]. Likewise, child vaccination/immunization results indicate substantial gains. By June 2010, 86% of children had received Penta 3/DPT 3 vaccine, 82% had received measles vaccine, and 62% had been fully immunized—an average annual increase in the number of fully immunized children of 15% since 2006 [34]. In addition, maternal health services coverage has shown progress: 85% of health posts could provide family planning services, 83% could provide antenatal care, 59% could perform clean deliveries, and 47% could provide postnatal care [35].

Awareness of HIV/AIDS has also improved, with the level of knowledge of condoms as a means of preventing HIV increasing by 78% in HEP villages and 46 in control villages. Again, seeking behavior for malaria treatment shows marked progress which results in in-patient malaria cases falling by 73% and deaths in children under five by 62% [36].

Overall, the HEWs program and the intervention in the foregoing show remarkable results. Its impact for reduction of maternal and child fatality rate has been substantial. In this connection the former Ethiopian Minister of Health, Kesetebirhan Admasu, underlines that "the HEWs have led the way to achieve major reductions in child and maternal mortality" [37]. In the same vein, regarding the contribution of HEWs with respect to the reduction of child mortality rates in the country, USAID Administrator Rajiv Shah notes:

> *... Between 2006 and 2010, infant mortality decreased by 23 percent and under-5 mortality by 28 percent. These achievements are largely a result of Ethiopia's investment in a community health system and a cadre of 35,000 health workers who provide front-line care [38].*

Global agencies, such as UNICEF, share the sentiment that the endeavor to deploy health workers to the most remote parts of the country has helped bring about a steep reduction in child mortality [37]. The WHO et al. report in 2014 establishes a significant increase of the maternal mortality rate from 740 in 2005 to 420 in 2013—showing progress towards improving maternal health [39]. Nevertheless, the implementation of the HEWs program has its own challenges.

3.3 The challenges of engaging HEWs

The task shifting from skilled providers to lower-level HEWs has been a model of success in Ethiopia for an extensive range of maternal and child services.

Nevertheless, while the commitment to introducing coherent and effective HEWs programs throughout the country is laudable, there are major obstacles.

First, HEWs lack the necessary knowledge and skills, which restricts the delivery of quality maternal and child health services [40]. A study by A. Medhanyie et al. has found that more than half (54%) of HEWs have poor knowledge about the contents of prenatal care counseling, and the majority (88%) have poor knowledge about danger symptoms, danger signs, and complications in pregnancy [39]. These workers lack the requisite skills to perform clean and safe deliveries. Research shows their basic health knowledge is quite poor regarding the major communicable diseases [40]. In one case, the parents of a 2-year-old child who had developed tonsillitis were taken to the Semera Health Post in Afar [41]. The health worker in charge prescribed amoxicillin pills. However, the next day the child's entire body became swollen, and he had to be taken back to the health post. The health professional in charge on that particular day noticed the complication the child had developed and referred him to a hospital in Dupti, but the child died by the time he reached the hospital. It was noted that the child would not have died had he been immediately referred to the hospital at early stage examination and that the inappropriate drug exacerbated his condition [41]. This clearly raises the need for a proper system to hold HEWs accountable to the community they serve.

Second, attrition and retention pose further challenges. In contexts where the health-care system is weak and characterized by a severe shortage of health-care workers, HEWs may be the rural community's only contact with the health-care system, placing a heavy burden on them, possibly resulting in them leaving their jobs. Often one of the HEWs is a member of the community (*Kebele*) and is required to serve in the political administrative cabinet, which adds to the burden [42]. As in some instance, HEWs reside at a distance from their work places; poor transportation and communication which results in job dissatisfaction remains as another challenge [43].

Third, the sustainability of community health projects depends on the availability of on-going funding, a diversity of funding sources and ability to mobilize volunteers or low-paid workers who in the face of their own poverty are willing to care for the needy in their communities. Nearly all the challenges that community health projects faced relate to inadequate and sporadic funding. Funding limitations further affect the availability of health goods and services such as supervisors, medical equipment, supplies of drugs for minimum curative services, furniture, and vehicles [44].

Fourth, administrative functions such as monitoring, supervision, coordination, and management are critical for successful community-based programs. Many HEWs perform their job alone or in small groups in distant sites, which results in a lack of meaningful supervision and reduces HEWs' ability to provide effective focused antenatal care [43].

Fifth, lack of commitment is yet another challenge. Although many HEWs work enthusiastically, there are a few who are not fully dedicated to their everyday activities [43]. This is mainly due to a failure to integrate HEWs as part of the state's responsibility for health-care delivery.

3.4 Implementation challenges in relation to goods and services

As previously noted, General Comment 14 clarifies the obligation of states to ensure maternal and child-friendly health services, goods, and facilities are available, accessible, acceptable, and of high quality. Although Ethiopia has improved health coverage through deploying HEP, health goods and services are threatened by myriad challenges.

With regard to availability, the Committee on Economic, Social and Cultural Rights (ESCR) notes:

> *The Committee is concerned that there is no universal health-care coverage. It is also concerned about the low number of qualified health-care professionals per capita in certain regions and critical shortages at health centres, both in medical equipment and staff. The Committee also notes with concern the high rate of maternal and infant mortality, and the low number of births that are assisted by a skilled attendant, especially in rural areas. It is further concerned that access to maternal and infant health care remains poor, in particular in the Somali National Regional State of Ethiopia [45].*

The United Nations Population Fund (UNPFA) equally observes:

> *Most of the health facilities which are far from Addis Ababa are either not fully staffed with skilled service providers or fully equipped with the necessary supplies and equipment that can provide quality services related to complications during pregnancy and childbirth. Limited human resources, especially midwives, hamper efforts to provide adequate services, especially in rural areas. Gaps in training and remuneration have led to attrition and turnover among public sector health care professionals. Public facilities routinely suffer stockouts and obstetric care equipment shortages due to budget deficits and poor management [46].*

The range of limitations in terms of availability of health-care facilities, goods, and services restricts the full realization of women's and children's right to healthcare and the underlying determinants of health.

With regard to accessibility, a myriad of challenges exist in the country. In one case story in 1980, an Ethiopian woman from the Oromo ethnic group was arrested without a court order. She was pregnant during her arrest and delivered her baby in prison without the help of a doctor. The baby's health was permanently damaged by the lack of timely help in her prison cell. This represents a clear case of limited access to health-care service to women and newborn babies in difficult situations. If there was a regard for human rights laws, the pregnant woman and her newborn baby would have had a health worker or professional who could have helped during childbirth [47].

A further challenge on access is, despite the improvements made in expanding access to health services, the disease burden is still high, and the service utilization rate remains low in the country, partly due to the burden of high out-of-pocket spending that restricts an already poor society from health-care utilization [48]. A recent survey by Berhan and Berhan in 2014 conducted in Ethiopia indicates that inaccessibility of transport, long distances from functioning health-care facilities, and a lack of confidence in the services provided are some of the barriers that impede access to maternal health facilities [49]. Similarly, the 2011 Ethiopian Demographic and Health Survey (EDHS) study shows that the major barriers for pregnant women to access health services are lack of transport to a facility (71%), lack of money (68%), and distance to a health facility (66%) [50]. Moreover, although child malnutrition has declined, many Ethiopian children continue to go hungry. Safe food is considered one of the underlying determinants of the right to health, but the rate of Ethiopia's stunted children (caused by malnutrition) is above the average of other African countries, the average rate for African countries being 38% and that of Ethiopia's is 58% [51]. Besides, although there are marked improvements in the coverage of access to child vaccination, clean water, and improved sanitation, the progress remains slow. This is likely to have a negative impact on the reduction of under-five mortality rates [52].

Acceptability of health-care services is another challenge. For instance, the Ethiopian Central Statistical Agency's study conducted in Ethiopia in 2014 shows that close to 90% of births occurred outside a health service facility for different reasons: 45% did not take place in a health facility because the mothers did not think it was necessary, and for 33%, mothers stated it was not customary [53]. In addition, it has been observed that the birthing position used at the health centers made the women feel uneasy and was one of the reasons for Ethiopian women choosing to deliver at home rather [53].

Further, the delay in providing obstetric and newborn care services and treatment is usually the major reason for the poor quality of service [49]. The following are identified as the main causes for delays in treatment: (1) the number of health professionals is insufficient; (2) available health professionals often exhibit poor knowledge and skill; and (3) nonfunctioning health facilities due to a lack of medical equipment essential to manage obstetric problems, such as drugs, supplies, reagents, a blood bank, oxygen, magnesium sulfate, and a broad spectrum of intravenous antibiotics [49]. The lack of these essential medical goods in laboratories, imaging facilities, delivery suites, and operating theaters further lowers the quality of treatment.

3.5 Judicial accountability

Judicial accountability mechanisms for women's and children's health provide avenues for remedies and redress for women, children, and their caregivers or representatives when their rights to health care are violated. In Ethiopia, the judiciary is vested with the power to consider women and children's rights matters, and the courts are guaranteed, under the FDRE Constitution, to do so free from interference or influence of any governmental body, government official, or any other source [29]. However, interpreting and applying the socioeconomic right to health of women and children in the constitution is arguably the most challenging task facing lawyers and courts in Ethiopia on various grounds.

First, there are problems with the law. The FDRE and the nine regional state constitutions each have a specific provision that deals with the rights of children. Nevertheless, women and children's right to survive, to health, to access to food and safe drinking water, to adequate standard of living, and to other rights relating to the underlining determinants of the right to health have not been explicitly recognized in these constitutions. The absence of explicit recognition might create ambivalence for the judges to enforce these rights when violated. Nor are there special laws that address these rights.

Second, awareness of children's rights is crucial for their overall implementation. However, knowledge about the rights of children has been considered the main challenge [54]. Parents' or guardians' limited knowledge of children's rights and violations of their rights present a challenge to developing proper judicial channels of accountability for children's rights to health or survival.

Third, vulnerable women and children are unlikely to be able to bring claims for violations of their rights on their own behalf. Human rights NGOs could play a major role in representing women and children's rights cases before courts, but the current Ethiopian CSO law limits the possibility of legal representation by civil society for violation of human rights by the state.

Fourth, although the debate over justiciability of socioeconomic rights seems to have been settled in many parts of the world, research shows this is not case within the Ethiopian judiciary and among Ethiopian practitioners [55].

Fifth, the requirement of vested interest or locus standi is a further challenge for judicialization of women and children's social right to health. For instance, according to the procedural law of the country, civil claims may be joined as a single case where they relate to the same transaction or series of transactions, such as in a case where a decision is sought by any group or person who is a member of or represents a group with similar interest [29, 56].

The foregoing renders the health inequality gap deeper and difficult among Ethiopian women and children and society at large. This challenge of inequality is in contradiction to the preamble of the FDRE Constitution, which underlines the need for Ethiopians to live on the basis of equality and without discrimination [29].

3.6 Non-transformative civil society

Ethiopia has adopted in 2009 the legislation to regulate the activities of CSOs [57] (at the time of writing this Chapter, a proposal was submitted to the Ethiopian parliament to amend this law). Three types of CSOs are classified under this new legislation, "Ethiopian Charities or Societies"; "Ethiopian Residents Charities or Societies"; and "Foreign Charities" [57]. The proclamation defines "Charitable Purpose" to include "the promotion of the rights of the disabled and children's rights" [57]. It indicates that CSOs are also mandated to promote child survival or health rights in Ethiopia, such as through litigation or advocacy or education. Nevertheless, the proclamation prohibits Ethiopian Residents Charities or Societies and Foreign Charities from engaging in issues, including, but not limited to, the advancement of human and democratic rights and promotion of the rights of the disabled and children's rights [57]. This is restrictive as these activities are left to Ethiopian charities or societies alone—which are also required not to generate more than 10% of their funding from foreign sources.

The majority of the Ethiopian population lives below the poverty line, and requiring nationals to raise 90% from domestic sources to form charities not only questions their formation but also their sustenance. The limitation on funding has therefore disabled the work of Ethiopian charities on human rights and democratization issues, which clearly affects advocacy on violations of the rights to health of women and children. Besides, the law has deeply affected the ability of international organizations to work in the field of human rights promotion and advocacy in the country.

4. Conclusion

Based on the conviction that an equitable health system is a core social institution and its potential for the realization of women's and children's right to health, this chapter argues that the essential HRBA features for ensuring maternal and child health rights in the Ethiopian context include (1) the explicit recognition of the right to health; (2) a national health plan encompassing human resources; (3) achieving health-care services that are available, accessible, acceptable, and of high quality; (4) accountability; and (5) a civil society that draws on the agency of vulnerable groups. Crucially, it examines the manner in which the Ethiopian system reflects such features and identifies the lacunae that exist in the country, including inadequate legislative framework and accountability mechanisms. To address these maladies, this chapter recommends the following: Firstly, the right of access to maternal and child health goods and services and processes to tackle causes of maternal and child mortality be explicitly enshrined in the national legislation. Secondly, the flaws in training, task allocation and supervision of HEWs need to be addressed, and adequate working conditions designed to boost HEWs' morale. Thirdly, programs and strategies must be implemented progressively to ensure that maternal and child health is accessible, available, acceptable, and of quality. Fourthly, accountability must be strengthened to monitor the implementation of the rights and the effectiveness of national programs tackling the issue of maternal and child survival. To enhance accountability, the legislature should amend legal provisions to allow CSOs to engage in human rights advocacy and litigation and promulgate legislation that creates a supportive and enabling environment for public interest litigation.

Author details

Solomon Tekle Abegaz
University of Gondar, Gondar, Ethiopia

*Address all correspondence to: solomomte@gmail.com

References

[1] International Conference on Primary Health Care. Declaration of Alma-Ata. USSR: World Health Organization; 1978

[2] Brigit T. The Right to Health as a Human Right in International Law. Oxford, Amsterdam: Hart/Intersentia; 1999. pp. 1-417

[3] Gunilla B, Paul H, Rajat K, et al. Health systems and the right to health: an assessment of 194 countries. The Lancet. 2008;**372**:1-39. DOI: 10.1016/S0140-6736(08) 61781-X

[4] Flavia B, Paul H, Sofia G, et al. Women's and children's Health: Evidence of Impact of Human Rights. Geneva: WHO; 2013. pp. 18-99

[5] Alicia EY. Toward transformative accountability: Applying a rights-based approach to fulfill maternal health obligations. SUR International Journal on Human Rights. 2010;7:94-120

[6] Committee on Economic, Social and Cultural Rights. The Right to the Highest Attainable Standard of Health: 11/08/2000. E/C.12/2000/4, CESCR General Comment 14. Twenty-Second Session, Geneva. 25 April–12 May 2000. Agenda Item 3. Available from: http://www.unhchr.ch/tbs/doc.nsf/(symbol)/E.C.12.2000.4.En [Accessed: 12 March 2018]

[7] Paul H, Gillian M. Impact Assessments, Poverty and Human Rights: A Case Study Using the Right to the Highest Attainable Standard of Health. Available from: http://www2.essex.ac.uk/ human_rights_centre/rth/projects.shtm [Accessed: 10 February 2018]

[8] Committee on the Rights of the Child. HIV/AIDS and the Rights of the Child. March 17, 2003. CRC/GC/2003/3. General Comment 3

[9] Committee on the Rights of the Child. Adolescent Health and Development in the Context of the Convention on the Rights of the Child. July 1, 2003. CRC/GC/2003/4. General Comment 4

[10] UN Convention on the Rights of the Child (CRC). New York: United Nations; 1989

[11] Committee on Economic, Social and Cultural Rights. The Right to the Highest Attainable Standard of Health: 11/08/2000. E/C.12/2000/4. CESCR General Comment 14

[12] UN General Assembly. Human Rights Council: Resolution/Adopted by the General Assembly, 17 April 2013, A/RES/22/32. Available from http://ap.ohchr.org/documents/alldocs.aspx?docid= 21600 [Accessed: 14 March 2018]

[13] Levy BS, Victor S, editors. Social Injustice and Public Health. New York: Oxford University; 2006

[14] Solomon TA. A rights based-approach to reducing child mortality in Ethiopia [thesis]. Pretoria: University of Pretoria; 2016

[15] Terre De Hommes. Human Rights-Based Approaches and European Union Development Aid Policies; 2008. pp. 1-6

[16] Zulufkar K, Mohammad A. Health status of marginalized groups in India. International Journal of Applied Sociology. 2012;**6**(2):60-70

[17] Singh JA, Govender M, Mills EJ. Do human rights matter to health? The Lancet. 2007;**370**(900):521-522

[18] The Right to the Highest Attainable Standard of Health: CESCR. 2000. General Comment 14

[19] Paul H, forward to Helen P. Accountability and the Right to the Highest Attainable Standard of Health. 2008. pp. 1-39

[20] International Human Rights Network. Our Rights, Our Future, Human Rights based Approaches in Ireland: Principles, Policies and Practice. 2005. pp. 1-56

[21] UNOHCHR. Principles and Guidelines for a Human Rights Approach to Poverty Reduction Strategies. 2006. Para 77. UN Doc HR/PUB/06/12

[22] Ibanez XA. The role of international and national courts: Human rights litigation as a strategy to hold states accountable for maternal deaths. In: Paul H, Tony G, editors. Maternal Mortality, Human Rights, and Accountability. London: Routledge; 2013. p. 47

[23] Leslie L. What is a human rights-based approach to health and does it matter? Health and Human Rights. 2008;**10**(1):65-80

[24] UN Office of the High Commissioner for Human Rights. Fact Sheet No. 31. The Right to Health. 2008

[25] Ministry of Health v Treatment Action Campaign (TAC). 5 SA 721 (CC), 2002

[26] Sisay Y. CSO law in Ethiopia: Considering its constraints and consequences. Journal of Civil Society. 2012;**8**(4):370-371

[27] Ayele B, Amenu D, Gurmessa A. Prevalence of maternal near miss and maternal death in Ayat Hospital, Ethiopia. Journal of Women's Health, Issues and Care. 2014;**3**(6):1-5. DOI: 10.4172/2325-9795.1000172

[28] UNICEF, WHO, The World Bank et al. The UN Inter-Agency Group for Child Mortality Estimation. New York: UNICEF; 2013. p. 11

[29] The Constitution of the Federal Democratic Republic of Ethiopia, 1995

[30] The Gambia: Purohit and Another v The Gambia. AHRLR 96 (ACHPR 2003); 2003

[31] WHO. Ethiopia. Available from: http://www.who.int/countries/eth/coopstrategy/en/ index1.html [Accessed: 11 May 2018]

[32] Araya AM. The Use of Health for Maternal Health Care in Ethiopia. Maastricht: Maastricht University; 2014. p. 27

[33] Alula S. The implementation of Ethiopia's Health Extension Program: An overview. Available from: http://www.ppdafrica.org/docs/ethiopiahep.pdf [Accessed: 12 March 2018]

[34] Kedir BN, Herbst C, Zhao F, et al. Health extension workers in Ethiopia: Improved access and coverage for the rural poor. In: Punam C, Manka A, editors. Yes Africa Can: Success Stories from a Dynamic Continent. The World Bank. 2011. p. 436

[35] Center for National Health Survey (CNHS). Functioning of Health Posts. Federal Ministry of Health of Ethiopia: Addis Ababa, Ethiopia; 2007

[36] Otten M, Aregawi M, Were W, et al. Initial evidence of reduction of malaria cases and deaths in Rwanda and Ethiopia due to rapid scale-up of malaria prevention and treatment. Malaria Journal. 2009;**8**(14):5

[37] In Ethiopia, a Far-Reaching Health Worker Programme has Helped Reduce Child Mortality Across the Country. Available from: http://www.unicef.org/infobycountry/ethiopia_70372.html

[38] USAID, Frontlines. Celebrating a Child Health Revolution. USAID: 2012

[39] Medhanyie A, Spigt M, Kifle Y, et al. The role of health extension workers in improving utilization of maternal health services in rural areas in Ethiopia: A cross sectional study. BMC Health Services Research. 2012;**12**(352):1-9

[40] Negusse H, McAuliffe M, MacLachlan M. Initial community perspectives on the health service extension programme in Welkait, Ethiopia. Human Resources for Health. 2007;**5**(21):1-5

[41] Interview conducted over a telephone with Mrs. Hawa Abdu. Maternal and Child Health Officer, Afar National Regional State Health Office. Addis Ababa, Ethiopia; 2015

[42] Improving Health Extension Program in Ethiopia. 2014. Available from: http://www.who.int/evidence/sure/pdimprovinghealth extensionprogramethiopia.pdf [Accessed: 11 May 2018]

[43] Awash T, Yayehyirad K, Asfawesen G, et al. Study of the working conditions of health extension workers in Ethiopia. Ethiopian Journal of Health Development. 2007;**21**(3):246-259

[44] Abebe B, Mengistu K, Mekonnen T. Preliminary assessment of the implementation of the health services extension program: The case of southern Ethiopia. Ethiopian Journal of Health Development. 2008;**22**(3):304

[45] UN Committee on ESCR, Consideration of Reports Submitted by States Parties Under Articles 16 and 17 of the Covenant: Concluding Observations of the Committee on Economic, Social and Cultural Rights-Ethiopia, 31 May 2012, E/C.12/ETH/CO/1-3, para 5. Available from: http://www.refworld.org/ docid/4ff6d0de2.html [Accessed: 21 June 2018]

[46] Integrated Regional Information Networks (IRIN), Ethiopia: Still Too Many Deaths in Childbirth. Available from http://www.irinnews.org/report/95356/ethiopia-still-too-many-deaths-in-childbirth [Accessed: 21 June 2018]

[47] Dhugassa BF. Women's rights and health: The case of Oromo women in Ethiopia. Health Care for Women International. 2005;**26**:149-169

[48] WHO. African Health Observatory: Ethiopia. Available from: http://www.aho.afro.who.int/profiles_information/index.php/Ethiopia:Analytical_summary_-Health_system_outcomes [Accessed: 21 June 2018]

[49] Yifru B, Asres B. Commentary: Reasons for persistently high maternal and perinatal mortalities in Ethiopia: Part III–perspective of the 'three delays' model. Ethiopian Journal of Health Science. 2014;**142**:137-148

[50] Central Statistical Agency (Ethiopia) and ICF International. Ethiopian Demographic and Health Survey 2011; 2012. 132p

[51] The African Child Policy Forum (ACPF). Africa's Children and the Post-2015 Development Agenda. Addis Ababa, Ethiopia: ACPF, 2014

[52] Audit Report Conducted on the Somali national regional state as regards measures taken to reduce maternal and child mortality. Addis Ababa, Ethiopia: Ethiopian Institution of Ombudsman; 2012

[53] Central Statistical Agency (Ethiopia). Ethiopia Mini-Demographic and Health Survey 2014; 2014. p. 50

[54] UNICEF Ethiopia. Child Protection Systems Mapping: The Case of Ethiopia. 2010. p. 26

[55] Salma Y. The rise of judicially enforced economic, social and cultural

rights. Seattle Journal for Social Justice. 2012;**10**:753-791

[56] The Civil Procedure Code of Ethiopia. Decree No. 52. 1965

[57] Proclamation to Provide for the Registration and Regulation of Charities and Societies. Proclamation No. 621/2009

Chapter 7

Food Security in Kazakhstan: Do Gender Inequalities Affect?

Maigul Nugmanova

Abstract

Kazakhstan has a large reserve of natural resources to provide the food self-sufficiency with domestic production. It could be three times more than population needs. However, Kazakhstan depends on food import and the agricultural sector accounts for 5% of GDP only. The actual poverty is higher than official data indicate, and it's about four times more in rural areas where 46% of population resides and one-fifth of the working-age population is employed. Women represent the majority among the poor and unemployed and face unequal treatment in labor market and burden of larger unpaid household workload. All of this decreases women's purchasing power, lowering economic access to quality food. This paper examines the interaction of gender inequality and food insecurity, applying the growth constraints analysis and engendering this approach and the empirical research on Karaganda oblast. It argues that gender inequality and rural poverty are linked to high economic costs and constraints in agriculture development and food security attainment.

Keywords: gender economics, food security, rural poverty, growth constraints analysis, Kazakhstan

1. Introduction

Kazakhstan is one of the top 9 countries in the world in terms of agricultural land and among 12 leading wheat exporters. It is among the top 15 countries in the world in terms of oil reserve. These resources could provide effective food self-sufficiency with domestic production of three times more than the population needs. However, Kazakhstan's local food production is much less than the present population needs. Kazakhstan is considered as an upper middle-income country [1] and has 2.8% of the population with income below the poverty line [2]. However, actual poverty is higher than official data, since the estimation of poverty line by the Kazakhstan Ministry of Labor and Social Protection of the Population does not correspond to international standards. Rural poverty is about four times more than in urban areas, and 46% of the population resides in rural areas. Agricultural sector in Kazakhstan comprises 5% of total GDP only, while it employs about one-fifth of the working-age population [3].

This paper focuses on gender dimension of economic issues needed to address gender inequality that continues to persist. It argues that gender equality is an important prerequisite to provide the food security. This research emphasizes on the impact of economic changes in Kazakhstan on women, their role in economy and unpaid household labor, and revealing of underlying causes of gender discrimination. Women in Kazakhstan comprise the majority among the poor and unemployed and face unequal treatment in labor market. And yet, women are the main economic agents of the country. In 2017, female labor force participation rate was 65.4% [4]. Women's daily work such as cooking; work in farms and household plots; food processing; and caring of livestock and other farm animals is crucial in the provision of the food security of country. "Gender-based constraints must be addressed to increase agricultural productivity; improve food security; reduce poverty; and build the resilience of rural population" [5].

This paper reviews the theoretical framework of the gender and macroeconomics and provides analysis of economic transition situation in Kazakhstan. It studies various economic transformation aftereffects under transition to identify their impact to rural people's well-being and food security. The paper also presents the issues of Kazakhstani agrarian sector and women status in this sector, applying the growth constraints analysis (hereinafter GCA) and engendering the GCA and the empirical research on Karaganda oblast. Based on growth diagnostics recommendations developed by Hausmann et al. [6], this paper examines the economic history of Kazakhstan and identifies the growth constraints of agriculture development. This paper considers different phases of the Hausmann's growth diagnostic decision tree, namely, "high cost of finance"; "bad local finance"; "low competition-high risk-high cost"; "low return to economic activity"; "bad infrastructure," etc. to define constraints to agricultural growth and food security in Kazakhstan. Gender issues are considered at all stages of the GCA. The paper examines food security issue in Kazakhstan through identification of gender differences in economic, social, and physical access to food. Also, it focuses on causes of gender distinctions and the extent to which they can affect agricultural growth and food security [7].

Analysis of the secondary data, review of reports, and the literature on gender and food security were used. Participatory observation is one of the methods of data collection. This paper includes results of the interviews with rural women of Karaganda oblast and with a professor in food safety. The interviews of rural women were done in 2015 in two rural regions of Karaganda oblast including Amangeldy sovkhoz and Abay village, to demonstrate the realities of rural women in Kazakhstan and their unpaid labor role in providing food security and to explore to what extent women's incomes can provide them with access to quality food.[1] Respondents were rural women engaged in household only and were selected from households with two parents and at least one child. Middle-income households with one cow or other farm animals and a small land plot were selected. Open questions with an open-ended choice of answers were used. The interview included questions on income sources and major expenditures; respondents' opportunities to get credits; challenges and benefits of working in private allotments; employment opportunities in formal sector; and starting own business. The study concludes that "more equal gender relations within household and communities lead to better agricultural and development outcomes including increases in farm productivity and improvements in family nutrition" [8].

2. Gender and macroeconomics: overview

To understand better the nature of gender relations, I focus on the pertinent social differentiations between women and men. "The concept of sex expresses

[1] Unpublished interviews with women of Sovkhoz Amangeldy and Abay village in Karaganda oblast in August 2015. Forty married women between the ages of 35 and 55 were interviewed, among them 20 interviews in Sovkhoz Amangeldy and 20 in Abay village.

two layers of reality: physiological and social. The first layer is the one a person is born with, while the second one, socio-sex (designated in literature as gender) is acquired in the process of socialization" [9]. "The concept of gender, like concept of class, is an analytical tool to understand social processes" [10]. Historically, the significant "changes in women's and men's status in the society were related to the development of material production activities and military art, when in demand were those socially significant attributes and abilities, which psychosomatically are more characteristic of men" [9]. Accordingly, women are often excluded "from prestigious activities, objectively placing" men in a dominant position in society and economy [9]. "Gender measurement of human reality starts settling in. At each level of human existence, certain gender roles are shaped and there arises social and economic inequalities between men and women" [9]. These distinctions in the social and economic status of men and women are maintained and reinforced by the process of economic development. "Due to persistence of gender discrimination, women play submitted roles, while men dominate in all areas of the society. Most important is that all laws and rules emerging in society have always been aimed at gratifying people's own egoism, especially in the men-women relationships. All legislative measures were worked out by men. Breaking this stereotype is a difficult task" [9].

According to Marxist economists, the root causes of gender discrimination raise from ownership relations, namely, the alienation of women from possession of resources [11]. Differences in economic status of women and men are subject to underlying laws of economic development. The basis of production and social relations are ownership relations that determine whether women can use their capabilities and convert opportunities. Marxist economists argue that, namely, ownership relations determine the economic opportunities of men and women. Cagatay et al. [10] analyzing different approaches to engendering macroeconomic modeling pointed out that "gender as a category of social and economic differentiation (like class and race) influences the distribution of work, income and wealth, the work productivity, and the behavior of agents in the economy." Consideration of gender relations in economy in terms of "access to capital and property, buying and selling of labour power, distribution of income and time resources" [12] shows that there is gender inequality in Kazakhstan and it constrains economic growth.

"According to the materialistic conception, the determining factor in history is the production and reproduction of the immediate essentials of life. This is of a twofold character. On the one side, the production of the means of existence, on the other side, the production of human beings themselves" [11]. However, "macroeconomics considers paid work and productive economy, but doesn't consider unpaid female labor and reproductive economy" [10]. Isolation of the reproductive sector from the productive one results in gender inequality [13]. The reproduction of the means of life and reproduction of life itself in fact are two inseparable components of social production. However, the reproductive sector is considered as a subordinate sphere [13]. The woman is the main agent of activity in the system of relations, which forms reproduction of life itself. Therefore, the position of a woman is secondary in the system of the economic relations [14]. Walters [13] criticizes the standard assumption of exogeneity of labor force and points out that labor force requires investments both in the productive and in the reproductive sectors. Considering the importance of health, education, and social infrastructure for labor force growth, he points out that on the whole the reproductive sector affects the quantity and quality of the labor force [13]. Women's unpaid labor in reproductive sector, such as childcare, food producing and processing, cooking, preschool training, etc., contributes to the development of quantity and quality of labor force and to the enhancement of economic growth in the future.

Sustainable food security deals with the sustainable environment and economic development, which promote "equal access to quality food, its availability, and economic ability of population to buy a quality food" [15]. Gender disparity in economy affects the solution of vital economic issues including food security [16]. Promotion of gender justice and sustainable development and engendering of economic policy with consideration of the own country specifics, traditions, and historical roots are crucial issues for Kazakhstan.

3. Growth constraints analysis

Analysis of economic transition situation in Kazakhstan and various economic transformation aftereffects in transition are necessary to identify the main constraints of the agriculture's growth and food security and mitigate the inequalities, which rural women face. It is necessary to consider the "country's economic history and performance, as many of the problems of the past as well as constraints for future actions are affected by macro concerns" [6].

The post-Soviet heritage of Kazakhstan was the one-sided development of the economy with specialization on grain, oil, gas, and coal that affected the country under transition. After the USSR collapse, between 1990 and 1998, there was an economic recession in Kazakhstan. The interest rates were high (about 300–400%) and this resulted in the reduction of credit and business growth. The populations purchasing power and incomes also declined, and poverty and income inequality increased. "Agricultural growth is the most effective way to reduce poverty and increase food security in low-income countries that depend heavily on agriculture" [5]. Agriculture was not a priority for the Government of Kazakhstan and it was funded on residual principles. Nevertheless, agriculture is the most crucial branch in the national economy. Kazakhstan, where 46% of population reside in the countryside, one-third of all employed is engaged in the agrarian sector, and 80% of land are the farming one, is considered as an agricultural country. Most part of agricultural land is disposed in the zone of risky farming and is dependent on weather. Moreover, agriculture is dependent upon state support. During Soviet time subsidies for agriculture were 10–12%, and after 1991 it was reduced to 2–3% [17]. Agricultural production dropped deeply as a result. It had adverse impact on the whole population but mostly on women. The number of men that lost their jobs in the agrarian sector moved to the cities to find the new ones. Work intensity of rural women was increased due to extra agricultural activities [18]. "When the length of the working day increases beyond a critical point, time spent on leisure, social activities, and even sleep is necessarily reduced, with the corresponding decline in well-being becoming unavoidable" [19].

During the 1990s, Kazakhstan's development has been characterized by privatization. As a result of privatization in agriculture, almost all of the "sovkhozes" (state farms) and "kolkhozes" (collective farms) were reorganized, and their farm lands and equipment were transferred to the farm members in the form of "pai" [share] [20]. It was a notional land or material share without personification and specific plot of land. Unfortunately, most of the rural citizens could not benefit from the privatization. The heads of former state and collective farms became the owners of privatized farm property due to the undeveloped land reform and corruption [20]. Private ownership of land was provided by the Land Code of the Republic of Kazakhstan of 2003. Unfortunately, by that time most of the rural people sold their "pais" for cheapest prices and had nothing to buy the land, neither "pai" nor money. In the second half of the 1990s, more than one-third of Kazakhstan population was poor, with income below the subsistence minimum.

Salaries were not paid for a long time, and sometimes workers received substitutes of salary in the form of equipment or food [20]. Women were worse off in terms of income, time resources, and position on the labor market and in the household. They did not participate in the reformation and privatization in agriculture due to lower access to the decision-making positions. They could not form individual farms due to lack of funds and entrepreneurial skills. Only 10% of farms were headed by women in 2005, 12% in 2008 [21], and 9% in 2014 [22]. Privatization promoted further property differentiation and gender discrimination. Women were unable to use advantages of privatization process.

Since 1999, Kazakhstan has reported economic growth. In the composition of economic growth, the share of agriculture among the other sectors of economy is significantly low [23]. The share of construction, services and utilities, oil and gas, and mining sectors is significant. Kazakhstan has prioritized the development of extractive industry, with low proportions of the sectors producing final, processed manufactures. National export consists of 97% of extractive industry products. Raw-material orientation of the Kazakhstani economy results in the decreasing in the economy competitiveness [24]. "Countries specializing in primary commodity exports, however, import mainly finished manufactured goods which have few spillover effects on productivity and output growth" [25]. There is "another side" of resource wealth. One of the poorest regions in the country is West Kazakhstan, and it is where most of the oil resources are concentrated. Stiglitz (in Ref. [26]) called it as a "resource curse." "Much of the natural resource base of the country is increasingly owned by foreign investors" [24]. Hausmann and Klinger [27] examined the economic growth of Peru and pointed out that the gap "between the growth rate of GDP and GNI demonstrates the share of domestic product which accumulated by foreign investors." In the case of Kazakhstan, we can see from **Figure 1** that since 1999, the growth rate of total GDP has been higher than GNI. This gap is not as large as in Peru (see in Ref. [27]) but still demonstrates a sizable difference, indicating therefore that some part of the domestic product is accumulated by foreign investors.

Extractive industry does not create a lot of jobs and moreover, it is a male-dominated sector. According to official statistics, only 1% of employed women and 4% of employed men work in the mining sector [28]. 78% of all employed in oil, gas, and mining sectors are men, and only 22% are women. Construction sector has the same picture that is 73% of men and 27% of women [28]. After 1999, a lot of constructions occurred in largest cities such as Astana and Almaty. This type of business favored the men employment. The development of the competitiveness of non-oil and non-construction sectors could create additional employment opportunities, especially for women.

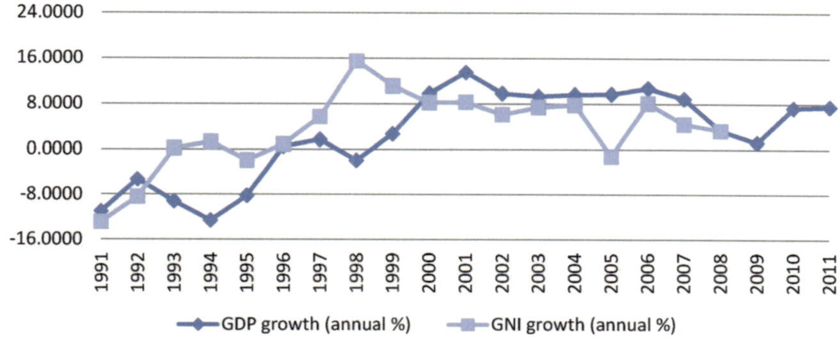

Figure 1.
Dynamics of GDP and GNI in Kazakhstan. Source: on the basis of World Bank [29].

Economic growth could create new opportunities for food security. Economic growth provided increase in the budget of the Ministry of Agriculture of the Republic of Kazakhstan from $174MM in 2001 to $931MM in 2008 [17]. In 2014, agriculture budget was $1200 MM. The question is "Who are the beneficiaries of these funds?" Why, in spite of the total GDP growth and decrease of budget and subsidies of the Ministry of Agriculture of the Republic of Kazakhstan, is Kazakhstan still food insecure, and why does it have a non-developed agriculture with low productivity and no competitiveness? First of all, there are the facts of misuse and insufficient, ineffective use of budget funds by the Ministry of Agriculture of the Republic of Kazakhstan. According to the Accounts Committee [30], the total amount of 79.6 billion tenge ($437MM) was used by the Ministry of Agriculture of the Republic of Kazakhstan with violation of the budget and other legislation. This Ministry has also used inefficiently the national budget and the state assets which are equal to 43.1 billion tenge ($237MM).

The 2003 Land Code of the Republic of Kazakhstan promoted the rise of quantity of individual farms (non-state enterprises). Currently, there is a state and private property of land in Kazakhstan with prevalence of private sector in agriculture. 93% of all agricultural lands are used by non-state enterprises. In 2010, there were 175,636 operating agricultural units, of which 5408 were non-state corporate farms; 170,193 family farms; and 35 state enterprises. It would be reasonable to consider private enterprises' constraints to invest in agriculture since there is a prevalence of private sector in agriculture.

According to Hausmann et al. [6], low levels of private investment and entrepreneurship are the constraint of the growth. There is a restricted access of agribusiness firms to finance. Only 3.5% of total commercial loans goes to agriculture in Kazakhstan [31]. In 2011, 71% of all bank assets were consolidated in five large banks in Kazakhstan, where the Government of Kazakhstan owned the considerable share [31]. It is obvious that there is no competition in financial sector and interest rate can be identified monopolistically. The largest banks have set a high interest rate of up to 14% annually.

According to the OECD [31] bank survey on interaction with the agribusiness sector, 45% of loans to agribusiness were provided to large-scale companies; 25% to medium-sized companies; and 30% to small farms. The share of loans to rural small enterprises is very low. However, it is a large sector that attracts most of the agricultural labor and produces 50% of agricultural output [3]. The majority of women entrepreneurs tend to be in small enterprises [32]. In 2015, the share of women entrepreneurs in small business of a country was 50%, and only 15% of large companies were headed by women [33]. Women have limited economic opportunities and therefore prefer small business which requires less resources, managerial skills, and documentation requirements [32]. Therefore, bank preferences to finance large enterprises restrict access of women to credit.

Investing in agriculture has high risks [31], high risks of banks deal with the low productivity of agriculture and nonperforming loans. Rural enterprises often default on the loans. Nonperformance on loans consists of 25% of gross total loans [31]. It constrains financial institutions from crediting to agribusiness. In order to compensate risks, banks raise the nominal interest rates and establish high collateral for lending. Cost of collateral for agricultural enterprises is higher than for other sectors [34, 35]. Mostly women cannot fulfill collateral requirements and therefore have lower access to credits. Agribusiness is characterized by low return on investment [31]. Low level of investment to agriculture results in the low productivity; low material-technical base; and insufficient use of seeds and fertilizers and bad infrastructure. 80% of farming machines are in technical rundown [36]. Labor productivity in agriculture is very low and accounts $3400/worker/year [37]. Despite the fact that agricultural infrastructure is already underdeveloped, the Government of Kazakhstan decreased expenditures on infrastructure from 16% in 2001 to 5% in 2009 [17]. All of these factors contribute to the production cost increase and no competitiveness of domestic food products.

According to the survey on Karaganda oblast, women are unaware about their opportunities on subsidies and credits (90% of the respondents). Women do not have appropriate qualification and management skills and proper knowledge to fill out documents and procedures on getting credits (90% of the respondents). Most of the women are reluctant to deal with banks or are anxious to take credits because of the unstable general financial situation in the country and non-confidence in their power to handle own business or mistrust to banks (77.5% of the respondents). Women are really concerned about the banks. Few of them who received credits (10%) pay high interest rates. Majority of women prefer to borrow money from their rich relatives and friends (70%). Usually, most of the credits women obtain are the microcredits which aren't enough to develop successful business.

There are almost no bank branches in rural areas of our country. It takes a lot of time for rural people to get nearest bank branches because of bad transportation. It contributes to the increasing of transaction costs. High transaction costs are also obstacles for small farmers and enterprises [31]. The situation with women is complicated by the fact that having a high "time intensity" [18], they cannot postpone their routine daily household duties such as cooking, child caring, and feeding of domestic livestock in order to go to the city looking for the bank [12]. So far the state support is needed to develop the women's entrepreneurship in terms of favorable tax system and conditions to access loans and trainings in business management.

4. Time use analysis

Considering constraints to agricultural growth and food security, it would be reasonable to take into account time allocation between men and women in household and then to consider how gender differentials in time allocation can impact food security. The Statistics Committee of Kazakhstan periodically conducts sample household survey in all oblasts of the country focusing on time use module [38]. This method allows examination of all kinds of household members' activities they do for a week; to determine their real work load; and moreover to demonstrate time use differences between women and men of urban and rural areas. The data were collected from all household members over 18, and the time scope was 7 days including all days of the week (**Table 1**).

According to the Statistics Committee of Kazakhstan data [38], respondents recorded the time spent for each activity performed by them within a day in chronological order. Data shows that women have larger workload and there is a time use discrepancy between men and women. Men in urban and rural areas spend more time for paid work. In agriculture men spend for paid work 6.8 h/week more than women. In urban area this difference is 4.8 h. Wage workers can accumulate more qualification and skills to increase their income. Wage employment is a stable source of income, which guarantees work experience benefits and contributions to the pension fund.

Data shows that women spent more time for chores. In agriculture women spend 17 h/week for cooking and dishwashing. It is approximately two times more than men allocate doing these jobs. Similar situation can be observed in performing other chores. Due to society's mentality, all housework is traditionally considered as women's one. Even if a man is temporary unemployed, he does not do "women's work" like cooking, laundering, and dishwashing. All of these works in household

+	Persons above 18 (person/hours)			
	Urban area		Rural area	
	Men	Women	Men	Women
Paid work	46.3	41.5	46.3	39.5
Getting to the work place	5.3	4.5	4.0	3.2
Work on the private land and housekeeping	14.1	13.6	16.0	17.3
Studying, in-service training, and self-education	34.5	31.5	38.3	32.5
Getting to the place of studying	4.6	4.4	4.6	3.4
Food shopping	3.3	4.4	2.6	3.4
Nonfood shopping	2.5	2.5	3.2	2.3
Attending consumer service houses	1.3	1.5	1.3	1.4
Cooking and dishwashing	9.5	16.2	9.0	17.0
Repair the housekeeping items	4.3	5.1	4.3	5.4
Laundry, ironing, clothes repairing	2.4	3.5	2.6	4.3
Childcare (children under 12) live in family	9.1	16.1	7.4	12.6
Caring for the elderly who need help	5.2	6.5	6.1	8.0
Attending museums, cinemas, concert, etc.	3.2	3.1	3.0	2.5
Watching TV	19.3	17.2	20.0	17.5
Attending fitness centers and sport clubs	2.4	2.4	1.6	1.5
Sleep	55.4	55.3	54.5	54.3
Free time	22.5	20.6	23.2	20.5

Table 1.
The time budget of all members of households during 7 days of the week according to the type of activity, the category of population, and gender in 2006 (according to the data of simultaneous research).

are unpaid and waste women's time which she could spend for training and paid work. The more time women spend for unpaid work, the fewer opportunities she has to increase income.

Table 1 shows that women spend 1.3 hours more than men working on the private land and doing housekeeping that equals 17.3 h/week. Actually this figure is higher because according to observation most rural women estimate their work on household plots as leisure. All respondents in Karaganda oblast answered they have a high burden in household and run around in circles between 6 A.M. and 12 P.M. Mentality of the society and heavy burden in the household set the restrictions for women, so they have no time, power, and energy for paid work. Low revenues do not allow family to mechanize housework and mitigate women's burden [18]. She was exploring interrelations between well-being and work intensity, pointing out that the lower the welfare of the household, the higher time and labor intensity.

Unfortunately, statistic agency's time use survey does not consider activities done simultaneously. Respondents registered their time on sequentially performed jobs during a week in chronological sequence. However, for example, in rural areas, women usually cook, work in the household plots, and care for children simultaneously [18]. She points out that "intensification of work ... by simultaneously performing two or more activities that require considerable energy or concentration is a qualitative dimension of time use that affects the well-being of the worker as well as the household" [18].

Both rural and urban men have more free time than women. Rural women have 20.5 hours of free time compared to 23.2 h of rural men. Free time is important to reproduce labor force [39] and to develop "internal freedom, creation of an inner world and a person's inner self-changes" [9]. "Free time is a space for human development [40]," for the comprehensive development of the human being. The lack of free time can result in human degradation to further enslaving division of labor. Women have a larger unpaid workload in household, they can spend a restricted time for paid work because of family preference, and therefore they have less opportunities to accumulate qualification and skills to increase income and have a low access to quality food.

5. Food security

There are numerous definitions of food security in the scientific literature, but they are all about "physical, social and economic access to all people at all times to sufficient, safe and nutritious food to meet their dietary needs and food preferences for an active and healthy life" [41]. Food independence, as a characteristic of food security, is critical for Kazakhstan. For a country with a fair number of natural resources, in order to provide the expanded reproduction of agricultural sector, domestic food production should be more than 80% of the country's food consumption [42]. When the country is specialized in certain types of food, its export should provide foreign trade surplus on food [42]. One of the main criteria of the country's food independence is connected with the financial ability to import the missing food and satisfy the demand of its population [42]. In Kazakhstan, "the most of domestic agro-food products were sold unprocessed, and higher quality processed foods were imported" [43]. In 2014 Kazakhstan had a positive foreign trade balance on agricultural products in the amount of US $198,7 million and the negative foreign trade balance on food products US $1782,2 million [42]. Kazakhstan is dependent from food import [44].

In 2017, food self-sufficiency, as a level of domestic agroproduction to the consumption standards, on meat and meat-based products was 62%; on milk 78%; on poultry meat 59%; and on fruits and berries 49%. The positive situation is with the self-sufficiency on grain 161% and potato 195% [44]. When calculating the level of food self-sufficiency, it would be more accurate data if loss of agricultural products will be considered. 30% of agricultural products do not reach consumers due to lack of storage conditions and imperfect economic relations between agribusiness companies and between producers, processors, and trade organizations [42, 45, 46]. So, we can conclude that domestic food supply is likely to be lower than official data. Kazakhstan is dependent from import on basic food stuffs. The more the import of food, the higher extent of dependence the country has from importers and market fluctuations and higher threat for the country's food security [47].

Nowadays, a significant part of the population's consumption of the country, especially in rural areas, consists of food produced on household plots and small peasant farms. Household plots calculated 1643.3 thousand units in 2016, and they produced 70% of potato; 50% of vegetables; 88% of milk; 76% of meat; 36% of eggs; and 68% of wool [23]. It is obvious that these farms are strategically important for food security of the country. They produce around half of the gross product. Women are the main economic agents in small peasant enterprises and household plots; therefore, they are important for food security of the country. However, household plots do not ensure women with high income. According to 2015 interview data on Karaganda oblast, the majority of respondents (90%)

answered that private allotments bring unstable and humble income. Women were undecided to name specific income data, and only 30% of them answered they had about 60,000–70,000 KZT/month from the sale of agricultural products at the time of vegetable and berry harvest. Perishables such as milk and cottage cheese require certain storage conditions or immediate sale. 60% of respondents have no transport to deliver products to the city market. Resellers offer cut prices. The majority of respondents (80%) noted that they often have no funds to purchase fertilizers, high-grade feed for livestock, and agrotechnics. Thus, according to the survey, low incomes from private farms and low productivity of private farms, along with weather conditions and time intensity, are associated with financial problems that aggravate purchase of quality fertilizers, feeds and necessary farming equipment, as well as problems in sales of products, due to undeveloped rural infrastructure and lack of transport.

Regarding expenses, 90% of respondents said that about 60% of the total household income is spent on food, the rest on clothing and footwear. 10% of respondents spend all their income to educate their children at the universities. 80% of women visit free medical institutions or self-medicate, and only 20% of them could afford paid medical services, since they were forced to do so due to medical prescriptions. Proper social support for women and infrastructure development could mitigate women's unpaid work in this sector and promote effective producing, harvesting, processing, and marketing of agricultural products and mitigate constraints to food security.

Economic access to food is assessed by the population's purchasing power and well-being [48]. According to official data, in the past several years, due to economic growth, population's welfare has improved. In 2014, the share of poor people was 2.8% in contrast with 6.5% in 2010 and 34.6% in 1996 [28]. In 2017, only 0.1% of population had earnings lower than subsistence minimum according to official data [3]. However, the Ministry of Labor and Social Protection of the Population of the Republic of Kazakhstan estimates the poverty line as 50% of the subsistence minimum (before January 1, 2018, it was calculated as a 40% of subsistence minimum). The Government of Kazakhstan uses this indicator to provide social assistance for poor people. The subsistence minimum in Kazakhstan is similar to the minimum consumer's basket cost, and in 2018 it equals to 28,284 KZT or $86, from which 60%, namely, $52 or 14,675 KZT, is the food basket. In 2011, the poverty line is 6243.6 KZT ($42) and in 2018 it is 14,142 KZT ($34). We can see that if in tenge this indicator grows, the dollar one falls. The quantity of goods and services that can be purchased for this amount is reduced. Quality processed food, medicines, clothing, and footwear are mainly imported, and their prices are set in accordance with the dollar exchange rate. In the past 8 years, the tenge has depreciated by almost 65%. Prices for local food products are also increasing, as production costs are rising: imported equipment, raw materials, vaccines, and fertilizers are used to produce them. Prices for gasoline, electricity, and the cost of a pitch in a market place are also increased. Thus, quality food products that are vital to a human being, such as fish, nuts, meat, olive oil, fruit, etc., are becoming less accessible to most of the population. The real purchasing power of population is falling. $86 (subsistence minimum in Kazakhstan) is not enough to cover vital human needs with consideration of the average family size which is 3.5 persons [21], while prices of utilities, energy, and medical services are increasing. Moreover, it is necessary to apply international standards to calculate the poverty line. Poverty line should be equal to subsistence minimum to guarantee proper social support for poor people. In 2015, poverty in rural areas was 3.6 times higher than in urban areas [23], and 45% of all unemployed reside in rural areas.

Women employed in agriculture have a lowest wage both compared to women of other economic sectors and to men of all sectors [49]. Earnings of 4.4% of the rural population are lower than the subsistence minimum [3]. Furthermore, counted subsistence minimum is inadequate for the upper middle-income country [50]. Moreover, in 2017, 23% of the working-age population was self-employed, and 62.4% of all self-employed people reside in rural areas [3]. 44% of all self-employed in agriculture are women [3]. Although there is not a single, unified definition of the "self-employment" notion in the current legislation of Kazakhstan, usually in practice self-employed people are more vulnerable in terms of stable incomes, social security, work experience records, and contributions to pension fund. They have a limited access to bank loans. So self-employed rural women are more vulnerable than wage-employed people in terms of incomes, position on the labor market, and access to quality food. The same situation is with informal employment. Around 70% of informal employees are engaged in agriculture [51]. Rutkowski (in Ref. [51]) pointed out that informal jobs are associated with low skills and productivity. Women prefer informal activity because working in the formal sector has a high cost including high taxes and document registration due to high bureaucracy. Women engaged in activities that deal with informal self-employment "encounter borrowing constraints, preventing their entry into the formal sectors" [52]. According to interview data in Karaganda oblast, 70% of women could not find decent jobs and have to work in their households only. 30% of respondents answered they do not want to work for low wages on low-skilled jobs outside the household.

On top of that, a woman's salary is 68% of the man's salary. Women have to choose low-paid jobs due to their responsibilities in terms of family and homework, limited access to retraining, and inability to work overtime on the paid job. Therefore, women are less suitable labor for employers. In 2017, the share of unemployed women was 53.6% of all unemployed, and 43% of all unemployed women resided in rural areas [3].

Over the last decade, according to the official data, the education and health expenditures have increased. However, these measures do not contribute to the welfare of the population due to inflation, which was 7% in 2017. Moreover, considerable assets have been spent to the elite educational institutions and hospital construction in Astana and Almaty cities. These elite schools, universities, and hospitals provide very expensive services that are unavailable for the majority of the population [53]. Last year's prices of quality medical services, utilities, electricity, and food have increased, and most of the public preschools have been closed. This has limited women's ability to find a paid work and has increased their unpaid work in household, thus increasing women's time pressure. The higher prices for food, the lower the consumption of quality food, which is usually more expensive. In Kazakhstan the consumption of meat, fish, and fruits has decreased. "Underconsumption of vital foods has result in the deterioration of immunity and health" [16]. Almost 40% of women in Kazakhstan suffer from anemia due to deficiency of iron [49].

One of the criteria of food security is the food quality. According to veterinary statistics, 20% of livestock in the country are infected by brucellosis or are located in areas where brucellosis was identified [54]. In 2012, 180 hearts of severe infectious diseases were registered. As a result, only less than 25% of cattle are in the regions where export is permitted [55]. At the interview with a professor from Agrarian University, he said the vaccines for brucellosis currently used in Kazakhstan are not effective in preventing brucellosis in our country and do not work against species of Brucella prevalent in our country. The professor proposed his own vaccine against Brucella that he has developed. Funding is required for further elaboration, testing, and implementation into production of new vaccines. Unfortunately, the Kazakhstani Ministry of Agriculture has not devoted funding for the development of his vaccine. Possibly the Kazakhstani Ministry of Agriculture has own benefits from buying ineffective vaccines. The vaccines, and not only vaccines for brucellosis, often are kept under conditions which do not meet the standards of vaccine storage.[2]

Moreover, the Ministry of Agriculture provides only diagnostic of disease on a cost-free basis, and farmers have to pay themselves for vaccines. The predominance of small-scale production in agriculture based on individual household plots and small farmers and the need for farmers and peasants to pay themselves for vaccination of animals also caused spreading of brucellosis. Farmers and peasants are not interested in spending money on vaccines due to low incomes. 80% of human diseases come from livestock and most livestock infections originate from poor countries. Women, as main economic agents who process meat and milk, are an at-risk group who can be infected by livestock diseases. Most of the domestic and imported food contains harmful substances [47, 56, 57]. According to the Sanitary-Epidemiological Committee of the Republic of Kazakhstan, around 70% of harmful substances enter into the human body with food [47]. Organic products are very expensive and inaccessible for the most of population. Two-thirds of the rural population has no access to safe water supply due to the insufficient technical condition of the existing water supply systems [58]. Very often the food import in Kazakhstan deals with import of low-quality cheap food from China. According to Kaigorodtsev (in Ref. [47]), there is a threat of "biological degradation of the population in terms of deterioration of the nutrition structure" [47]. "Governance focuses mostly on output, quantity, but not on the issues of effective allocation of resources, quality of product or social issues" [43].

Despite all the challenges, Kazakhstani people had rich qualities; "they recognized martial prowess, hospitality, respect for elders, love for children, and ready aid to kinsmen as virtues" [24]. According to Kazakh national traditions, children will maintain their old parents, more rich relatives help the poor ones, and men have full responsibility for the family's well-being. Maybe these national characteristics will help poor households and women to survive also in the future.

6. Conclusions

As an agricultural country, Kazakhstan should prioritize the agricultural growth in order to provide food security and mitigate poverty. For a country with a large reserve of natural resources and largest employment share in agriculture, food self-sufficiency is an important prerequisite of food security. Literature review and data analysis show that in spite of the growth in total GDP and budget increase for the Ministry of Agriculture of the Republic of Kazakhstan, Kazakhstan is still food insecure and has the underdeveloped agriculture. Kazakhstan is dependent from food import. Fieldwork data analysis has determined that economic access to safe and nutritious food is limited by low purchasing power and well-being of whole rural population, but women are relatively worse off than men.

The empirical analysis revealed that the access of rural women to finance is limited by the high cost of finance, which is the result of the high interest rate, high risks for banks in lending of agriculture, and high transaction costs. It primarily

[2] Unpublished anonymous interview with a professor of Kazakh National Agrarian University on food security issues, 2013

affected the small enterprises and women who can handle only small business. Deficiency of skills and training opportunities; unpaid household work; high time and work intensity; low access to land, equipment, and quality fertilizers; and mentality of the society on "women's work" demonstrate gender inequality in Kazakhstan's agriculture sector which constrain agricultural growth and the national food security.

Cultivation of household land plots became a main survival strategy of a family, in terms of individual consumption of the products in the household and in terms of income from the sale of the surplus product in the markets. Unfortunately, this sector cannot provide women with the sufficient income due to low productivity and lack of resources to buy fertilizers, livestock feed, and agricultural equipment. Most women have not any market experience and often face challenges in selling their products. Such a situation becomes keener due to bad infrastructure which increases women's business costs and work burden.

This paper calls the attention of Kazakhstan's policy makers to the importance of gender mainstreaming in food security programs; women's role in economy; and unpaid labor in household. Proper state support for women and infrastructure development is needed to mitigate women's unpaid work and free up time for further training and for decent paid work in the formal sector. It could promote effective producing, harvesting, processing, and marketing of agricultural products and mitigate constraints to food security provision. This paper provides analytical examination of interaction of gender equality and food security and concludes that gender discrimination affects the national food security.

Kazakhstan has elaborated and signed a number of documents on gender equality. However, there is a gap between the creation of legislative documents and their actual implementation. Nowadays the major question is how the declared tasks should be implemented. Gender mainstreaming into food security is about not just women's issues in agriculture but also poverty, unequal access to resources, unequal distribution of income, as well as wealth and corruption. All human beings, especially decision-makers, shall be "responsible for results. Personal characteristics of employees (including potential negative demonstrations such as personal ambitions, incompetence", and preference to personal interests) "may differently affect public interests" [9]. "The rate of divergence between the set objective and its actual implementation is the measure of personal" and moral responsibility of each member of the society [9]. This gap "may affect the quality of outcomes, in our case resulting in gender inequality remaining" [9]. Spiritual and moral crisis is the main "cause of all other forms of global crisis" including economic, ecological, and social crises [59] and corruption. To overcome the spiritual and moral crisis, the humanization of people is needed and changing the outlook of people and their attitude to other people and the environment. Efforts to achieve gender equality must include personal spiritual revival and promotion of a truly civilized society, where absolute values and norms of life are freedom, equality, and security of everyone.

Acknowledgements

I would like to express my special thanks to adjunct professor of the University of Eastern Finland Heimo Mikkola for the scientific guidance, technical assistance, and moral support.

I am very grateful to the Fulbright Visiting Scholar Program for financial support and for the great opportunity to conduct research and to get consultations at the American University and World Bank in Washington, DC.

Author details

Maigul Nugmanova
Gender Economics Research Center, Narxoz University, Almaty, Kazakhstan

*Address all correspondence to: maigulnugmanova@yahoo.com

References

[1] World Bank. Kazakhstan overview. February 2013. Available at: http://www.worldbank.org/en/country/kazakhstan/overview

[2] The Organisation for Economic Co-operation and Development (hereinafter OECD). Multi-dimensional review of Kazakhstan. In: Initial Assessment, OECD Development Pathways. Vol. 1. Paris: OECD Publishing; 2016. DOI: 10.1787/9789264246768-en

[3] Statistics Committee of Kazakhstan. 2018. Available at: http://stat.gov.kz/

[4] TheGlobalEconomy.com. 2018. Available at: www.theglobaleconomy.com/Kazakhstan/Female_labor_force

[5] WB, Food and Agriculture Organization of the United Nations (FAO) & The International Fund for Agricultural Development (IFAD). Gender and Climate-Smart Agriculture. Module 18 for the Gender in Agriculture Sourcebook. Washington, DC: World Bank Group; 2015. Available at: http://www.fao.org/3/a-az917e.pdf

[6] Hausmann R, Klinger B, Wagner R. Doing Growth Diagnostics in Practice: A 'Mindbook', CID Working Paper N177. Center for International Development at Harvard University; 2008. Available at: http://siteresources.worldbank.org

[7] Millennium Challenge Corporation (MCC). Millennium Challenge Corporation Compact Development Guidance. Gender Integration Guidelines. March 2011. Available at: https://assets.mcc.gov/guidance/guidance-2011001054001-genderintegration.pdf

[8] Farnworth C, Colverson K. Building a gender-transformative extension and advisory facilitation system in Sub-Saharan Africa. Journal of Gender, Agriculture and Food Security;**1**(1):20-39. Cited in Gender in Climate-Smart Agriculture: Module 18 for Gender in Agriculture Sourcebook. Agriculture Global Practice. Washington, DC: World Bank Group. 2015

[9] Nugmanova M. Reported in UNDP Kazakhstan CO Gender Mainstreaming Strategy. The strategy was elaborated by author as a National Expert to the UNDP CO in Kazakhstan; 2007. Available at: http://europeandcis.undp.org/gender/kazakhstan/show/08FCC922-F203-1EE9-B3360D15BA11580A

[10] Cagatay N, Elson D, Grown C. Introduction. World Development. 1995;**23**(11)

[11] Engels F. The Origin of the Family, Private Property and the State. Moscow: Progress Publishers; 1968

[12] Corner L. Women, Men and Economics: The Gender-Differentiated Impact of Macroeconomics (With Special Reference to Asia and Pacific). United Nations Development Fund for Women (UNIFEM) Asia - Pacific Regional Office; 1997

[13] Walters B. Engendering macroeconomics: Reconstruction of growth theory. World Development. 1995;**23**(11):1869-1880

[14] Rimashevskaya N. Women in Society: Realities, Issues, Prognosis. Moscow: Nauka; 1991. p. 11

[15] Faures J. FAO's common vision, principles and approach for the transition towards sustainable food and agriculture. In: Knowledge and Information for Sustainable Food Systems. A Workshop of the FAO/UNEP Programme on Sustainable Food Systems. Rome: Food and Agriculture Organization of the United Nations; 2016

[16] WB, FAO and IFAD. Gender in Agriculture Sourcebook. Washington, DC: HTM; 2009. Available at: http://www.fao.org/docrep/011/aj288e/aj288e00

[17] Pomfret R. Kazakhstan's agriculture after two decades of independence. In: Central Asia Economic Paper, No. 6. Elliott School of International Affairs, George Washington University; 2013. Available at: https://app.box.com/s/frv8c7f4zz0u0b3w5ds9

[18] Floro M. Women's well-being, poverty, and work intensity. Feminist Economics. 1995;**1**(3):1-25

[19] Floro M, Pichetpongsa A. Gender, work intensity, and well-being of Thai home-based workers. Feminist Economics. 2010;**16**(3):15-44

[20] Esentugelov A. Economy of Independent Kazakhstan: The History of Market Reforms. Almaty: CIMEK; 2007. 355 p. 11

[21] Statistics Committee of Kazakhstan. 2009. Available at: http://stat.gov.kz

[22] Doing business in Kazakhstan. Kazakhstan regions SMEs development indicators comparison. 2015. Available at: http://doingbusiness.gov.kz/ru/analysis-statistics/Kazakhstan-regions-SMEs-development-indicators-comparison.php#/ru/about-us

[23] Statistics Committee of Kazakhstan. Kazakhstan National Economy Ministry. 2016. Available at: http://www.stat.gov.kz/faces/PressServicePage/PressServiceNews/newsPage

[24] Brown R. Culture, chaos and capitalism: Privatization in Kazakhstan. University of Pennsylvania, Journal of International Economic Law. 1998;**19**(4)

[25] Seguino S. Gender inequality and economic growth. World Development. 2000;**28**(7):1211-1230

[26] Stiglitz J. From Resource Curse to Blessing. Project Syndicate. August 2012

[27] Hausmann R, Klinger B. Growth Diagnostics in Peru. CID Working Paper No. 181. Center for International Development at Harvard University; 2008. Available at: http://research.hks.harvard.edu/

[28] Statistics Committee of Kazakhstan. 2014. Available at: http://stat.gov.kz/

[29] World Bank Data. World Development Indicators (database). Washington, DC: World Bank; 2012. p. 2012. Available at: http://data.worldbank.org/data-catalog/world-development-indicators

[30] Accounts Committee for control over execution of the Kazakhstan republican budget. 2015. Press Releases 06/02/2015. Available at: http://esep.kz/rus/showin/article/2048

[31] OECD. Improving Access to Finance in Kazakhstan's Agribusiness Sector. Private Sector Development Policy Handbook. Paris, France: OECD Publishing; 2013

[32] Tambunan T. Women entrepreneurship in Asian developing countries: Their main constraints and personal reasons. In: Policy Discussion Paper Series. Center for Industry, SME & Business Competition Studies, Trisakti University; 2009. Available at: http://www.online.fe.trisakti.ac.id/pusatstudi_industri/index4.html. No. 7/08/09

[33] Statistics Committee of Kazakhstan. Kazakhstan National Economy Ministry. Business-register 'Key indicators of the number of legal entities and individual entrepreneurs in Kazakhstan'. 2015. Available at: www.akorda.kz/ru

[34] World Bank. Kazakhstan—Country Partnership Strategy for the Period FY12-FY17. Washington,

DC: World Bank; 2012. Available at: http://documents.worldbank.org/curateden/2012/03/16220488/kazakhstan-country-partnership-strategy-period-fy12-fy17

[35] National Bank of Kazakhstan. 2012. Available at: http://www.afn.kz/index.cfm?docid=476

[36] Ministry of Agriculture. 2013-2015 Agriculture Ministry Strategic Plan. Astana. 2013. Available at: http://mgove.kz/wp-content/uploads/2013/05/2

[37] Kazakhstan Agricultural Development Program for 2013-2020 (KADP). Astana, Sep. 2012. Available at: http://www.krgagri.kz/programma-po-razvitiyu-agropromyshlennogo-kompleksa-v-respublike-kazahstan-na-2013-2020-gody.html

[38] Statistic Agency of Kazakhstan. Women and Men in Kazakhstan. Statistical Bulletin. Astana, 2008

[39] Marx K. Capital. Vol. 1, chapter 23, part VIII. In Marx K, Engels F, editors. Full Collected Works, 2nd ed., Vol. 23. Moscow: Politizdat, Marksizm-Leninizm Institute; 1961

[40] Marx K. Salary, Price and Profit. 2nd ed. Vol. 16. Moscow: Politizdat; 1960. pp. 101-155

[41] Food and Agriculture Organization of the United Nations (FAO). Declaration of World Summit on Food Security. 2009. Available at: http://www.fao.org/fileadmin/templates/wsfs/Summit/Docs/Final_Declaration/WSFS09_Declaration.pdf

[42] The Concept of Food Security of Kazakhstan up to 2030, Decree of Kazakhstan. 2015. Available at: http://mgov.kz/wp-content/uploads/2015/04/Kontseptsii_rus.docx

[43] Pomfret R. Cited in the OECD Review of Agricultural Policies: Kazakhstan 2013. Chapter 1, p. 60. Paris: OECD Publishing; 2008. DOI: 10.1787/9789264191761-en

[44] Kazakhstan Agricultural Development Program for 2017-2021 (KADP). 2017. Available at: http://mgov.kz/ru/aza-stan-respublikasyny-a-k-damytudy-2017-2021-zhyldar-a-arnal-an-memlekettik-ba-darlamasy/

[45] Kaigorodtsev A. Economic and Food Security of Kazakhstan (questions of theory, methodology and practice). Scientific monograph. Ust-Kamenogorsk: Media-Alliance; 2006

[46] Hon E. Self-Sufficiency of Food Security of Kazakhstan. Kazakhstan Strategic Studies Institute under the President of Kazakhstan, Republican Economic Newspaper "Delovoy Kazakhstan", 13.02.2012. Available at: http://kisi.kz/en/categories/economy-and-energy/posts/self-sufficiency-of-food-security-of-kazakhstan418

[47] Kaigorodtsev A. Mechanism of functioning and development of the food security system in Kazakhstan [Author's thesis]. Ust-Kamenogorsk. 2009

[48] Food and Agriculture Organization of the United Nations (FAO). Corporate Document Repository; 2016. Available at: http://www.fao.org/docrep/x0262e/x0262e16.htm

[49] Statistic Agency of Kazakhstan. Women and Men in Kazakhstan (2009-2013). Statistical Bulletin, Astana. 2014

[50] World Bank. The World Development Report. Gender Equality and Development. Washington, DC: The World Bank; 2012

[51] Rutkowski J. Promoting formal employment in Kazakhstan. In: Paper presented at IZA/World Bank workshop on institutions and informal employment in emerging and transition

economies, IZA, Bonn, 9-11 June. 2011. Available at: http://www.iza.org/conference_files/InfoETE2011/rutkowski_j1928.pdf

[52] Asian Development Bank (ADB). Gender Assessment Report: Kazakhstan. Mandaluyong City, Philippines: ADB; 2013. Cited in Mussurov A, Arabsheibani R. Informal self-employment in Kazakhstan. IZA Journal of Labor & Development. 2015;**4**:9, pp. 42-43

[53] Analysis of the Impact of Income Sources and Social Programs on the poverty eradication in Kazakhstan. Almaty: Scientific Research Center "Sange"; 2011. Available at: www.stat.gov.kz/getImg?id=WC16200013454

[54] Ivanov P. Antibrucellosis Vaccination. Information-Advertising Newspaper Agroinfo, December. 2015;**30**. Available at: http://agroinfo.kz/vakcinaciya-protiv-brucellyoza/

[55] Ministry of Agriculture. Modernization of Kazakhstan Veterinary System: International Standards. 2013. Available at: http://www.mgov.kz/wp-content/uploads/2013/07/Veterinariya-rus.doc

[56] Mamytbekov A. Kazakhstan Agriculture Ministry Report. Central Communications service's briefing under the Kazakhstan President, June 27, 2013. Available at: http://mgov.kz/doklad-ministra-sel-skogo-hozyajstva-rk-na-brifinge-v-sluzhbe-tsentral-ny-h-kommunikatsij-pri-prezidente-rk-27-06-2013-g/Ministry of Agriculture

[57] Yergozhin Y, Beketov K. Actual problems of chemical security of Kazakhstan. Kazakhstan Chemical Journal. 2010;**N2**(29)

[58] UNDAF. United Nations Development assistance framework for the Republic of Kazakhstan, 2010-2015. Astana. 2009:16

[59] Rerikh N. Theory of Alive Ethics. Minsk: MCR; 1994

Chapter 8

Decolonizing Indigenous Law: Self-Determination and Vulnerability in the Mapuche Case

Jorge Aillapán Quinteros

Abstract

In the present essay, the author—and Mapuche, at the same time—critically analyzes the construction of the Mapuche people as a "vulnerable human group" under the International Human Rights Law and then, according to decolonial option, proposes a hypothesis: if the indigenous people are vulnerable, by definition, to claim the right to self-determination, in the Mapuche case, it is an oxymoron.

Keywords: indigenous peoples, Mapuche, modernity, decoloniality, human rights, vulnerability, victimhood, right to self-determination, racism

1. Introduction

Today, Art. 1 of "Indigenous Act," No. 19.253, recognizes nine "Chilean" indigenous peoples. Among these, the Mapuche stand out not only because they have the highest population but also because of their claim to self-determination, which they have been carrying out under the current legal paradigm of the International Human Rights Law (IHRL), specifically, based on the recognition of this right made by the ILO Convention No. 169 (1989), United Nations Declaration on the Rights of Indigenous Peoples (2007), and, lately, the American Declaration on the Rights of Indigenous peoples (2016), normative triad that constitutes the "right to autonomy or self-government" in the context of "Indigenous Law," scilicet, the set of national and international norms dictated to regulate the cultural, environmental, and patrimonial peculiarities of the native peoples.

After the "invention" of America [1], the Indianous Law came to define Indigenous subjectivity. At present, this task has been entrusted to the IHRL; hence, the indigenous are born and die under the logical and conceptual scheme of human rights. This has brought certain benefits because intercultural policies have made it possible to review the historical situation of indigenous people and advance in the recognition and enjoyment of certain rights, even when these are cultural or "folkloric" kind. In the case of political rights, on the other hand, the said recognition and enjoyment has not been successful, especially when what is claimed is territorial control, self-government, and self-determination.

The purpose of this essay is to give an account of the current state of autodeterminist Mapuche's claim, reminding the reader that perseverance in this juridical argument, under scheme of Indigenous Law, will not lead to either an internal autonomy or, much less, an external sovereignty. From the "colonial difference" [2] brought about by modernity and my Mapuche-Chilean "border" position, I propose to advance in the construction of a proper, local, and pertinent discourse on the situation of the Mapuche-Chilean as a way to advance toward the decolonization of Indigenous Law and, definitely, that the Chilean State recognizes and validates the Mapuche as a sovereign people, politically, legally, and territorially. For this, my essay is divided into two sections. Into the first, entitled "The indigenous people as a vulnerable human group," I review the main subjectivity assigned by imperialism—from the colonial category of "amentes" to the current classification of "vulnerable"—always under the assumption that the Indigenous people are disabled. In the second section, the title corresponds to the hypothesis offered by this essay—"Mapuche self-determination, an oxymoron?"—since, under the current legal configuration, it becomes a paradox, not because Indigenous Law itself and the Chilean courts deny it, but because the IHRL constitutes a paradigm of contemporary imperialism and the "coloniality of power" [3] under which not only political self-determination is closed, but even cultural is extremely limited.

2. Indigenous peoples as vulnerable people

2.1 The invention of America: the indigenous peoples and their status as "miserables of Castilla"

Indigenous peoples have been defined as those ethnic groups within the State that are characterized by a very long-term settlement within a given territory, an ancestral linkage with the land, and a high vulnerability to progress [4]. It is a very widespread definition: these people have a special connection with their ancestral territory, but these lands do not pertain to them.

In Chile, before their independence from the Spanish Crown, the Mapuche occupying the present territory were subjected to the draconian statute compiled under the label of "Laws of the Indies" norm that—on the pretext of protecting them—grouped them into "encomiendas" which were delivered to the Spanish "encomenderos" for their administration and care. Regrettably, both the "encomenderos" and the "general protectors of natives" abused the natives, forcing them to pay annual tributes, depriving them of all political representation, and providing, in fact, a slave trade despite the fact that the laws proclaimed their freedom [5].

It is known that, once installed in America, the conquerors denied humanity to the indigenous people. Later, they were considered human beings, although abject, almost beasts, because in the opinion of the Europeans, the natives were simply "amentes" since psychological or cognitive abilities of them were clearly diminished, a policy that endorsed the extermination, only appeased for the mercy of a sector of the Catholic Church, specifically through the discourse of the activists like Fray Bartolomé de las Casas or Francisco de Vitoria [6]. Even so, both agreed on the need to provide them with tutelage, for that reason the Catholic Church became the classic protector and defender of the indigenous people, in the Latin American context, and the Indianous Law granted them the legal status of "miserable of Castilla," assigning them "patrons" because, despite recognizing own political organization and own law, the Europeans said that the Indians were not able to self-determine, and, therefore, facing the hegemonic law, they were "relatively incapable" [7].

2.2 Republican Chile: indigenous are equal citizens (but incapable)

Chile declared its independence from the Spanish empire in 1810, and, along with it, it freed itself from that hegemonic law. For the indigenous peoples who occupied this territory, however, the situation worsened because, henceforth, they had to submit to the yoke of the new Chilean elites that—as heirs of the European cultural imaginary—began the stage of "internal colonialism" [8]. It is somewhat paradoxical to assume it, but despite the conquest or "invention" of America, the Spanish empire continued recognizing some ways of self-government for Mapuche people, specifically in the title "Of the Indians of Chile," included in the "Digest of the Laws of Kingdoms of the Indies" (1680). After the formation of the Chilean republic, however, Mapuche's Law came to be considered as a mere "indigenous custom." This sovereign law—validated and respected by the Spanish empire—was victim of the modern Chilean "epistemicide," because the validity and application of this custom was subject to the decision of the Chilean legislator.

Art. 1146 of the Chilean Civil Code prescribes: "All person are legally capable, except those that the law declares incapable" and, subsequently, in Art. 1447 lists those people considered incapable. And although neither at the time of its coming into force (1857), nor now, this Code has expressly declared the indigenous as incapable, the truth is that different Chilean laws have prohibited indigenous people from carrying out certain legal acts—in particular, alienating their lands—hence it has been affirmed that it is one of the "most notable disabilities" [9].

Chile, after the advent of the republic, even recognized the indigenous constitutionally, benefiting them with equality, freedom, and ability to exercise their legal rights and obligations, even though the latter was extremely limited, particularly with regard to the autonomy of the will and the possibility of selling their lands, an issue that continues to this day as a mark of the historical treatment as incapable. On this, Chilean legal scholars criticized in his opportunity the equality of rights granted to the natives, because it was harmful for them, they were easily deceived and granted contracts of sale of their land for ridiculous prices, or they were not paid [5].

However, that disability has not only been considered in free traffic of goods and services but also into Chilean criminal law. In this sphere, indigenous peoples have been declared inimputable due to their "amencia," that is, it is assumed that they have a psychological, social, or economic inferiority that prevents them from adapting to the normative requirements imposed by the modern State and ratified by the "Ingenious Act" and Chilean criminal code. This is an extremely controversial issue at the time of its practical application, because it is influenced by legal issues, both in substance and form. However, the "essentialist" construction of indigenous peoples—which "internal imperialism" continues to do up to now—turns out to be decisive, since it is assumed that they continue to live in barbarous and uncivilized conditions and, therefore, are unable to comply the standards of civilized, Christian, and Western conduct set by the IHRL [10].

As a corollary to this section, we can affirm that currently in Chile, in order to manifest consent and validly bind themselves before the law, people must be fully able. The legal disabilities, on the other hand, can be physical or biological, as well cognitive or psychological as it happens, for example, with deafness, muteness, or dementia. Some are congenital, but there are also supervening ones, considering also those of human ontogenesis as occurs, for example, with childhood and old age. Probably, the historical explanation for this would have to be sought at a time when subjective rights were considered "able-do" faculties, in other words, that human rights could have as many rights as their physical and mental capacity allow [11]. However, other disabilities have been included in Chilean legislation, linked to race, gender, or working population. In fact, this was the case until 1943 with the so-called civil death that prevented the individual who issued religious solemn vows to retain or acquire ownership of things. The same happened until 1989, because the Civil Code declared married woman incapable; only with the enactment of the Act

No. 18.802 was it possible to eliminate this impediment, despite the fact that it will continue to doubt their full legal capacity [12].

Regarding the indigenous people, on the other hand, this incapacity continues to affect us; for that reason, to consider ourselves fully autonomous or capable before the Chilean law is highly questionable. In fact this happens, for example, as a result of racism and discrimination that prevents us, among other things, access to good jobs even having merits for it: "socioeconomic inequality in Chile has had an ethnic and racial connotation," said a recent study by the United Nations Development Programme (UNDP). What is more, when categorizing surnames and social position—in people born between 1940 and 1970—"Aillapán" is one of the 50 surnames whose family does not have a single prestigious professional in this country [13].

In the legal sphere, the antecedents are diverse, beginning with that established in Art. 13 of Act No. 19.253, and by virtue of which it is limited to the natives to freely dispose of their lands [14]. However, the most important precedent comes from IHRL because it recognizes to indigenous peoples' "right to self-determination" and "self-government," but conditioning their exercise to respect human rights and fundamental rights was agreed internationally by the States. In a sentence, right to self-determination will be effective—only—"to the extent possible," as prescribed in Art. 7.1 of the ILO Convention No. 169.

2.3 The indigenous peoples as a "vulnerable" human group protected under the international human rights law

Through the twentieth century, the historic exclusion suffered by many groups of people came to be shored by means of the anti-discrimination law, identifying those groups "disadvantaged" or "especially vulnerable" to then propose new paradigms of coexistence through positive discrimination and affirmative action [15]. During the first years of the current millennium, however, the social sciences have turned to redefining the concepts of "vulnerability" and "vulnerable human groups."

The concept of vulnerability is not new to western law. However, its current understanding and complexity responds to a typically European development [16]. And although these terms are not explicitly recognized in the European Convention on Human Rights (1950) or in another regional instrument, the truth is that its theoretical elaboration has been received and promoted by various human rights organizations attached to the UN and has even been expressed in the European jurisprudence of national and regional courts [17]. Subsequently, it has also spread to Latin America and Chile, a country that often describes indigenous peoples as "vulnerable," language used not only in academic area but also by the courts, by the government, and, in general, by citizens [18].

One of the current world references of the thesis on "vulnerability," in the juridical field, is the American Martha Albertson Fineman. She says that all human beings are "vulnerable" and, thus, has tried to redefine the traditional operative concepts in anti-discrimination law, particularly, the liberal tendency that denies people their vulnerability, under the pretext of avoiding social stigmatization [19]. Yet, this thesis has received some critics that aim at the "universalization" of the vulnerability, because not all human experiences it in the same way [20], a question that Fineman has tried to explain. The problem, however, is that Fineman ignores that the state structures or "regimes" are constructed precisely to justify and validate inequities or "subordiscriminations," in order to justify the classic liberalism's calls for equality before the law for all peoples. Nevertheless, only recognizing and transforming the systems—structures and relations—of power, like the State, can better respond to the typically "systemic" vulnerability.

According Fineman, human resilience is enough to overcome vulnerability's situations [21]. However, structural changes are neither influenced by this resilience nor even exercising a responsible and participatory citizenship. First of all, people should be treated as able of self-determination—individually or collectively—to organize themselves, to decide their future, and, just there, try to solve the situations of vulnerability that can affect them. Recall that in the basis of human rights theories, from political liberalism, underlies the widespread idea that not all human beings are holders of all rights, since only autonomous individuals can claim ownership and capacity to exercise their rights. In contrast, those who are disabled—voluntarily or involuntarily—to self-determine or lack economic or material sufficiency become dependent beings, that is, nonself-sufficient and, therefore, are justified to be deprived of the ownership of all or some of the rights or the ability to exercise them [22]. Special consideration deserves, in this point, the case of the indigenous peoples and the submissive relation that maintains with the western law, especially when Article 7.1 of the ILO Convention N° 169 recognizes self-determination, but only "to the extent possible."

2.4 Victimhood: a strategy for recognition and enjoyment of indigenous rights

Also linked to vulnerability—and in the context of the IHRL—is the phenomenon of "victimhood," that is, the legitimacy that certain people have to access the recognition and enjoyment of certain benefits as forms of State reparation after violations of their human rights are committed, generally, by agents of the State.

On the juridical sphere, the situation of victims has historically been approached from the perspective of civil law and, also, of criminal law. However in the political sphere, this happened during the twentieth century, linked to the so-called processes of "transitional justice" and where, the victim became a construction not only legal, but also historical, social, cultural, economic and political wide and with a precise objective: to establish the criteria or legal requirements so that people who qualify as victims can access repair plans and, in general, government assistance [23].

Currently, vulnerability is determined by "human embodiment" [24]. Previously, it had been argued that for the contemporary moral economy, the body and its suffering were extremely useful when it came to claiming and accessing the rights offered by the capitalist democracies. There is no doubt that this "politic of suffering" is extremely useful for those States that, without to change their structures of exclusion and discrimination, manage to respond to the claims of groups historically violated, indemnifying them and reintegrating them into their citizenship, although that yes: under the condition of "victims" [25, 26]. Certainly, we must not forget that if one or several people are recognized as victims, this may imply to enjoy a series of benefits [27], demonstrating why "victimhood," in the context of transitional justice, turns out to be extremely useful to the time to negotiate and generate repair programs. Moreover, this strategy of victimhood is being useful to those convicted of crimes against humanity who, claiming their status as "victims," demand respect for their human rights and the possibility of opting for prison benefits [28].

However, as I will explain below, despite the fact that "victimhood" entails certain benefits, this strategy is ineffective and even paradoxical when it comes to claiming self-determination and self-government, in the context of the IHRL. At least, in case of Mapuche people.

3. Self-determination into Mapuche's claims: an oxymoron?

3.1 The international human rights law as a paradigm of modernity/coloniality

In addition to the individual perspective, the modern theory of human rights is inexorably determined by questions relating to the national sovereignty of States. However, in the case of indigenous peoples, and their right to self-determination, these issues are often ignored. And although the "Indigenous Law" has been outlined, during the last decades, as an autonomous discipline within the IHRL, it is pertinent to remember that the concern for situation of them, arose due to the terrible working conditions in which they was, and not for questions of sovereignty. It was the International Labor Organization (ILO) that in 1921 began to show concern and to study —from the labor perspective, not the political perspective— the situation of indigenous workers. This is confirmed by one of the main antecedents to the "right to self-determination," included in ILO Convention No. 169, that it does not pretend to be a basis for declaring the indigenous self-government.

The human rights are often understood as a set of faculties and institutions that, in each historical moment, specify the requirements of human dignity, freedom, and equality, which must be positively recognized by the legal systems legal issues at national and international levels [29]. Paraphrasing to Costas Douzinas, we must ask ourselves the question: Are indigenous people "completely" human or, in contrast, are they only "partially" human, with very limited rights? This question is not trivial, especially assuming that the concept of "humanity" was defined by Eurocentric modernity, heir to that Athenian-Roman citizenship: masculine, white, plutocratic, heterosexual, and so on. And of course, the barbarians —and among them the indigenous— have gradually been integrating ourselves into this "humanity," despite the fact that this membership continues to be an imperial arbitrariness, decided from Europe or the United States [30].

Now, I will do analyze the classic criticisms against human rights. However, in a lot of them it is possible to discover arguments that would allow us to move toward the "decolonization" [31] of indigenous law, demonstrating why it is an oxymoron that indigenous peoples rely on the same colonial grammar to achieve their political self-determination.

Considering the historicist critique, it is already possible to understand the refusal of western States—and, in our case, Chile—to respond to the main indigenous claims. In the other hand, Karl Marx did not consider this demand in his analyses; however, a rereading of their texts would predict that indigenous claims—in the key of human rights, not in terms of subjective rights as such—can never be satisfied, because the content and the positivization of these rights depend totally on the convenience of the bourgeoisie and its benefit, in the context of a neoliberal and highly individualistic economy. Even assuming that the reformulation of the principle of equality has made it possible to improve the relationship between the bourgeoisie and the indigenous peoples, we must not lose sight of the fact that this reformulation aimed at "equality of exploitation of the labor force" [32, 33]. However, it should be noted that both Marxism and capitalism constitute nemesis of the indigenous worldview, since both depend on the exploitation of the land and its natural resources [34].

It has been pointed out that human rights are the hallmark of modernity, an ideal habitat for the concretion of the liberal Kantian myth that speaks of a fully autonomous, invulnerable, cosmopolitan, multicultural, and tolerant humanity. Paradoxically, as postmodernist criticism points, during the twentieth century, there were more violations of those rights than in any of the preceding and less enlightened times. However, it is forgotten that modernity began in the sixteenth century, precisely with the genocide and "epistemicide" against people who inhabited the American continent at that time [35]. Now, with regard to postmodern criticism, we should also make certain clarifications. It is possible to assume that human rights are a mark of postmodernism, although taking into account that most critics speak from Eurocentrism or "postmodern reason." For me, on the other hand, the International Human Rights Law is a paradigm of "modernity/coloniality," understanding "coloniality" as the dark and macabre side with which modernity has been operating historically. These are the political instrument—by excellence—of contemporary imperialism and for which it fights battles in its name, freeing people from regimes, practices, and barbaric customs, pontificating universal morality, and even breaking their own ethical standards. Contradictorily, these same principles of human rights and national sovereignty that have served the great powers to legitimize the new legal, social and economic order have served to evade the criticisms and questions on the flagrant violations of human rights that these same powers discuss.

On the other hand, as the configuration of IHRL depends on European and American imperialism, it can be said that there is no hope of self-government or self-determination for "non-Western" people [36]. Douzinas has explained it better by saying that the universality of human rights, although it was an invention of the west, today is used by the south and the east to access the distribution of the world product, trying to achieve a full coexistence between different peoples and the same participation in the enjoyment of the planetary wealth, when in fact the agreements of concessions of aid, ordinarily, only impose privatization, the market economy, and human rights as the gospel of liberation. In the case of indigenous people, history repeats itself: the imperialism offers a possibility of conversion, although not to Catholicism, but to neoliberalism and its representative democracy [26].

3.2 Mapuche self-determination: toward a decolonial turn

I am not going to ignore that the IHRL has been extremely useful when it comes to raising and justifying Mapuche demands. And although, since the beginning of the 1990s, "institutional" ways have been configured that distance themselves from those that claim "political violence," the truth is that there is no known Mapuche actor who tries to avoid the imperialist doctrine of human rights to support both their political and juridical plaint as such.

In my opinion, however, the Mapuche, in turning to the IHRL—as a political and legal basis for its national liberation strategy—errs, because self-determination, under that perspective, is only allowed for those issues that do not involve territorial control or sovereignty. The Declaration on the Rights of Indigenous Peoples UN (2007) recognizes in its articles 3 and 4: "Indigenous peoples have the right to self-determination." However, Art. 46.1 warns: "Nothing in this Declaration may be interpreted as implying for any State, people, group or person any right to engage in any activity or to perform any behavior against the Charter of the United Nations or construed as authorizing or encouraging any action which would dismember or impair, totally or in part, the territorial integrity or political unity of sovereign and independent States."

The Mapuche people do not exist beyond the IHRL. In other words, there is no possibility of self-determination beyond the limits set by imperialism in the matter of human rights. This is reaffirmed by Article 34 and 46.2 of Declaration of the year 2007, articles V, XXXV, and XXXVI of the American Declaration of Indigenous Peoples OAS (2016) and articles 8.2 and 9.1 of ILO Convention No. 169. From a critical perspective, this type of writing should not be surprising since the establishment and interpretation of the Treaties, in the matter of human rights, always go under direction desired by imperialism, both global and internal [37]. It is a matter of reviewing, for example, the recommendations of the "Ruggie framework" (UN) that advocating respect for indigenous territorial control does not establish sanctions for States or companies that disobey their commitments in the area of extractive industry. In the Chilean context, on the other hand, the policies of returning land to the Mapuche people seek to repair the spoils suffered in ancestral territories, under a human rights approach, although responding only to those communities validated by the State—in attention to the homogenizing concept of "intermediate group" used by the 1980 Constitution—and without ever granting territorial control or self-government and, even, subtracting the said lands from the normal judicial traffic. The same concept "land" responds to a purely western vision—i.e., the land is indivisibly inserted into the broader concept of "territory"—and the criterion of Chilean jurisprudence remains invariable in this topic, mainly through the implementation of the "indigenous consultation" to which the Chilean State has been obliged when it ratified ILO Convention No. 169 [38].

In Chile, the Mapuche people can only aspire to a "cultural" self-determination but, even so, tolerated in the "to the extent possible," as stated in Art. 7.1 of the ILO Convention No. 169. Thus, for example, the Chilean Supreme Court has recently ratified it, allowing the practice of rituals in ancestral lands—now occupied by other people—but immediately denying the possibility of recovering them[1]. Politically, and under the prism of post-dictatorial Chilean governments, Mapuche self-determination will be achieved through the dedicated parliamentary seats in the National Congress, with or without prior constitutional recognition. However, in my opinion, this only confirms to Chile like a "pluricultural" society, but not that the political self-determination or self-government of the Mapuche people will be allowed. And with that, as has been argued, the victorious revolutionaries and their legislators could be as tyrannical as their predecessors, and this has been the case in Chile, especially if we consider that, after the overthrow of Pinochet, the governments of "center-left" have imprisoned and killed more Mapuche than the right-wing governments. Finally—and although it is painful to assume it—although codification is one of the basic guarantees of fundamental rights, this does not guarantee love, respect, and affection toward others [26], and this has been demonstrated in recent years because, despite the sanctions and recommendations of international human rights organizations, Chile continues to apply a racist politic against the Mapuche people. Even, the Supreme Court has recognized this. It happened in 2016, when a Mapuche woman was imprisoned and forced to give birth while she was chained. On that occasion, the Supreme Court accepted an appeal for amparo in her favor, noting that the Chilean State discriminated doubly for being a woman and an indigenous person.[2]

In my opinion, Mapuche self-determination implies the reorganization and free administration of the ancestral territory but mainly to recover the lost nomogenetic capacity, independently of the relationship that may exist with the Chilean State toward the future. It is known that, at international sphere, the right to self-determination, for indigenous, has been configured from the 1980s. In the case of ILO Convention No. 169, this happened in 1989: "The peoples concerned shall have the right to decide their own priorities for the process of development as it affects their lives, beliefs, institutions and spiritual well-being and the lands

---

[1] Recitals 3 and 6 of the judgment, dated July 26, 2018, case N° 9021–2018, "Painepe con Sociedad Agrícola Las Vertientes Limitada."

[2] This jugment was delivered on December 1, 2016, in case N° 92.795–16.

they occupy or otherwise use, and to exercise control, to the extent possible, over their own economic, social and cultural development." However, Chile only introduced this Treaty into its internal legislation in 2008, a disdain that has characterized to governments that succeeded Pinochet, refusing to recognize the quality of the "people" of the Mapuche, precisely to avoid claims of self-determination a posteriori. In this sense, the opinion expressed by the Constitutional Court, in the year 2000, remains the rule: "(...) the expression 'indigenous peoples', should be considered within the scope of said treaty, as a set of persons or groups of people of a country who possess in common their own cultural characteristics, who are not endowed with public powers (...)".[3] The formula proposed by the Chilean State to relate to it is not that of sovereign political peers—as historically it was—but the one inherited from the Iure Belli: the victorious State of offering mercy to the vanquished and thus, acknowledging or not their past mistakes, conditions the Mapuche to dialog in a state of subjection, under the rules and standards set by the Chilean State itself in signature tune to the international "humanitarian reason" [39]. As a result, it will not be the international law of sovereign States that will elucidate the issues between Chile and the Mapuche people, but only the IHRL, regulations before which the Mapuche only acquire relevance in a context of vulnerability and victimization.

Considering the Kantian autonomic proposal, we could argue that the Mapuche people are still in a stage of "tutelage" or "nonage." And in attention to this plan, we could say that when a person decides to become independent, abandoning the paternal or maternal lap, he can achieve it in different ways. So, you can live outside the family home but maintained by your parents. Others—more dignified, in my opinion—will realize their independence by accepting, in the beginning, small gifts or the impulse of their parents to achieve their definitive economic emancipation. Even, there are even people who claim their own self-sufficiency but without accepting any kind of family support, regardless of whether they break or retain the family bond that unites them. And using the analogy, we could see our relationship with the Chilean State in the same way because if self-determination is what we want, we must decide if we are going to break all political and territorial relations with Chile, if we are going to negotiate a personal status that identify us in the whole country, if a "plurinational region" will be defined, and so on. Precisely, that is the legal explanation why the relationship between the Mapuche people and the Chilean State is not governed by International Public Law, as it happens between sovereign States, and at the same time, it allows us understand the strategy that transforms the juridical or legal claims in "facts of political transcendence" [40], in order to access protection provided by the International Human Rights Law.

4. Conclusions

Bearing that what the Mapuche people want is a political self-determination, in attention to International Public Law, the autonomous movement should consider the following suggestions:

1. Define preliminary issues. From the reading, the analysis, and the praxis of the Mapuche autonomist movement, it is not possible to clearly extract what is the scope of the self-determination sought, the territory that will encompass, as well as the personal status that will define who can be considered "Mapuche."

[3] This text corresponds to the recital N ° 44 of the judgment issued on August 4, 2000, in case N ° 309.

2. Vulnerability. Taking on the above, whatever the option, it is fundamental that the Mapuche people abandon their self-identification with the "vulnerable human groups," promoted by the indigenists and human rights activists. There is no doubt that the recognition of a catalog of human rights for indigenous peoples has allowed their visibility at the international ambit, but it is true that this also perpetuated their dependence on current imperialism—external and internal—which in exchange for "cultural rights" exploits the indigenous ancestral territories, submerging in poverty the people who inhabit them and forcing the exodus to the metropolis; without going any further, in Chile, the vast majority of the Mapuche—about 70 or 80%—have been born and are currently living in Santiago. In my opinion, vulnerability is another symptom of the "coloniality of being" which, through racism and the taxonomy imposed by modernity, continues to perpetuate the classification between superior and inferior human beings.

3. Victimhood. It would be prudent, too, that the Mapuche will not continue using the policies of "victimhood," designed by the Chilean governments following the Pinochet dictatorship, since they only perpetuate a dialectic of violence and submission of the Mapuche people with respect to the Chilean State. Instead of empowering indigenous peoples, it ends up decimating them, dehumanizing them, atomizing their collective struggles through "clientelism," and exposing their situation through the "emblematic cases" that would apparently benefit an entire population, but in truth they only end up giving revenues to the people, activists, and Chilean political parties that are behind these claims. In my opinion, victim status is just a transitory situation. For the rest, remember that self-flagellation perpetuates the oppression [41].

4. Toward decolonization of the indigenous law. In the end, it is worth remembering that the law is one of the areas that has served most to regulate and impose the modern colonialism, which is why its development and control have always remained in the hands of the elites, who always seek to preserve their privileges, through the promotion of capitalism and representative democracy, as constitutive expressions of the "coloniality of power." That is why the emancipation of indigenous peoples is impossible without removing that "colonial matrix of power," without reaching a "second decolonization" [42] that puts us again before the dilemma: rebuilding a "negative or oppressive identity" that keeps us in the vulnerability and dependence or, instead of that, reconstructing a "positive or emancipatory identity" that leads us toward self-determination and a sovereign political existence.

5. Recovery of Mapuche's nomogenetic capacity. In general, for Latin America, it is affirmed that the indigenous' own law managed to survive, notwithstanding the "epistemicide" applied by European colonialism [43]. That's why within the movement for self-determination, there is a sector that interpellates the Chilean State to recognize what was agreed in various treaties signed between the seventeenth and nineteenth centuries, in which the Mapuche was considered as a free and sovereign people over their territories [44]. In other words, the survival of the obligations acquired by the pre-republican and republican authorities before the Mapuche people is raised, providing arguments in favor of the recognition of the nomogenetic capacity of the latter and legal pluralism in the Chilean legal system.

DOI: http://dx.doi.org/10.5772/intechopen.89020

Author details

Jorge Aillapán Quinteros
Center of Mapuche Studies and Research "RÜMTUN", Santiago, Chile

*Address all correspondence to: abogado@aillapan.cl

References

[1] Quijano A. Colonialidad del poder y clasificación social. In: Castro-Gómez S, Grosfoguel R, editors. El giro decolonial. Reflexiones para una diversidad epistémica más allá del capitalismo global. Bogotá: Iesco/Instituto Pensar/ Siglo del Hombre; 2007. pp. 93-126

[2] Mignolo W. Historias locales/diseños globales. Colonialidad, conocimientos subalternos y pensamiento fronterizo. Madrid: Akal; 2003. 456 p

[3] Maldonado-Torres N. Sobre la colonialidad del ser: contribuciones al desarrollo de un concepto. In: Grosfoguel R, Castro-Gómez S, editors. El giro decolonial. Reflexiones para una diversidad epistémica más allá del capitalismo global. Bogotá: Iesco/ Instituto Pensar/Siglo del Hombre; 2007. pp. 127-168

[4] Torrecuadra S. Los pueblos indígenas en el orden internacional. Madrid: Dykinson; 2001. 192 p.

[5] Claro Solar L. Explicaciones de Derecho civil chileno y comparado. Tome I. Vol. 5. Editorial Jurídica: Santiago; 1979. 617 p

[6] De Vitoria F. Relecciones sobre los indios y el Derecho de guerra Madrid. Espasa-Calpe S.A.; 1975. 147 p.

[7] Dougnac A. Manual de Historia del Derecho Indiano. México: UNAM; 1994. 465 p

[8] Dussel E. El encubrimiento del otro: hacia el origen del mito de la modernidad. La Paz: Plural/UMSA; 1492, 1994. 219 p

[9] Alessandri A. Derecho civil. De los contratos. Santiago: Editorial Jurídica Ediar-ConoSur Ltda; 1988

[10] Mignolo W. Who speaks for the "human" in human rights? In: Barreto JM, editor. Human Rights from a Third World Perspective: Critique, History and International Law. Newcastle: Cambridge Scholars Publishing; 2012. pp. 44-64

[11] Hobbes T. In: Curley E, editor. Leviathan, with Selected Variants from the Latin Edition of 1668. Indianapolis: Hackett Publishing; 1994. 627 p

[12] Domínguez C. La situación de la mujer casada en el régimen patrimonial chileno: mito o realidad. RCHD. 1999;**26**:83-103

[13] PNUD. Desiguales. Orígenes, cambios y desafíos de la brecha social en Chile. Santiago: PNUD; 2017. 412 p

[14] Martinez C. Aplicación de la ley N° 19.253 en materia de contratos. Análisis jurisprudencial y comentarios [thesis]. Concepción: Facultad de Derecho de la Universidad de Concepción; 2012

[15] Aillapán J. La discriminación Racial en el Derecho Interno e Internacional [Thesis]. Concepción: Facultad de Derecho de la Universidad de Concepción; 2005

[16] Peroni L, Timmer A. Vulnerable groups: The promise of an emerging concept in European human rights convention law. I-CON. 2013;**11**:1056-1085. DOI: 10.1093/icon/mot042

[17] Besson S. La vulnerabilité et la structure des droit de l'homme. L' exemple de la jurisprudence de la Cor Européene des droit de l'homme. In: Burgorgue-Larsen L, editor. La vulnérabilité saisie par les juges en Europe. Paris: Pedone; 2014. pp. 59-85

[18] Nash C. Derechos humanos y pueblos indígenas. In: Análisis jurisprudencial para procesos de consulta en el marco del Convenio N° 169 de la OIT. Vol. 147. Santiago: Centro

de derechos humanos, Facultad de Derecho de la Universidad de Chile; 2014

[19] Fineman M, Grear A, editors. Vulnerability. Reflections on a New Ethical Foundation for law and Politics. Farnham: Ashgate; 2013. 236 p

[20] Mackenzie C, Rogers W, Dodds S, editors. Vulnerability: New Essays in Ethics and Feminist Philosophy. New York: University Press; 2014. 318 p.

[21] Fineman M. The vulnerable subject and the responsive state. Emory Law Journal. 2010;**60**:1-42

[22] Barranco Avilés M. Vulnerabilidad, derechos humanos y empresas. Cuadernos electrónicos de Filosofía del Derecho. 2016;**34**:1-16. DOI: 10.7203/CEFD.34.8925

[23] Gugliemucci A. El concepto de víctima en el campo de los derechos humanos: una reflexión crítica a partir de su aplicación en Argentina y Colombia. RES. 2017;**35**:83-97. DOI: 10.7440/res59.2017.07

[24] Fineman M. Feminism, masculinities, and multiple identities. Nevada Law Journal. 2013;**13**:619-640

[25] Fassin D. Moral economies revisited. Annales. Histoire, Sciences Sociales. 2009;**64**:1237-1266

[26] Douzinas C. El fin(al) de los derechos humanos. Anuario de Derechos Humanos. 2006;**7**:309-340

[27] Todorov T. Les abus de la mémorie. Paris: Arléa; 1995. 61 p.

[28] Salvi V. De vencedores a víctimas. In: Memorias militares sobre el pasado reciente en la Argentina. Buenos Aires: Biblios; 2012. 229 p.

[29] Pérez Luño A. Los derechos fundamentales. 8th ed. Madrid: Tecnos; 2004. 239 p.

[30] Grosfoguel R. Descolonizando los universalismos occidentales: el pluri-versalismo transmoderno decolonial desde Aimé Césaire. In: Castro-Gómez S, Grosfoguel R, editors. El giro decolonial, reflexiones para una diversidad epistémica más allá del capitalismo global. Bogotá: Iesco/Instituto Pensar/Siglo del Hombre; 2007. pp. 63-78

[31] Mignolo W. Desobediencia epistémica: retórica de la modernidad, lógica de la colonialidad y gramática de la descolonialidad. Buenos Aires: Ediciones del Siglo; 2010. 126 p.

[32] Tible J. José Carlos Mariátegui: Marx e América Indígena. CCemarx. 2009;**6**:97-114

[33] Peces-Barba Martínez G. Tránsito a la modernidad y derechos fundamentales. In: Ansuátegui Roig F, Rodríguez Uribes J, editors. Historia de los derechos fundamentales. Madrid: IDHBC, Dykinson; 2003. pp. 15-263

[34] Teale T. The Silko road from Chiapas or why native Americans cannot be marxist. Melus. 1998;**23**:157-166. DOI: 10.2307/467833

[35] Quijano A, Wallerstein I. La americanidad como concepto, o América en el moderno sistema mundial. Revista Internacional de Ciencias Sociales. 1992;**34**:583-592

[36] Chomsky N. Humanitarian Imperialism: The New Doctrine of Imperial Right [Internet]. 2008. Available from: https://monthlyreview.org/2008/09/01/humanitarian-imperialism-the-new-doctrine-of-imperial-right/ [Accessed: 2018-11-15]

[37] Douzinas C. Human Rights and Empire. The Political Philosophy of Cosmopolitanism. Abingdon: Routledge-Cavendish; 2007. 336 p

[38] Rojas Bastidas D. Análisis conceptual del derecho a la tierra de

los pueblos indígenas según el Derecho internacional [thesis]. Santiago: Instituto Nacional de Derechos Humanos; 2014

[39] Fassin D. Humanitarian Reason. A Moral History of the Present. University California Press; 2012. 352 p

[40] Tiscornia S. Activismo de los derechos humanos y burocracias estatales. In: El caso Walter Bulacio. Buenos Aires: Editores del Puerto-CELS; 2008. 309 p.

[41] Taylor C. Multiculturalismo y política del reconocimiento. México: Fondo de Cultura Económica; 1993. 157 p

[42] Castro-Gómez S, Grosfoguel R. Prólogo. Giro decolonial, teoría crítica y pensamiento heterárquico. In: Castro-Gómez S, Grosfoguel R, editors. El giro decolonial. Reflexiones para una diversidad epistémica más allá del capitalismo global. Bogotá: Iesco/Instituto Pensar/ Siglo del Hombre; 2007. p. 307

[43] Garzón López P. Pueblos indígenas y decolonialidad. Sobre la colonización epistemológica occidental. ARIS. 2013;**10**:305-331. DOI: 10.29092/uacm.v10i22.278

[44] Contreras Painemal C. Los Tratados Mapuche en la bibliografía. EL. 2011;**31**:105-120

Chapter 9

Uprising and Human Rights Abuses in Southern Cameroon-Ambazonia

Nanche Billa Robert

Abstract

In 2016, lawyers, teachers and students in the two Anglophone regions initially led demonstrations and strikes, which eventually involved a wider section of the population. This mobilization was against their marginalization by the Francophone-dominated government in which they were chronically under-represented in all aspects of national life: political appointments and professional training and had been treated as second-class citizens since their reunification. They argued that their vibrant economic and political institutions had been completely erased, and their education and judicial systems had been undermined and degraded. Activists spread videos that show security forces abusing human rights (by suppressing peaceful gatherings, beating, harassing, arresting and killing protesters, burning their houses, schools and hospitals) in order to produce a counter-narrative to the 'official story' that main-stream media had been producing. We collected and analyzed 30 videos to better appreciate the human rights abuses. The videos provide information that cannot be provided by other types of data. They are used as 'proofs of facts' and they contain much more visual information on bodily movement and acoustic data. The videos show appalling images not just of how French-speaking soldiers tortured Anglophones but also their inability to communicate with them adequately although they share the same country.

Keywords: protest, cultural hegemony, human rights, uprising, videos, alternative media, Ambazonia, judiciary and education

1. Introduction

It seems people everywhere are questioning the ability of traditional political actors to represent their interests and are increasingly seeking a more direct and unmediated relations to the decisions that affect their lives [1]. The Southern Cameroon-Ambazonia crisis commonly known as the Anglophone crisis revolves around the marginalization of the Anglophones and the dilution of their cultural identities especially concerning education and the judiciary by the Francophones in their attempt to assimilate them. Anglophones have therefore collectively given voice to their grievances and concerns and are demanding that something be done about them and they have taken extra-institutional actions by arming themselves to defend themselves against the government security forces who abuse their human rights by arbitrarily arresting, torturing, detaining, killing them, burning their houses, raping their women and also refusing them the right to self-determination.

The collective challenge that from the onset of the crisis was predominantly regressive, that is, a return to federation as it was from 1961 to 1972, changed due to Cameroon government's failure to listen to their plights. They overwhelmingly became progressive, that is, they wanted absolute independence except for their elite (parliamentarians, ministers and other prominent government workers) still clamoring for federation and a unitary state because they benefitted from the government and were afraid of losing their jobs. The question we ask is: how have Anglophones historically sustained social solidarity with their common opponent, which is the government of Cameroon, in order to attain their desired policy change? What means have they used to make their voices heard in the international scene? And finally, how have the government responded to their protest?

The rise and spread of new ICTs have transformed the way that society is organized, which of course include social movements. Internets and SMS messaging for examples have enabled activists to coordinate protest in record time, giving rise to the 'flash mob' phenomenon. 'Flash mob' is a term that originally referred to social experiments and countercultural movements to reclaim 'public spaces' Salmond [2]. The Anglophone movement can be dubbed as the 'Twitter Revolution' or 'Facebook Revolution' emphasizing the role of social media in diffusing videos of human rights abuses and to organize protest mobilizations both at the local and international levels.

The videos were diffused all over the world thereby creating huge impact in the international community. Diffusion is the process through which movements import and export ideas, tactics, strategies, organizational forms and cultural practices as Entman [3] puts it, by framing: a way of selecting and highlighting a particular claim to mobilize supporters, demobilize antagonists and convince observers of the worthiness of their course. The frame Ambazonian highlight is that their union with Francophone is fake and it never took place because there is no certificate of union and that they are culturally different, therefore the need for the restoration of their independence. Their frames are deeply rooted in local or national political and cultural context and are more open to diffusion especially as it concerns the abuse of human rights. They use a frame that makes them to think globally and act locally, that is, they take a political action frame that links global problems with local action.

Many videos have been spread on the brutality of the security forces that disrespected the universal declaration of human rights. They can easily be downloaded from the Internet clearly showing that due to the age of Twitter and Facebook revolution, the images have been globalized in order to gain international attention from organizations and countries that matter in the world. The spreading of these videos and other information led to the shutting down of the Internet in Ambazonia for 93 days.

The objective of this work is to collect and analyze short videos and journalists' reports for television stations using social movement theory.

2. Origin of the Ambazonia uprising: dominant not consensual cultural hegemony

The Ambazonia crisis is an attempt of Southern Cameroonians to break the dominant Francophone cultural hegemony. Since 1972, La République du Cameroun has dominated the Southern Cameroonians, which came into union with them from a weaker position with a population numerically smaller. As a result, La République du Cameroon has been making efforts not just to dominate them but to absorb them into the broader Francophone cultural system. They silently destroyed the dignity and statehood of Anglophones-not by the French-speaking community at large, but by the government which was led and dominated by Francophones.

Marx and Engels [4] famously argued that, in any epoch, the dominant ideas are the ruling ideas in society that serve to maintain the dominance of the ruling classes. Those who have the means of economic production also have control over the production of ideas, and the class which is the material force of society is at the same time the ruling intellectual force. The ruling class, rules also as thinkers and as producers of ideas and regulate the production and distribution of ideas of their age. Similarly, La République du Cameroon has been producing ideas to suppress Southern Cameroonians because of their dominance over the economy, judiciary and political institutions. When the crisis started in order to dilute it, they produced many unsuccessful concepts such as the promotion of Bilingualism and multiculturalism, the national disarmament and demobilization and reintegration committee all headed by Anglophones and whose reports were dropped in the dustbins. Finally, they gave Anglophones what they termed 'Special Status,' which Anglophones rubbished as being empty. How did these two separate entities come together and form a union?

Cameroon was initially a German's territory from 1887 to 1914 before the British invaded it from Nigeria in 1914 and the German surrendered in February 1916. After the war, the League of Nations partitioned the colony between the United Kingdom and France on June 28, 1919, and France gained the larger geographical share. French Cameroon became independent as La République du Cameroun in January 1960 and Nigeria was scheduled for independence later that same year, which raised question of what to do with the British territory. A plebiscite was agreed on and it was held on February 11, 1961, and the British Southern Cameroon voted to join Cameroon as West Cameroon I.CB Dear [5]. To negotiate the terms of the union, the Foumban Conference was held on July 16–21, 1961 in which the Federal Constitution was drafted. It stated in Article 47.1 that "No bill to amend the constitution may be introduced if it tends to impair the unity and integrity of the federation."

This poorly conducted re-unification was based on centralization and assimilation, and has led the Anglophone minority feeling politically and economically marginalized as their cultural differences are ignored. "On the 1st September 1966 the Cameroon National Union (CNU) was created by the union of political parties of East and West Cameroon. Most decisions were taken without consultation, which led to widespread feelings amongst the West Cameroonian public that although they voted for reunification, La Republique du Cameroon was absorbing or dominating them," Wikipedia [6].

Achankeng [7] states that although the plebiscite was an expression of willingness to associate with French Cameroon, no necessary discussions took place to arrive at an agreed document and set the legal basis of the federation. So it never took place and neither were any agreements subsequently signed between the two countries.

In 1972, President Ahidjo (the President of the Republic of Cameroon) conducted a referendum on the form of the state. Although the West Cameroon lawmakers heavily opposed and rejected it on the ground that it was a violation of the 1961 Federal Constitution, he went ahead with the referendum and the Federal Republic of Cameroon became the United Republic of Cameroon [8]. All these events were calculated attempts meant to incorporate a former colony into another state. Bongfen [9] and Ajong [10] state that it abolished "all federal legislative, judicial and administrative institutions, and removed all guarantees that protected the rights of the minority Southern Cameroonians in the federation. Unlike during the plebiscite of 1961 wherein only Southern Cameroonians voted to decide on their destiny, the May 1972 referendum was extended to all the people of la République du Cameroun. It was 'a creeping annexation than unification'. However, the dissenting voices of Southern Cameroonians rejecting the centralized United Republic of Cameroon were dwarfed by the wide majority of La République. Many Southern Cameroonians regard 20th May, - the national day of today's Cameroon – as a day when they lost their freedom".

In 1984, Paul Biya removed one of the stars from the flag and changed the official name of the country to the Republic of Cameroon (La République du Cameroon), which Cameroon had before her unification with Southern Cameroon. Some Anglophones such as Gorji-Dinka, Bernard Fonlon and Carlson Anyangwe from the Southern Cameroon considered it as the dissolution of the 1961 union.

Citizens from these regions, that is, the Anglophone regions, have been mobilizing against their marginalization by the Francophone-dominated government. They complain about chronic under-representation in all issues of national life, including political appointments and professional training. They argue that since their reunification, they have been treated as second-class citizens. Their vibrant economic and political institutions have been completely erased, and their education and judicial systems have being undermined and degraded.

Gorji Dinka and Albert Mukong: Southern Cameroonian nationalists who protested the ill-treatment of their people by the central regime were arrested and detained. Representatives of southern Cameroonians in the tripartite talks of 1991 proposed a return to the federation, but the leaders of La République du Cameroon ignored them. In 1994, John Ngu Focha and Salomon T. Muna both former Prime Ministers of the Southern Cameroons returned to the United Nations in New York and demanded separate independence for the Southern Cameroons. The mission to the UN preceded the All Anglophone Conference (AAC 1), which took place in Buea in April 1993 bringing together all Southern Cameroon citizens who unanimously called for the restoration of the statehood of the Southern Cameroons. A second All Anglophone Conference (AAC 2) was held in Bamenda in May 1994, at which the decisions of AAC 1 were reiterated and a reasonable time was given to French Cameroon to accept a return to the two state federations or Southern Cameroon would revive its statehood and independence. The implementation of AAC 1 and AAC 2 was however stalled by the brutal arrests and incarceration of the leaders of the AAC with several others escaping into exile.

The ACC was renamed the Southern Cameroons Peoples Conference (SCPC), and later the Southern Cameroon People's organization (SCAPO), with the Southern Cameroon National Council (SCNC) as the executive governing body. Southern Cameroon National Council younger activists formed the Southern Cameroons Youth League (SCYL) in Buea on May 28, 1995.

When they felt their demands were met with contempt and total disregard, the SCNC took their case back to the United Nations led by John Foncha and protested against La République du Cameroun annexation of their territory. Their focus has been maintained on the restoration of the statehood of Southern Cameroon, and the government brutal repression has helped to unify them.

Police routinely disrupted SCNC activities: On March 23, 1997, gendarmes killed about 10 people in a raid in Bamenda. The police arrested between 200 and 300 people, mostly SCNC supporters as well as members of the Social Democratic Front. In the subsequent trials, Amnesty International and SCNC found substantive evidence of the government torturing and using force on them. The raid and trial resulted in a shutdown of SCNC activities. On October 1, 1999, SCNC militants took over Radio Buea to proclaim the independence of Southern Cameroon but failed to do so before security forces intervened. After clashes with the police, the SCNC was officially declared illegal by the Cameroonian authorities in 2001. In 2006, a faction of SCNC once again declared the independence of Ambazonia Lansdorf, ed. [11].

Although Cameroon is bound by the international law and its own constitution to respect human rights and freedoms, many human rights have been violated in Southern Cameroon. This work pays particular attention on the cruel treatment of people who exercise the right to association and peaceful assembly. We use videos to show how these rights were violated in Ambazonia. We argue that the videos helped to globalize the crisis and attract the attention of the international community to the severity of the killings and abuse.

3. Data collection and interpretation

In the age of smartphones, images or video-making has become less problematic as most people even in the third world possess a smartphone with a built-in camera. They take pictures of what is relevant to them in their daily lives. They usually film the remarkable, the extraordinary, the exceptional and not the ordinary or everyday activities [12]. From the onset of the Anglophone crisis, participants made many videos to expose the human right abuses of the military and they flooded the Internet. That was why the government cut-off the Internet in the English-speaking areas to stop them from circulating incriminating images.

We decided then to collect 30 videos to analyze them because they provide information that cannot be provided by other types of data. They are used as 'proofs of facts' and as it is often said, a picture or video is more, and different, than a thousand words because they contain much more visual information on bodily movement and include acoustic data. Although images are specific reality constructions, ambivalent, subjective and diffuse, their interpretation must be substantiated in words [13].

The videos collection contribute toward answering a research question and are interpreted by providing verbal accounts and linked to the theoretical concept of cultural dominance and media and information communication. The questions we asked concerning each of the videos were similar to those asked by Becker [14]: What are the acts of violence and human rights abuses in each video? How can they be interpreted and linked to our theoretical concept? What insight do they generate and substantiate? What different kinds of people are there? We link observations to theoretical concepts such as status, groups, norms, rules, and common understandings, deviance and rule violation, sanctions and conflict resolution.

4. The Ambazonia uprising

The relationship that exists between Southern Cameroon and La République du Cameroon is one of two people, two inheritances, and two divergent mentalities: one struggles for its liberation, while the other suppresses and abuses its human rights or struggles to maintain control over it by using its mighty state military. They speak different languages with little or no rapprochement although they live in the same country. The various videos below clearly show the differences. The oppressors' troops speak in French, while the oppressed speaks in Pidgin English. A country divided predominantly by language although language is not the cause of the Anglophone crisis: it is the history of people. This shows the struggle between the two people and languages while one is resisting the onslaught and domination, the other is trying very hard to overcome and crush them. Having been oppressed for long, the oppressed is not willing to give up and the oppressor is not willing to let her leave her unitary state, and then the struggle of two people stiffens. The government that has been in power for over 38 years does everything to suppress the uprising by sending its brutal security forces to harass the Anglophones who are striking for a just course.

According to Cameroon Concord News 2019 [15], "being Anglophone or francophone in Cameroon is not just the ability to speak, read and use English or French as a working language. It is about belonging to the Anglophone or Francophone ways including things like outlook, culture and how local governments are run. Anglophones have long complained that their language and culture are marginalized". They thought it necessary to protect their judicial, educational and local government systems. They wanted an end to annexation and assimilation and more respect from government for their language and political philosophies. They preferred a total separation by creating their own independent state if the government failed to listen to them.

According to www.Amnesty.org [16], "towards the end of 2016, the two Anglophones regions were rocked by demonstrations and strikes, initially led by lawyers, teachers, students, and eventually involving a wider section of the population. They protested against what they viewed as the growing marginalization of the Anglophone linguistic, cultural, educational traditions and systems in various sectors such as the failure to use the Common Law in courts and Standard English in classrooms, as well as the improvement of their representation in politics".

They decided to express their grievances by protesting. The protests began in the streets of Anglophone cities as thousands of Anglophone Cameroonians, from lawyers and teachers as well as irate youth, protested against the Francophone hegemony. Handfuls of videos show young men manifesting determination and strength for change in the Southern Cameroon-Ambazonia. They collaborated especially when one of them was shot because they were conscious of their marginalization. They knew the police would shoot them but they moved on. This shows that a disillusioned unemployed youth is very dangerous for the health of a country. They all hungered for independence and not even federalism that some elite would talk of. Although largely, but not always peaceful in nature, these protests were met with sustained repressions from the Cameroon authority and security forces. Some peaceful protesters were killed during the demonstrations; hundreds of people were arrested and detained without trial. Our objective in this work is to analyze the confrontation between the protesters and security forces using amateur videos secretly taken by the protesters.

4.1 Cultural domination in the judiciary section

The protest began on October 6, 2016, as a sit-down strike initiated by the Cameroon Anglophone Civil Society Consortium (CACSC), an organization consisting of lawyer and teacher trade unions from the Anglophone regions of Cameroon. Barrister Agbor Balla, Dr. Fontem Neba and Tassang Wilfred led the strike.

According to Wikipedia [17], "the common lawyers of Anglophone Cameroon were said to have written an appeal letter to the government over the use of French in schools and courtrooms in the English-speaking regions of Cameroon. In an effort to protect the English culture, they began a sit-down strike in all courtrooms on October 6, 2016. Peaceful marches began with marches in the cities of Bamenda, Buea, and Limbe calling for the protection of the common law system in Anglophone Cameroon and the practice of the Common Law sub-system in Anglophone courts and not the Civil Law as it was used by French-speaking magistrates". They equally demanded for the creation of a common law school at the University of Bamenda and Buea [18].

More so, Francophones occupied all the juicy positions in the Supreme Court. Although Francophones had little or no knowledge in English and the Common Law, most of the magistrates and bailiffs in the Anglophone zone were Francophones. Anglophones lawyers were disgruntled of the domination of the Civil Law as if Cameroon was uniquely a Civil Law country. There was equally a problem of translating the Business law for Africa (OHADA) uniform acts, CEMAC code, and others because the Francophones wanted to assimilate the Common Law sub-system.

In Africanews Morning call [19], Barrister Bobga Harmony declared that the government of Cameroon had completely ignored them, which was a violation of the right to self-determination. According to him, "since 1972, they have been a progressive, an inexplicable, illegal and illegitimate erosion of the common law." He regretted that Francophones had been replacing the Common Law with the French Civil law as if Anglophones "were a conquered people." The lawyers had complained for years through writing to competent authorities before realizing that if they did not take concrete actions, they would be swallowed up by the dominant Francophone system. So they held a Common Law conference on the May 9, 2015, which was followed by a second conference in Buea where they made a declaration reinforcing their position.

Although they had sent a communiqué to the presidency of the Republic of Cameroon, nobody listened to them. Instead of defending the Common Law lawyers, the Minister of Justice insulted them in the government newspaper: Cameroon Tribune. As a result, they protested and insisted to talk only with the president of the Republic of Cameroon or his properly mandated agent because they had exhausted all negotiation with the executive and the legislature. They had filed a petition to the national assembly and the senate and they were planning to file a petition to the constitutional council for the determination of the question of whether there had been any act of union between West Cameroon and East Cameroon. They planned to proceed to the international jurisdiction like the African Commission for Human and People's Right, the Human Right Commission if the government did not listen to them. Bobga Harmony said "We are going to seize the international community because these are grave abuses of human rights. The international community cannot fold its arms and allow us to be brutalized in our land," Barrister Bobga Harmony said in Africanews Morning Call [19].

4.2 Cultural domination in the educational section

Teachers and the general public joined the lawyers in the strike. They reportedly opposed what was described as the "imposition of French in schools in Anglophone parts of the country." According to Catherine Soi reporting for Aljazeera [20], students battled on their own at school because even private school teachers had deserted classroom in support of the public sector teachers and so many classrooms and schools across Ambazonia were empty. They wanted the government to stop sending teachers who spoke only in French or Pidgin English. Even students supported the strike action because after completing school, they were unable to find jobs.

"For over fifty years Anglophone students have not been able to have a headway in Cameroon in most disciplined that bring about development: science and technology because the government has refused to train teachers for our schools," declared Tassang Wilfred over Aljazeera (2016).

According to University of Buea strike Report [21], a mammoth crowd of students came out protesting in order to attract the authority of the university attention to their plights. A student carried a placard on which it was written: "enough is enough." They had a variety of complaints: the non-payment of the 50,000frs CFA that the government had promised them, the cancelation of the 10,000frs CFA penalty fees for the late payment of school fees, and the payment of fees before being given a semester result, and as it was the general cry with the secondary and high schools in the Anglophone zone, they also demanded the removal of French-speaking lecturers from the faculty of the university.

They stood in front of the Administrative Block wishing to meet the Vice Chancellor to tell her their problems but instead security forces took her away and a huge number of security forces were sent to dispatch them. As they arrived, the students ran into different directions and the atmosphere became very misty because the security officers had thrown teargas and fired gun shots in the air. The students shouted no violence as they ran away for safety. Although students were beaten and arrested, it did not dampen the spirit of the strike action so the students left and marched into the street.

4.3 The white coffin revolution

According to Bamenda protest close to one hundred wounded [22], protesting residents voice other grievances, including – poor roads, no jobs and water. "On November 21, 2016, Mancho Bibixy, the newscaster of a local radio station, stood in an open casket in a crowded roundabout in the Anglophone city of Bamenda. Using a blow horn, Bibixy denounced the slow rate of economic and structural development in the city."

"When that Chinese them di come, m-e-y they come tell we when they dig road, na we di fix'am back," he declared his discontent with the bad state of roads that Chinese would only construct but would not repair. He showed his defiant attitude by declaring he was ready to die while protesting against the social and economic marginalization of Anglophone in the hegemonic Francophone state.

"I don tell them, if na teargas I go drink'am."

"Let them chase me....it won't mean anything to me," he declared.

He emerged as a key leader in the Anglophone political movement who were among the first to be arrested and he was later slammed a 15-year prison term (**Figure 1**).

In a video entitled "Bamenda Protest Close to 100 wounded," [22] it shows how the white coffin was carried about and a mammoth crowd of young men followed it with Bibixy himself leading.

"We can never be defeated by the police," they declared when the police came to stop them. They rounded-up one of them and chased the others who came to stop their peaceful march. One can clearly hear a voice saying in the video:

"You no take hi gun?" asking whether he has not taken his gun.

"Cameroon must change,"

"That independent na today where i go start o-o," which means: the independence will start today.

Young men came in their bikes honing while those who were on foot shouted. Protesters were all over the whole streets.

"I say... bamenda di hot yah," they said in the background.

"We need change in Bamenda," they said.

"whosai the police them dey where they di try their nonsense, make them come now," they declared with determination.

Then suddenly trucks of military men arrived shooting in the air and killed a good number and wounded about a hundred.

Figure 1.
The White Coffin Revolution. Source: https://www.google.com/search?q=picture+of+white+coffin.

"Jesus, they are killing us in Bamenda," they said. Another truck arrived on which it was written "Gendarmerie Nationale" and it sprayed huge amount of water on a hostel: Grand Plaza; certainly where some of the protesters were hiding. The video shows how two persons hurriedly took away a shot person on a bike and some were taken and given private treatment at homes.

In a video entitled: Bamenda Boiling, they Escaped Teargas, on December, 8th 2016 [23], shows some young men shouting loudly and running away as fast as they could from the police who were throwing teargas on them to stop them from manifesting. Some covered their nostrils with handkerchiefs to prevent them from inhaling the toxic gas.

The struggle as well was not only between the Francophone and Anglophone but also between the Anglophone and their elite who enjoyed juice positions in the government and were not ready to resign from their positions. They were enablers: the government used them to crush their own people. They always would preach anti-struggle campaign and would bring other Francophone authorities to fight against their people. Each time they visited the Anglophone zone, there was always a battle between them and their people. The elite wanted to maintain the status quo, while the general population wanted a change.

The video Bamenda Boys against CPDM [24] shows a comic scene where a young man brought a large catapult and took a stone to support the big stick and another one pulled the rope from behind him and then they took the catapult to confront the CPDM barons. According to Zigolo Tchaya 2016 [25] reporting for France 24, when the Prime Minister of Cameroon (an Anglophone) and the Secretary General of the Cameroon People's Democratic Movement, the party of the government in power, went to Bamenda to hold a pro-government rally with its militants to calm down the striking lawyers and the teachers' association, who had been striking for 2 months, a group of young men burnt the CPDM party uniform of an elderly person who was going to attend the rally. The angry youth blocked the hotel where the Prime Minister and Secretary where lodging and there was a confrontation between them and the security. According to Gigova [26], it led to four deaths and several wounded and about 50 arrested. The Prime Minister, The CPDM Secretary General, the Governor of the North West region, and the national security adviser were forced to go into hiding.

5. Government response and human rights violations

Cameroon 2018 Human Rights Report [27] states that "although the law provides for freedom of peaceful assembly, the government often restricted this right. The law requires organizers of public meetings, demonstrations, and processions to notify officials in advance and does not require prior government approval of public assemblies, nor does it authorize the government to suppress public assembles that it has not approved in advance. However, officials routinely asserted the law implicitly authorizes the government to grant or deny permission for public assemblies".

It equally states that, "the government often refused to grant permits for gatherings and used force to suppress assemblies for which it had not issued permits. Authorities typically cited "security concerns" as the basis for deciding to block assemblies. The government also prevented civil society organizations and political parties from holding press conferences. Police and gendarmes forcibly disrupted meetings and demonstrations of citizens, trade unions, and political activists, arrested participants in unapproved protests, and blocked political leaders from attending protests."

In the Stream: Alzeera 2017 [28], Anne Marie Befoune put it as "The strike action is a reflection of a bigger problem, people have had a lot of pains, frustration and anger in their hearts and they were just looking for the slightest opportunity to express what they feel." The irony is that each time the security forces brutalized the protesters, they instead united against the common enemy, which was the government security forces.

Government responded by cruelly torturing and exerting inhuman or degrading treatments or punishment on demonstrators. Although the constitution and law prohibit such practices, there were reports that security force members beat, harassed, or otherwise abused citizens, including separatist fighters. Cases have been documented of how security forces severely mistreated suspected separatists and detainees [27].

Below we show videos that demonstrate gross human rights violation of the lawyer, the students and the general public.

5.1 Molestation of lawyers

The government sent over 5000 troops to thwart the Anglophone crisis. According to Zigolo [25] reporting for France 24 [25], the crisis was considered to be "a strong organized and well-coordinated violence from angry protesters and government did not want to allow that part of the country to be destroyed and the protesters too said they would not stop protesting until the government solved their problem".

According to *StopBlaBlaCam* [29], policemen blew the 'the men in uniform': lawyers with their batons in Buea. The whole city was also under lockdown, monitored by Special Rapid Response (ESIR), the police and gendarmerie. There was also a strong police presence to face the demonstrators. Incidentally, the policemen were demanding that the lawyers hand over their black robes.

On November 10, 2016, the demonstration of lawyers in Buea in the Southwest region met with heavy-handed police response. Lawyers were reportedly brutalized, their offices ransacked, and their wigs and gowns seized by police. Many were injured and harassed in their cars. Their phones were seized and destroyed, and some were barred from joining the demonstrators. Police reportedly raided hotels in search for lawyers and were harassed by law enforcement officers (**Figure 2**).

Figure 2.
Confrontation between the police and lawyers. Source: Cameroon Online [30].

The video entitled: Uprising 4 Police Brutality on Lawyers [31] clearly shows the commotion that took place in the Muea police station. One sees a police officer running after a young lawyer and then another lawyer is pushed into the police station by yet another policeman. Another lawyer is beaten and pushed out of the police station. The police kicks another who falls down and his watch falls off but the police pulls him up by dragging his coat. A female fat police encourages her colleague to hit the lawyer by clearly articulating the phrase in French "frappe," "frappez-lui" over and over.

The episodes of police brutality in Cameroon were not limited to lawyers only; it extended to University of Buea students as well as the general public. Many were molested by police and disturbing videos show police officers armed with stick hitting or rolling them in water, invading students' quarters and beating them.

5.2 Molestation against university students

The videos show appalling images of how French-speaking soldiers, who were alienated from the sufferings of English-speaking citizens, inflicted pains on them. Although they were in the same country, they could not communicate because they spoke different languages.

The video Police and Gendarmes severely torturing University Students in Buea strike [32] certainly was filmed while in the house because of the iron bars of the window. In it, two policemen force a student to lie down very fast: "Couches-toi" the police ordered him to lie down.

"Comment ca," the young man retaliated by asking why.

"Couche-toi vite," he ordered again.

"Ne parle pas," "viens ici," "Enleve la cle ci," "viens d'abord ici, regarde la bas," they continuously ordered him. Then one of them raises his baton and hits him while the other forces him to lie down while they hit him counting the number of strokes in French. The police standing by takes the baton from his colleague and asks the students to roll on the soil while he hits him with all his force. "Tourne, c'est votre pays-ci?" he asked whether it was his country. "Vous savez que vous allez gravez?" he asked while hitting him whether he knew they would go on strike.

The video entitled "2 police and Gendarmes severely torturing University Students in Buea, Buea strike [33] shows with a lot of noise in the background, two policemen harassing university students in their neighborhood. Three university students are laying down, one in a puddle and a female student is brought in and the police man brutally pushed her in the puddle.

"Attend d'abord, je vais te giffler hei," the policeman said in French threatening to slap the girl and then the girl's leg is pulled and is forcefully pulled in the puddle, rubbing her head in it.

"They go kill man," they camera man exclaimed that they would kill them.

The Southern Cameroon updates: Police Brutality at UB 28/11/2016 [34] certainly taken from a story building shows how a group of police and gendarmes in the street of Molyko molested a young man. While one of the policemen was pulling him ahead, another one came from behind and kicked him and he fell down. It is clearly seen how one of the security officers had wounded a female student's head, one also sees a student whose t-shirt had been torn and blood dripping from his head.

The video: Université de Buéa - les forces de l'ordre entrent dans les residences et tortuent des etudiants [35] starts with the camera woman inviting fellow students to run for safety. "Yuna enter o-o-o-h," she invited other students. Then students are seen running very fast into their residence for safety as scores of security men followed them behind with batons. They caught some married women and hit them severely. "They go kill we that married woman them, I swear," the camera women lamented. A woman is drawn from her house and mercilessly hit by the security officers. "Pour les hommes faire les descendre," an order is given in French to bring out all men. "Faire descendre tout les hommes," the order is repeated for emphasis. A boy is removed from his house and the French-speaking security officers hit his head with their batons.

"Amenez-le, ca va," an order is given and the boy is held from his belt.

The Centre for Human Rights and Democracy in Africa [36] reported that at least 14 student hostels were attacked that day. More than 140 rooms were vandalized, their occupants tortured on the Buea (Molyko) main boulevard, and some students were asked to sing that "an Anglophone will never rule the country." Even though most students were finally released, several of them spent 3 days in detention facilities in overcrowded cell conditions, with little or no communication with their families.

5.3 The molestation of the general public

The video Bamenda in turmoil today December, 2006, part 1 [37] shows a group of predominantly young men lamenting because a police had shot one of the protesters who wore a t-shirt with white and red lines on it, stained by blood and mud. He lay helplessly in the hands of his comrades.

"Oh my God, wait, wait. Bring he s-o, hold i hand," they held him and he dangled in their hands while those around him lamented.

The video This is Bamenda [38] shows a group of young men carrying peace plants and marching very fast in a street in Bamenda. They were carrying a dead young man to the main street in Bamenda called the Commercial Avenue. The commentator said "Bamenda is turning into something else," which means that many people are dying in Bamenda, and then he calls on "BBC, CNN and Alzeera, you guys need to support us, people are dying," he said. The spectators and the participants shouted and lamented.

"Y-e-e-u-h Bamenda, Bamenda, Bamenda, Bamenda," he shouted several times.

"w-e–e–e-h massa," he shouted several times again. Then the dead man is shown with a blue band that fastened him to the stick he was tied. He is being carried away by other young men marching very fast and singing: "Amba, Amba, Ambazonia." It means they identify themselves more with Ambazonia than Cameroon.

5.4 Internet shutdown

The various videos incriminated Cameroon security forces and therefore as a result as [27] shows Cameroon experienced its first Internet shutdown in January 2017 for 93 days. It came after Anglophone teachers, lawyers, and students went on strike over alleged social bias in favor of Francophones. Education, financial, and health-care institutions as well as businesses that relied on Internet access were stunted. International bodies applied pressure on the government to restore Internet access. Despite Internet access being restored in April 2017, there were continuing reports of network instability. In October 2017, the government effected a second Internet blockade, targeting social media and apps such as Whatsapp and Facebook where such videos as those described above were sent. It continuously affected the country economically, and many citizens were forced to travel back and forth to regions with Internet access for business or information.

6. The Ambazonian war

Two weeks into the protests, more than 100 protesters were arrested, and six were reported dead [39]. Throughout September, separatists carried out two bombings: one targeting security forces in Bamenda Quartz Africa [40], and while the first bombing failed, the second injured three policemen Reuter [41]. On September, 22, Cameroonian soldiers opened fire on protesters, killing at least five and injuring many more [40]. On November 30, 2017, the president of Cameroon declared war on the Anglophone separatists Sun Newspaper [42].

"I have learned with emotion the assassination of four Cameroonians military and two policemen in the South of our country --- things must henceforth be clear. Cameroon is victim of repetitive attacks claiming a secessionist movement. Facing these aggression acts, I would reassure Cameroonians that everything has been put in place to take out of the dark these criminals so that peace and security reigns all over the territory." This marked the start of a very violent confrontation between government forces and armed separatists.

Non-state actors, including local armed groups, also bear much responsibility for the violence. Separatist militias are battling government forces as well as pro-government "self-defense" forces that consist of what separatists term criminal gangs who are terrorizing local inhabitants and wreaking havoc. The military also conducts a deliberate violent campaign against civilian population. Lawyer Right Watch Canada [43], "There is evidence that much of the violence is intentional and planned, including retaliation attacks on villages by government security forces, often followed by indiscriminate shooting into crowds of civilians, invasion of private homes and the murder of their inhabitants, and the rounding up and shooting of villagers."

According to the International Crisis Group, at least 1850 people have been killed since 2017; the ICG reports that at least 235 soldiers and police officers and 650 civilians, and close to 1000 separatists have lost their lives; and Anglophone federalists estimate 3000–5000 dead, and separatists estimate 5000–10,000 dead.

6.1 The consequences of the war

6.1.1 Arbitrary arrests and detentions

The Centre for Human Rights and Democracy in Africa [44] reports that in early January 2017, the Cameroon Anglophone Civil Society Consortium (Consortium or CACSC) agreed to meet with the government about the release of protesters arrested during a 2016 demonstration in Bamenda. The Consortium accused the government for shooting four unarmed youth and proceeded to declare "Ghost Towns" on January 16 and 17. The reports equally state that, "in response, the government cut the Internet and banned the activities of two groups: the Southern Cameroon National Council (SCNC) and the Consortium on January 17, 2017. The same day, two prominent Anglophone civil society activists who headed the Consortium: Dr Felix Agbor NKongho and Dr Fontem Neba were arrested".

On January 9, 2017, armed soldiers forcibly entered the home of Mr Mancho Bibixy, a journalist and Newscaster of "Abakwa" (a local radio program reporting on the rights of the Anglophone minority), and arrested him, along with six other activists. He was taken to a vehicle with neither shoes nor identification papers and was arbitrarily detained for 18 months and his hearings were postponed for more than 14 times.

On May 25, 2018, Bibixy and his co-accused were sentenced to between 10 and 15 years of prison each by a military court, for acts of terrorism, secession, hostilities against the state, propagation of false information, revolution, insurrection, contempt of public bodies and public servants, resistance, depredation by band, and non-possession of national identity card. He was being held in an overcrowded cell at the Kondengui Central Prison, a maximum-security prison in Yaoundé.

Between September 22 and October 17, 2017, 500 people were arrested, with witnesses describing the detainees as being packed into jails in the South West region. In December 2017, a group of about 70 heavily armed Cameroonian soldiers and BIR sealed the village of Dadi and arrested 23 people returning from their farm or were in front of their homes.

On January 5, 2018, 47 separatist activists, including Sisiku Ayuk Tabe of the proclaimed Interim Government of Ambazonia, were arrested and detained by Nigeria authorities in Abuja. The detainees were repatriated afterwards and imprisoned in Yaoundé incommunicado for 6 months awaiting trials. They were not given access to their lawyers nor charged with any offense.

Mass arrests and detentions have caused harsh and often life-threatening prison conditions in Cameroon, including gross overcrowding, lack of access to water and medical care, and deplorable hygiene and sanitation. Prisoners are transferred out of the region to other more secure areas.

6.1.2 Internally displaced persons (IDPS)

Several hundred thousand persons abandoned their homes in some localities of the Northwest and Southwest Regions because of the socio-political unrest. Estimate of IDPs varied depending on the source, with the government estimating 74,994 IDPs as of June, while the United Nations estimated 350,000 IDPs from the Northwest and Southwest as of September.

On December 2017, the Senior Divisional Officer for Manyu: Oum II Joseph asked the population of Manyu residents in Akwanga, Eyumojock, and Mamfe sub-division to relocate or they would be considered accomplices or perpetrators of ongoing criminal occurrences registered on security and defense forces [45].

By the end of December 2018, the crisis had forced mass displacement of the population in the North West and South West regions, with estimates of between 450,000 and 550,000 displaced persons. This represents more than 10% of the region's population. Cameroon now has the sixth largest displaced population in the world. Many are fleeing violence as a result of raids on villages and surrendering areas. They take refuge in the forests where they lack hygiene, health services, sanitation, shelter and food. The United Nations Office for the Coordination of Humanitarian assistance estimates that approximately 32,000 Cameroonians are registered refugees in Nigeria. More than 200 villages have been partly or completely destroyed, forcing hundreds of thousands of people to flee. The rate of attacks has increased steadily, usually causing significant damage. An additionally 30,000 to 35,000 people have sought asylum in neighboring countries.

6.1.3 Destruction of schools and villages

Separatist activists who seek an independent state for the country's English-speaking regions began to set fire on schools and attack teachers and students to enforce a boycott they had declared on local schools. In June 2018, UNICEF reported that at least 58 schools had been damaged since the beginning of the crisis in 2016. Human Rights Watch documented 19 threats or attacks on schools, and 10 threats or attacks on education personnel (**Figure 3**).

Most children in the two regions have been deprived of the right to an education, with 30, 000–40,000 children affected. As of June 2018, armed separatists

Figure 3.
Government soldiers supervising the burning of a school and a burnt school [46].

Figure 4.
Genocide in Ambazonia, burning of villages and IDPs [45].

had reportedly attacked 42 schools, at least 36 of which were burnt down; the Cameroonian's figure indicated that they had burnt at least 120 schools. Rural areas are especially affected.

Anglophone villages suspected of harboring separatists or arms have been burned and pillaged in both the South West and North West regions. Homes have been burned to ashes, sometimes with their inhabitants. About 206 settlements have been raided and partially destroyed by state defense forces during attempts to crack down on armed separatists. Several villages in Mbonge and Konye subdivision have been completely emptied of their population. Civilian witnesses say that army attacks are routinely followed by the ransacking of houses and shops, the destruction of food stocks, and the rounding up and mistreatment or killing of civilians, often as reprisals for their killing of a member of the defense and security forces (**Figure 4**).

7. Discussions

One of the key ways social movements engage in cultural resistance is by means of the production and dissemination of multiple forms of media in order to mobilize support, to reach out for supports beyond those already in agreement with movement claims, and to increase the legitimacy of their claims and demands. Social movements operate at a considerable disadvantage when trying to influence news portrayals of issues than do their better-funded opposing groups and organization.

Anglophones or Ambazonians who are defending themselves from the Cameroon security forces that kill them are presented in the state television and other media as "terrorists" and never as those fighting for a just course, whereas as seen above, they did not start the war; it was declared on them. The main stream media equally promoted hate speech and incitement to violence, which radicalized separatist groups the more. Government officials refer to protesters in dehumanizing or incendiary terms, such as "dogs" and "terrorists" in the main stream media. When the security agents who terrorize the population are presented in mainstream media, they are considered as valiant and patriotic agents of the republic who protect the population. Did they really protect the population when they tortured them, arbitrarily arrested them, and burned their houses as seen above?

Therefore, media serve to propagandize and serve the interests of the powerful that control and finance them. The propaganda model shows that media function to represent the agendas of the dominant social, economic and political groups that exercise power nationally and globally. Therefore, social movements face difficulties in their attempts to transmit their claims and to traverse the gap between their intended messages and their target audiences.

Activists in the Ambazonian crisis created a strategy that Mattoni [47] considered as alternatives that are the creation of their own independent media or public forums of communication in order to communicate for a lack of interest or bias by established media. Alternatively, in the Ambazonian crisis, many videos were produced that facilitated the mobilization and production of a counter-narrative to the 'official story,' which indicates that there is no Anglophone problem in Cameroon and the professionalism of the security forces. The Internet makes the process of sharing easier and faster and with a potentially larger audience than ever before. These messages in the videos from the alternative media environment have made their ways into mainstream mass media like the various reports carried by BBC, France 24, TV5 Monde, etc.

8. Conclusion

The Ambazonia crisis was triggered by the Southern Cameroonians' attempt to break the dominant Francophone cultural hegemony. They came into union with them from a weaker position with a population numerically smaller. As a result, La République du Cameroon has been making efforts not just to dominate them but to absorb them into the broader Francophone cultural system. They silently destroyed the dignity and statehood of Anglophones-not by the French-speaking community at large, but by the government that was led and dominated by Francophones.

Toward the end of 2016, the two Anglophone regions were rocked by demonstrations and strikes, initially led by lawyers, teachers, and students and eventually involving a wider section of the population. They protested against what they viewed as the growing marginalization of the Anglophone linguistic, cultural, educational traditions and systems in various sectors such as the failure to use the Common Law in courts and Standard English in classrooms, as well as the improvement of their representation in politics.

Many videos were produced showing their repressive response of the government, which were opposed to the official narratives produced by the main stream media. We collected 30 of them because they provide information that cannot be provided by other types of data. They are used as 'proofs of facts.' The videos show appalling images not just of how French-speaking soldiers tortured Anglophones but also their inability to communicate with them adequately although they share the same country.

The government response to the demonstration led to the violation of the following rights: the right to life, liberty, and security of persons; the right to be free from torture or cruel, degrading and unusual treatment; the right to be free from arbitrary arrest and detention; the right to association and peaceful assembly; the right to equality before and equal protection of the law; the right to take part in the conduct of public affairs; the right to have criminal charges and rights determined by a competent, impartial and independent tribunal (and in the case of civilians, a civilian court); the right to a fair trial, representation by a lawyer of choice, and (where the defendant does not have means to pay for legal representation) legal aid; the right to prompt, detailed notice of charges in a language understood by the defendant and adequate time and facilities to prepare a defense against them and communicate with counsel; the right to an interpreter where required; the right to appeal; the right not to be persecuted for any act or omission that was not a crime when committed; and the right to self-determination.

Author details

Nanche Billa Robert
Department of Sociology, Anthropology and Social Sciences for Development, Faculty of Arts, Letters and Social Sciences, University of Maroua, Cameroon

*Address all correspondence to: nanchefile@yahoo.co.uk

References

[1] Christina F. Sociology for Globalising Societies: Social Movements and Globalisation—How Protests, Occupations and Uprising are Changing the World. New York: Palgrave Macmillan; 2014

[2] Salmond M. The power of momentary communities. Aether. 2010:90-100

[3] Entman R. Framing. Journal of Communication. 1993;**43**:51-58

[4] Marx K, Engels F. The German Ideology. New York: International Publishers Co; 1970. p. 1845

[5] I.C.B. Dear, editor. The Oxford Companion to World War II "United Nations Trusteeship Council, 1961. Report of the United Nations Commissioner for the Supervision of the Plebiscites in the Southern and Northern Parts of the Trust Territory of the Cameroons Under United Kingdom Administration" PDF; 1995

[6] Wikipedia, Free Encyclopedia. History of Cameroon. Available from: https://en.wikipedia.org/wiki/History_of_Cameroon

[7] Achankeng F. The Foumban constitutional talks and prior intentions of negotiating: A historico-theoretical analysis of a false negotiation and the ramifications for political developments in Cameroon. Journal of Global Initiatives: Policy; Pedagogy, Perspective. 2014;**9**:129-154

[8] Takougang J, Amin JA. Post-Colonial Cameroon: Politics, Economics, and Society. New York: Lexington Books; 2018. pp. 78-80

[9] Chem-Langhee B. The road to the unitary state of Cameroon 1959-1972. 2004

[10] Ajong Mbahpndah Laurean. Is Independence the Answer for S. Cameroon? Peace and Conflict Monitor. University for Peace; 2006. Available from: http://www.monitor.upeace.org/archive.cfm?id_article=378

[11] Lansdorf T. "Cameroon". Political Handbook of the World 2016-2017. CQ Press; 2017. pp. 236-246

[12] Ebele TS. Collecting Images as Data in Qualitative Data Collection. In: Flick U, editor. London: London Sage Publication; 2018

[13] Collier J, Collier M. Visual Anthropology: Photography as a Research Method. Albuquerque: University of New Mexico Press; 1986

[14] Becker HS. Visual evidence: A Seventh Man, the specified generalisation, and the work of the reader. Visual Studies. 2002;**17**(1):3-11

[15] Cameroon Concord News. 2019. Available from: http://www.cameroonconcordnews.com/category/life/page/3/

[16] Available from: www.Amnesty.org

[17] Wikipedia, Free Encyclopedia. 2016-2017 Cameroonian Protest. 2019. Available from: https://en.wikipedia.org/wiki/2016%E2%80%932017_Cameroonian_protests

[18] Anglophone Cameroon: Common Law Lawyers Protest—Contra Nocendi International. Contranocendi.org; 2017

[19] Africanews Morning Call: Cameroon's Lawyer. 2016

[20] Catherine Soi. Cameroon Language Strike. English Teachers Say No to French. Aljazeera; 2016

[21] University of Buea Strike Report. Available from: https://www.youtube.com/watch?v=w70vJprHtdU

[22] Bamenda Protest Close to One Hundred Wounded. Available from: https://www.youtube.com/watch?v=c0IfFQV7zvc

[23] Bamenda Boiling, they Escaped Teargas. 2016. Available from: https://ambaland.com:/b [Accessed: 8 December 2016]

[24] Bamenda Boys Against CPDM. Available from: https://www.youtube.com/watch?v=c0IfFQV7zvc

[25] Zigolo T. Les Anglophone de Bamenda France 24. 2016. Available from: https://www.youtube.com/watch?v=0zfvcnbapSU

[26] Gigova R. Rights Groups Call for Probe into Protesters' Deaths in Cameroon, CCN. Available from: https://www.cnn.com/2016/12/15/world/cameroon-protesters-deaths/index.html [Accessed: 15 December 2016]

[27] Cameroon. Human Rights Report: Country Reports on Human Rights Practices for 2018 United States Department of States. Bureau of Democracy, Human Rights and Labour; 2018

[28] Stream: Anglophone Protes over Cameroon Francophone Administration. Alzeera; 2017

[29] StopBlaBlaCam. (True or False?) Two Anglophone Lawyers beaten up in Buea. 2007. Available from: http://stopBlaBlacam.com/culture-and-society/1511-177-two-anglophone-lawyers beaten-up-in-Buea

[30] Cameroon Online: Crise Anglophone: Buea and Bamenda sous forte Militarisation. Available from: https://237cameroun.online/en/node/14527 [Accessed: 28 September 2017]

[31] Uprising 4: Police brutality on Lawyers. 2016. Available from: https://www.youtube.com/watch?v=-feBb4WWmn8

[32] Police and Gendarmes severely torturing University Students in Buea strike Nov 28, 2016 (1). Available from: https://www.youtube.com/watch?v=SRpENBgjnRg

[33] Police and Gendarmes Severely Torturing University Students in Buea, Buea Strike. 2016. Available from: www.youtube.com/watch?v=v-p9Yw.2my4 [Accessed: 28 November 2016]

[34] The Southern Cameroon Updates: Police Brutality at UB. 2016. https://www.youtube.com/watch?v=HoF33CYSZWo [Accessed: 28 November 2016]

[35] Université de Buéa - les forces de l'ordre entrent dans les residences et tortuent des etudiants. Available from: https://www.youtube.com/watch?v=SNX5Y3d54E8

[36] The Centre for Human Rights and Democracy in Africa: Cameroon Unfolding Castatrophe. Evidence of Human Rights Violations and Crimes against Humanity; 2019

[37] Bamenda in Turmoil Today December, 2006 Part 1. Available from: https://www.youtube.com/watch?v=Oh_KOlMIkXo

[38] This is Bamenda. Available from: https://www.youtube.com/watch?v=HpeUsylzcH0

[39] BBC NEWS. Arrests in Cameroon Language Protest. 2016. Available from: http://Web.archive.org/web/20170911183649http:/www.bbc.com/news/world-africa38078238

[40] Quartz. The crisis in Cameroon's English-Speaking regions has turned violent with Bombing. 2017. Available from: http://qz.com/1084943/cameroons-anglophone-crisis-turns-violent-as-president-paul-biya-speaks-at-unga-2017/

[41] Reuter. Suspected Separatists Bomb Wounds "Police in Cameroon's Anglophone Region. 2017. Available from: http://www.reuter.com/article/us-cameroon-politics-blast/suspected-separatist-bomb-wound-3-police-Cameroon-anglophone-regioniduckcinbw2C9

[42] Biya Declares War on Anglophone Separatists- The Sun Newspaper, Cameroon; 2017 [Accessed: 05 December 2017]

[43] Lawyer Right Watch Canada. Cameroon's Unfolding Castrophe/ Report; 2019

[44] Centre for Human Rights and Democracy in Africa Reports 553,775 Persons Displaced. Upsurge of IDPs in Cameroon's Anglophone Regions. 2018. Available from: https://chrda.org/2018/12/20/upsurge-ofidps-in-cameroons-Anglophone-regions// [Accessed: 20 December 2018]

[45] Available from: https://ambazoniagenocidelibrary.com

[46] Available from: https://www.google.com/search?sxsrf=ACYBGNSTGWizo2P9-P9Wj1aj

[47] Mattoni A. Media Practices and Protests Politics. Burlington: Ashgate; 2012

Chapter 10

Humans: The Biggest Barrier to Realising Human Rights - A South African Perspective

Erika Serfontein

Abstract

In demarcating the law, human rights, and human behaviour, the objective is to explore the tension between safeguarding human rights and promoting individual autonomy. While international human rights law signifies the potential of creating dignified life experiences, the behaviour of humans, and, specifically, of those in government incited my focus on the effect of human behaviour on the realizsation of human rights. By studying human rights through a philosophical lens, a (a) conceptual clarification of human rights is provided, (b) the most prominent human rights are identified, (c) general and specific justifications of human rights discussed, and (d) the normative implications of human right claims explored. Focus is placed on South Africa although the value and potential generalisation generalization of the data for evaluating the effectiveness of human rights in achieving their social goal globally, are acknowledged. Reviewing literature, an overview is provided of the law and human rights; the different dimensions of human rights; and human behaviour. Persistent human rights violations, albeit legal protection, are delineated and the significant role played by human behaviour during such violations are highlighted. Given that human behaviour is influenced by various ethical, social, and legal principles, governments are urged to be mindful of the well-being of the humans they are ethically and legally obliged to serve.

Keywords: human rights, human rights law, human behaviour, law, natural law, ethics, morals and values, human dignity, respect, South Africa, philosophical views

1. Introduction

When Nelson Mandela became the President of South Africa in 1994, he identified one major challenge that lied ahead, namely, the establishment of a social order in which individual liberty truly entails the freedom of the individual. To meet this challenge, he advocated behaviour aimed at restoring the human dignity of each and every South African as guaranteed, alongside a wide variety of other individual fundamental rights, in the Constitution of the Republic of South Africa, Act 108 of 1996 (hereafter the Constitution).

Mandela noted the importance of human rights as well as their practical realisation to give effect to such rights. Whether the formal acceptance of internationally recognised human rights in their constitutions and other national legislation by governments around the globe is a mere symbolic gesture or a true reflection of a commitment to and an internalisation of the demarcated norms associated with human rights and is however yet to be established [1]. In this regard, the tension that arises between the protection of humans from being exploited and their fundamental rights violated, on the one side, and the promotion of individual autonomy and respect, on the other, needs consideration.

Given the significant role played by governments (consisting of humans) in determining the structures, formations, and circumstances under which effect can be given to human rights within their respective countries, this chapter explores the practices, norms, and values adhered to by humans and how they correspond or conflict with the goals of international human rights law through a philosophical lens. By describing and analysing both the legal and normative impact of human nature and behaviour, this chapter contributes to the understanding of contemporary sociolegal changes and its consequential implications on the effective realising of human rights. Consideration is taken of the practical reality mirroring the worldwide occurrence of daily human right infringements by humans through their behaviour, making it clear that neither the existence of natural laws nor the ratification of human right treaties is necessary congruent with their day-to-day governance of nations and that a gap exists between philosophical views pertaining to natural moral rights, idealistic legal documents guaranteeing human rights, and reality. In order to continue the philosophical debate regarding human rights, a conceptual clarification of what human rights entail is firstly provided.

2. What are human rights?

Human rights are regarded by Heard [2] as being a product of a global philosophical debate that has prolonged for over 2000 years. As a result, human rights are viewed as a continuation of the natural rights tradition which focused on the moral properties of human beings and, thus, emerged long before the adoption thereof in legal documents [3]. They encompass moral entitlements that belong to humans whether recognised by legal systems or not [4]. As moral rights and claims, they present minimum standards pertaining to human treatment to which humans are morally entitled to [5] simply because of them being human [6]. In this regard, Nussbaum [7] identified the need for a list of minimal goods or opportunities required by all humans to live decent lives—an issue that soon became a central topic in the debate on the philosophical foundations of human rights. Gusman [3] agrees by stating that the question is not whether human rights have value but rather whether their special status as being essential to ensure humans a valuable life is recognised. Along the same trend, Grotius [8] viewed human rights as part of universal laws of nature not only guiding the interaction between humans but also allowing for individual (moral) rights to self-determination.

Various authors [9–12], however, argue that rights cannot exist without being provided legal status ensuring mechanism for their enforceability. In referring to the views of philosophers such as Burke, Bentham, and Rousseau, Heard [2] similarly argues that human rights do not automatically belong to all humans detached from human endeavour as they are, par excellence, created by human action. As such, human rights are the product of both human co-existence and legal systems. Although philosophers were initially reluctant to scrutinise human rights as embedded in international and national legal systems [13], Kirchschlaeger [14] identified four different dimensions to human rights aiming at guaranteeing the safeguarding of every human in respect of the crucial areas and elements of basic human existence (life and survival). These four dimensions are forthwith employed as a framework in obtaining a holistic and integrated view of human rights.

DOI: http://dx.doi.org/10.5772/intechopen.88912

2.1 The ethical dimension of human rights

Considering the philosophical emphasis on basic moral or natural rights as well as on the very nature of rights, the ethical dimension of human rights is firstly analysed. Although philosophers measured human behaviour during premodern times against the will of God (adherence to natural moral obligations), modern times necessitate the consideration of human behaviour as being morally good or bad by measuring its degree of adherence to legally sound human rights [15]. This is due to human rights becoming central to the ethical and political discourse, indicating a weighty shift regarding how humans understand the foundations of morality.

By itself, human rights incorporate norms that are perceived to allow humans to live civilised and honourable/dignified lives [6] or lives worth living as long as they know and recognise these rights and behave according [16]. It has, moreover, become crucial for humans to be aware of the fact that they are part of a dynamic world, co-existing amongst other humans. This entails the dichotomy of man—as an individual complete whole, humans strive at self-survival placing them in basic competition with one another on the one side, whilst they, as members of a social unit, on the other side, should be dedicated to group survival [17–19].

Since human rights derived from human nature, and humans are, by nature, egoistic in that they selfishly seek individual autonomy at the cost of others [19], legal systems aim at limiting and guiding human behaviour by combining human rights with corresponding duties [17]. This entails that the human rights of others need to be respected at all times even if it may be detrimental to individual needs [13]. Human rights, subsequently, do not only provide legitimate claims, they also oblige—by way of successive waves of responsibilities—all humans to respect them and to withhold themselves from infringing upon the human rights equally conferred to others as well as to, for unselfish reasons [20, 21], protect and support those whose rights are abused or denied. With regard to the latter, Keith [1] and Kirchschlaeger [14] draw specific attention to vulnerable, marginalised human beings and those belonging to discriminated against minority groups having to endure the violation of their human rights because they simply do not possess sufficient knowledge or means to claim their rights and, thus, cannot make their voices heard. It is in this regard that Changeux [22] proposed that humans need to discern and explain the different aspirations and beliefs of human beings regarding their own mental health and life expectations to each other through extensive dialogue in order to ensure the good life all desire and to achieve a more harmonious balance between the rights of the individual and the needs of human society.

The international legal recognition of human rights aiming at giving effect to human rights is regarded as one of the greatest moral achievements of humankind [23]. This is due to the perception that an ethical system functions as a framework for the creation, manifestation, and enforcement of legal principles. In this regard, Kirchschlaeger [14] believes that a just law is a code made by humans to reflect their moral convictions, whilst unjust law comprises of codes that is not in harmony with moral laws. Since the practical realisation of human rights depends upon the conscious willingness of humans themselves to follow moral acceptable behaviour towards others [13], human rights will continue to have a strong moral foundation regardless of their legal status.

2.2 The legal dimension of human rights

According to Habermas [24], the legal dimension of human rights has not solely developed in reaction to wars of aggression and mass crimes on humankind nor can its advances be limited to a human rights regime. He contends that globalisation was the main reason behind this dimension as it highlighted the necessity to standardise moral human behaviour across national borders, thus requiring governance beyond the nation-state and the conversant legal principles that has, until now, been effective. As a direct consequence, the sovereignty of national governments (the subjects of international law) was affected, and their ability to control human behaviour was limited as they were left with less independent decision-making power regarding their traditional functions, ranging from protecting peace and physical security to warranting freedom, the rule of law, and democratic legitimation (creators of social security for its citizens). In this regard, the international human rights regime has adopted a more behavioural tone during the twenty-first century [25]. This is in line with the philosophical views of Burke, Bentham, and Rousseau [2], namely, that human rights are a product of a specific society and its prevailing legal system due to their interdependency on human behaviour rather than belonging to humans merely based on their humanness.

Because of its international legal recognition, human rights are defined by various authors [4, 25–27] as universal rights which emerged as an ideal from legal imperatives as reflected in various declarations, conventions, and treaties leading to a universal culture of human rights. International human rights law, although existing beyond the determination of specific societies [2], essentially serve as individual legal entitlements primarily against all States and State entities. Such entitlements allow humans to legitimately claim equal protection of their basic human needs, respect for their dignity, and the fulfilment of their ideal to live a life worth living [1, 6] regardless of where they live. This is in line with the philosophical views of Rousseau, claiming that people agree to live alongside others if society protects them and if human rights are used as an ethical yardstick to globally determine and criticise governments' treatment of their inhabitants [2].

Different authors [14, 23, 28, 29], to the contrary, believe that international human rights law is not universal in the sense that it cannot substitute national laws but only complement them. They believe that human rights are incompatible with their own universality as they simply apply within a specific geographical area once accepted by societies as part of their positive national legal doctrine. For human rights to have universal status, Gusman [3] contends that they must be justifiable from different moral cultures and acceptable by the majority, though not necessarily all, cultures around the globe.

In criticising the individualistic approach to universal human rights derived from Western cultures [6, 30], Mkabela [31] voices his concern over universal human rights negating the importance of a unique set of values guiding human behaviour in different communities. He opines that the significance of unique values lies in them serving as the foundation for developing practices, codes, and ethical as well as cultural standards and for directing attitudes regarding ethical behaviour amongst humans irrespective of class, ethnicity, or gender. To substantiate his argument, Mkabela [31] refers to ubuntu, a traditional value system pertinent to the African continent, incorporating moral values such as humility, modesty, conformity, and empathy forming the basis upon which individuals are viewed through a lens placing more emphasis on individual duties and responsibilities than on individual human rights.

Prominence is placed on moral values based on the mutual acceptance that the humanity of individuals is conveyed through personal interactions with others in a specific community. In view hereof, it is evident that human rights law needs the support of an equivalent moral awareness and ethos to be effective and regarded as being just. Humans do not follow legal principles purely because they fear its sanctions but rather because they believe in and share the ethical principles underscored by legal imperatives [14]. This is consistent with the nature of humans to constantly, consciously, and unconsciously adapt their behaviour in order to regard themselves as being moral persons [32].

In considering the amount of prevalent human rights violations occurring worldwide despite the existence of moral and/or legal human rights, Wolfgang [30], to the contrary, casts doubt on the social validity of human rights to bring about mutual respect amongst humans. Posner [23], likewise, criticises human rights law as he could find little evidence of it improving the general well-being of humankind. In this regard, Ajey [6] notes that the values cherished in international human rights documents arise mainly from liberal conceptions of humans and society, which gave rise to the prioritisation of civil and political rights over socio-economic rights (the rights to work, health, or education) as well as the rights of community members, despite their developmental value for humankind. In agreement, Wolfgang [30] cautions against a too optimistic view steered by the conviction that globalisation, economic growth, and legal actions alone can foster human rights. Mention is, in this regard, made of the inherent weaknesses of international human rights law to respect traditional community practices as well as the diversity amongst nations, which he regard as being incompatible with the idea of universal human rights. This leads to necessity of also taking regard of the political element influencing human rights.

2.3 The political dimension of human rights

The extent to which human rights are legally recognised within a society is directly influenced by the different political struggles societal members had to endure [2].

Experiences gained through a variety of political struggles occurring worldwide against human injustices, nevertheless, led to political deliberation, the formation of political grounded opinions and political theories, as well as the following of political processes to achieve mutually agreed upon resolutions that could enjoy global acceptance in order to prevent the reoccurrence of such injustices. This, in turn, allowed for moral human rights to be schematically transformed into legally protected human rights with the aim of ensuring their enforceability, warranting a more controlled and well-disciplined judging system as well as assuring the selection of the elements of human existence that essentially requires special protection [14].

Since the outcome of political decisions may, by itself, give rise to gross human rights infringements when extreme political action and military intervention are undertaken, justified by an attempt to bring an end to individual human rights violations [33], the law, in turn, places specific limitations on political State power [28]. By guaranteeing political rights as well as rights to development, social, economic, and cultural rights, the law moreover promotes the active political participation of individuals in political decisions affecting them, thus allowing their voices to be heard when it comes to their rights and their own lives. This is achieved through effective democratic processes and the full realisation of political and civil rights [20], thus ensuring that all States function within their legal boundaries when dealing with individuals being subjected to their behaviour [28].

In this regard, Pacilli et al. [32], however, caution that too strong identifications with political groups may lead to the dehumanisation of others not belonging to such groups. It is in this regard that emphasis must be placed on democracy as entailing more than just a political institution but rather signifying a representational and moral concept. Of its own accord, democracy embodies a value system which surpasses many aspects of social life, starting with individuals who strongly identify with democracy, filled with passion to build true democracies around the world [28]. The value of robust, safe and unwavering democracies for the realisation and protection of human rights to bring about human security cannot be overstressed [34]. The efficiency of democracies must, subsequently, be measured by the extent to which all of its members, including governments, are dedicated to ensure that human rights and laws are throughout equally respected and upheld [20]. Such dedication can be measured by dissecting the establishment and maintenance of positive human life experiences relating to political stability, economic prosperity, workable democracies, and peaceful co-existence in societies amidst the existence of potentially opposing divisions [35]. In this regard, Heard [2] emphasises that the rights of man must be held sacred, however great a sacrifice governments must make.

2.4 Human rights in its historical dimension

The historical fight for human rights started with philosophical and/or theological ideas and concepts underscored by Hobbes, Locke, and Kant regarding the need to respect the inherent worth of humans which gradually spilled over to the political sphere of national governments and, eventually, to the international domain [14]. In acknowledging the prominence of the values embedded in human rights, Gearty [36] even opines that their recognition across political and ideological borders symbolised the end of all ideologies and, thus, the end of history. It brought an end to historical periods during which human beings were not treated with dignity nor equally protected to the extent to which they deserved and, consequently, started a new moral era [23] which can be inherited by future generations [16]. In order to delineate the efficiency of such an inheritance, the human rights most prominent for current and future generations need identification.

3. Which human rights are pertinent to meaningful human existence?

After analysing various definitions proposed by researchers, Doğanay and Öztürk [37] follow a philosophical natural rights approach as underscored by numerous philosophers [38–42] by defining human rights as entailing, par excellence, universal concepts of fairness and equality. In doing so, focus is placed on the generalisation and global application of human rights as well as its origin being the very existence of humans (life, self-esteem, and the intrinsic value of dignity [6]) in relation to equality (all human beings are born equal and should be treated equally—a concept initially based on the spiritual assumption that all humans possess a soul and are part of Christ's redemption plan [5]), which they consider to be the main feature of all human rights. Based on the intrinsic worth shared by all human beings, Metz [21] contends that humans are entitled to significant moral claims to receive equal treatment. This entails treating all humans in a special manner by virtue of their capacity to cooperative rather than by an endeavouring to balance conflicting human needs and interests within society.

To Staerkle et al. [28], the rights to individual freedom and political participation are prominent as they are inherent to human nature. Ercan et al. [16], in turn, emphasise the essence of human dignity, tolerance, peace, respecting others' rights, brotherhood, solidarity, and friendship. From a philosophical point of view, the rights to human freedom/liberty and property also merits prominence although it has all along been recognised that humans naturally possess liberty [3]. Guaranteeing human freedoms has, nevertheless, became essential as humans, according to Rousseau [43], longed for their natural freedom when entering into a social contract with others, thus accepting legal systems governing their behaviour.

In the South African context, the newly appointed democratic government of 1994 adopted a final Constitution in 1996, in which mostly individual fundamental rights are guaranteed. This Constitution is regarded as a transformational document aiming at replacing the previous apartheid regime due to colonisation, riddled with racism and the unequal treatment of humans based on their individual characteristics. It is a value-driven Constitution guaranteeing fundamental rights to every human being and pertinently providing for constitutional values including transparency, democracy, equality, human dignity, and the achievement of each human's potential.

Given their prominence in the new South Africa, the rights to equality (section 9), human dignity (section 10), and life (section 11) are firstly assured. Due to its history of past inequalities towards humans and their current diverse population, the right to equality deserved special attention. It entails respecting the equal worth (mutual recognition) of all humans although they differ regarding their nature, life conditions, social circumstances, as well as personal biographies and decisions [30].

Although the Constitution does not provide for a hierarchical structure of human rights, the standing of human dignity and the right to life was elevated above all other fundamental rights in the landmark case of *S v Makwanyane,* 1995 (3) SA 391 (CC) (para. 144). The Constitutional Court made a specific mention of the political and social factors dominant in South Africa which caused a climate of aggression, revenge, and vengeance disregarding the worth and life opportunities of its inhabitants. In view hereof, it is safe to say that lived experiences in a particular society influences the manner in which human rights may be prioritised, interpreted, and perceived [26]. For South African's specifically, the rights to liberty, education, and personal gain may, for example, be more important than building a better life for future generations. As a direct result, they may be more selective of which human rights they support and which activities they demand from government to make their lives worthwhile [3].

The legal recognition of human rights on international level by the United Nation's Declaration on Human Rights placing emphasis on the fact that all human beings are born free and equal in dignity and rights as well as that humans are naturally gifted with reason and conscience that allows them to interact with others in a spirit of comradeship is also not without appraisal. Bentham [9], for example, critiques the notion of equality as an anarchical myth by noting that humans are clearly born unequal pertaining to status, property, genetic talents, and wealth, and access to the social determinants of good health and in numerous other aspects. As a direct result, he disregards the existence of natural rights and underscores the importance of legally recognised human rights. He points out that the moral componence of human rights is in direct conflict with their presumed legal status. Bentham also states that humans are not born free as babies are absolutely dependent on others for their survival. Along the same lines, he argues that human rights refer to rights which must be legally guaranteed to humans and not merely justified by legal systems. As such, he argues that the human rights discourse has moved outside the scope of moral and legal philosophers and into the hands of politicians deciding which human rights will deserve prioritisation.

The right to equality is, furthermore, criticised by Donnely [44] on the basis that humans by nature function in hierarchical relations with other humans within a society, thus automatically leaving them prone to inequalities and competition for better life opportunities. Based on the prominence of human rights and the critique against them, the justification of such rights merits discussion.

4. Can human rights be justified?

The potential of protecting human rights for enabling all humans to live quality lives lies in the fact that human rights guide humans to cope with the burdens of a dynamic society whilst influencing their own physical, mental, and emotional well-being, their economic status, knowledge wealth, access to basic services, and social security which, in turn, positively impacts on their general behaviour towards others [45].

Intrinsically, every human being must be regarded as an end in itself and as the subject of their own lives [30]. This view is embedded in the widely accepted ethical notion that human autonomy is grounded upon universal dignity representing a philosophical belief which suggests an objective moral principle, on the one side, and the recognition of equal human rights, on the other side [46]. All humans consequently have equal dignity; it is a heritage of humanity [47].

The attachment of responsibilities to human rights is necessary to allow for a moral, ethical, and balanced justification thereof, especially due to the individualistic nature of human rights. It serves as a reminder to all that individual freedom necessitates restriction and that human beings are not mere right-holders but also duty-bearers in order to harmonically co-exist with others. Each human being is, thus, not only a beneficiary of human rights but also confined by duties towards family and society members, the State, as well as the international community [48]. In this regard, the United Nation's Declaration of Human Rights ([49], article 1) recognises that all human beings are gifted with reason and conscience and obliged to adopt a spirit of brotherhood towards one another during their interactions. Individuals or specific groups of humans can, thus, not be excluded from access to human rights [14]. They play a key normative role in human existence within a broader society [50], requiring a dynamic understanding of diverse human needs that must be met. In recognising that diverse human needs may conflict with each other, the normative effect of human rights necessitates clarification.

5. What are the normative implications of human rights claims?

Heard [2] argues that the leading rhetorical advantage of human rights is that they should triumph over all other legitimate claims within a society due to their basic and fundamental value for human existence. The recognition of a human rights culture in South Africa, for example, abruptly brought an end to the adverse effects resulting from the historical apartheid era which made it impossible for instilling democratic principles that could guarantee an equitable and thriving society [45, 51].

Empowering humans with legal entitlements to have their human rights respected, fulfilled, and promoted, however, reflects only one side of a coin. Since communities consist of a combination of affect-laden interactions amongst their diverse members, cognisance must be taken of the degree to which such members and government are willing to commit themselves to a uniform set of norms, values, and cultures pertaining to a shared history and common identity [52]. In this sense, commitment entails a deeply rooted dedication and not merely a shallow confirmation of the value of human rights [53]. Humans need to be tolerant towards differences, requiring of them to respect, accept, and appraise human differences positively [54] if they want to live together peacefully [48]. In this regard, Staerkle et al. [28] caution that democracy, allowing for a government by the people for the people, must not be viewed as a natural or automatic consequence of the recognition of the worth of every community member but rather as a result of a combination of historical, cultural, social, and economic factors present in communities gradually leading to the acceptance of some form of democracy. Heard [2], alongside, opines that there may remain a need to safeguard humans from utilitarian decision-making even amongst governments that are sincerely committed to moral obligations. This is mainly due to the potential of conduct being regarded as being in the best interests of the greater good of the entire society to lead to sacrifice or exploitation of minority interests. Since a harmonious balance needs to be obtained between diverse human interests, insight into the nature and behaviour of humans being the ultimate bearers of human rights warrants further understanding.

6. Understanding human nature and behaviour within the moral and legal framework of human rights

The disputed concept of human nature can be explained as incorporating a grouping of genetic and cultural factors decisive to human ethics, feelings, and behaviour [17]. It is due to the generic or biological factors inherent in humans that man has the capacity to develop ethics, namely, to anticipate consequences of behaviour, adopt societal standards, feel empathy, and make moral choices. Cultural factors, on the other side, emanate from society itself in which the actual morals, ethics, and norms applicable in a specific society naturally follow from the development of culture within such a society [17].

Although it is obvious that tension may arise between the genetic (individual egoism) and cultural (group identity) elements that guide human nature, thus influencing human behaviour, scientists have rarely linked these factors to human rights [17]. It is, however, argued that human rights cannot be studied in isolation—they unavoidably embrace unique human developmental opportunities, interpersonal and domestic elements, as well as broader institutional and societal issues prevalent in different social contexts [55]. Societal concerns, in turn, affect human attitudes, behaviour, and even the extent to which men are willing to adopt a social identity and are prepared to recognise and support human rights [48].

Seeing that human behaviour is subjective to an individual's unique personal philosophy, political opinions, and goals, humans tend to choose the rights they are willing to support [26]. The adherence to human rights and, thus, the success of an idealistic human rights culture are depended upon a better insight into the genuine attitudes of and behaviour towards human rights in general [26]. It must, therefore, be acknowledged that individual, self-contained values such as social justice, equality, loyalty, and care [4, 55] as well as the social conditions in which humans live **predict** their behaviour [25]. This, consecutively, poses challenges for the realisation of universal human rights aiming at regulating human behaviour across national borders, underscoring a more globalised application [24]. In this regard, Moghaddam and Vuksanovic [26], however, opine that the attitudes and behaviour of humans towards the human rights of others should be consistent and should not change as a function of who they are and where they live.

Although humans have a natural tendency to follow morally grounded rules of behaviour even in the absence of formal legal principles, the adoption of a legal system assists in giving recognition to rights which can be claimed when humans behave unjustly and infringing on the rights of others. It can, therefore, be argued that there can be no society without rights regulating human behaviour whether being part of government or on a personal level [3, 15, 19, 56]. It is, however, important to identify and understand the main features guiding humans to commit and subject their own behaviour to legally entrenched human rights even when it is not totally favourable to themselves.

The Declaration of Human Rights [49], alongside, recognised that every individual and each societal institution should strife at educating themselves and others in respect of human rights and freedoms. Since then, numerous authors have stressed the importance of human rights education and education in general for influencing human behaviour. Kramers-Olen [55], for example, in researching the violation of the human rights of people with intellectual disabilities, found that the meaningful realisation of human rights inevitably intersects with the educational level of humans. It was concluded that such humans are often the victims of human rights abuses purely due to their lower intellectual functioning. As a direct result, the same author underlines the importance of obtaining loyalty amongst all societal members and institutions towards respecting human rights. In researching the violation of humans living with albinism, Mswela [29], similarly, found that such humans are marginalised and even killed due to misconceptions held by community members regarding them as being a curse on community or considering their body parts as being beneficial used as a muti.

It is in view hereof this respect, that the importance of human rights **education** in increasing knowledge, skills, understanding, attitude and mindfulness; all essential for preserving, endorsing and promoting fundamental rights and freedoms [37] and obtaining peace, cooperation, tolerance as well as democracy; is stressed [16]. The positive effect of education on changing humans' attitudes regarding their behaviour towards protecting human rights in general and even for future generations is highlighted [37]. Mkabela [31], conversely, cautions that human rights education should not negate traditional and indigenous values but rather be receptive to unique community perspectives in order to close the gap between the conceptualisation and practice of human rights by members belonging to different cultural groups. Mkabela's research results displayed the negative consequences of education taking a too globalised approach. It led parents to start relinquishing their roles of inculcating values to their children and to blame the education system for presenting human rights education in schools which encourages unacceptable behaviour in their communities. Human rights education should, according to Cohrs et al. [33], include more general anti-authoritarian and democratic or egalitarian values and attitudes for them to become more dominant and give rise to more positive orientations towards human rights.

Ercan et al. [16] advocate the starting of appropriate human rights education at primary schools to positively affect learner behaviour through knowledge and socialisation. They highlight the fact that learners at this developmental level are more open to adopting lifelong tolerance, awareness, and the ability to compromise, obtain overall positive attitudes towards human rights, and assume self-reported behaviour, thus being less inclined to violate such rights. Ongoing civic education or education for democracy as part of school reform is, nevertheless, encouraged.

From an interdisciplinary point of view, Kirchschlaeger [14] opines that both the law and education can establish an ethical foundation upon which legal systems can be changed in order to make provision for morally laden human rights. In this regard, he points out that the realisation of human rights cannot be automatically achieved; they necessitate a suitable ethos that ensures their enforcement. They need to be truly lived by, by both humans and governments; they are not a gift but a human task. Humans must be educated on how to behave in ways that compliment human rights, they need to be prepared to take action on behalf of fellow human beings, and they must be taught to have sympathy for others and remain committed to obtaining social justice and peace [14]. The eminence of human rights education is underscored by the fact that gross human rights abuses continue to take place globally.

7. Persistent human rights violations

Although political leaders globally vowed in 2000 to do all within their power to endorse and respect internationally recognised human rights, more than 800 million people around the globe still live under very poor and inhumane conditions [30]. Albeit being different in degree, all countries experience human rights problems hampering the respect such rights are entitled to in practice [57]. All modern societies consist of groups enjoying more power, social status, and wealth than subordinated groups, replicated by forms of discrimination such as sexism and racism, being justified as so-called hierarchy-augmenting legitimising myths [33].

In Islamic countries, for instance, women are still not viewed as equals, religious rebels are victimised, and political participation is only partially recognised. Political dominance is also central in countries such as Russia, Turkey, Hungary, and Venezuela. Xenophobia is flourishing in Europe and South Africa, whilst slavery still continues in some countries [23]. There are still more than 150 countries (out of 193 belonging to the United Nations) engaging in human anguish, and the amount of authoritarian governments is increasing. As such, reality shows that human rights law has failed to achieve its goals.

The ability of human rights to emancipate and dominate, protect, and control can, however, not be ignored. They have become a means for regulating human life and, thus, became tools of public power (the authority to withhold, revoke, or violate protection, provision, or participatory rights [48]). They are used as justification for a new configuration of political, economic, and military power [36]. Human rights, as colonialism in the guise of moralism, are often employed as a political alibi by governments tolerating and ignoring persistent inequities and unashamed injustices [58]. The rise of mass democracies around the globe during the twentieth century has given way to the protection of some humans whilst neglecting the needs of others comprising the poor and those struggling to live adequately and to find employment, thus leaving them to squad in illegal settlements, making illegal use of water and electricity, and even to commit immoral behaviour such as stealing, cheating, intimidating, abusing, and even murder just to survive [21]. Forced to behave outside the parameters of the law, such humans tend to want to be excluded from rights if rights are the law in order to escape, at least, a small part of the totalising system of governmentality that is served by the common purchase on human rights. As such, human rights have become a myth for those who suffer constant violations by, ironically, those who underscore the victory of human rights [36].

The constitutional rights of so-called loyal citizens are protected, whilst others are denied access to such safeguards [59]. Human rights are selectively misused to justify violations at the cost of many humans. They are camouflaged by states, identified as the main violators of human rights, as a form of justice-seeking [60]. Gearty [36] blames the incorporation of human rights into law as it imprisons and restricts human rights to the sphere of the law. To avoid this, Wolfgang [30] advocates the following of, as opposed to a totalitarian approach, a pluralistic ethical approach based on the principle that everyone matters equally and that all have access to rights by virtue of their humanity, not only as citizens but also as non-citizens, in order to avoid the exclusion of certain humans.

The practical realisation of human rights, nevertheless, necessitates some form of legal protection. Crimes against humanity, in essence committed by humans themselves, being it through governments or on an individual level, can only be corrected if such crimes are indeed legally punished [27]. Whilst some States are not able to protect human rights, others simply do not want to [57]. It is often contended that giving effect to human rights, especially socio-economic rights, is just too costly. Ferreira [61] criticises such an argument by pointing out that human rights are more complex than such a contentment allows for, as human rights cannot merely be interpreted as entitlements to some good. The inability of States to provide for the necessary infrastructure within which the human rights of all regarding housing, medical care, education, employment, and food can be realised as a global concern as it denies humans their right to have their basic human needs to be met that will enable them to live dignified lives [61].

South Africa is, with regard to governments, merely not wanting to effectively realise human rights, a good example. Whilst this country's unemployment and poverty rates are increasing, government is misusing State funds for their own personal gain—corruption amongst State members is at the order of the day. Pensioners are, for example, left without resources as government used their funds to build e-tolls on its public roads. Increasing conflict amongst society members over employment opportunities and wages, the showing of intolerance towards diversity, the discrimination between inhabitants by way of name-calling through the social media and even from political platforms, the political upheavals from government scandals, as well as constant violent protests by the black majority who have yet to fully benefit from the transition from apartheid to democracy, all contribute to the unwillingness of the South African government towards creating a society reflecting a human rights culture. To this, the corruption-plagued governance of old President Zuma, supporting the rights of oppressors over their victims, can be added [62].

Regarding the political dimension of human rights, Gilbert [63] remarks that politicians are only concerned about being re-elected and will do everything and promise anything as long as they achieve their goal, without any true commitment to respecting the human rights of those electing them. Politicians tend to adopt a culture of control characterised by dismissing societal welfare pertaining to alleviate poverty, bring about equality, and create better life and employment opportunities as well as punishing crime by using expressive, emotive, and moralistic rhetoric to demonise those who seek State assistance as they are progressively marginalised from the economy [64].

In other parts of the world, the rise of secret terrorist activities are also used to secretly, without any legal justification, intrude the lives of humans of which the events of 11 September 2001 in the USA is but one example [36]. States are, likewise, using the protection of national security (the common good [21]) as a main means of restricting the individual rights belonging to humans. They fail to balance conflicting rights and competing interests effectively.

In South Africa, the acceptance of a human rights-driven Constitution and that of democracy instilled new hope for a better life for all South Africans. However, government soon turned to uplift themselves at the cost of those in a dire need of equal life opportunities. As a result, faith was lost in this country's ability to meet the needs of its inhabitants which led South Africans displaying new behaviour to obtain the attention of the world. They have turned to, amongst other, drug abuse, murders, aggressive strikes, land grabbing, and brutal aggression towards foreigners, gangsterism, hate speech, and human trafficking.

The South African Constitutional Court, despite repeated attempts to convince it to do so, has even on numerous occasions [*Government of the Republic of South Africa v Grootboom* 2001 (1) SA 46 (CC) paras 32-3; *Minister of Health v Treatment Action Campaign* 2002 (5) SA 721 (CC) paras 34-9; *Nokotyana v Ekurhuleni Metropolitan Municipality* 2010 (4) BCLR 312 (CC); and in *Mazibuko v City of Johannesburg* 2010 (4) SA 1 (CC) fn. 46] refused to adopt a minimum core approach to the realisation of individual's socio-economic rights in order to oblige the government to give effect to such rights. Thus, even the judiciary indicated its lack of commitment towards the realisation of human rights by opting for rather maintaining good relationships with the executive authority by showing empathy to the latter's limited available resources. Rudman [65] disapproves of such an approach by stating that Constitutional Courts, par excellence, established to protect constitutional rights, should be much more flexible in their approach as to enable them to be stricter when it comes to the violations of human rights. The unwillingness of courts is criticised by Barak [34] to the extent that the judiciary's main duty is to guard the effective implementation of human rights and, thus, to stand up to a government guilty of abusing its powers. Courts should not negate their responsibility to ensure that governments do not exceed their powers to the detriment of humans [66]. If courts remain unwilling to assist humans in this regard, humans will come to distrust judicial systems to adjudicate human rights infringements effectively [36].

It is evident that the Constitution presupposed an efficient government with the capacity and commitment to meet the hopes of its inhabitants in their desire for a participatory and efficient democracy, the realisation of their human rights, peace and security, equal developmental opportunities, social justice, and integration [24]. In this quest, it must be recognised that humans themselves do not just live in a democracy; a constitutional State does not embody a complete structure but is rather imperfect, revisable, subtle, and delicate in its aim at recognising human rights afresh under dynamic circumstances. As such, the responsibility lies with all living in contemporary South Africa to endorse human rights and inspire government to do the same [54]. In a democracy humans are obliged to actively participate and take responsibility for the realisation of human rights and cannot, as the case in authoritarian regimes, exclusively blame government for human rights violations [28].

8. Conclusion

In studying human rights through a philosophical lens, this chapter succeeded in recognising the moral or ethical dimensions lying at the foundation of human rights. Although it was acknowledged that humans by nature tend to behave ethically, it became evident that persistent human rights violation through human behaviour necessitates the inclusion of human rights within a legal framework. This allows for obliging not only governments but also private individuals to adhere to the responsibilities indispensably linked to human rights. It also empowers those whose human rights are violated to legitimately claim compliance to normative legal imperatives.

The interplay between the egoistic nature of humans and the need for humans to harmoniously co-exist in society amongst other humans depicted the effect of society-specific conditions on human behaviour. It came to the fore that humans, with their own individual set of morals and beliefs, need to be well educated in order to adopt and adapt to mutually acceptable behaviour that would be to the benefit of all living in such a society.

Reference to the persistent occurrence of human rights violations globally underscored the gap, despite the widely acceptance of human rights in their ethical, legal, political, and historical dimensions that remains to exist between both moral and legal ideals and the extent to which effect is given to human rights in reality. This keeps the gate open for furthering the debate pertaining to how human behaviour needs to be adopted to realise human rights, at least those pertinent to meaningful human existence, to their fullest potential.

Author details

Erika Serfontein
North-West University, Vanderbijlpark, South Africa

*Address all correspondence to: erika.serfontein@nwu.ac.za

References

[1] Keith LC. Human rights instruments. In: Cane P, Kritzer HB, editors. The Oxford Handbook of Empirical Legal Research. Vol. 2010. United State: Oxford University Press; 2010. pp. 353-375

[2] Heard A. Human Rights: Chimeras in Sheep's Clothing? [Internet] 1997. Available from: http://www.sfu.ca/~aheard/intro.html [Accessed: 18 December 2018]

[3] Gusman J. The concept of human Rights: Political and moral approaches [thesis]. Political Science: Radboud University; 2015

[4] Twose G, Cohrs JC. Psychology and human rights: Introduction to the special issue. Peace and Conflict: Journal of Peace Psychology. 2015;**21**(1):3-9. DOI: 10.1037pac000008

[5] Douzinas C. Human Rights and Empire: The Political Philosophy of Cosmopolitanism. United Kingdom: Routledge; 2007. 313 p

[6] Ajey MO. Human rights in a moderate communitarian political framework. South African Journal of Philosophy. 2015;**34**(4):491-503. DOI: 10.1080/02580136.2015.1119920

[7] Nussbaum M. Creating Capabilities: The Human Development Approach. Cambridge: Harvard University Press; 2011

[8] Australian Human Rights Commission. All human rights explained, fact sheet 3 [Internet]. 2009. Available from: www.humanrights.gov.au/education/hr_explained/ [Accessed: 17 December 2018]

[9] Bentham J. Anarchical fallacies. In: Jeremy Waldron J, editor. Nonsense Upon Stilts: Bentham, Burke, and Marx on the Rights of Man. London: Methuen; 1987

[10] Geuss R. History and Illusion in Politics. Cambridge: Cambridge University Press; 2001. 144 p

[11] Darby D. Rights externalism. Philosophy and Phenomenological Affairs. 2004;**68**:620-634

[12] Martin S. Rights as enforceable claims. Proceedings of the Aristotelian Society. 2003;**103**:133-147

[13] Cruft R, Liao SM, Renzo M. The philosophical foundations of human rights: An overview. In: Cruft R, Liao SM, Renzo M, editors. Philosophical Foundations of Human Rights. Philosophical Foundations of Law. Oxford: Oxford University Press; 2015. pp. 1-41

[14] Kirchschlaeger PG. Adaptation—A model for bringing human rights and religions together. Acta Academica. 2015;**47**(2):163-191

[15] Muis J. Human rights and divine justice. HTS Theological Studies. 2014;**70**(1):1-8. DOI: 10.4102/hts.v70i1.2740

[16] Ercan R, Yaman T, Demir SB. Human rights attitude scale: A validity and reliability study. Journal of Education and Training Studies. 2015;**3**(6):220-231. DOI: 10.11114/jets.v3i6.1031

[17] Marks P. The past and future of the separation of human rights into categories. Maryland Journal of International Law. 2009;**24**:208-241

[18] Gerard RW. The rights of man: A biological approach. In: Maritain J, editor. Human Rights: Comments and Interpretations. London/New York: Allan Wingate—Originally Issued as UNESCO Doc. PHS/3 (Rev.); 1949. pp. 205-206

[19] Wilson EO. The Social Conquest of Earth. WW Norton & Co: New York/London; 2013. 330 p

[20] Bribena K. What if there was no human rights in Africa: The musing of a human rights scholar. Gender and Behaviour. 2017;**15**(4):10090-10100

[21] Metz T. African values and human rights as two sides of the same coin: A reply to Oyowe. African Human Rights Law Journal. 2014;**14**:306-321

[22] Changeux J. The Physiology of Truth. Neuroscience and Human Knowledge, Cambridge, MA: Harvard University Press; 2002. 236 p

[23] Posner E. The case against human rights. The Guardian. 2017. Available from: /ael.eui.eu/wp-content/uploads/sites/28/2017/05/De-Burca-03-Posner.pd [Accessed: 13 May 2018]

[24] Habermas J. The constitutionalisation of international law and the legitimation problems of a constitution for world society. Constellations. 2008;**15**(4):444-455. DOI: 10.1111/j.1467-8675.2008.00510.x

[25] Woods AK. A behavioural approach to human rights. Harvard International Law Journal. 2010;**51**(1):51-111

[26] Moghaddam FM, Vuksanovic V. Attitudes and behaviour toward human rights across different context: The role of right-wing authoritarianism, political ideology and religiosity. International Journal of Psychology. 1990;**25**:455-474. DOI: 10.1080/0020759 9008247877

[27] Asomah JY. Cultural rights versus human rights: A critical analysis of the trokosi practice in Ghana and the role of civil society. African Human Rights Law Journal. 2015;**15**:129-149. DOI: 10.17159/1996-2096/2015/v15n1a6

[28] Staerkle C, Clemence A, Doise W. Representation of human rights across different national contexts: The role of democratic and non-democratic populations and governments. European Journal of Social Psychology. 1998;**28**:207-226

[29] Mswela M. Violent attacks against persons with albinism in South Africa: A human rights perspective. African Human Rights Law Journal. 2027;**17**: 114-133. DOI: 10.17159/1996-2096/2017/v17n1a6

[30] Wolfgang H. Human rights and globalisation—Are human rights a "Western" concept or a universalistic principle? NGTT. 2014;**55**(1):117-137. DOI: 10.5952/55-1-2-518

[31] Mkabela QN. Ubuntu as an axiological framework for human rights education. Indilinga, African Journal of Indigenous Knowledge Systems. 2014;**13**(2):283-291. DOI: 10520/EJC166448

[32] Pacilli MG, Roccato M, Pagliaro S, Russo S. From political opponents to enemies? The role of perceived moral distance in the animalistic dehumanization of the political outgroup. Group Processes and Intergroup Relations. 2016;**19**(3):360-373. DOI: 10.1177/1368430215590490

[33] Cohrs JC, Maes J, Moschner B, Kielmann S. Determinants of human rights attitudes and behaviour: A comparison and integration of psychological perspectives. Political Psychology. 2007;**28**(4):441-469. DOI: 10.1111/j.1467-9221.2007.00581x

[34] Barak A. Foreword—A judge on judging: The role of a Supreme Court in a democracy. Harvard Law Review. 2002;**16**:19-162

[35] Law DS. Constitutions. In: Cane P, Kritzer HB, editors. The Oxford Handbook of Empirical Legal Research. United State: Oxford University Press; 2010. pp. 376-398

[36] Gearty C. Human rights: The necessary quest for foundations. In: Douzinas C, Gearty C, editors. The Meanings of Rights: The Philosophy and Social Theory of Human Rights. Cambridge: Cambridge University Press; 2014. pp. 21-38

[37] Doğanay A, Öztürk A. Developing attitudes towards human rights through socio-scientific issues in science courses: An action research. Multidisciplinary Journal of Educational Research. 2017;7(3):253-286. DOI: 10.17583/remie.2017.2873

[38] Grotius H. In: Barbeyrac J. The Rights of War and Peace. Vol. 3. Indapolis: Liberty Fund; 2005. Available from: https://oll.libertyfund.org/titles/1877. 8/22/2019

[39] Von Pufendorf S. Of the Law of Nature and Notions: Eight Books. 4th ed. New Jersey: Lawbook Exchange Ltd; 2005. pp. 1018. ISBN: 13:978-1584773948.

[40] Locke J. Two Treaties of Region: A Principal Component Analysis Government. Available from: https://www.earlymoderntexts.com/assets/pdfs/locke 1689a pdf

[41] Kant I. The Metaphysics of Morals. Edited by Gregor MJ. 2013. ISBN: 9780511809644. DOI: 10.1017/CB09780511809644

[42] Hobbes T. Leviathan; 1651. ISBN: 13:978-1730901539. pp. 293

[43] Rousseau J. Discourse on the Origin of Inequality, Originally Published 1755, Quoted from the Social Contract and Discourses, Translated by Cole GDH, Editor. London: Orion Publishing; 1993. 53 p

[44] Donnelly J. International Human Rights in Theory and Practice. 2nd ed. Ithaca/ London: Cornell University Press; 2003. 16 p

[45] Oke AE, Aigbavboa CO, Cane TK. 2017. Expected Quality of Life of Smart City Citizens. Available from: www.researchgate.net/...Oke/.../Expected-quality-of-life-of-smart-city-citizens [Accessed: 16 October 2018]

[46] Steinmann R. The core meaning of human dignity. PER. 2016;**19**:1-32. DOI: 10.17159/1727-3781/2016/v19i0a1244

[47] Strydom H. The human rights side of the human genome. TSAR. 2003;**1**: 37-55. ISSN 0257-7747

[48] Ziemens J, Abb H. Strong identities and endorsement of human rights: Conflictive or complementary? South African Journal of Higher Education. 2017;**31**(6):151-166. DOI: 10.28535/31-6-1636

[49] United Nation. Declaration on Human Rights 1948: GA Res 217A (III). Adopted by the United Nation's General Assembly on 10 December 1948

[50] Joas H. Die Sakralität der Person. Eine neue Genealogie der Menschenrechte. Berlin: Suhrkamp; 2011

[51] Greyling TA. Composite Index of Quality of Life for the Gauteng City-region: A Principal Component Analysis Approach. Johannesburg, Gauteng: Gauteng City Region-Observatory; 2013 Handle.net/10539/17365

[52] Etzioni A. Creating good communities and good societies. Contemporary Sociology. 2000;**29**(1):188-195. SSRN: ssm.com/abstract=1438224

[53] Partington M. Empirical legal research and policy-making. In: Cane P, Kritzer HB, editors. The Oxford Handbook of Empirical Legal Research. United State: Oxford University Press; 2010. pp. 1002-1024

[54] Belasheva IV, Petrova F. Psychological stability of a personality and capability

of tolerant interaction as diverse manifestations of tolerance. International Journal of Environmental and Science Education. 2016;**11**(10):3367-3384

[55] Kramers-Olen A. Sexuality, intellectual disability, and human rights legislation. South African Journal of Psychology. 2016;**46**(4):504-516. DOI: 10.1177/00812463 16678154

[56] Griffin J. Discrepancies between the best philosophical account of human rights and the international Law of human rights. Proceedings of the Aristotelian Society. 2001;**101**:1-28

[57] Sarkin J. Balancing national security and human rights: International and domestic standards applying to terrorism and freedom of speech. African Human Rights Law Journal. 2016;**16**(1):265-282. DOI: 10.1080/13876980500513335?scr=recsys

[58] Hopgood S. The End Times of Human Rights. Ithaca, New York: Cornell University Press; 2015. 272 p

[59] Sheka KR, Pederson J. Reconceptualising human rights attitudes: Understanding outcomes and determinants. In: Proceedings of the Association, Political Economy of the World-System section of the American Sociological. Power and Justice in the Contemporary World-Economy; New York. 2013

[60] Keet A. Refractions: Social theory, human rights and philosophy. Acta Academica. 2014;**46**(4):132-158. DOI: Handle.net/10520/EJC165375

[61] Ferreira N. Feasibility constraints and human rights: Does 'ought' imply 'can'? THRHR. 2012;**28**:483-505. DOI: 10.1080/199962126,2012,11865057

[62] Africa Country Benchmark Report. 2017;(1):236-245. Available from: http://www inonafrica.com/2017/11/10/africa-country-benchmark-report-acbr-2017 [Accessed: 18 July 2018]

[63] Gilbert P. Human rights, yeah right ... Without Prejudices. 2014;**14**(10):82. DOI: Handle.net/10520/EJC164046

[64] Garland D. The Culture of Control: Crime and Social Order in Contemporary Society. Oxford: Oxford University Press; 2001. 324 p

[65] Rudman A. The protection against discrimination based on sexual orientation under the African human rights system. African Human Rights Law Journal. 2015;**15**:1-27. DOI: 10.17159/1996-2096/2015/v15n1a1

[66] Dbe A. Balancing human rights and national security. South African Law Journal. 2007;**124**(1):57-75. DOI: 10.1080/13876980500513335

Chapter 11

Problems of Social Rights Enjoyment by Persons Diagnosed with Epilepsy: Legal Aspect

Anton Petrovich Gertsen
and Vladimir Vladimirovich Rumyantsev

Abstract

Epilepsy is a disease that creates many problems for people with such a diagnosis in the enjoyment of their social rights. Despite the existing regulatory legal acts governing the protection of health and the social rights enjoyment by citizens with epilepsy, there are many questions on this topic both regarding accessibility of these norms to people with epilepsy and in terms of compliance of the current legislation with the norms of the Constitution of the Russian Federation. In this article, we tried to reflect the basic norms of the current legislation in the Russian Federation governing the provision of medical care to people with epilepsy, providing them with free medications, admission of patients with epilepsy and epileptic syndrome to various types of work, education, military service, possession of weapons, driving, and pay attention to the problems of people diagnosed with epilepsy.

Keywords: epilepsy, clinical guidelines, drug provision, work with a diagnosis of epilepsy, study with a diagnosis of epilepsy, driver's license, military service, disclosure of the diagnosis

1. Introduction

Article 7 of the Constitution of Russia proclaims the Russian Federation as a social state, the distinguishing feature of which is an active policy in the fields of science, education, health care, culture, etc. [1], as well as a high level of social responsibility of government to citizens.

Constitutional norms provide a person with a wide range of diverse rights and freedoms that cover all major areas of life and activity. The fundamental rights and freedoms enshrined in the Constitution of the Russian Federation are inalienable (Article 17) and equal (Article 19) for everybody. Everyone has the right to work (Article 37), to health protection (Article 41), and to education (Article 43).

2. Problems of the social rights enjoyment by persons with a diagnosis of epilepsy

The impact of epilepsy on the social life of citizens is very diverse. Fundamentally important issues in epilepsy are problems of diagnosis, modern treatment, the impact of the diagnosis of epilepsy on employment, military service, the ability to drive a vehicle, etc.

2.1 The right to free medical care

The legal basis of the state's obligation to develop and implement measures to protect the health of citizens is the provisions of Article 41 of the Constitution of the Russian Federation, which enshrines the right of citizens to health care and medical assistance, which is provided to citizens free of charge at the expense of the corresponding budget, insurance premiums, and other incomings. Thus, the right to medical care is among the constitutionally protected values and is an indispensable and inalienable benefit belonging to everyone from birth. This is a fundamental, initial legal establishment, basic for the entire system of specific rights and freedoms assigned to a person in the field of health care, which has the highest legal force [2].

To date, the main body of legislation in terms of the public health protection has been formed both at the federal and regional levels. At the same time, the modern legal framework does not fully ensure the constitutional right of citizens to health protection and medical care. At the moment, there are a number of gaps in federal legislation that prevent the full enjoyment of the right of citizens, including people with a diagnosis of epilepsy, to health protection, which will be discussed further below.

First of all, it seems necessary to eliminate the uncertainty of the status of the documents, on the basis of which patients are diagnosed and treated, and the quality of medical care is assessed. According to clause 1 of Article 37 of Federal Law No. 323-FZ dated November 21, 2011, "On the Basics of Health Protection of the Citizens in the Russian Federation" (hereinafter referred to as Law No. 323-FZ), medical care is arranged and provided in accordance with the procedures for providing medical care that are binding in the territory of the Russian Federation for all medical organizations, as well as on the basis of medical care standards [3]. At the same time, as follows from the explanation of the press service of the Ministry of Health of the Russian Federation dated 05.09.2017, the standards are flow charts developed on the basis of clinical guidelines, which are a list of services, medicines, medical devices, and other components of treatment that can be used for a particular disease with the average frequency and multiplicity of their representation in the group of patients with this disease. Standards cannot be used by the attending physician, as these are the documents used by the organizers of health care for planning and economic calculations, in particular when preparing the program of state guarantees of providing free medical care to citizens [4]. According to the abovementioned message of the press service of the Ministry of Health of the Russian Federation dated 05.09.2017, the documents that establish the algorithm for patient management, diagnosis, and treatment are clinical guidelines. They do not establish uniform "patterned" requirements for the treatment of all patients, but contain the logistic structure of the doctor's actions, using diagnostic methods and treatment that have proven their effectiveness. At the same time, at present, federal legislation does not contain any indication of the obligatory observance of clinical guidelines. But from 01.01.2022, medical assistance will have to be carried out on the basis of, inter alia, clinical recommendations in accordance with Federal Law No. 489-FZ dated 25.12.2018 "On Amending Article 40 of the Federal Law "On Mandatory Medical Insurance in the Russian Federation" and the Federal Law "On the Basics of Health Protection of the Citizens in the Russian Federation" concerning clinical recommendations," where it is said that clinical recommendations are documents containing structured information based on scientific evidence on prevention, diagnosis, treatment, and rehabilitation, including patient management protocols (treatment protocols), options for medical intervention, and the description of the sequence of actions of a medical worker taking into account the course of the disease, the presence of complications and comorbidities, and other factors affecting the results of medical care.

In accordance with clause 2 of Article 76 of Law No. 323-FZ, clinical guidelines on the provision of medical care are developed, among other things, taking into account the results of clinical testing, and are approved by medical professional nonprofit organizations in accordance with Article 37 on the arrangement of medical care. Developed and approved clinical guidelines are posted on the website of the Federal Electronic Medical Library of the Ministry of Health of the Russian Federation (www.femb.ru). The functional responsibilities of any medical practitioner include systematical reviewing and tracking the replenishment of the base with new clinical guidelines.

To date, more than 1200 clinical guidelines on various diseases and conditions have been developed and are in force. Despite the fact that epilepsy is one of the most common diseases of the central nervous system, which has a wide variety of forms, radically different in treatment tactics and prognosis, unfortunately, clinical guidelines have not been approved on any of them by medical professional nonprofit organizations of neurologists and epileptologists operating in Russia, based on which an ordinary neurologist, regardless of length of service and experience, using the prescribed algorithm, could provide qualified assistance and referring to which could prescribe the necessary drugs to the patient free of charge, regardless of their value. In addition, in the presence of prescribed clinical guidelines, an epileptologist could ensure the start of treatment not only with classical drugs but also with the use of modern medicines and could decide in time on the need for surgical treatment of diseases. It is known that in many situations in patients with epilepsy, the time of the treatment start is the key to a complete cure and/or lack of disability.

It can be stated that the combination of "legislative inaction of public organizations" with the fact that the adoption of various kinds of bylaws (from the relevant orders of the Ministry of Health of Russia to the legal acts of health authorities in the constituent entities of the Russian Federation), developing the provisions of Law No. 323-FZ, is catastrophically late or nonexistent [5] and does not allow epileptologists to provide full assistance to patients with a diagnosis of epilepsy. Thus, there is a paradoxical situation. Clinical guidelines are given a leading role in the development of standards of care, the treatment of patients suffering from epilepsy, and assessing the quality of care. However, these fundamental documents that directly or indirectly regulate many legal relations in the field of health care of patients with epilepsy are absent. This situation requires immediate actions to develop and adopt all the necessary clinical guidelines for the treatment of patients with a diagnosis of epilepsy, which will be drawn up taking into account new medicines and medical technologies.

2.2 The right to free provision of medicines

Another topical issue concerns the availability of free drug provision for patients with epilepsy. Unfortunately, the rights of all citizens to access free drug provision are "not officially recognized, which goes against international agreements on human rights adopted at the UN level" [6]. Most of our citizens exercise their right to free drug provision in accordance with legal guarantees for compulsory health insurance programs, in the so-called general legal regime. Along with the general one, it is also possible to single out a special legal regime for drug provision on the basis of the fact that the citizens have a particular disease, assigned by the legislator to the corresponding list, or a certain legal status [7]. In actual fact, the existence of such a special legal regime means nonobservance of the Constitution of the Russian Federation and is discriminatory against the majority of citizens in terms of free drug provision.

Within the framework of a special legal regime, drugs are provided to citizens from among the categories listed in Article 6.1 of Federal Law "On State Social Assistance" No. 178-FZ dated 17.07.1999 [8] (hereinafter referred to as Law No. 178-FZ): disabled people, participants of the Great Patriotic War, combat veterans, residents of besieged Leningrad, etc. Resolution of the Government of the Russian Federation No. 890 dated 30.07.1994 established a list of population groups and disease categories, for outpatient treatment of which drugs are dispensed on medical prescriptions free of charge [9]. By letter of the Ministry of Health and Social Development of the Russian Federation No. 489-BC dated 03.02.2006 "On dispensing medicines to the population on medical prescriptions for outpatient treatment free of charge or with a 50% discount," it is explained that Resolution of the Government of the Russian Federation No. 890 dated 30.07.1994 provides for financing of expenses when paying for drugs to certain population groups at the expense of funds of the constituent entities of the Russian Federation and other sources attracted by them for these purposes [10]. According to these documents, drug provision to certain categories of citizens, including people with epilepsy, is carried out both at the federal and regional levels. At the same time, patients with an established diagnosis of epilepsy have the right to be provided with free medicines, regardless of the presence or absence of disability and other preferential grounds.

At the same time, the constituent entities of the Russian Federation have the right to establish their own circle (including the extended one) of recipients of drug provision. Taking into account the fact that citizens from the categories listed in Law No. 178-FZ, as a rule, reside in the territory of certain constituent entities of the Russian Federation, they are entitled to drug provision as both federal and regional benefit recipients. Hence, it follows that they are entitled to receive drug provision for two reasons. At the same time, in the event of refusal from drug provision of one level, for example, a regional level, they retain the right to drug provision of another level-the federal level. However, in fact, the rights of certain categories of citizens to drug provision are often violated, and for various reasons, more often of an economic nature, they are denied free medicines.

Another topical issue is the discrepancy between the federal program [11] and regional programs of state guarantees of free medical care to citizens. According to clause 3 of Part 1 of Article 16 of Law No. 323-FZ, the development, approval, and implementation of the territorial program of state guarantees of free medical care to citizens, including the territorial program of compulsory medical insurance, are the powers of the state authorities of the constituent entities of the Russian Federation. The federal legislator, empowering the state authorities of the constituent entities of the Russian Federation with the above powers and including the legislation of the constituent entities of the Russian Federation to the system of legal regulators in the field of health, at the same time established the scope and limits for the implementation of the regulatory powers of the state authorities of the constituent entities of the Russian Federation in this field, stipulating the provisions in parts 1 and 3 of Article 81 of Law No. 323-FZ, according to which the state authorities of the constituent entities of the Russian Federation approve territorial programs of state guarantees of free medical care to citizens in accordance with the Federal Program. The prescription on the need to adopt a territorial program in accordance with the Federal Program is also contained in the third paragraph of Section I (General Provisions) of the Federal Program. Federal legislation does not provide the constituent entities of the Russian Federation with the right to adjust territorial programs downwardly. Moreover, by virtue of Part 3 of Article 81 of Law No. 323-FZ, territorial programs of state guarantees of free medical care to citizens, subject to the compliance with financial standards established by the program of state guarantees of free medical care to citizens, may contain additional types and conditions of medical care, as well as additional volumes of medical care, including those providing the possibility of exceeding the averages established by medical care standards. Resolution of the Government of the Russian Federation dated December 10, 2018, No. 1506 "On the Program of State Guarantees for Providing Free Medical Care to Citizens for 2019 and for the Planning Period of 2020 and 2021" [12] for the first time directly instructs regions to form a list of drugs dispensed to the population free of charge, in the volume not less than the list of essential and most important medicines approved by the order of the Government of the Russian Federation for the corresponding year. Nevertheless, almost everywhere, the executive authorities of the constituent entities of the Russian Federation, due to the lack of funds in regional budgets, deviate from the guarantees established at the federal level and violate the rights of residents of the regions to receive state guarantees of free medical care in the amount determined by the Government of the Russian Federation. Regional lists of drugs, dispensed free of charge, are, in most cases, much less than federal. Such situations become the subject of consideration by the Supreme Court of the Russian Federation, which, as a rule, acknowledges the existence of violations. The Supreme Court of the Russian Federation adopted such decisions in Amur [13], Vologda [14], Bryansk [15], Penza [16], Novgorod [17] Regions, Altai [18], Krasnoyarsk [19] and Perm [20] Territories, the Chuvash Republic [21], and many other constituent entities.

Based on the decisions of the Supreme Court of the Russian Federation, the committed violations of the established federal guarantees of medical care are subject to elimination. At the same time, the judicial practice in many cases proceeds from the fact that the inability to obtain the necessary drug on medical prescription due to the absence of the drug on the Drug List cannot violate the patient's right to receive the necessary treatment. However, it is necessary to understand that only a small part of legally literate patients, whose rights to receive free drugs were violated, go to court. In practice, even such a limited list of population groups and disease categories does not guarantee the unconditional right of citizens who meet the requirements of these lists to free medicines. The current drug provision system does not comply with Article 41 of the Constitution of the Russian Federation on the right of everyone to free medical care at the expense of the relevant budget, insurance premiums, and other incomings.

According to experts, the introduction of universal reimbursement for medicines to ensure the availability of medicines would make it possible to radically change the situation and shift the focus of state support from the treatment of the late stages of the disease and the prevention of death to the prevention of diseases and the prevention of their development [22].

2.3 The right to receive drugs, unregistered in the Russian Federation

Many drugs that can save the lives of patients or improve their life quality are absent in the territory of the Russian Federation, as they are not registered by the Ministry of Health of the Russian Federation. The use of unregistered drugs is possible in the territory of the Russian Federation subject to the additional rules set out in Order of the Ministry of Health and Social Development of the Russian Federation No. 494 dated August 9, 2005, "On the procedure for using drugs by patients for health reasons" [23], Federal Law No. 61-FZ dated 12.04.2010 "On the

Circulation of Medicines" [24], Rules for the Importation of Drugs for Medical Use into the Territory of the Russian Federation, approved by Resolution of the Government of the Russian Federation No. 771 dated September 29, 2010 [25].

According to the legislation, if a patient has the right to free drug provision and he/she has vital indications for the use of a drug unregistered in the country, this drug shall be provided free of charge. But the procedure for the importation of such unregistered drugs is extremely complex and requires a significant investment of time and money. In this regard, such drugs are practically inaccessible to the majority of patients. And only if the patient has the opportunity to purchase such drugs at his/her own expense, he/she can do this when traveling abroad with the minimum amount of bureaucratic complications.

It should be noted that such a difficult-to-surmount barrier to the widespread use of modern medicines in the treatment of citizens is created by the current rules for registration of drugs in the Russian Federation, which are very complex, opaque, costly, and disadvantageous to foreign pharmaceutical companies. The domestic procedure for registration of drugs is obstructing in nature and leaves some patients with epilepsy, including children, without access to modern medicines. The inaccessibility of modern drugs for some patients with epilepsy and, as a result, the impossibility of obtaining high-quality medical care affects their future social life.

2.4 The right to work

The prevalence of epilepsy in the Russian Federation is 2.98 people per 1000 people of the population [26]. Of all persons suffering from epilepsy, no more than 10% need inpatient care, but the majority (over 90%) are outpatients, of which about 60% of adult patients are able-bodied and work in a team of healthy people [27]. However, the problem of work and employment of this category of citizens remains unresolved. Despite many years of remission (drug or nondrug), these citizens are subject to the same legal restrictions as people with an incurable form of epilepsy [28].

The current legislation of the Russian Federation does not regulate the procedure for the removal of the diagnosis of epilepsy, and this diagnosis remains with the person for life. A history of diagnosis of epilepsy gives rise to a large number of problems for citizens in the enjoyment of their social rights.

The right to work is one of the basic human rights playing an important role in the life of everyone, since most people meet their vital needs in connection with their work activities. That is why ensuring equal access to work is at the center of social and economic policies throughout the world.

However, the analysis of the norms defining the legal status in the sphere of labor of citizens suffering from epilepsy suggests that not all the issues have found normative consolidation and legal regulation. Thus, given the above constitutional norms that establish binding requirements, the current labor legislation is so ambiguous about the establishment and regulation of rights guaranteed by the Constitution of the Russian Federation, which suggests its discriminatory nature in relation to citizens diagnosed with epilepsy. In modern society, discrimination is one of the most common signs of regression. It is based on unlawful comparisons among people, nonobservance of the Constitution of the Russian Federation, and disregard for the principles of equality and freedom. There is no doubt that when hiring it is necessary to adhere to such parameters as education, qualifications, experience, skills, and abilities. No other reasons can serve as justified grounds for refusing an employee to provide a workplace [29].

Essential characteristics of labor freedom, reflecting the modern needs of society, have been consolidated in the regulations of the new generation. It is no coincidence that the slogan of Part 1 of Article 37 of the Constitution of the Russian Federation "labor is free" is developed by the principal clause "everyone has the right to freely dispose of their abilities to work", and only then the right to choose his/her occupation and profession follows" [30]. According to Part 4 of Article 15 of the Constitution of the Russian Federation generally recognized principles and norms of international law are an integral part of the legal system of the Russian Federation [31]. Article 23 of the Universal Declaration of Human Rights enshrines the right to work, including free choice of work, fair and favorable working conditions, protection from unemployment, and receipt of fair and satisfactory remuneration ensuring a decent life for himself/herself and his/her family.

Articles 6, 7 of the International Covenant on Economic, Social and Cultural Rights [32] enshrine the right to work, including the opportunity to earn a living by freely chosen labor in fair and favorable conditions that provide a satisfactory remuneration for the workers themselves and members of their families. Clause 5 of Resolution of the Plenum of the Supreme Court of the Russian Federation "On some issues of the application of the Constitution of the Russian Federation by courts in the administration of justice" No. 8 dated October 31, 1995, explicitly states that the courts shall be guided by the provisions of the Universal Declaration of Human Rights and the International Covenant on Economic, Social and Cultural Rights. Since the Constitution of the Russian Federation establishes the unconditional priority of international conventional rules over the rules contained in domestic legislation [33], the determination of the right to work in the territory of the Russian Federation shall be guided by the listed international norms. In accordance with Part 3 of Article 37 of the Constitution of the Russian Federation: "Everyone has the right to work in conditions that meet the requirements of safety and hygiene, to remuneration for work without any discrimination and not lower than the minimum wage established by federal law, as well as the right to protection against unemployment."

These constitutional provisions were developed in the Labor Code of the Russian Federation (hereinafter referred to as the Labor Code of the Russian Federation). Article 2 of the Labor Code of the Russian Federation establishes the principle of equal rights and opportunities for workers. This is one of the basic principles of labor law, in which "principles of a higher (constitutional) level were embodied, which, from the point of view of content, express rights and freedoms in the field of labor and thereby directly condition the basic rights and freedoms of an employee" [34]. Application enshrined in Article 2 of the Labor Code of the Russian Federation, the principle of equal rights and opportunities for workers, excludes the possibility of presenting different requirements to persons performing work functions of the same content. The establishment of any restrictions is permissible only when it is due to the specifics and characteristics of the work performed, and the differences in the legal status of workers shall be based on their belonging to categories that are different in terms of conditions and type of activity [35].

Article 2 of the Labor Code of the Russian Federation prohibits discrimination in the field of labor. What is meant by discrimination is specified in Article 3 of the Labor Code of the Russian Federation: "Everyone has equal opportunities to exercise their labor rights. No one can be restricted in labor rights and freedoms or receive any benefits regardless of gender, race, color, nationality, language, origin, property, family, social and official status, age, place of residence, attitude to religion, political beliefs, affiliation or non-affiliation with public associations, as well as of other circumstances unrelated to the professional qualities of the employee" [36]. Resolution of the Constitutional Court of the Russian Federation No. 19-P dated December 27, 1999, (clause 4) states that "the freedom of labor involves the provision of everyone with the opportunity to enter into labor relations on equal terms with other citizens, realizing their abilities to work" [37].

In practice, these provisions are not always implemented. First of all, labor law provides for restrictions related to harmful and dangerous working conditions. Harmful production factor by virtue of Article 209 of the Labor Code of the Russian Federation is a production factor, the impact of which on an employee may lead to his/her illness. According to clause 4 of Article 14 of Federal Law "On Special Assessment of Working Conditions" No. 426-FZ dated December 28, 2013, [38] harmful working conditions are working conditions under which the levels of exposure to harmful and (or) hazardous production factors exceed the levels established by standards (hygienic standards) of working conditions. Article 213 of the Labor Code of the Russian Federation states that harmful and (or) dangerous production factors and work, during which mandatory preliminary and periodic medical examinations are carried out, the procedure for which is determined by the federal executive body authorized by the Government of the Russian Federation. In pursuance of the provisions of Article 213 of the Labor Code of the Russian Federation, the Ministry of Health and Social Development of the Russian Federation by Order No. 302-n dated April 12, 2011, approved the "List of harmful and (or) occupational hazards and works that require mandatory preliminary and periodic medical inspections (examinations), and the Procedure for conducting compulsory preliminary and periodic medical inspections (examinations) of workers engaged in heavy work and work with harmful and (or) dangerous working conditions" [39]. According to subsection 2 of clause 3 of Annex 3 to the order of the Ministry of Health and Social Development of the Russian Federation No. 302-n dated April 12, 2011, periodic medical examinations are carried out in order to identify diseases that are medical contraindications to continue work related to exposure to harmful and (or) hazardous industrial factors. According to clause 31 of the same order, at the end of the periodic inspection, the medical organization draws up a medical report.

The list of works that require mandatory preliminary and periodic medical inspections (examinations) of workers includes work at height, maintenance, and repair of existing electrical installations, work in specific geographic regions with significant remoteness of work sites from medical institutions, work directly related with the maintenance of pressure vessels, work directly related to the use of flammable and explosive materials, work in militarized security services, special communication services, collection apparatus, banking structures, other agencies, and services that are allowed to carry and use weapons, work performed by the gas rescue service, militarized mining and mine-rescue services of ministries and departments, and fire protection, work performed by emergency rescue services for the prevention and elimination of natural and man-made emergency situations, etc.

Clause 48 of section IV. Medical contraindications for admission to work of the "Procedure for conducting compulsory preliminary (when applying for a job) and periodic medical inspections (examinations) of workers engaged in hard work and work with harmful and (or) dangerous working conditions," approved by the same order of the Ministry of Health and Social Development of the Russian Federation No. 302-n dated April 12, 2011, indicate that workers (persons entering the work) are not allowed to perform work with harmful and (or) dangerous working conditions, as well as work that require the conduct of preliminary and periodic medical inspections or examinations (that is, all of the above types of work) in order to protect public health and prevent the occurrence and spread of diseases, if there are legally established general medical contraindications, which include diseases accompanied by consciousness disorders: epilepsy and epileptic syndromes of various etiologies and syncopal syndromes of various etiologies.

At the same time, there is no indication in the document that epilepsy ceases to be a medical contraindication to performing work with harmful and (or) hazardous working conditions after stopping dispensary observation due to persistent long-term remission (recovery). On the one hand, this can be seen as a concern for legislators about the health and well-being of citizens with epilepsy, but in practice, this means a lifelong ban on many professions and a narrowing of life horizons, regardless of the actual state of health, the duration of remission with or without medication.

Similar contraindications also exist for other works.

- For example, the diagnosis of epilepsy (G40) prevents the admission to the state or municipal service according to order of the Ministry of Health and Social Development of the Russian Federation No. 984n dated 14.12.2009 "On the approval of the Procedure for medical examination by state civil servants of the Russian Federation and municipal employees, the list of diseases that prevent admission to the state civil service of the Russian Federation and the municipal service or its performance, as well as the forms of conclusion of a medical institution" [40].

- In accordance with Resolution of the Government of the Russian Federation No. 733 dated 26.08.2013 "On medical examination of persons for the presence (absence) of a disease that prevents them from entering the service in the bodies and institutions of the Prosecutor's Office of the Russian Federation and performing the duties of a prosecutor's office employee" [41] in this case epilepsy is a contraindication.

- Epilepsy and epileptic syndromes of various etiologies are included in the list of diseases that impede the appointment of a judge, approved by Decree of the Council of Judges of the Russian Federation No. 78 dated 26.12.2002 [42].

- Order of the Ministry of Health and Social Development of the Russian Federation No. 989n dated 26.08.2011 approved a list of medical contraindications for work using information constituting a state secret, the procedure for obtaining and the form of a certificate of the absence of medical contraindications for working using information constituting state secret [43]. Epilepsy (G40) is included in this list.

- Epilepsy is in most cases a contraindication for service in the internal affairs bodies and internal troops, in the federal migration service, the federal fire service of the Emergencies Ministry in accordance with Article 21 of the diseases time-table of Annex 1 to the Instructions on the procedure for conducting a military medical examination and medical inspection in the internal affairs bodies of the Russian Federation and the internal troops of the Ministry of Internal Affairs of the Russian Federation, approved by order of the Ministry of Internal Affairs of the Russian Federation No. 523 dated 14.07.2010. The assignment of various categories of citizens to be examined to the relevant columns (I, II, III) of the diseases time-table is regulated by articles 104 – 106 of the specified instructions. If a citizen enrolled in a service (study) has a history of at least one seizure entered into medical records, or there are pathological changes on an electroencephalogram at rest or with functional loads (paroxysmal activity and hemispheric asymmetry), certain categories are considered to be limitedly able [44]. On May 14, 2018, this order became invalid on the basis of Order of the Ministry of Internal Affairs of Russia dated 02.04.2018 No. 190, but the requirements for the state of health of citizens entering the service of the internal affairs bodies of the Russian Federation regarding persons diagnosed with epilepsy remained the same [45].

Thus, the state of health of an employee directly affects the possibility of concluding an employment contract. If a certain type of work requires undergoing a medical examination, its result is of paramount importance for the conclusion of an employment contract.

The state of health further influences the employment relationship: it can serve as a basis for transfers of both permanent and temporary nature (Articles 72, 254 of the Labor Code of the Russian Federation), for suspension from work, contraindicated for health reasons (Article 76 of the Labor Code of the Russian Federation), and determines the content of the employment contract (reduction of working time for persons with disabilities; conclusion of a fixed-term employment contract with persons who, due to their state of health, are only allowed to work temporarily in accordance with the medical certificate). Finally, it can also play the role of a legal rights-terminating fact (Articles 77, 81, 83, 341 of the Labor Code of the Russian Federation). At the same time and in the case of long-term remission, citizens with a diagnosis of epilepsy in history are subject to the same legal restrictions.

2.5 The right to study

The above contraindications apply not only to labor relations. Resolution of the Government of the Russian Federation dated 14.08.2013 No. 697 approved a list of specialties and areas of training, when applying for which applicants undergo mandatory preliminary medical inspections (examinations) in the manner prescribed at the conclusion of an employment contract or employment-related contract for the relevant position or specialty [46]. This means that since 2013 it is impossible to get an education in the desired profession, if it is included in the established list of contraindications.

2.6 The rights of citizens with a diagnosis of epilepsy to be called up to military service

Another topical issue is the conscription into the armed forces of persons suffering from epilepsy. From the analysis of statistical data obtained during the medical examination of citizens to be called up to military service, it follows that for health reasons in Russia every third conscript is currently exempted from military service and the number of citizens who are to be released from call-up for health reasons continues to grow. According to Article 5.1 of Federal Law "On Military Duty and Military Service" No. 53-FZ dated March 28, 1998, citizens, at military registration, conscription, or entering military service under a contract, as well as those previously recognized as limitedly able to perform military service for health reasons, shall undergo medical examination by medical specialists: a therapist, a surgeon, a neuropathologist, a psychiatrist, an ophthalmologist, an otorhinolaryngologist, a dentist, and, if necessary, doctors of other specialties [47].

In accordance with Clause 4 of Section 1 of the Regulations on Military Medical Examinations, medical inspection refers to the examination and assessment of the state of health and physical development of citizens at the time of inspection in order to determine their suitability for military service, training (service) in certain military occupational specialties with a written opinion [48]. Doctors managing the work on medical inspection of citizens, according to the results of a medical inspection, give an opinion on the suitability of a citizen for military service in the following categories:

A—able to perform military service
B—able to perform military service with minor restrictions
B—limitedly able to perform military service
G—temporarily unable to perform military service
D—unable to perform military service

With the presence of a diagnosis of epilepsy, according to Article 21 of the Diseases Time-Table in the Annex to the Regulations on the military-medical commission, citizens, when initially undergoing military registration and military service call-up, with epileptic seizures with a frequency of five or more times a year fall into category D (unable to perform military service). In the presence of epileptic status, with a confirmed permanent diagnosis of epilepsy, citizens fall into category D, regardless of the frequency of epileptic seizures.

With a single epileptic seizure in a history of the last 5 years or rare epileptic seizures with a frequency of less than five times a year, citizens fall into category B (limitedly able to perform military service). In cases when medical documentation confirms the established diagnosis of epilepsy in the past, but over the past 5 years epileptic seizures have not been observed, citizens fall into category B, regardless of the results of electroencephalography during the inspection.

In epilepsy, which comes out only in simple partial epileptic seizures or epileptic seizures that develop only in sleep, citizens also fall into category B, regardless of the frequency of seizures. According to Part 1 of Article 23 of the Law "On Military Duty and Military Service," citizens who are recognized as being limitedly able to perform military service for health reasons are also not subject to military service and are exempted from military service.

With a single epileptic seizure in history (more than 5 years) or the presence of epileptiform activity, identified by the results of electroencephalography (peaks, sharp waves, all types of peak-wave complexes, polyspikes, and photoparoxysmal reaction) without clinical manifestations, citizens, at initial military registration and military service, fall into category B-4 (able to perform military service with minor restrictions and can serve in the guard and defense units of combat missile systems, communications units, radio engineering units and other units of the armed forces of the Russian Federation, other troops, and military formations).

It should be noted that Article 21 of the Diseases Time-Table does not take into account whether remission occurs on the background of continuous drug therapy or in its absence.

The presence of a seizure shall be confirmed by medical supervision, and other medical documents confirming an epileptic seizure can also be taken into account. To confirm the presence of an epileptic seizure, written evidence from eyewitnesses can be taken into account, if the description of the seizure gives grounds to consider it epileptic. At the same time, the authenticity of the signatures of eyewitnesses for epileptic seizures shall be notarized.

Article 21 of the Diseases Time-Table does not include seizures associated with the cancelation of alcohol, developed immediately after (up to 10 weeks) a brain injury caused by a brain tumor, drugs or other chemical agents, caused by somatogenically caused metabolic encephalopathies, encephalopathies caused by effects of adverse physical factors, and febrile seizures.

2.7 The right to driving vehicles

The state of health affects almost all aspects of human life. One of the consequences of the diagnosis of epilepsy is **a ban on driving vehicles**. According to clause 1 of Article 23 of Federal Law "On Road Safety" No. 196-FZ dated December

10, 1995, medical inspection of candidates for vehicle drivers is mandatory [49]. The receipt, replacement, and restoration of driving licenses are performed only if there is a medical certificate, which is issued after passing a medical examination in a licensed medical institution.

The presence of documented epilepsy is a medical contraindication to driving a vehicle. According to clause 1 of Article 23.1 of the Law "On Road Safety," medical contraindications to driving a vehicle are diseases (conditions), the presence of which impedes the ability to drive a vehicle. The "List of medical contraindications to driving a vehicle," approved by Resolution of the Government of the Russian Federation No. 1604 dated December 29, 2014, states that epilepsy is a disease of the nervous system, which is a contraindication to driving a vehicle. At the same time, this List does not indicate that epilepsy does not cease to be a medical contraindication to driving a vehicle even after termination of dispensary observation due to persistent remission (recovery) [50].

In accordance with order of the Ministry of Health and Social Development of the Russian Federation No. 302-n dated April 12, 2011, diseases accompanied by disorders of consciousness (epilepsy and epileptic syndromes of various etiologies, syncopal syndromes of various etiologies, etc.) are contraindications for admission to work related to driving a vehicle.

2.8 Medical secrecy

2.8.1 Medical secrecy and concealment of the diagnosis

In view of the above, a question arises about the consequences of concealing the diagnosis of epilepsy. The following should be answered in this regard:

- By virtue of Article 92 of Federal Law No. 323-FZ dated 21.11.2011 "On the basis of health protection of citizens in the Russian Federation," personalized accounting for medical activities is the processing of personal data about persons receiving medical services. Information about persons, who receive medical services, is classified as restricted access information and is subject to protection in accordance with the legislation of the Russian Federation.

- In accordance with clauses 1 and 2 of Article 13 of Federal Law No. 323-FZ dated 21.11.2011 "On the basis of health protection of citizens in the Russian Federation" information about the fact that a citizen applied for medical care, his/her state of health and diagnosis, other information received at his/her medical inspection, and treatment constitute a medical secrecy. The disclosure of information constituting medical secrecy, including after the person's death, by persons to whom it became known during training, working, and performing professional, official, and other duties is not allowed.

- According to Article 9 of Law of the Russian Federation No. 3185–1 dated 02.07.1992 "On psychiatric care and guarantees of the rights of citizens when it is provided" [51] information about the fact that a citizen applied for psychiatric care, his/her mental health and the diagnosis of mental disorder, and other information received during the provision of psychiatric care constitute medical secrecy protected by law.

Thus, the constituent elements of the above medical secrecy are the fact and date of application for medical care, diagnosis, treatment, status, history of the disease, information about associated diseases (sexually transmitted infections, HIV infection, infertility, other gynecological pathology, genetic abnormalities, etc.), and history of life (adultery, homosexual orientation, sexual perversions, abortion, the concealment of true paternity in legal marriage, suicide attempts, etc.). The disclosure of this information can not only degrade the honor and dignity of patients and contribute to their discrimination in society but also cause auto-aggressive reactions (suicides). Similar consequences may also occur due to the disclosure of other diagnoses, for example, cancer and neurological, in particular epilepsy.

It should also be noted that the disclosure of information constituting medical secrecy is the basis for bringing to administrative and criminal liability. According to Article 13.14 of the Code of Administrative Offenses of the Russian Federation, disclosure of information, access to which is restricted by federal law (except for cases when disclosing such information entails criminal liability), by a person who has obtained access to such information in connection with the performance of official or professional duties shall be subject to an administrative fine of citizens in the amount of from 500 to 1000 rubles and of officials from 4000 to 5000 rubles [52]. In accordance with clause 2 of Article 137 of the Criminal Code of the Russian Federation [53], illegal collection or spreading of information about the private life of a person which constitutes his personal or family secret, without his consent, or the distribution of this information in a public speech, in a publicly performed work or in the mass media, committed by a person using his/her official position, shall be punishable with a fine in the amount of from 100 thousand to 300 thousand rubles, in the amount of the wage or salary, or any other in come of the convicted person for a period of from one to two years, or by deprivation of the right to hold specified offices or to engage in specified activities for a term of from two to five years, or by forced labor for a term of up to four years accompanied by deprivation of the right to hold specified offices or to engage in specified activities for a term of up to five years or without such, or by arrest for a term of from four to six months, or by deprivation of liberty for a term of up to four years accompanied by deprivation of the right to hold specified offices or to engage in specified activities for a term up to five years.

Thus, a doctor who made and/or supervises a patient with a diagnosis of epilepsy does not have the right to disclose the diagnosis, except in cases established by the Law (such a case would be, for example, a request from a prosecutor or a judge in a specific criminal or administrative proceeding).

A different matter is the concealment of the diagnosis by the doctor who participates in mandatory preliminary and periodic medical inspections when admitting to various types of work and driving a vehicle, where he/she is individually responsible for the decision made. Here, the responsibility for concealing a diagnosis is directly proportional to the consequences of a given violation.

2.8.2 Medical secrecy and a regional fragment of a unified state information system in the field of healthcare

Issues of disclosure of medical secrecy have been developed with the introduction of a regional fragment of a unified state information system in the field of health care due to its inconsistency with the norms of modern legislation of the Russian Federation (RMIS).

RMIS as an element of the national information system created to ensure effective information support for bodies and organizations of the health care system, as well as citizens in the framework of health care management processes and its direct receipt. The development of the system is governed by the Concept of creating a unified state information system in the health sector, approved by order of the Ministry of Health and Social Development of the Russian Federation No. 364

dated April 28, 2011 [54], as well as a number of guidelines and functional requirements for individual components of the system, which are annexes to the order.

According to Article 23 of the Constitution of the Russian Federation, everyone has the right to privacy, personal and family secrets, and protection of his/her honor and good name. Everyone has the right to confidentiality of correspondence, telephone conversations, and postal, telegraph, and other communications. Under personal privacy, the Constitution of the Russian Federation and federal legislation imply noninterference in privacy, the inviolability of personal and family secrets (privacy secrets). Restriction of this right is allowed only on the basis of a court decision.

By virtue of Article 92 of Federal Law No. 323-FZ dated 21.11.2011 "On the Basics of Health Protection of the Citizens in the Russian Federation," personified accounting for medical activities is the processing of personal data about persons who receive medical services. Information about persons, who receive medical services, is classified as restricted access information and is subject to protection in accordance with the legislation of the Russian Federation.

According to Article 9 of Law of the Russian Federation No. 3185–1 dated 02.07.1992 "On psychiatric care and guarantees of the rights of citizens when it is provided," information about the fact that a citizen applies for psychiatric care, his/her mental health and the diagnosis of mental disorder, and other information obtained during the provision of psychiatric care constitute medical secrecy protected by law.

It should be noted that the above program does not provide the necessary conditions for the protection of the information it contains, which creates the prerequisites for violating the norms of current legislation. The RMIS program contains confidential information, namely: the fact and date of applying for assistance, diagnosis, treatment, mental status, history of the disease, information about associated diseases (sexually transmitted infections, HIV infection, infertility, other gynecological pathology, genetic abnormalities, etc.), and history of life (adultery, homosexual orientation, sexual perversions, abortion, the concealment of true paternity in legal marriage, suicide attempts, etc.). The disclosure of this information can not only degrade the honor and dignity of patients and contribute to their discrimination in society but also cause auto-aggressive and aggressive tendencies (including to medical staff). Similar consequences may occur due to disclosure of diagnoses, for example, oncological and neurological, in particular epilepsy.

Moreover, the information contained in the RMIS program is currently not adequately protected and can be changed, replaced, deleted, stolen, and also made public in the media, including the Internet. The presence of an electronic signature in the doctor's account does not eliminate the possibility of such violations. As practice shows, due to insufficient protection of confidential information in the RMIS program, patients repeatedly refused to be examined and withdrew consent to treatment and to the processing of personal data.

Such a discrepancy between the information system and legal requirements violates the constitutional rights of citizens to privacy, personal, and family secrets.

3. Conclusions

In terms of the implementation of social rights of citizens with a diagnosis of epilepsy, there are the following problems:

1. There are no clinical guidelines on the provision of medical care to patients with epilepsy, approved by the Ministry of Health of the Russian Federation,

which makes it difficult for patients with a diagnosis of epilepsy to have access to modern treatment.

2. The current system of drug provision does not ensure the right of people suffering from epilepsy to free modern effective drugs and does not comply with the unconditional right of everyone to free medical care stated in the Constitution of the Russian Federation.

3. In employment relationships, citizens with long-term remission (drug or non-drug) fall under the same legal restrictions as people with an incurable form of epilepsy.

To date, an employer may dismiss or may not hire an employee who has been diagnosed with epilepsy or syncope condition (due to inconsistency with the position held), suggesting to an employee (if possible) employment in an alternative position (which he/she corresponds to). At the same time, contraindications to work with a diagnosis of "epilepsy" according to the list of general medical contraindications for admission to work with harmful and (or) dangerous production factors, as well as to work, during which the preliminary and periodic medical inspections (examinations) of workers are required (state and municipal services, prosecutor's office employees, judges, etc.) are saved for life not only for patients with epilepsy and epileptic syndromes of various etiologies (G40.0–G40.9) but also for patients with syncope syndromes of various etiology.

4. Since 2013, it is impossible for citizens with a diagnosis of epilepsy to get an education in the desired profession if it is included in the established list of medical contraindications.

5. Military service (including using a weapon) is possible with a single epileptic seizure in history (more than 5 years) or the presence of epileptiform activity detected by electroencephalography, without clinical manifestations.

It is also important that the military-medical examination for epilepsy does not include seizures, which are the clinical manifestation of the acute condition of G40.5 (for example, alcohol poisoning, drugs poisoning, febrile seizures, etc.).

6. The ban on driving a vehicle remains for life, regardless of the severity of the seizures, their number and etiology (G40.0–G40.9), prolonged remission due to drug therapy, or in its absence.

7. Information insecurity in the regional fragment of the unified state information system (RMIS) violates the patients' rights to privacy and the rights of the doctor to medical activities.

Conflict of interest

The authors declare no conflict of interest.

Author details

Anton Petrovich Gertsen[1]* and Vladimir Vladimirovich Rumyantsev[2]

1 Orenburg Regional Clinical Psychoneurological Hospital of War Veterans, Regional Center for the Diagnosis and Treatment of Epilepsy, Orenburg, Russia

2 EPILEPSY56 LLC, Orenburg Region, Orenburg, Russia

*Address all correspondence to: antngercen@yandex.ru

References

[1] Constitution of the Russian Federation. 2014. Available at: http://www.consultant.ru/document/cons_doc_LAW_165801/3d0cac60971a511280cbba229d9b6329c07731f7/ - dst100009 [Internet]. http://www.consultant.ru/document/cons_doc_LAW_28399/ (as amended on 21.07.2014)

[2] Komarova VV. Social statehood of Russia and the right to health protection, medical care. Law and the State: Theory and Practice. 2014;**2**:35

[3] Federal Law No. 323-FZ dated November 21, 2011. On the Basics of Health Protection of the Citizens in the Russian Federation (as amended on 27.12.2018) [Internet]. Available at: http://www.consultant.ru/document/cons_doc_LAW_121895/

[4] Report of the press service of the Ministry of Health of Russia dated September 5, 2017 on the topic of the application of clinical guidelines [Internet]. Available at: https://www.rosminzdrav.ru/news/2017/09/05/6045-soobschenie-press-sluzhby-minzdrava-rossii

[5] Timofeyev IV. On the problems of legal regulation of the medical care quality, reducing the effectiveness of the implementation of the constitutional right to health protection and medical care in the Russian Federation. Medical Law. 2016;**3**:14

[6] Meshkovsky AP. On the problems of drug provision of the population. Medical Technology. Evaluation and Selection. 2015;**3**(21):21-33. P. 21 [Internet]. http://mt-choice.ru/mt_21_2015-3_21-33/

[7] Putilo NV, Volkova NS, Tsomartova FV, et al. In: Putilo NV, editor. The Right of Citizens to Drug Provision: Monograph. M: IZiSP, Contract; 2017. p. 27

[8] Federal Law "On State Social Assistance" No. 178-FZ dated 17.07.1999 (as amended on 27.12.2018) [Internet]. Available at: http://www.consultant.ru/document/cons_doc_LAW_23735/

[9] On the state support for the development of the medical industry and improving the provision of the population and health care institutions with medicinal products and medical devices. Official Gazette of the Russian Federation. Resolution of the Government of the Russian Federation No. 890 dated 30.07.1994. 08.08.1994, No. 15, Art. 1791

[10] On the dispensing of medicines to the population on medical prescriptions during out-patient treatment free of charge and with a 50% discount. Letter of the Ministry of Healthcare and Social Development of the Russian Federation No. 489-BC dated 03.02.2006. [Internet]. Available at: https://base.garant.ru/4183218/

[11] Program of state guarantees of free medical care to citizens for 2018 and for the planned period of 2019 and 2020: approved by Resolution of the Government of the Russian Federation No. 1492 dated 08.12.2017. Official Gazette of the Russian Federation. 18.12.2017, No. 51, Art. 7806

[12] On the program of state guarantees of free medical care to citizens for 2019 and for the planned period of 2020 and 2021. Resolution of the Government of the Russian Federation No. 1506 dated December 10, 2018 [Internet]. http://www.consultant.ru/document/cons_doc_LAW_313205/

[13] Appellate Decision of the Supreme Court of the Russian Federation No. 59-APG17-11 dated 27.12.2017 "On leaving unchanged the decision of Amur Regional Court dated 27.07.2017, which invalidated paragraphs 3, 4, 6,

9, 12, 13, 15, 16 of Section VII of the territorial program of state guarantees of free medical care to citizens for 2017 and for the planning period of 2018 and 2019, approved by Resolution of the Government of Amur Region No. 19 dated 24.01.2017 [Internet]. Available at: http://www.consultant.ru/cons/cgi/online.cgi?req=doc&base=ARB00 2&n=524840#05862020361830658

[14] Appellate Decision of the Supreme Court of the Russian Federation No. 2-APG17-15 dated 13.09.2017 "On leaving unchanged the decision of Vologda Regional Court dated 22.05.2017, which partially satisfied the administrative petition to declare invalid in part of the Program of state guarantees of free medical care to citizens in the territory of Vologda region for 2017 and for the planning period of 2018 and 2019, approved by Resolution of the Government of Vologda region No. 15 dated 25.01.2017 [Internet]. http://www.consultant.ru/cons/cgi/online.cgi?req=doc&base=ARB 002&n=515208#05781082757960796

[15] Appellate Decision of the Supreme Court of the Russian Federation No. 83-APG17-13 dated 30.08.2017 "On leaving unchanged the decision of Bryansk Regional Court dated 26.05.2017, which invalidated certain provisions of Resolution of the Government of Bryansk Region No. 74-пdated 13.03.2017 "On the territorial program of state guarantees of free medical care to citizens for 2017 and for the planned period of 2018 and 2019" [Internet]. http://www.consultant.ru/cons/cgi/online.cgi?req=doc&base=ARB 002&n=513191#04418926657394773

[16] Appellate Decision of the Supreme Court of the Russian Federation No. 29-APG18-1 dated 28.03.2018 "On leaving unchanged the decision of Penza Regional Court dated 30.10.2017, which invalidated certain provisions of the territorial program of state guarantees of free medical care to citizens in Penza Region for 2017 and for the planning period of 2018 and 2019, approved by the Government of Penza region No. 660-ppdated 29.12.2016." [Internet]. http://www.consultant.ru/cons/cgi/online.cgi?req=doc&base=ARB00 2&n=536675#0789044349995315

[17] Appellate Decision of the Supreme Court of the Russian Federation No. 84-APG17-12 dated 27.12.2017 "On leaving unchanged the decision of Novgorod Regional Court dated 11.09.2017, which invalidated certain provisions of the territorial program of state guarantees of free medical care to citizens for 2017 and for the planning period of 2018 and 2019, approved by Resolution of the Government of Novgorod Region No. 43 dated 08.02.2017" [Internet]. Available at: http://www.consultant.ru/cons/cgi/online.cgi?req=doc&base=ARB00 2&n=525594#08265906324676541

[18] Appellate Decision of the Supreme Court of the Russian Federation No. 51-APG17-14 dated 13.09.2017 "On leaving unchanged the decision of Altai Regional Court dated 27.04.2017, which satisfied the administrative claim for invalidation of certain provisions of the territorial program of state guarantees of free medical care to citizens for 2017 and for the planning period of 2018 and 2019, approved by Resolution of the Administration of the Altai Territory No. 457 dated 30.12.2016 [Internet]. Available at: http://www.consultant.ru/cons/cgi/online.cgi?req=doc&base=ARB 002&n=515224#02411298700308315

[19] Appellate Decision of the Supreme Court of the Russian Federation No. 53-APG17-37 dated 11.10.2017 "On leaving unchanged the decision of Krasnoyarsk Regional Court dated 06.06.2017, which satisfied the administrative claim for invalidation in the part of the territorial program of state guarantees of free medical care to citizens of the Russian Federation in the Krasnoyarsk Territory for

2017 and for the planning period of 2018 and 2019, approved by Resolution of the Government of the Krasnoyarsk Territory No. 682-pdated 27.12.2016 [Internet]. Available at: http://www.consultant.ru/cons/cgi/online.cgi?req=doc&base=ARB002&n=517349#05769377896171882

[20] Appellate Decision of the Supreme Court of the Russian Federation No. 44-APG17-17 dated 25.10.2017 "On leaving unchanged the decision of Perm Regional Court dated 28.06.2017, which invalidated certain provisions of the Program of state guarantees of free medical care to citizens for 2017 and for the planning period of 2018 and 2019, approved by Resolution of the Government of the Perm Territory No. 1191-pdated 30.12.2016" [Internet]. Available at: http://www.consultant.ru/cons/cgi/online.cgi?req=doc&base=ARB002&n=518603#02093156965570936

[21] Appellate Decision of the Supreme Court of the Russian Federation No. 31-APG17-9 dated 11.10.2017 "On leaving unchanged the decision of the Supreme Court of the Chuvash Republic dated 16.06.2017, which partially satisfied the administrative claim for invalidationin part of the program of state guarantees of free medical care to citizens in the Chuvash Republic for 2017 and for the planning period 2018 and 2019, approved by Resolution of the Cabinet of Ministers of the Chuvash Republic No. 602dated 30.12.2016"[Internet]. Available at: http://www.consultant.ru/cons/cgi/online.cgi?req=doc&base=ARB002&n=517493#04034208977023762

[22] Meshkovsky A. On the problems of drug provision to the population. Medical Technology. Evaluation and Selection. 2015;**3**(21):21-33. P. 7. [Internet]. http://mt-choice.ru/mt_21_2015-3_21-33/

[23] Order of the Ministry of Healthcare and Social Development of the Russian Federation No. 494 dated August 9, 2005. On the Procedure for Using Medicinal Products in Patients for Salvage Purposes [Internet]. Available at: http://www.consultant.ru/document/cons_doc_LAW_55425/

[24] Federal Law "On Circulation of Medicinal Products" No. 61-FZ dated 12.04.2010 (as amended on 27.12.2018) [Internet]. Available at: http://www.consultant.ru/document/cons_doc_LAW_99350/

[25] Resolution of the Government of the Russian Federation No. 771 dated 29.09.2010 (as amended on 28.12.2016) "On the procedure for the importation of medicinal products for medical use into the territory of the Russian Federation" (together with the "Rules for the importation of medicinal products for medical use into the territory of the Russian Federation") [Internet]. Available at: http://www.consultant.ru/document/cons_doc_LAW_105543/

[26] Gekht AB, Hauser VA, Milchakova LY, Gusev YI. Epidemiology of epilepsy in the Russian Federation. In: Materials of the X Congress of Neurologists with International Participation. Nizhny Novgorod: Publishing house "Darts Grupp"; 2012. p. 277

[27] Kekelidze ZI, Tyumenkova GV. Stigmatization of Patients with Epilepsy: Guidelines. M: Yustitsinform; 2009. p. 4

[28] Gertsen AP, Rumyantsev VV. Topical issues of the social rights enjoyment by people with a diagnosis of epilepsy: The legal aspect. Russian Journal of Pediatric Neurology. 2018;**13**(1):42-53. DOI: 10.17650/2073-8803-2018-13-1-42-53

[29] Ostapenko AG, Shumayeva KV. Discrimination in labor law. Eurasian Union of Scientists. Legal Science Series. 2015;**11**(20):145-146

[30] Zhernakov VV. Freedom of labor and the prohibition of forced labor in the modern labor law. Perm State University Bulletin. Legal Science Series. 2013;**3**(21):90

[31] Cherdantsev AF. Theory of State and Law. M: Yurayt; 2002. p. 224

[32] International Covenant on Economic, Social and Cultural Rights (adopted on 16.12.1966 by Resolution 2200 (XXI) at the 1496th plenary meeting of the UN General Assembly) [Internet]. Available at: http://www.consultant.ru/document/cons_doc_LAW_5429/

[33] Marchenko MN. Theory of State and Law. M: TK Velby, Prospekt; 2004. p. 498

[34] Dmitriyeva IK. Main principles of the labor law: Extended abstract of the D.Sci.Jus. dissertation: 12.00.05. 2004. p. 12

[35] Orlovsky YP. In: Orlovsky YP, Nurtdinova AF, editors. Labor Law of Russia. M: Contract, Infra-M; 2008. p. 48

[36] Labor Code of the Russian Federation No. 197-FZdated 30.12.2001 (as amended on 27.12.2018) [Internet]. Available at: http://www.consultant.ru/document/cons_doc_LAW_34683/

[37] Resolution of the Constitutional Court of the Russian Federation No. 19-Pdated December 27, 1999 on the case on verification of the constitutionality of the provisions of clause 3 of Article 20 of the Federal Law "On Higher and Postgraduate Professional Education", in connection with the complaints of citizens Malkov VP, Antropov YA, as well as a request of Vakhitovsky district court of Kazan [Internet]. Available at: http://www.consultant.ru/document/cons_doc_LAW_25870/

[38] Federal Law "On the Special Evaluation of Working Conditions" No. 426 dated 28.12.2013 (as amended on 27.12.2018) [Internet]. Available at: http://www.consultant.ru/document/cons_doc_LAW_156555/

[39] Order of the Ministry of Healthcare and Social Development of Russia No. 302 ndated 12.04.2011 (as amended on 06.02.2018) "On approval of the lists of harmful and (or) hazardous production factors and works, during which mandatory preliminary and periodic medical inspections (examinations) are carried out, and Procedure for conducting mandatory preliminary and periodic medical inspections (examinations) of workers engaged in heavy work and work with harmful and (or) hazardous working conditions (as amended on 06.02.2018) [Internet]. Available at: http://www.consultant.ru/document/cons_doc_LAW_120902/2ff7a8c72de3994f30496a0ccbb1ddafdaddf518/

[40] Order of the Ministry of Healthcare and Social Development of the Russian Federation No. 984 ndated 14.12.2009 "On approval of the procedure for medical examination by state civil servants of the Russian Federation and municipal employees, the list of diseases that impede admission to the civil service of the Russian Federation and municipal service or its performance, as well as opinion forms ofmedical institutions"(Registered at the Ministry of Justice of the Russian Federation on 29.12.2009 No. 15878) [Internet]. Available at: http://www.consultant.ru/document/cons_doc_LAW_96619/

[41] Resolution of the Government of the Russian Federation No. 733 dated 26.08.2013 "On medical examination of persons for the presence (absence) of a disease that prevents them from entering the service in the bodies and institutions of the Prosecutor's Office of the Russian Federation and performing

their duties as a prosecutor's office employee" (together with the "Rules for conducting a medical examination of a person for the presence (absence) of a disease that prevents him/her from entering the service in the bodies and institutions of the Prosecutor's Office of the Russian Federation and performing his/her duties as a prosecutor's office employee") [Internet]. Available at: http://www.consultant.ru/document/cons_doc_LAW_151258/

[42] Resolution of the Council of Judges of the Russian Federation No. 78 dated 26.12.2002 "On the Approval of the List of Diseases Preventing the Appointment to the Position of a Judge" [Internet]. Available at: http://www.consultant.ru/document/cons_doc_LAW_40411/ca1820d99f2c758e82d835816b28c0a34417dc33/

[43] Order of the Ministry of Healthcare and Social Development of the Russian Federation No. 989ndated 26.08.2011 "On the approval of the list of medical contraindications for work using information constituting a state secret, the procedure for obtaining and the form of a certificate of the absence of medical contraindications for working with information constituting a state secret. [Internet]. Available at: http://www.consultant.ru/document/cons_doc_LAW_120463/2ff7a8c72de3994f30496a0ccbb1ddafdaddf518/

[44] Order of the Ministry of Internal Affairs of Russia No. 523 dated 14.07.2010 (as amended on 26.08.2013) "On the approval of the Instruction on the procedure for conducting a military-medical examination and medical inspection in the internal affairs bodies of the Russian Federation and the internal troops of the Ministry of Internal Affairs of the Russian Federation" (Registered at the Ministry of Justice of Russia on 10.11.2010 No. 18929) [Internet]. http://www.consultant.ru/document/cons_doc_LAW_106964/ became invalid from 14.05.2018 on the basis of order of the Ministry of Interior of Russia No. 190dated 02.04.2018)

[45] Order of the Ministry of Internal Affairs of Russia No. 190 dated 02.04.2018 "On requirements for the state of health of citizens entering the service of the internal affairs bodies of the Russian Federation, and employees of the internal affairs bodies of the Russian Federation, lists of additional mandatory diagnostic studies conducted prior to the start of a medical inspection, forms of documentation required for the activities of military medical commissions, the procedure for conducting a control examination and re-examination and on the recognition of invalidation of certain regulatory legal acts" (together with the "Requirements for the state of health of citizens entering the service in the internal affairs bodies of the Russian Federation, and employees of the internal affairs bodies of the Russian Federation, depending on their positions and the characteristics of serving in certain positions", "Procedure for conducting a control inspection and re-examination according to the results of an independent military-medical examination") (Registered at the Ministry of Justice of Russia on 03.05.2018 No. 50952) http://www.consultant.ru/document/cons_doc_LAW_297538/

[46] Resolution of the Government of the Russian Federation No. 697 dated 14.08.2013 "On the approval of the list of specialties and areas of training, when applying for training under which applicants undergo mandatory preliminary medical inspections (examinations) in the manner prescribed at the conclusion of an employment contract or employment-related contract for the relevant position or specialty" [Internet].

http://www.consultant.ru/document/cons_doc_LAW_150768/

[47] Federal Law "On Military Duty and Military Service" No. 53-FZdated 28.03.1998 (as amended on 22.05.2018) [Internet]. http://www.consultant.ru/document/cons_doc_LAW_18260/

[48] Resolution of the Government of the Russian Federation No. 565 dated 04.07.2013 "On the approval of the Regulations on the military-medical examination" (as amended on 30.01.2019) [Internet]. Available at: http://www.consultant.ru/document/cons_doc_LAW_149096/

[49] Federal Law "On Road Safety" No. 196-FZdated 10.12.1995 (as amended on 27.12.2018) [Internet]. Available at: http://www.consultant.ru/document/cons_doc_LAW_18260/

[50] Resolution of the Government of the Russian Federation No. 1604 dated 29.12.2014 "On the lists of medical contraindications, medical indications and medical restrictions to driving a vehicle" [Internet]. Available at: http://www.consultant.ru/document/cons_doc_LAW_173211/

[51] Law of the Russian Federation No. 3185-1 dated 02.07.1992 "On psychiatric care and guarantees of the rights of citizens in its provision" (as amended on 07.19.2018) [Internet]. Available at: http://www.consultant.ru/document/cons_doc_LAW_4205/

[52] "Code of the Russian Federation on Administrative Offenses" No. 195-FZdated 30.12.2001 (as amended on 06.02.2019) [Internet]. Available at: http://www.consultant.ru/document/cons_doc_LAW_34661/

[53] "Criminal Code of the Russian Federation" No. 63-FZdated 13.06.1996 as amended on 25.04.2018 [Internet]. Available at: https://www.wipo.int/edocs/lexdocs/laws/en/ru/ru080en.pdf

http://www.consultant.ru/document/cons_doc_LAW_10699/

[54] Order of the Ministry of Healthcare and Social Development of Russia No. 364 dated 28.04.2011 (as amended on 12.04.2012) "On the Approval of the Concept for Establishing a Unified State Information System in the Field of Healthcare" [Internet]. Available at: http://www.consultant.ru/document/cons_doc_LAW_113731/

Chapter 12

Abortion, Criminal Law and the Ten Thousand Women: Portraits of the Inquisition in Contemporary Brazil

Alexandra Lopes da Costa

Abstract

The deleterious effects of the criminal law, which deals with abortion in Brazil, the restriction of reproductive rights and their impact on women's health will be the subject discussed in this chapter from an analysis of the "case of the ten thousand," as it became known the emblematic reproductive rights violation of a universe of almost ten thousand, women, occurred in Campo Grande, Mato Grosso do Sul (MS), in 2007, when a doctor's office was invaded by the police after a television report denouncing the establishment for abortion practices. This chapter discusses this paradigmatic case of violation of privacy and disrespect to reproductive health by making critical considerations about the implications of the criminalization of abortion on the physical and emotional integrity of women, highlighting the discursive contradictions between the Brazilian law and the United Nations Documents that deal with the consequences of unsafe abortion in the female population worldwide.

Keywords: criminal law, abortion, reproductive rights, reproductive health

1. Introduction

The criminal law that deals with abortion on the Brazilian territory walks against the progress of reproductive rights on the international board, of scientific evidences that highlight health risks caused by the criminalization and the positive experiences of safe abortion services on countries where it is legalized. It is a police assumption, a crime normalized by justice, a sin for many people and a serious public health problem, a controversial field of discussion, delicate and prickly.

On this conflicted combat ring I present the "ten thousand case," as it became known a Dantesque episode of reproductive rights' violation in an universe of almost ten thousand (9896) women, that took place in Campo Grande, capital of Mato Grosso do Sul (MS), provoking controversy between, on one side, the defenders of embryonic cells' life since conception and, on the other, the ones who defend the dignity of life and autonomy of women.

Mato Grosso do Sul is a state in the Midwest region of the Brazilian territory considered one of the country's granaries in planting grains and raising cattle. In this state with agrarian characteristics and conservative norms of gender perseveres the contrasts of concentration of income, of the power of the oligarchies and of the large rural properties that reinforce the bases of Coronelismo and Machismo, besides the oppression of the women in the city, countryside, indigenous villages, border regions and Quilombola communities.

It was in this hostile environment that the greatest act of violation of women's rights occurred in the history of the Midwest region, with the accomplishment of the journalistic material on the Family Planning Clinic, of the former doctor Neide Mota Machado, in the largest television network of the region that denounced abortion practice without obtaining convincing evidence.

Remembering, on the 10th day of April in the year 2007, a medical clinic named "Familiar Planning Clinic," owned by an anaesthesiologist named Neide Mota Machado, was invaded by police after the exhibition of the news report that reported the place for performing abortions. On the occasion, police confiscated the medical records of ten thousand women, violating their right to privacy and medical confidentiality about health questions which concerned only them.

In Brazil, the juridical instrument that deals on abortion is the Criminal Code, dated from 1940, where, on its articles 124–128, condemns abortion in every case, with or without the pregnant' consent; excluding two exceptional situations: if the pregnancy results from rape or presents real risks to the woman's life. There is still a recent measure promulgated that allows the therapeutic anticipation of child-birth when it presents anencephalic fetus.[1]

Despite the severe criminalization of abortion (excluding the three cases mentioned above) the prison sentence has weak application in the country, due to the expressive numerical proportion of women that resort, daily, to this popularly used practice, unable to be imprisioned in a system that is already overcrowded and deficient. But it looms upon them the fear of being discovered, the threat of being denounced to police, stigmatized by society and the risk of punishment by justice [1–6].

About one in every five Brazilian women around 40 years old already interrupted a pregnancy at least once. In 2015 alone, the estimatives pointed 416 thousand abortions in all country. The clandestine abortion entails, frequently, countless sequels on health or even death, and imposes an expressive factor of mortality among women: it is the fifth biggest cause of maternal death, in its vast majority preventable if abortion was legalized, free and safe.[2]

Even before imminent risks, there are many women who dribble the law and exercise the right to choose to interrupt an unplanned, unwanted and rejected pregnancy, generally, clandestinely and without proper medical assistance. The restrictive criminal law, thus, fulfil a misogynistic pedagogical objective: the maintenance of compulsory maternity and the male guardianship over the feminine governability of their own body and destiny.

It is a disciplinary correction device that punishes legally and symbolically women that dare to enjoy the freedom of choice and self-care, with discernment and ethic authonomy, on the most intimate, hard, painful and delicate decision for abortion. "In practice, the laws concerning abortion has less prescriptive function

[1] In 2004, the National Confederation of Health Workers (Confederação Nacional dos Trabalhadores na Saúde/CNTS) filed a petition of an Argument of Fundamental Precept Violation (Arguição de Descumprimento de Preceito Fundamental (ADPF 54), arguing that the prohibition of child-birth anticipation of ananencephalic fetusis a violation of the mother's dignity. In 2012, the Federal Courtof Justice approved the permission for anticipation on this case.

[2] Information available at the electronic address (in Portuguese): https://www.huffpostbrasil.com/2018/07/31/aborto-no-brasil-como-os-numeros-sobre-abortos-legais-e-clandestinos-contribuem-no-debate-da-descriminalizacao_a_23486575/ [Accessed on: July 2018].

then symbolic disciplinary function; although not effective, it makes a normative environment that punishes the women psychologically socially" ([2], p. 38).

This article presents the history of the case of the ten thousand that was marked as a kind of contemporary witch hunt, with legal, symbolic and moral punishment and stigmatization of the feminine, that is, a methodology to condemn thousands of women using the sensationalism bonfire of mass communication vehicles, the religious dogmatism of the speech in support to life since conception, the coercive effects of a law about freedom of choice and the power of conservative forces that culminated with the inquisition of four women before a Popular Jury.

On the next part of this essay the text explores the relationship between gender relations and legal devices and the legislator's perspective on the differential treatment of male and female in various historical moments, highlighting also the influence of dogmatic religious groups and other conservative forces that press Brazilian parliaments in contemporaneity, in an attempt to enact antiquated laws that weaken or even disregard human rights, especially with regard to sexual and reproductive rights. After this subitem, it will focus on the story of the Familiar Planning Clinic since the start and highlight the paths that employees of such establishment took to the Jury trial, as well as the events that resulted on the violation of privacy and disrespect of reproductive health of the ten thousand. On the next section I talk about the most striking moments of the Jury Court and, lastly, I weave critical considerations about the implications of abortion criminalization on the physical and emotional integrity of women, highlighting the discursive contradictions between the Brazilian law and United Nations documents that deal with the consequences of insecure abortions among the female population around the world.

2. Juridical devices, disciplining of bodies: two-way street?

Themes like abortion, maternity and law devices on the reproductive scope cannot be dissociated from gender conventions immersed on the historical context of each period, culture and society. On Classical Antiquity, for instance, many philosophers believed that men were transmitters of humanity oriented by the understanding that semen generated life in the receptacle of the female body. Women were conceived as a territory to seed and the ones at fault in case of sterility [7].

Women's anatomy was defective and deficient, said Aristoteles. Men, on the other side, were endowed with the creation act by the qualities inherent to their sex, of their breath and fertility of their seed when fertilizing the cold vessel of the women made life sprout, superiodr dimension of the masculine (omni)potence [8]. However, on the Greco-Roman world the decision for abortion did not suffer moral or legal condemnation. But the apparent freedom and autonomy of women on the control of their body was subordinated to the meticulous appraisal of the husband's or master's decision.

Thereby, abortion was only allowed when it did not go against the will of progeny and many were the men that accused women of denying them this right. On those cases, the crime was not about the abortion of the fetus, but to contradict the masculine's interests and will [7, 9].

On the Middle Ages, the Christianization of the West by the roman caused the collapse of the ancient pagan traditions, cults, belief and the rich pharmacopeia became stigmatized, hunt down and condemned. The women's knowledge became a heresy and a threat to the know-power of the first herbalists (doctors), proof of witchcraft and union with the devil in consequence of their weak and diabolical personality.

The evil and vile inclination of the feminine character is highlighted on Malleus Maleficarum, the most important known guide of identification and fight against witchcraft. This document became something like a churchman Criminal Code indispensable to the catholic judges on the race against the witches. Born from a crooked rib, women are mysterious beings, of fragile sex, treacherous and cunning that distill the damnation above everyone, imperfect animals and liars worse than death. "Without the malignancy of women, not to mention the witchcraft, the world would keep existing immune to numerous hazards," speculates the bull of the inquisitors ([10], p. 53).

Essentially related to sexuality and the mysteries of the universe, to the limits between life and death, like abortion, witches were nothing more than the peasants, lovers, prostitutes, midwives, healers, mourners, women that defied the church dogmas by holding knowledge and power about diseases relief and control of the body [11], like phytotherapeutic knowledge of medicinal teas, passed on from generation to generation through oral tradition, which united women, because the herbs were cultivated on the backyards, close to the kitchen, denoting a familiar and intimate knowledge of the feminine, highlighted Del Priore [12].

From Plato to Aristotle, going through the church philosophers, to the example of Saint Augustine and Thomas Aquinas[3], many are the treaty that reaffirm the inequality of women in relation to men, highlights the historian Mary Del Priore [13]. According to her, the philosophical thinking of centuries XVIII and XIX justified the masculine domination in various ways.

Even the illuminists from the French Revolution (1789), carriers of new ideologies in the name of reason, freedom and equality and opponents to the church dogma when proclaiming the quality of rights to men, excluded women equating in some aspects to the conservatism and intolerance of the medieval catholic morality. Remember the french feminist Olympe de Gouges, that when elaborating the Declaration of the Rights of Woman and of the Female Citizen, in counterpoint to the Declaration of the Rights of Man and Citizen, was criminalized, condemned to death and decapitated in a public square under the accusation of subverting the designs of nature. The principles of Human Rights were, notoriously, erected grounded on the masculine [14, 15].[4]

Despite the resistance and women's fights for civil and politic rights, the secondary place delegated to them in the family and society ruled expressively on the Victorian Age. It was evident, so, that abortion was not allowed. With the ascension of social medicine there is a reinforcement of binary representations of gender versed as a science threshold. The fragility, the pudency, the affective characteristics in detriment of the rational ones and the subjection of sexuality to the maternalism constituted the medical normalizations for the feminine [14, 15].

The association of women to maternity, considered an innate biological instinct, built the normality parameters to the feminine sex prescribed by the masculine

[3] However, it is important to note: the Catholic Church has not always considered abortion a sin or a crime and it cannot be said that there was consensus on the subject over time. St. Augustine in the fourth century and Thomas Aquinas, a thousand years later, for example, considered the embryo a life only after 40 days of gestation (6 weeks). We can also cite the encyclical Apostolicae Sedis (1869), promulgated by Pope Pius IX, in Italy, which came to condemn abortion radically. But the reasons were not so much humanitarian as politics. It was the time of the unification war of Italy, and the pope needed Napoleon's army. In exchange, Bonaparte asked Pius IX to declare that the soul and human life were given from the conception, since the French low birth rate was a hindrance to the French emperor. See the article "The Catholic Church has not always been against abortion." Available from: https://www.revistaforum.com.br/igreja-catolica-nem-sempre-foi-contra-o-aborto/ [Accessed on: December 19, 2018].

[4] Even under this hostile atmosphere, women have claimed a different position in society claiming the right to education, work, political participation and full citizenship through a series of manifestations and protests.

DOI: http://dx.doi.org/10.5772/intechopen.89014

gaze. The will to generate, give birth and motherhood were preponderant facts on the definition of a healthy and balanced organism settling the natural fate of women: get married, give birth, raise children, take care of the house, the husband and the children [9].

Such aspects also influenced the juridical world, because the definition of crime and offense followed a stereotype vision of the proper conduct to men and women. Cesare Lombroso, Italian doctor and criminologist and one of the most famous exponents of the racist and mysoginist thinking of this phase of history, believed that women with outstanding erotism and intelligence did not have the maternal feeling, there so, were abnormality and dangerous creatures composing the group of the criminal, prostitutes and crazy that should be banished from society (Lombroso and Ferrero apud Soihet, [15]).

In general lines, those gender norms disseminating a world order unequal to men and women enrolled in Latin America from the European colonization remaining along the XIX century. In the scope of social relations, the masculine privileges on the field of economy, culture, politics and sexuality were backed by law, church recommendations and medical corporations that timidly were emerging [16].

The gender conventions dictated the life rules of men and women as outlined by the Civil Codes of the past centuries, drawn under the inspiration of Spanish and Portuguese law, heavily based on canonical principles. In them, women were banned from acting in the public scope and their rights to property, property management, inheritance, and decision making in marriage remained limited. In addition, criminal law judged the crimes committed by the male and the female sex differently, whose judgments involving human rights honesty and male honor highlighted these sexist distortions [16].

And in spite of the cultural atmosphere instituted by the bourgeois revolutions (Industrial and French Revolution) in Europe to have influenced the revision of canon law in Latin societies in the mid-XIX century, the new legal body processed to reiterate the family model already prescribed in the Canonical Code: religious, heterosexual, monogamous and undissolvable marriage, as well as the husband's authority over his wife and children (Patria potestas) [16].

Regarding Brazil, in 1830, in the Criminal Code of the Empire, a device that considers abortion a crime that jeopardized security and human life itself, with the exception of non-punishment when abortion was committed by the pregnant woman herself. The Criminal Code of the Republic of 1890 also did not punish women, but presaged punishment for the practice of abortion performed by third parties, with or without the consent of the pregnant woman, with aggravation if this resulted in her death.

Later in time, the Brazilian Criminal Code of 1940, which deals with abortion in Articles 124–128, allowed abortion only in cases of risk to the woman's life or due to rape and criminalized it in other situations. Concerning the permission of abortion involving sexual violence, the conception of jurists in general pointed out that the rape severely damaged male honor and dignity and tainted the offspring of the man who did not accept to support illegitimate children and pass on his inheritance. Therefore, it was a mentality that followed patriarchal period customs and not necessarily a concern for women, their physical and emotional health.

Although dated from 1940, the provisions of the Criminal Code concerning abortion remain in force, but are obsolete and anachronistic for the contemporary society. It is important to say that this legislation was promulgated in the government of Getúlio Vargas, president who took over the country through a coup. That is, the law that governs abortion in Brazil was drawn in full dictatorial regime, in a socio-cultural context of rigid gender customs: few women worked outside home, drove cars, had a college degree, could choose whether or not to have children or even participated in movements, unions or actively on the political life of the nation. But it could be said that, paradoxically, it was advanced for the time, especially if we consider the countless bills, contrary to sexual and reproductive rights, that are currently being processed in the National Congress and the more flexible achievements, values and customs and from the point of view of gender relations that we find today.

The laws, roughly written by men, do not escape gender representations inserted in long term history. As remembered by Fausto [17], on the literary work "Crime and Routine," a study about criminality in São Paulo city between 1880 and 1924, the efficiency of the criminal action is not only technical, but is related to social discrimination working as a repressive practice that can even criminalize behaviors apparently nonchalant to criminal law, like the imprisonment of prostitutes, homosexuals and women who opted for abortion.

That is, the inappropriate behavior according to sex within the family and society, as well as ethnic-racial characteristics influence the conception and definition of the offense and on the application of punishment on the transgression scope. Furthermore, Fausto [17] signaled the existence of criminal behavior that did not draw police's attention, like assaults practiced by husbands and certain sexual crimes.

In 1945, the country resumed the redemocratization process and decades later, in 1964, suffered a new coup d'etat orchestrated by the military, which overlapped the Democratic State and initiated a period of strong censorship, political persecution, torture and death. Even in this context, feminists denounced the oppressions of a patriarchal society, raised the flags of "personal is political," preached the end to domestic violence, of defense of sexual freedom, of the non-demonization of contraceptive methods, of the right to control their own body and reproductive self-determination. Those discussions were also influenced by the emergence, on 1960, of the contraceptive pills.

The politization of the body, sexuality and reproduction gets special attention on the women's movements. The slogan "our body belongs to us" was fundamental to think the diverse forms of subjugation of women and target of political action fundamental on a conception of citizenship that retrieved the autonomy and freedom of women in the experience of sexuality and reproduction [18, 19]. The search for economical, subjective and social autonomy also became essential to this feminine body in the process of emancipation and the existence of the feminist movements that insurged, which also helped to delimit a self-fight field concerning other social movements [18].

Since then Brazilian women obtained a series of achievements, like more space and participation in society, public politics and specific laws to prevent and reduce violence against women and changes on the conservative mentality on the field of gender relations in the sense of more equality. Many of these achievements were driven by International Conferences related to women rights promoted by United Nations (UN) on the decade of 1990 in conjunction with feminist activism.

Stands out the International Conference on Human Rights, held in Vienna in 1993 [20]; that states in its article 18 that rights of women and girls are inalienable; the International Conference on Population and Development, in Cairo in 1994, asks the Estates for investment on familiar planning politics, the reduction of maternal mortality and the review of punitive laws that concern abortion; and the IV World Conference on Women, at the city of Beijing in China in 1995, that requested to the government the use of gender perspective on the development of policies for women [21].

These UN meetings also helped to transpose the generic parameter of man (western, white, heterosexual) as a synonym for humanity, marking the liberal conception of the text of the Universal Declaration of Human Rights of 1948 [22], extending the horizon of human rights for the inclusion and visibility of new subjects. They also revealed that the specifications, diversities and differences between men and women and among women themselves must be integrated into the discourse of human rights as factors of inequality and discrimination [23, 24].

However, the inequalities between men and women are still significant in Brazil. The voluntary abortion is not allowed by law yet, the participation of women on parliaments is minimal, the rates of domestic violence, of feminicide and maternal mortality are very high and, broadly, they still have the lower wages in the market for the same work developed when comparing to men.

In the last decades, the reversal has been enormous. On the field of reproductive self-determination it can be highlighted the dozens of legislative proposals (written under strong influence of conservative, fundamentalist sectors and dogmatic religious groups) that seek to restrict women's sexual and reproductive rights on process in the National Congress, like the Legislative Proposal 478/2007–called Statute of the Unborn (Estatuto do Nascituro), which prohibits abortion in all cases, even rape, and turns the insecure abortion into a heinous crime; the Legislative Proposal 3748/2008, which provides child support to the mother for giving birth to children conceived through a rape crime; the Legislative Proposal 1413/2007, which prohibits the distribution of emergency contraceptive (known as morning-after pill by SUS–the Health Unic System (Sistema Único de Saúde)) and its commercialization in drugstores, among others.

Thus, there are many initiatives in parliaments throughout the country that try to stop achievements in the field of human rights when it involves sexuality and reproduction. To be more emphatic, they are bills that try to prohibit emergency contraception, which strengthen the obstacles to the criminalization of homophobia and the recognition of rights to the homosexual population, as well as opposing the reformulation of restrictive legislation regarding abortion and of sex education programs in schools.[5]

From the religious field to the government policy scope there is a resurgence of fundamentalism and conservative forces that threaten the rights and lives of women. One of the strategies of the conservative groups is to keep the National Congress always on the agenda of discussing abortion as a crime and incompatible with human values in defense of life. An example of this is the numerous appealing projects cited above. The actions of conservative groups, such as the appealing projects cited above, generate tensions and wear and tear on the allied fronts of feminists, but are part of a well-orchestrated strategy by self-entitled "pro-life" for the strengthening of their ideals.

The pressure and interests at stake are so many that even in relation to the so-called "allied politicians," the expected result and compromise are not always achieved. Former President Luiz Inacio Lula da Silva (PT), a progressive force, for example, who has already spoken publicly about the right of women to decide, signed the agreement with the Vatican in 2008, which preaches religious teaching in schools, financial support and a number of other measures in the countercurrent of the Lay State.[6]

[5] We cannot forget the bill "School Without Party", that seeks to suppress discussions of gender, religion, sexuality and politics in the classroom and in the school space as a whole, setting a censorship and limitation of content to be teached mode, with punishment to the teacher if denounced by the student.

[6] The agreement between the Government of the Federative Republic of Brazil and the Holy See concerning the Legal Status of the Catholic Church in Brazil, signed in the Vatican City on November 13, 2008, was ratified by Decree No. 7107 of February 11, 2010. Available from: http://www.planalto.gov.br/ccivil_03/_ato2007-2010/2010/decreto/D7107.htm

In the sowing of patriarchal values, fundamentalists, oligarchies and religious sectors are the groups that most represent the obstacles to advancing the fight for the decriminalization of abortion in Brazil. Generally, they have a conservative discourse from the point of view of biomedical science and the laity of the state. In the dispute for the concept of life, what prevails is the discourse of biological life from orthodox biomedicine and the mix of values of the State and Church, with strong articulation in the Executive.

And if in one hand reproduction and motherhood continue to be treated as the fated destiny of women, on the other, adoption is not yet a valued alternative to motherhood. In addition, the dispute in the field of reproduction also occurs through the market, with the industry of products for babies and pregnant women, new reproductive technologies, last generation ultrasonographies, etc.

Among this context, the neoliberal field advances in the Brazilian political culture, going through the health issue with the growth of foundations and private health plans to the detriment of the Unified Health System (SUS), It is also evident a scenario of high urban violence and at the same time indifference to this violence in most Brazilian urban centers. The marches that preach peace and not abortion, understood as a threat to life, start to appear, generally formed by the middle class who have a conservative vision of peace, since the fear of violence is what drives this kind of reaction by the average layers and other conservative groups, centered on their own navel.

There are also the strategies that the media has been adopting in relation to abortion, polarized by messages through soap operas and programs that are veiled or expressive against legalization and the frequent reports displayed in newspapers about the overflowing appearance of clandestine clinics in various regions of the country, as well as women leaving hospital in handcuffs for reports of unsafe abortion by doctors and other health professionals to the police.

A series of reports conducted by journalist Paula Guimarães, from the *Portal Catarinas*, named "From the emergency room to the penal system,"[7] carried out all over the country, portrays cases of criminalization of patients attended at the Health Posts or in hospitals, due to complications by badly done or even spontaneous abortions, evidence that health professionals have often reported to the police the injured women who entrust their lives to them.[8]

A research carried out by the Public Defense of Rio de Janeiro points out that the delations made by health institutions and professionals during emergency care for women by the practice of self-medication are more common than one can imagine and one of the main means of entry of patients into the penal system. To get an idea, in 65% of cases they were reported during emergency medical care, and in 20% of cases, by relatives and neighbors.[9]

[7] Consult the series "From the Emergency Room to the Penal System", produced by Paula Guimarães. Available at the electronic address: https://outraspalavras.net/outrasaude/do-pronto-socorro-ao-sistema-penal/ [Accessed on: December 20, 2012].

[8] To keep track of this reality, the Collaborative Map of Criminalization by Abortion was launched, which compiles information and journalistic material on the cases of patients reported to the police while receiving medical care in health centers throughout Brazil. The Abortion Criminalization Collaborative Map can be accessed at this electronic address: http://especiais.catarinas.info/mapa-colaborativo-da-criminalizacaoo-das-mulheres-por-aborto/ [Accessed on: December 20, 2012].

[9] To keep track of this reality, the Collaborative Map of Criminalization by Abortion was launched, which compiles information and journalistic material on the cases of patients reported to the police while receiving medical care in health centers throughout Brazil. The Abortion Criminalization Collaborative Map can be accessed at this electronic address: http://especiais.catarinas.info/mapa-colaborativo-da-criminalizacaoo-das-mulheres-por-aborto/ [Accessed on: December 20, 2012].

In Campo Grande, in the year 2017, a case of spontaneous abortion was reported to the police by professionals from the Emergency Mobile Service (SAMU) and widely reported in the local press, suggesting that it was an intentional abortion and disseminated negative representations of the patient. Parts of a fetus were found in the toilet at the house of a married woman who requested emergency assistance from SAMU. The medical help turned into a police case. After receiving care at the residence by the SAMU team, she was taken by ambulance to Rosa Pedrossian Regional Hospital, where she received other medical care, but was kept under police surveillance and was released only after being interviewed.[10]

The sensationalism of the press regarding abortion strengthens the representations of women's biological determinism as mother (maternalisms). It is common the reports that disclose the cases of patients who provoked abortion, sought medical services resulting from complications, who leaves health institutions handcuffed after the care and are taken directly to the police station, in addition to the materials that denounce the clandestine clinics and their process of invasion by the police. The media spectacle on the news report that explore the closure of clandestine establishments that allegedly carry out procedures for intervention of unwanted pregnancies was evident in the case of women criminalized for abortion in Campo Grande, when the police, a public prosecutor and a judge of the jury created a task force for the massive indictment of the ten thousand women who passed through the Family Planning Clinic of Neide Mota over the 20 years of its operation, subject of the last two sections of this text.

3. The case of the ten thousand: the criminal chase and the "witches" exposition in Brazil

Clandestine clinics of abortion in Brazil have been, frequently, target of media reports and spectacularization. One of the involvement marks of media on public revelation of places that supposedly performed pregnancy interruption surgeries was the case of the ten thousand. This story started on April 10, 2007, at Campo Grande city, when a news report made with a hidden camera,[11] operated by a fake pregnant couple looking for abortion, denounced the existence of a Familiar Planning Clinic in function for over 20 years at the capital downtown.

On April 11 the police started the investigation and on April 12 the state's General Prosecutor was visited by representatives of the National Congress' Mix Parliament Front on Life's Defense (against abortion) that put pressure on authorities for the establishment of a criminal process against the owner of the place, the doctor and anaesthesiologist Dr. Neide Mota Machado [25, 26].

The pressure had effect. On April 13, 2007, policemen with a search warrant closed the clinic without the doctor being there, and confiscated surgical instruments, medicines, syringes, needles and patient's private documents. The medical reports of 9896 women were scrutinized by the police and, lately, by justice strong-arms [25, 26].

---

[10] To keep track of this reality, the Collaborative Map of Criminalization by Abortion was launched, which compiles information and journalistic material on the cases of patients reported to the police while receiving medical care in health centers throughout Brazil. The Abortion Criminalization Collaborative Map can be accessed at this electronic address: http://especiais.catarinas.info/mapa-colaborativo-da-criminalizacaoo-das-mulheres-por-aborto/ [Accessed on: December 20, 2012].

[11] Later, another report was made, this time with camera in sight, in which the medical anesthesiologist NeideMota Machado reported to the journalist HonórioJacometto the abortion requested by the clients, but in a safe manner and with all appropriate medical care.

After 3 months, the state's Prosecution Office offered a suit against NeideMota and other six of her employees for the crime of abortion and criminal association [27]. The medical reports (9896) of the patients, handled without the presence of an expert, were included on the process as proof for the indictment. In order for the crime not to prescribe, the prosecution denounced all the ten thousand women [25, 26].

That is, the medical reports served as basis to the process, especially the ones that had ultrasonography, positive pregnancy tests and forms signed by women authorizing the medical procedures. Cases of prescription and ones with information judged incomplete by justice were discarded [25, 26, 28]. Such a measure resulted on the accusation of 1500 women for crimes of abortion.

Of these, the first called to attend to the police station did not know what the intimation was about and were submitted to questioning without clarification of their rights, like the right to keep silent or having the presence of a lawyer or public defender. This fact represents a violation of the right to full defense and the minimal judicial guarantees [27]. To some of them, it was offered the process' suspension so they would not be taken to jury, as long as they accepted to collaborate with investigations and under some conditions. Only five men were sued on this stage [26] and, as the story went, it is estimated that less than 10 were indicted.

Through 3 months, the process were available for public consultation on the Justice Court of MatoGrosso do Sul's (TJ/MS) website and many people had access to the names, accusation and address of the women who supposedly had had abortions, violating the constitutional right to privacy [26].

During the judicial treatment of the case there was a sentence reversion (based on the law 9.009/95) on the alternative sentences and many women were able to choose to pay a fine, community service or donation of a basic products list. Poor women, generally, opted for community service, where they were obligated to make it on day care centers and schools, bringing moral and emotional embarrassment and strong self-blaming. The Judge's declaration to the press revealed that this condemnation was on purpose: they should take care of children and regret what they had done [26].

It is established that the police mandate to close the Clinic did not authorize the apprehension of medical reports. The delegate that took the case, Dra. Regina Márcia Rodrigues de Brito affirmed to Ipas Brasil: "if we were investigating a clinic where they did not make abortions, we would not have taken the medical reports" ([26], p. 6). She also affirmed that it would not be possible to sue the women without information that were on the reports [26].

According to Art. 154 of the Penal Code, to reveal secrets to someone without fair cause concerning a role or profession and which revealing could cause damage to another is punishable with 3 months to 1 year of detention and a fine. Art. 102 of the Brazilian Medical Ethic's Codedescribes methods to secure the confidentiality and protect patient's privacy on criminal investigations. Not even a judicial ordercan suppress the mandatory protection of professional secrecy.

Resolution n° 1.605/2000 of the Federal Medical Council, on the Art. 4, is another document that determines the procedures: "if a judicial authority demands the presentation of medical reports during a criminal process, the doctor will provide those documents only to a legal expert named by the judge that will analyse the question" (p. 6, [26]).

In light of that, only 1500 women were indicted, but them all (around 10,000) had their rights violated, even though both medical secrecy and their privacy were disrespected. After all, the medical reports were handled by police and justice employees without the presence of an expert, damaging the women's right to medical secrecy, which concerns only them since it involves the intimacy of their bodies [26, 27].

As the investigation unrolled, NeideMota Machado (clinic's owner) and four of her employees were pronounced, by all the Court Judges of TJ/MS, to be judged by a popular jury. However, something new and unexpected happened: the enigmatic death of NeideMota.

On the afternoon of November 29 of 2009, a Sunday, Neide was found dead inside her car on a road near the farmhouse where she lived: "On her right hand she had a 10 ml syringe and between her legs there was another one, without a needle. There was also an used bottle of Lidocaine Hydrochloride, and a letter written by pencil between her bench and the passenger."[12] The content of the letter asked for no panic, trauma or pain, on the day before, Neide had registered on a public notes' office the desire to be cremated.

After police investigations the case was filed as suicide, but feminists from all around the country and many people in town brought up the hypothesis of "file burning," since the mysterious death was not well explained by the competent authorities. About 3 years after the closing of the Family Planning Clinic, the jury trial that led to judgment the four employees that worked at Dr. Neide Mota Machado's clinic started on Campo Grande's Forum.

4. Jury trial or witch-hunt?

The Jury trial that submitted the four former workers from the Family Planning Clinic, Libertina de Jesus Centurion, Rosângela de Almeida, Maria Nelma de Souza and Simone Aparecida Cantagessi de Souza to the scrutiny of a popular jury had its first run on April 8, 2010, at 8 a.m., on the 2nd Section of the Jury Court on the Justice Forum of Campo Grande-MS county, lasting for 2 days.[13]

Despite the intense disclosure of the case on vehicles of mass communication, there were few people where the judgment took place. It was noticeable the attendance of friends and family of the defendants, students, law operators, and just five feminists from the city, among other actors made the timid and simple audience made by a group of a little more than 30 people. There were no banners, outcries or any kind of public manifestation on the front of the Forum, contrasting the intense acting of the Brazilian feminist organizations to stop the conviction of the clinic's patients, criminalized for abortion over the past 3 years.

Three members of the Prosecution Office, four defense lawyers, the judge, employees of the Forum and, posteriorly, the four indicted (who entered escorted by policemen), and the seven juries members of the Verdict Council composed the actors framework in plenary. It all seemed too serious and gloomy, except for the striking presence of the press. Journalists from various TV stations, from printed and online newspapers, made the event coverage with media ratio breaking the ice from the formalities and sobriety atmosphere.

The magistrate AluízioPereira dos Santos started the trial by communicating the criminal process instruction in plenary and identifying all the actors involved: the presiding judge (that is, himself), the prosecutors, defense lawyers and indicted.

After the initial instructions from the judge, the judgment started with the argumentation of Siufi, defense lawyer of Simone Cantagessi, who questioned the judge about to whom had been delivered the expert forensic medical report about

---

[12] Information available on the website: https://alias.estadao.com.br/noticias/geral/livro-de-joseph-frank-e-mais-que-uma-biografia-de-dotoievski/70002482374 [Accessed on: August 15, 2018].

[13] The first date of the judgment was supposed to be on February 24, 2009, but it was changed by the judge due a question of order argued by the defense that pointed violation of natural principles and excess of accusations.

the medical records apprehended at the clinic. By highlighting that the results of the document's analysis does not prove the materiality of the crime, Siufi asks the judge the postponement of the Jury, an arguing that will insistently resume during the moments granted to the defense time.

> *"If it was delivered to someone who's part of the Prosecution Office, I ask Your Honor for it to be officiated to the National Council of the Prosecution Office to take appropriate action, because I'm sure that if this document was here, the decision of the crime would be another"* [29, 30].

Siufi alerted that the report of indirect corpus delicti forensic exam already mentioned the material collected at the clinic, sustaining that the reports do not prove the materiality of the crime. This fact would show the existence of ungrounded questions and would allow blurred inductions of the case assessment. In face of that, the lawyer defended the postponement of the Popular Jury in view of the wide possibility of conducting the legal process through tortuous ways. Another two requirements are worded by the lawyer: the withdraw of the police escort around the defendants and the removal of two of the present prosecutors under the allegation of over charge.[14] Judge Aluízio Pereira dos Santos says:

> *"Concerning the escort, the escort remains. The treatment that they will have will be the same as the others that were here, and we will ask the policemen to keep their distance because they're not dangerous, but in order to avoid some unpredictable situations the police will stay. Concerning the forensic reports, this is in protocol and we will see about that. Concerning the accusation questions, there are many, they exceed 512, but they are temporary, the wording is temporary, I will see the pleas and we will get to the end of the judgement to a wording that comes to attend the defense, the Prosecution Office and above all the judge's interests. [...] because we received a document from the court judge that I read carefully and it says that the jury can't be postponed. Concerning the presence of prosecutors in the plenary, they will stay as observers, the question is solved" (Aluízio Pereira dos Santos).*

Obeying the lawyer's request about the presence of the police in an oppressive position and repressing the defendant during the judgment, the judge kept the escort, but asking for a bigger distance between the police and the women. The speech of the magistrate seems to suggest an implicit consent shared by other actors in scene about the fact that the defendants are not "criminals," but had just committed acts adverse to the legislation and should answer for that. It also reveals a sense based on gender stereotypes, in which the feminine essence is not seen as dangerous or menacing by nature [31]. However, it does not redeem the situation.

The judge Aluízio dos Santos also informed the possible review of the accusation questions due to the volume of material and decided for the maintenance of the two original prosecutors in plenary only as observers,[15] being replaced by the prosecutor Douglas Oldergardo Cavalheiro dos Santos. Resuming session the judge explained the procedures for formation and acting of the juries council, highlighting the principle of incommunicability between the members of the jury and, then, handed

[14] Until this moment the responsible for the case were promoters Paulo Cesar Passos and Luciana do Amaral Nagib, being replaced when the judgment started by promoter Douglas Oldergardo Cavalheiro dos Santos.

[15] Lately those promoters left the room to avoid pretexts that could help canceling a future decision on the judgment.

over copies of a document containing guidance to the juries staff. Concluding this act, the judge requested the entry of the four indicted in the plenary.

A mix of apprehension, anxiety, emotional exhaustion and fear was painted on the face of the defendants followed by female police officers. On the chairs pointed by his honor, the corporal image of the defendants revealed certain submission and gentleness characteristic of feminine socialization. The curved silhouettes and the heads slightly bowed down indicated a clear attempt to hide or to look away, possibly scared, bewildered and embarrassed before the police escort ahead, the press' spotlight and the audience of little more than 30 people.

One of them was visibly shaken and tears ran down her face. It was then that the judge explained to the indicted she could wait on the adjoining room or even leave the court if she wanted, pointing out that the legislation did not define the mandatory presence of the defendants during the course of the judgment. On this specific matter, the judge considered that the Court presents a democratic characteristic.

The next stage consisted on the sortition of seven names among the 25 possible present juries. The defense refused two juries and the prosecutors three, requiring new draws until the final composition of the seven juries, composed by five women and two men. Then started the ritual procedure of commitment of the juries with the justice, wrought by the classic "So I promise."

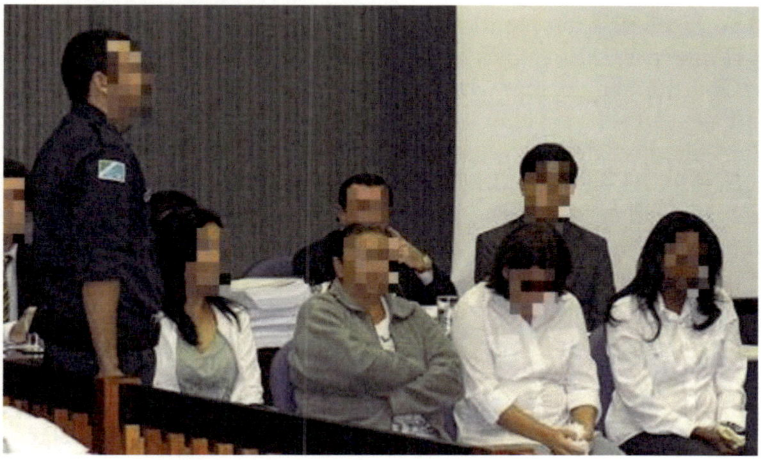

On the next pages it will be described the most important moments of the trial starting with some considerations from the magistrate, followed by the testimony of the defendants, the prosecutor's speech and the defense pleas.

The synthesis of the accusation sentence read by the judge pointed the television coverage as the catalyst of the elements that provided the criminal investigation. His honor referenced the first material shown on TV, two reporters with a hidden camera disguised as a couple looking for an abortion at the clinic, subject to financial charging, and the second where Neide Mota admits openly in interview to the journalist Honório Jacometto to perform abortions by clients request. The defendants were indicted for involvement in 26 procedures of abortions in 25 women, totalizing 26 cases and 25 prosecution witnesses, at the Family Planning Clinic.[16]

The judge revealed that 51 witnesses were heard and that wiretaps were requested at the start of the process. He informed that he defended the temporary arrest of doctor Neide and Simone for 5 days but the Justice Court ordered their

[16] One of the defense witness had two abortion at the clinic, resulting in a total of 26 abortions that happened at the place.

arrest. The members of the jury understood that there was sufficient evidence as to criminal authorship and proof of materiality. Thereafter, this sentence was altered, but the prosecution appealed and the conviction was kept.

The questions period came next, when questions directed to the defendants referred to the time they knew Neide Mota, if they had knowledge about the abortion of living fetuses, if the judicial pardon was offered and another about the value of the appointments, the business hours, the procedures made at the clinic, if the doctor had patients designated by other doctors, if they identified the presence of patients that were on social columns, etc. The three nurses gave similar answers, saying they did not knew Neide Mota before working at the clinic, and also their role on the clinic, like checking the blood pressure, weighing the patients and the medical screening. They also pointed they did not knew about the removal of living fetuses alleging that the clinic only made the procedure of removal of retained abortions, cysts, curettage and DIU (Intra uterine device) placement.

They also stressed that women of low and high class attended the clinic, and many of them attended pointed by other doctors. One of them said it was usual the presence of notable personalities, influent and known people that were mentioned on social columns and that it had occurred the removal of a living fetus by court order, probably involving rape or fetal anomaly incompatible with life. Another one pointed that the clinic had operation license and went through frequent supervision of the Prefecture, also highlighting that the doctor always took part of Nursing Weeks in educational institutes where she gave lectures about contraceptive methods. Two of the three nurses conciliated the work at the clinic with services at other hospitals ant the three denied peremptorily the accusation of criminal association. But they offered to collaborate on the process as to obtain judicial pardon. They highlighted they did not knew the values charged and what happened during the appointment because Neide made the appointments alone with the patients in the room and that they, assistants, only obeyed the doctor's orders according to notes on the patients' medical records.

Simone Cantagessi was the only defendant that confirmed abortions at the clinic, but did not plea guilty on the criminal association charge. Unlike the information spread by the press, Cantagessi said she worked at the place for 6 months only, after moving from Goiânia to Campo Grande. She said she did not knew the city, did not find regular work and that her function was to make the patients' medical screening.

At the appointment she questioned women about the reasons that made them look for an abortion, talked about contraceptive methods, explained the facts, the procedures and showed other options. She emphasized that the role of the psychology professional is not one of convincing and that interrupting the pregnancy was a decision that should be made by the pregnant women. She also revealed the impossibility of knowing if the patients went back because of the psychological treatment and that to her what really mattered "was their life, what they would chose for their life." She emphasized never have mentioned a price list[17] about the costs of having a child and even told the patients the story of a cousin who managed to sustain all her children working as a housekeeper. Her work consisted on simply clarifying the situation and talking about alternatives besides abortion.

---

[17] The price list containing information about the costs of raising a kid was found in one of the walls at the clinic and highlighted by press' ballyhoo. However, the information on this paper, taken from a magazine, did not work as a document that was related to the appointments with local workers and was a minor data on the case.

> *"I know that in my country abortion is a crime. If regret could kill, I would be dead. I could have attended women at my clinic and would do it the same way. It bothered me the interview saying I worked five years at the clinic, but it was only 5 or 6 months when I arrived from Goiânia. Daniela was the former psychologist. All I hope is that justice will be done. But too many things were distorted. I regret what I did there. My council, the CRP (Regional Psychology Council) did not remove my license. I acted within my profession. I'm not the one who kills children, against life, like the press made me look" [29, 30].*

Following the jury, what was seen was an exaggeration of prosecution's powers that imposed inquisitorial emphasis upon the defendants, but that also exposed contradictions and a thirst for the conviction of the women, which will be shown forward on this text by the defense lawyer speech and reasoning. During some moments, the court resembled a big staging show, like a persuading game, rhetoric and eloquence on a fierce duel between promoter and the defense.

At the start of the accusation charges, Douglas Oldegardo Cavalheiro dos Santos exhibited the TV report where Neide Mota confirmed to performing abortions. The prosecutor signalized that the journalistic material showed facts that should be of everyone's knowledge due the placement on television, warned the jury to be careful on not making judgments based on previous opinions. It was also said that the case of the Family Planning Clinic had, possibly, the biggest amount of procedural documents on the history of the Mato Grosso do Sul Court. One of the biggest concerns of the prosecutor revealed on the court was "the inductive detour of this polemic's process," because it was not about being pro or against abortion. The discussion should be linked to the law, despite the pressure of NGOs that, according to the prosecution, would report to international instances the case on Mato Grosso do Sul. It was explained that the case of the Family Planning Clinic was one of violation of the right to live because there is no place in the world, not even where abortion is legal, that it is made on the first time a woman arrives to a clinic.

The prosecution alleged that abortion has nefarious effects on the psychological integrity of the women and highlighted the financial interests, the mercantilist character and the social segregation of abortion on Dr. Neide's clinic. They also said that the clinic had expired medications, veterinary medications used for "pig abortions"[18] and a "disgusting fetus absorbing machine." At this moment, the promoter requested that the materials collected at the clinic were brought and took from a transparent plastic box the "disgusting absorbing machine," showing it to the plenary. Concerning the medical records and apprehensions, the prosecutor said that they did not prove the materiality, but corroborated with the materiality. Concluding, he said that there were the pro-life and pro-choice groups, but no feminist movement would be favorable to what happened at Doctor's Neide Mota Machado clinic.

The prosecution then made explicit the accusation made by the 25 witnesses, that is, the women that confessed having an abortion. Each one of the four defendants there at the jury's mercy was accused for involvement on intervention of 26 aborts for working at the clinic, however, not having participated on the same way on each one of the 26 procedures, because the effective support varied according to professional competence and their work hours. For instance, in some cases, there was no even contact between the employee and the patient. That means that the charging

[18] Promoter refers to the medication Cytotec. In some moments of his exposition, it could be seen the use of the word "kids" instead of "fetuses".

points by which they were being accused were not similar for all the defendants, because they were elaborated according to the participation on the facts. The prosecution persisted with the presentation emphasizing the importance of individualization of each case being judged, that is, in line with the specificity of the involvement of the defendants and meticulous analysis of the charging points on account of the high numerical proportion.

Following, they listed the accusations: abortion assistance, patient's persuasion, patient's medication with abortive drugs, among others. However, it was recognized that they did not have proof enough for five of the confessed abortion cases and that other six witnesses had not spoken about the involvement of the health professionals. It was then pointed 15 accusations made by witnesses and the judge received the request of conviction of the three nurses. One professional should be condemned for one case and participation on two abortions; the other assistant should be condemned on five cases of abortion and the third defendant for collaborating on four abortions. For the nurse was requested the condemnation on four occurrences and involvement on other five with minor participation; for the psychologist, the prosecution requested condemnation for acting on five episodes and minor participation on another four. The prosecution finished pointing out that the defendants had good nature, but would still pay for the mistakes made at the clinic, remembering that 12 out of the 13 women that alleged to having aborted declared regret. Furthermore, it was insisted that the treatment at the clinic was a system that privileged the abortion in detriment of protection of the patients or of another option on the pregnancy.

Only two defense lawyers requested speaking time. The first emphasized that the defendants cooperated with the investigation, but without the grants of judicial pardon like many patients attended at the clinic. He reiterated once again that the reports about the medical records does not prove the materiality of the crime and, therefore, there should be no prove, only mere assumptions. He argued that the 1988 Federal Constitution, Brazil's supreme law, requires the materiality for conviction. Lawyer Siufi initiated his speech showing one of the tv news that originated the charge: the news report recorded with a hidden camera on which his client is shown guiding a supposedly pregnant couple looking for abortion. He highlighted the illegal character of the recording from TV Morena, affiliate of Rede Globo, mocking: "a TV channel that preaches morality, see the example set by Big Brother" and accentuating society's hypocrisy.

Siufi's exposition was marked by questionings about the methods used for producing evidence, contradictions, arbitrariness and the lack of sustainability of the condemnations. Adding to the reading of the prosecutor about the accusation of abortion practice involving Simone Cantagessi, he alleged that the incrimination had no grounds, since there was no determining participation of the healthcare professional in many of the cases pointed out by the prosecution. Going through the testimonies of some accusation witnesses read by the prosecution, the lawyer detailed that there was no participation from the psychologist. In three cases Simone just had a talk with the patient. In one of them the accusation witness alleged to having a spontaneous abortion at home and did not look for the clinic again, on the other two, accusation related the fact that the psychologist did not induce or persuaded them about abortion. Siufi explained that it was within the competence of the psychologist to talk with the patient, being that the professional did not talk or, much less, decided and encouraged the interruption of pregnancy. "That was her job," asserted the defense. In other nine cases there was no participation of the psychologist, since the witnesses did not even mention her name or guaranteed they did not talk to her.

The defense also recalled that judicial pardon was considered due to Simone's collaboration on investigations and the prosecution recognized her collaboration, signaling at judicial pardon, but during final allegations looked down on Simone's help and did not grant the pardon.

Unlike his client, Siufi highlighted that some patients at the clinic had a different procedural treatment and received judicial pardon. The defense then questioned who were those women, sharpening public's curiosity: The question that remains is who are they? Were they rich? Congressmen's lovers? Authorities' daughters? High class people? According to the defense, this discrepancy on treatment aroused suspicions about the suitability of the judicial procedures, because the judge's decision left behind doubts for benefiting people who also had participation on the events.

Another point discussed was the early access by the Prosecutors Office to the expert report of medical records. The lawyer emphasized that prosecution already had privileged information long before the other parts, even the defense. Lawyer Siufi also warned to the time required to evaluate in detail each point to be judged. Due to the high number of questions under examination, the defense speech said that if the review of each question point took 5 minutes, it would be necessary more than 2 days to finish the trial.

The defense also insisted pithily on reflecting about the motivations who took a big quota of women to opt for interrupting the pregnancy, like the lack of financial condition, pressure of a partner who does not want the child or the male abandonment before the pregnancy, as well as emotional conditions, the delicate dilemmas and the most intimate feeling of each woman before a unwanted or unplanned pregnancy.

> *"Did the person have no way of raising a child or the father did not want to recognize it? Were they forced by their boyfriend, husband or fiancées? How many people we know that were forced to give up their child for adoption because they had no conditions of raising it? Am I saying any lies here? Those kids at the streets in Campo Grande, it's not about being pro or against abortion, no! It's necessary to see the inward of everyone. How can I get into the heart of someone who's sweet, that no one knows? How can I? Campo Grande has around 800 thousand people. Those 10 thousand women, they are about 5% of the population over those 20 and some years. That was on Dr. Neide's office, it was a medical document, it was in her office"* [29, 30].

One of the peaks of the judgment was Siufi's revelation about the lack of proof on the presumed abortions that happened at the clinic, according to the information subsidized by the expert report regarding the content of the medical reports. He stressed that the proof of crime is given by the materiality of the crime, that is, the report of the corpus delicti examination. Therefore, it is not about speculating or judging if the woman committed or not the abortion. And the material proofs, the report of the indirect corpus delicti examination did not prove the abortions.

> *"There was no participation of Simone on Aline's case or in any other. There's no way to know, the reports don't prove. There's no way to know if it was DIU placement, spontaneous abortion, cyst or curettage. There's no way to know. And even in doubt there is a conviction against Dr. Simone. If she had no part, she did not participate in anything. Your excellencies will have to absolve her. Without the first accusation point all the others are harmed. And also the judicial pardon and the penalty reduction, there's no need of all that and the other accusation points. Tatiana also had no participation, nothing, from Dr. Simone. I'd like you to judge this case correctly"* [29, 30].

As it was, there would be no proof of Simone's participation in any case since there was no material proof, Siufi concluded saying that "to judge you peer is not something easy" and asked the jury to vote "no" on all the first accusation question and, in that way, absolve the defendants.

> *"They even say that this is the only power that men took from God's hand, because there's the power to convict and the power to absolve. I know that the late hour is tiring, but I want to say to Your Excellencies, I'll ask Your Excellencies to say no to that [...] if Your Excellencies understand the condemnation and have any doubt in your mind, when it's time to cast the vote, say no to the first question [...] Say no to this here, which is the portrait of hypocrisy, because it cannot be the fight between the rock and the sea and make the seashell suffer the consequences. No. But I wish that Your Excellencies say no to all the first questions: No. And after Your Excellencies leave this Court, after all the work and love given to the justice's cause, I wish the regret of having convicted four innocents do not keep you company"* [29, 30].

The judge notifies that he finished the discussions and grants the prosecutor the right to a replica, but he does not use the contestation. After that he relates to the jury that he will explain about the accusation questions on the secret room and how the procedures will take place, when he will also answer questions about "the matter of facts." The meeting was finished with "more than 600 questions," highlighted the judge, concluding to the jury: "about the questions we'll explain what the prosecutor and the defense thinks."

The trial decision happens on the next day. On April 9, 2010, 2:50 pm, the magistrate publicly advertised the decision of the jury to convict the defendants. The result of the sentence presented a negative balance for the clinic's workers: Maria Nelma was convicted to 4 years on semi-open regime; Libertina to 1 year and 3 months on semi-open regime; Rosângela de Almeida to 7 years on semi-open regime; Simone was condemned to 6 years and 4 months on the semi-open.

To finish, the judge thanks the jury, the lawyers, the prosecution and concludes the judgment. But something unusual happens, because there would still be a manifestation against the decision of the Jury closing with golden keys the scenario of "the case of the ten thousand" as a miraculous movie story. Undismayed by the final sentence, Simone Cantagessi's husband (who is also a judge) makes a touching plea and public protest, but without obtaining a favorable result, since the case had already been judged and decreed finished by the judge. On October 8, 2010, the employees from the former doctor Neide Mota Machado's clinic had their penalty reduced by the Justice Court of MatoGrosso do Sul: Maria Nelma had her penalty reduced to 2 years, Libertina was limited to 10 months, Rosângela's was reduced to 1 year and Cantagessi two.

5. Final notes: the deleterious effects of criminal law and the right to health

Themes like abortion, maternity and law devices on the reproductive scope cannot be dissociated from gender conventions immersed on the historical context of each period and society. The Brazilian Criminal Code from 1940, on its article 128, which proscribes abortion, was promulgated on Getúlio Vargas' government, in full dictatorship, and with inflexible gender traditions: few women worked outside home, had a college degree, could choose about having or not having children or even voted.

In 1945, the country resumed the redemocratization process and decades later, in 1964, suffered a new coup d'etat orchestrated by the military, that overlapped the Democratic State and initiated a period of strong censorship, political persecution, torture and death. Even in this context, feminists denounced the oppressions of a patriarchal society, raised the flags of "personal is political," preached the end to domestic violence, of defense of sexual freedom, of the non-demonization of contraceptive methods, of the right to control their own body and reproductive self-determination.

Since then Brazilian women obtained a series of achievements, like more space and participation in society, public politics and specific laws to prevent and reduce violence against women and changes on the conservative mentality on the field of gender relations in the sense of more equality. Many of these achievements were driven by International Conferences related to women rights promoted by United Nations on the decade of 1990 in conjunction with feminist activism.

Stands out the International Conference on Human Rights, held in Vienna in 1993 [20]; that states in its article 18 that rights of women and girls are inalienable; the International Conference on Population and Development, in Cairo in 1994, asks the Estates for investment on familiar planning politics, the reduction of maternal mortality and the review of punitive laws that concern abortion; and the IV World Conference on Women, at the city of Beijing in China in 1995, that requested to the government the use of gender perspective on the development of policies for women [21].

However, the inequalities between men and women are still significant in Brazil. Abortion is not allowed by law yet, the participation of women on parliaments is minimal, the rates of domestic violence, of feminicide and maternal mortality are very high and, broadly, they still have the lower wages in the market for the same work developed when comparing to men.

In the last decades, the reversal has been enormous. On the field of reproductive self-determination it can be highlighted the dozens of legislative proposals that seek to restrict women's reproductive rights on process in the National Congress, like the Legislative Proposal 478/2007–called Statute of the Unborn (Estatuto do Nascituro), which prohibits abortion in all cases, even rape, and turns the insecure abortion into a heinous crime; the Legislative Proposal 3748/2008, which provides child support to the mother for giving birth to children conceived through a rape crime; the Legislative Proposal 1413/2007, which prohibits the distribution of emergency contraceptive (known as morning-after pill by SUS–the Health Unic System (Sistema Único de Saúde)) and its commercialization in drugstores, among others.

The laws, roughly written by men, do not escape gender representations inserted in long term history. Fausto [17], on the literary work "Crime and Routine," a study about criminality in São Paulo city between 1880 and 1924 considers that the efficiency of the criminal action is not only technical, but is related to social discrimination working as a repressive practice that can even criminalize behaviors apparently nonchalant to criminal law, like the imprisonment of prostitutes, homosexuals and women who opted for abortion.

Therefore, the inappropriate behavior according to sex within the family and society, as well as ethnic-racial characteristics influence the conception and definition of the offense and on the application of punishment on the transgression scope. Furthermore, Fausto [17] signaled the existence of criminal behavior that did not draw police's attention, like assaults practiced by husbands and certain sexual crimes.

This question highlights the police convenience with social mentality in the process of naturalization of violence against women, including there the denial to women of their faculty of reproductive choice, on the domestic and family scope throughout history. It became evident on the case of the women criminalized for abortion in Campo Grande, when police, a prosecutor from the Prosecution Office and a judge from the Jury Court made a task-force for the massive indictment of ten thousand women who went to the Familiar Planning Clinic from Neite Mota over the 20 years it operated.

The ten thousand women from Campo Grande and a million more that perform abortions every year on the Brazilian society reveal that the prohibitive criminal law is innocuous and detrimental in case of the voluntary intervention of pregnancy. Either because it does not prevent thousands of women to perform an insecure abortion, at large, precariously and onerously, opting for illegal clinics, midwives, with the help of people without proper qualification or even in a solitary way, using medicines from the clandestine market, the consumption of teas or introducing objects in the genital tract intending to pierce the uterus, often without any professional guidance, sterilization processes, emotional support or the minimal hygiene and safety conditions. Either because it does not respect the dignity and autonomy of women as ethical beings capable of mature and conscious choices about their lives.

It is known that the condition of illegality makes it difficult to quantify accurately the number of abortions practiced in Brazil. According to research developed by the National Feminist Network for Health and Reproductive Rights, in 1991, based on a methodology developed by the Alan Guttmacher Institute, which calculates the data by the use of surveys of hospitalizations for abortion in the health services, pointed out the occurrence of 700,000–1.4 million abortions in the country. More recent studies identify that this estimate remains the same.[19]

If in one hand, the advent of the birth control pills on the decade of 1960 contributed to the exercise of a sexuality unlinked to reproduction, on the other, the existence of contraceptive methods with low hormonal dosage or compatible with organisms of different women are not always available by the public politics on Mato Grosso do Sul and the whole country.

According to the "Dossier on insecure abortion for advocacy: the impact of abortion illegality on women's health and quality of reproductive health care in Campo Grande and Corumbá, Mato Grosso do Sul," published in 2010, there are deficiencies in the Family Planning Programs, the distribution of medicines and the quality of care provided to women in the local public health system, which make it difficult for women to acquire contraceptives, as well as seeking and adhering to routine medical treatments and appointments. The failures are mainly "related to the quality of medical care, maintenance of the stock of medicines and consequently the continuity of the supply of contraceptive methods" ([32, 33], p. 4). One of the health managers interviewed by the research team of this Dossier, who was then responsible for following the Family Planning Program of the capital, openly exposes the problem:

> *"...we don't have the monthly injectable contraceptive in the system, there's no implant, levornogestrel IUD, vaginal ring and contraceptive patch. The SUS (Health Unic System) still cannot get even close of a bold and modern familiar planning. We also don't have the proper "provision" of the IUD short stock (for women with hysterometry smaller than 7 cm); and of the quarterly injectable. Frequently there's no appropriate provision of the stock; many women discontinue the use because of the lack of the quarternal."*

[19] On that, consult the 2016 National Research on Abortion (PNA 2016). Available from: http://www.scielo.br/pdf/csc/v22n2/1413-8123-csc-22-02-0653.pdf [Accessed on: December 18, 2012].

Add to this the difficulties that many women feel when negotiating the condom use with their partners and the fact that any contraceptive can fail. That is, women and men do not have the same power, risks and benefits on the sexuality and reproduction scope. It is upon the feminine body that falls the damage caused by the continuous use of birth control pills and there is no fair distribution of the risks if we consider the organisms of men and women.

Furthermore, the differences on the social conditions of the feminine population affects the greater or lesser access to quality of life, information, medicines and health care. And they are the ones who get pregnant and are given most of the responsibility for care and education of children–in most cases, without the help of the father. It is also little emphasized the male responsibility on the administration of fertility and contraceptive medicines that are efficient for men lack in the research field [2].

> *On the other side, it is important to rethink that the fact that the gestation develops inside the feminine body has particular relevance. If the right to privacy involves the power to exclude heteronomous interventions on the owner's body, it is hard to conceive an intrusion so intense and severe upon someone's body, like the imposition on pregnant women to keep a pregnancy, for 9 months, against their will [5, 6].*

Although the male participation on an undesired pregnancy is an elementary evidence, the onus of an illegal abortion falls upon the feminine population's organism, including the risk of damage to health and of death, as well as criminalization by justice, weakening the right to health disposed on the Article 6° of the Brazilian Federal Constitution and the recommendations of international agreements from the United Nations signed by the country.

According to the document formulated by the UN Special Rapporteur for the Right to Health in 2011 [34], named "The right of every person to experience the highest level of physical and mental health," the prohibitive criminal laws about abortion contradict the human dignity, a fundamental principle of Human Rights, because it affects the mental and emotional health of women and interfere on the freedom to make decisions without the state's intervention.

Still according to the document, when criminal law is used to regulate and restrain sexual and reproductive conducts, the State imposes itself forcefully submitting and canceling the desire, conscience, autonomy and the life project of the individual. Like this, the penalization of abortion represents a violation of the right to sexual and reproductive health and a severe interference of the state on women's life. "The criminal laws that punish and restrict the induced abortion are the paradigmatic example of the unacceptable barriers that prevent women from exercising their right to health and, consequently, should be eliminated" ([35], p. 9).

It is relevant to remember that the case of the ten thousand was structured based on the medical reports seized at the Clinic. However, the police order did not authorize the seizure of the medical records, which violated the right to medical confidentiality of the patients, their intimacy and privacy. On this subject please note that the Federal Constitution of 1988, on its article 5°, subsection X, underlines: "Inviolable are the intimacy, the private life, the honour and image of people, and is guaranteed the right to indemnity for material or moral damage derived from its violation" ([36], art. 5°, subsection X).

Additionally, the expertise examination on the seized medical records did not prove the abortion practice, even so around 1500 women were sued by justice and four employees condemned by the institution of the Jury. The judge, prosecutors and the police detective declared at various times to the press the fact that abortion is a crime in Brazil, therefore, they should obey the law. However, this plea was not utilized in respect to the lack of materiality of the crime, which makes the trial before a popular Jury, in a country where the population is mostly catholic, strategic to condemnation.

After all, the role of the judge in the Jury Court is to basically police and preside over the tasks, falling upon the juries the verdict without the need of legal justification on the decision [37]. Another aggravating factor to the situation is the fact that we live in a culture strongly influenced by religious dogmas that are contrary to abortion. Moreover, the disclosure of the case by mass communication vehicles informed and misinformed, cultivated judgments and helped to shape a sentence in the consciousness of each citizen, aspect that needs attention for the fact that the judgment was submitted to decision of a popular jury [37].

The ballyhoo of the press around the abortion commerce on the Familiar Planning Clinic highlighted the financial gain over the women's suffering evoking the idea of social selectivity. The commodification of abortion is a point that tends to weigh on the balance in many cases of clinics taken to the judiciary, notes Oliveira (2010). It was one of the pleas used by the prosecution during the Jury trial, as if the charge of financial honorariums was something even more inhuman in the context of a voluntary interruption of pregnancy.

The health market was not invented by doctor Neide's clinic. Just see how much it costs the obstetric follow-up during the 9 months of pregnancy, the price of medical exams, the value of child-birth charged by private doctors, the room rate in the maternity ward and the corporative interests linked to the powerful medicine market. In our society, the solution for pain, the treatment and cure of patients becomes, many times, a merchandise as any other inscribed in the trade and consumption circuit.

A little addressed challenge by the local press was the perception of sexual and reproductive rights comprehensively. For Corrêa and Petchesky [2], it is necessary to consider the relation between power and resources available to women concerning the decision-making on the sexual and reproductive scope. These authors highlight the necessity to understand these rights beyond the "particular freedoms" or "individual choices," but related to social, cultural, economic, gender, class, race, ethnicity conditions and the public policy devices available for each woman particularly and jointly and, like this, seek to understand the specifications of the decision for abortion.

The right to health needs to be understood interconnected to the other rights considering the body of the individual, its subjectivity, relation, material and economic conditions and the whole existence of its life in society, including there, the structural transnational violence and the world around them. According to the World Health Organization (WHO), health does not mean absence of diseases, but envelops comprehensive bio-psycho-social aspects that affect the quality of life and well-being of people.

Therefore, the abortive itineraries cannot be treated for the criminal aspect, as determined by many international conferences, pacts and conventions on the field of human rights of which Brazil is a signatory, among them the documents deliberated on the International Conference on Population and Development (ICPD) and in the IV World Conference on Women, that reiterates the commitments of the ICPD and highlights that abortion is a public health problem and not a crime [21].

In this context, to judge an equal in the face of such dramatics, intimacies and human vicissitudes that mark the existence of thousands of women in all country is an act of disrespect of human rights, aggravated by the time limitation for reflection of the high numerical proportion of question appreciated by the juries in the case of

Campo Grande. It is not enough to emphasize the legal particularities of the process and the importance of individualization of cases for each of the employees on the defendants' bench, as indicated by the prosecutor during the trial. It is difficult to understand the reasons that took many women to interrupt a pregnancy, the intense physical and emotional suffering lived with the maintenance of a forced pregnancy, the paths, sensitivities, consciousness and reasons that lead four salaried workers to service at the Familiar Planning Clinic.

> *Each citizen is a stand-alone agent capable of making decisions based on personal values, ideologies, beliefs and reasons, specific life situations and plans for the future, using freedom as guide. However, to the extent that women and men are differently affected by the impact of reproduction on the organism, to force women into unwanted pregnancy violates integrity, hurts the dignity and reduces their bodies to mere reproduction instruments. This creates the necessity of legal guarantees that protect the individuality and decision of women. The restrictive criminal law, however, is a punishment for women. On the "case of the ten thousand," for instance, only five men were indicted [24].*

That way, what was observed on the case of the ten thousand was a mass criminalization of the feminine gender, once only a few men were sued by justice. This shows the gender inequality on the field of right to health and on the juridical treatment on the abortion matter, damaging the fundamental right to freedom, equality and the guarantee of the principle of reproductive self-determination to the female population [24].

The secularism of the State, the freedom of conscience and beliefs are premises defended by the Federal Constitution of 1988 that, in its article 5°, subject VI, disposes: "It is inviolable the freedom of conscience and beliefs, being assured the free exercise of religious cults and guaranteed, in the form of the law, protection of places of cult and its liturgies." And Article 19, subsection I, of the mentioned Constitution, prohibits the Union, the States, the Federal District and the Cities to "establish religious cults or churches, subside them, impair their operation or keep with them or their representatives dependency relationships or alliance, excepted, in the form of the law, the collaboration of public interest." The Brazilian State is secular, thus, the country cannot legislate nor build universal public policies guided by moral or religious beliefs.

In regard to the principle of equality, as established by the Article 5°, subsection I, of the Magna Carta, the prohibition of abortion leads to a context of gender discrimination, because it imposes greater onus on women than men, as well as among women themselves depending on their social conditions, since the consequences of clandestine abortion reach more drastically women in situations of economic vulnerability.

Still on this premise, we must remember that the condemnation for the women from the Familiar Planning Clinic was uneven. The richer could convert their sentence to a fine, but the poorest, considering black women together, in general, had to provide community services at schools and daycare centers where they lived with children and a likely feeling of guilt and emotional suffering.

One may conceive that the poor majority left their homes at dawn to provide the community service and, lately, went to work, usually poorly paid domestic work, and at night they still took care of their own home and family, a strenuous journey. Punished by their social condition, deficient services of juridical defense and precarious services of familiar planning, women from the popular layers and employees from Dr. Neide Mota's clinic, were the most penalized. This is an example of how the gender, ethnicity, race and class categories pass through the institutional, medical and legal structures. The social construction of the feminine is, like that, indispensable to think about the differential treatment that women had if compared to men in the case of the Familiar Planning Clinic. As explained by Corrêa:

> *Because the social construction of the feminine and of the feminine bodies is strongly associated to the signs of guardianship, they are constructions that conceive the feminine as "out of order," like bodies and subjects that has no capacity of taking care of themselves. They are bodies destined to give birth to children for the State, the capital, the job market, the family and, because of that, women should be protected. The poorer and financially dependent the person, heavier are the protection and vigilantism rules on them.*

During the Jury Court, the defense of life was a plea used by the prosecution to condemn the women. However, defense of life is not compatible with the option for abortion. Within the sciences the concept of life has many meanings. In biology, to exemplify, a line of research identifies life in the origin of cells. Other biologists seek to investigate the essence of what determines the entity of the being or even speculate whether life resides in the transmission of hereditary traits through genes. There are still those who consider life a relational process between organisms and the environment. "The organism subjectively interprets the world and itself and, in so doing, constructs its environment" ([38], p. 21).

In this relational perspective the notion of life and its sacredness is perceived as communication. Thus, biological science must invest in researches that are capable of capturing the signs relations more than, purely, the relations between molecules. That is, "life is not something possessed or donated to a given entity" (Coutinho et al. 2008, p. 22) or just something of a material substance. It is, above all, a continuous process of semiotic relations between organisms and the environment. "In reality, the name 'life' is merely the reification of the process of being alive. It does not exist as an independent reality" ([38], p. 2).

Thus the theoretical, philosophical, or metaphysical speculative search for the concept of life, more emphatically about which moment can be considered as living, does not seem to be so relevant to biology in the face of the pressing need for empirical research. The author of this text also believes that it is not primordial to sociology to lean on studies to identify the exact moment in which one begins the life before the necessity of the empirical investigation, that, in the case of the abortion, must analyze and understand each concrete and particular case of the experiences of the women involved and their relationships with the environment.

> *"If we can understand the controversy about abortion as a discussion linked to other differences of religious and philosophical opinions, we'll understand better in what and why we diverge. We will also be in better condition of emphasizing the points in which we agree and of noticing in which way our divisions, however profound and painful they may be, are still rooted to a fundamental unity of humanitarian conviction. What we share is more fundamental that our divergences about your better interpretation"* [39].

Therefore, in many countries where abortion is legalized, that is, more than half of the world, the constitutions protects the life of the fetus and allow the voluntary interruption of pregnancy [5, 6]. And in those countries, it is not too much to highlight, the abortion and mortality by abortion rates go down if compared to the period of zero tolerance of the punitive prohibitionism.

In many of these legislations that allow abortion and ponder about the life of the fetus and the pregnant woman, the resource to abortion is foreseen in cases of risk to physical and emotional women health. And also due to economic, social and varied familiar issues, sexual violence and fetus with incurable anomaly, besides the recommendation of dialogs with the pregnant woman in search for alternatives before abortion, teaching us the necessity to ponder with respect, wisdom and sensibility how to equate the reasonableness of rights between the life of the fetus and of the women without maculating our most precious good: the human life [40–45].

Like this, the life of women, complete human beings, that have histories, families, friends, feelings, desires, pains, joys, projects, frustrations and dream, it is preponderant, in many laws of the nations that allow abortions, in relation to the intrauterine life. In life inside the uterus there is no person or complete subject capable of enjoying the fundamental rights. That is, the embryonic cells are not an integral person yet, a human being that suffers, lives, toil, has problems, yearnings, realizations and difficulties. There are also various other laws in which there is no primacy between the right of women and the life of the unborn, but an equivalence between the two, that in the impossibility of harmony it is necessary to admit the prevalence of only one right based on the context and on the delicate relation established between the pregnant woman and the fetus [5, 6].

It is necessary to consider the stories and life experiences, the paths, the present conditions and projects for the future, the power imbalances in relationships between women and men, the assorted economic, physical and emotional conditions, the masculine subtle coercion modes to engage sexual relations without the use of preservatives, among a series of situations, reason and the most intimate and inviolable feelings that provokes certain behaviors and the choice for abortion, to think about such a delicate and controversial theme. The scarcity of familiar planning services, the high number of insecure abortions in the Brazilian society and the public health problem generated by the punitive prohibitionism of the law, are necessary contexts, moreover, for the reflection about the need to revise or dispose of such legislation.

Women health cannot be put at risk by an antiquated legislation, a religious morality, misogynist conventionalisms, biopolitics interests in the population control or by the coercive power of the State on the restriction of freedom and interference in the individual privacy. The tutelage over their bodies and consciousness, be it by men, the church, the judiciary, the medics, on the intimate and essential decision-making for their bio-psycho-social well-being, life quality and project for the future, prevents women for being acknowledged as subjects, whole people with ethical capacity and autonomy of making choices by themselves that are better or less harmful to them and their environment. Democracy and the exercise of full citizenship will only be possible with a law that guarantees human, sexual and reproductive rights of women in detriment to the preconceptions embedded in society. It is time to change a situation that stigmatize, penalize, mistreats and reap life of thousands of women every year in Mato Grosso do Sul and all over Brazil.

Author details

Alexandra Lopes da Costa
Federal University of Mato Grosso do Sul, Brazil

*Address all correspondence to: alexasociais@yahoo.com.br

References

[1] Gonçalves TA. Aborto e religião nos tribunais brasileiros. São Paulo: Instituto para a Promoção da Equidade; 2008

[2] Corrêa S, Petchesky R. Direitos Sexuais e Reprodutivos: uma perspectiva Feminista. PHYSIS–Revista de Saúde Coletiva, Rio de Janeiro. 1996;**6**(1-2): 147-177. Available from: http://www.scielo.br/pdf/physis/v6n1-2/08.pdf [Accessed on: August 2013]

[3] Ardaillon D. O Lugar do Íntimo na Cidadania do Corpo Inteiro. Estudos Feministas, Florianópolis. 1997;**5**(2):376-378. Available from: https://perioddicos.ufsc.br/index.php/ref/article/view/12155/11425 [Accessed on: August 2018]

[4] Gonçalves TA, Lapa TS. Instrumentos jurídicos e o aborto nos tribunais brasileiros. In: Arilha M, Lapa TS, Pisaneschi TC, editors. Direitos Reprodutivos e o Sistema Judiciário Brasileiro. São Paulo: Oficina Editorial; 2010. pp. 49-85

[5] Sarmento D. Legalização do aborto e constituição. In: Cavalcanti A, Xavier D, editors. Em defesa da vida: aborto e direitos humanos. São Paulo: Católicas pelo Direito de Decidir; 2006. pp. 111-168

[6] Sarmento D. Filosofia e Teoria Constitucional Contemporânea. Vol. 1. Rio de Janeiro: Lúmen Júri; 2009. pp. 147-170

[7] Galeotti G. História do Ab( )rto. Vol. 70. Gráfica de Coimbra, Portugal: Edições; 2007

[8] Perrot B. Minha história das mulheres. Contexto: São Paulo; 2007

[9] Badinter E. Um Amor Conquistado: o mito do amor materno. Rio de Janeiro: Nova Fronteira; 1985

[10] Kramer H, James S. Malleus Malleficarum. Rio de Janeiro: O Martelo das Feiticeiras; 2001

[11] Zordan PBMBG. Bruxas: figuras de poder. Estudos Feministas, Florianópolis. 2005;**13**(2):256

[12] Priore MD. Ao sul do corpo. Condição feminina, maternidades e mentalidades no Brasil colônia. Unesp; 1993

[13] Priore M. Del. História das mulheres: as vozes do silêncio. In: Freitas MC, editor. Historiografia brasileira em perspectiva, São Paulo, Contexto; 2003. p. 217-235

[14] Soihet R. Violência Simbólica. Saberes masculinos e representações femininas. Revista Estudos Feministas. 1997;**5**(1)

[15] Soihet R. Formas de Violência, Relações de Gênero e Feminismo. In: Piscitelli A, Melo HP, Maluf SW, Puga VL, editors. Olhares Feministas. Brasília: Ministério da Educação: Unesco; 2009. pp. 369-391

[16] Pecheny M, de la Dehesa R. Sexualidades e políticas na América Latina: um esboço para discussão. In: Corrêa S, Parker R, editors. Sexualidade e política na América Latina: histórias, intersecções e paradoxos. Rio de Janeiro: ABIA; 2011

[17] Fausto B. Crime e Cotidiano. A criminalidade em São Paulo (1180-1924). Brasiliense; 1984. pp. 9-80

[18] Portella AP. Corpo, sexualidade e reprodução. Recife: SOS Corpo–Instituto Feminista para a Democracia; 2009. Série Formação Política

[19] Schild V. Feminismo e neoliberalismo na América Latina. Revista Outubro. 2016;**26**:59-77

[20] Declaração de Vienna, 5 de Junho de 1993. Available from: http://www.dhnet.org.br/direitos/anthist/vienna/vienna.html [Accessed on: August 2013]

[21] Brasil. Presidência da República. Secretaria Especial de Políticas

para as Mulheres. In: Instrumentos Internacionais dos Direitos das Mulheres. Brasília: Secretaria Especial de Políticas para as Mulheres; 2006

[22] Nações Unidas. Declaração Universal dos Direitos Humanos de. 1948. Available from: http://bit.ly/9SrcBE [Accessed on: August 2013]

[23] Piovesan F. Direitos Reprodutivos como Direitos Humanos. In: Reprodução e Sexualidade: Uma Questão de Justiça. Porto Alegre: Fabris; 2002. pp. 61-79

[24] Costa AL. Modern-day Inquisition. SUR 19. 2013. Available from: http://sur.conectas.org/en/modern-day-inquisition/ [Accessed on: 04 October 2018]

[25] Campos CH. Aborto: estratégias de (des)criminalização. In: Seminário Internacional Fazendo Gênero 8–Corpo, Violência e Poder. Florianópolis: Universidade Federal de Santa Catarina; 2008. Available from: http://bit.ly/MwATQz [Accessed on: August 2013]

[26] IPAS (Brasil). Processos judiciais evolvendo abortamento: Negação dos Direitos Reprodutivos das Mulheres em Mato Grosso do Sul. 2008. Available from: http://bit.ly/MHup0p [Accessed on: 18 April 2012]

[27] Galli B, Campos CH. Mulheres processadas pela prática de aborto em Mato Grosso do Sul: direitos humanos e reprodutivos em questão. Revista de Saúde Sexual e Reprodutiva, Informativo eletrônico de IPAS Brasil. 2008;(38). Available from: http://bit.ly/KIYLRE [Accessed on: August 2013]

[28] Campos CH. Mass prosecution for abortion: Violation of the reproductive rights of women in Mato Grosso do Sul, Brazil. In: Case Studies on Resisting and Challenging Fundamentalisms. AWID; 2011. Available from: http://bit.ly/nZHgEC [Accessed on: August 2013]

[29] Siufi R. Depoimento. Tribunal do Júri–caso Neide Motta. Campo Grande, MS. 1 arquivo. (mp3) (18′31″). 2010

[30] Souza SAC. Depoimento. Tribunal do Júri–caso Neide Motta. Campo Grande, MS. 2010

[31] Ferreira MM. História, tempo presente e história oral. In: Topoi. Rio de Janeiro. 2002, pp. 314-332. Disponível no endereço eletrônico: http://www.ppghis.ifcs.ufrj.br/media/topoi5a13.pdf, consultado em 08 de out. 2009

[32] Costa AL, Ziolkowski NE, Galli B, Viana P. Dossiê sobre aborto inseguro para advocacy: o impacto da ilegalidade do abortamento na saúde das mulheres e na qualidade da atenção à saúde reprodutiva em Campo Grande e Corumbá, Mato Grosso do Sul. Recife: Grupo Curumim; 2010. Available from: http://www.aads.org.br/arquivos/dossieMS.pdf [Accessed on: August 2013]

[33] Costa AL. Punição, aborto e resistência: uma análise do caso Neide Mota e as dez mil mulheres. In: Narciso TE, Maciel JG, editors. Prisões, violência e sociedade. Paco Editorial; 2017. pp. 261-294

[34] Relator Especial sobre o Direito à Saúde. 2011. Right of everyone to the enjoyment of the highest attainable standard of physical and mental health. Doc ONU A/66/254, 66ª Sessão

[35] Nações Unidas. Relator Especial sobre o Direito à Saúde. In: Right of Everyone to the Enjoyment of the Highest Attainable Standard of Physical and Mental Health. Doc ONU A/66/254, 66ª Sessão. 2011

[36] Brasil. Constituição Federal de 1988. Available from: http://bit.ly/MGKy4K [Accessed on: August 2018]

[37] Oliveira GM, Costa AL, Pereira M, da S. Da histeria coletiva ao

esquecimento: mídia e poder público no enredo da caça às bruxas do aborto no Mato Grosso do Sul. Seminário Fazendo Gênero 9: diásporas, diversidade e deslocamentos. 2012. Available from: http://www.fazendogenero.ufsc.br/9/resources/anais/1278279535_ARQUIVO_Dahisteriacoletivaaoesquecimento.pdf

[38] Coutinho FA, Maia MB, Silva FAR. A polissemia do conceito de vida. In: Direito de Decidir: múltiplos olhares sobre o aborto. Belo Horizonte: Autêntica Editora; 2008. pp. 9-28

[39] Dworkin R. Domínio da vida: aborto, eutanásia e liberdades individuais. 2nd ed. WMF Martins Fontes: São Paulo; 2009

[40] Comissão Econômica Para a América Latina e o Caribe (CEPAL). Indicadores de Saúde Reprodutiva na América Latina e no Caribe. Santiago, Chile: Nações Unidas; 2010. Série mujer y desarrollo 103

[41] Ikawa D, Piovesan F. Feminismo, direitos humanos e constituição. In: Sarmento D, editor. Filosofia e Teoria Constitucional Contemporânea. Vol. 1. Rio de Janeiro: Lúmen Júri; 2009. pp. 147-170

[42] Instituto Brasileiro de Geografia e Estatística. 2013. Available from: http://cod.ibge.gov.br/AS5 [Accessed on: April 7, 2012]

[43] Torres JHR. A inconstitucionalidade da criminalização primária do aborto. In: Arilha M, Lapa TS, Pisaneschi TC, editors. Aborto medicamentoso no Brasil. São Paulo: Oficina Editorial; 2010. pp. 41-79. Available from: http://www.ccr.org.br/uploads/ciclodedebates/volume_2_Aborto_medicamentoso_no_Brasil.pdf [Accessed in: August, 2013]

[44] Ventura M. Descriminalização do aborto: um imperativo constitucional. In: Cavalcanti A, Xavier D, editors. Em defesa da vida: aborto e direitos humanos. São Paulo: Católicas pelo Direito de Decidir; 2006. pp. 181-188

[45] Zaffaroni ER. La cuestión criminal 2. Página 12, Argentina, quinta-feira, 02 de junho. Suplemento Especial. 2012. Available from: http://www.pagina12.com.ar/diario/especiales/18-175157-2011-08-23.html [Accessed on: 10 February 2012]

Chapter 13

Globalization of the Cruise Industry: A Tale of Ships Part II - Asia Post 1994

Andrew O. Coggins

Abstract

Cruising has grown over 7% a year since 1980. Sustained rapid expansion in North America, followed by local expansion in Europe and Asia, has made cruising a global industry, with 365 ships and estimated sales of $37.8 US billion (CIN, 2017). This global development has been fueled by innovation and introduction of market changing resident ships appealing to the mass traveler which were quickly matched by competitors, establishment of industry and port marketing organizations, awareness of cruising as a vacation option, and availability of suitable port and berthing facilities. When these four conditions coexisted the industry experienced rapid growth. Since 1966, the cruise industry has developed from a Miami-centered industry to a global industry centered in North America, Europe, Asia, and Australia/New Zealand. Given the high cost of state-of-the-art ships, their deployment is a good indication of industry's confidence in market growth. This chapter chronicles the development of the Asian cruise industry from 1994 through 2017. Data from *Cruise Industry News Annual Reports* (CIN) and *Berlitz Complete Guide to Cruising and Cruise Ships* (Ward) are examined and conclusions are drawn.

Keywords: innovation, cruising, Asia, tourism, globalization

1. Introduction

Shipping by its nature has always been global. With the development of alternative means of transporting passengers and mail and the subsequent demise of national fleets (ships built in the owner's country, registered in that country, crewed by citizens of that country, and in some cases constructed in that country), shipping has become even more global. Owners (cruise companies) are incorporated in and ships registered in the best countries from taxation purposes. Ships are constructed on a worldwide basis based on which shipyard offers the best deal. Crews are sourced on a worldwide basis according to who is willing to work for the salaries and under the conditions offered by the owners. Specific to the cruise industry, Oivind Mathisen, Editor of *Cruise Industry News Annual Report 2017–2018* (CIN 2017–2018) [1] writes:

> *"Despite a variety of geopolitical events and incidents, the industry has prospered and grown with a nearly unbroken record of profitable years for the publicly traded companies.*

> *The business model is unique. The cruise companies incorporate overseas as shipping companies to avoid U.S. corporate income tax; build ships in countries that have experienced shipyards and offer export financing; hire officers and crews from maritime nations and from an international labor pool; source passengers from different markets based on demand and ability to pay the highest rates; and deploy ships that generally follow the sun, all while delivering an exceptional product.*
>
> *It is a formula that has worked successfully for 50 years, going on 51 (p. 6)."*

Cruising, unlike most shipping, including passenger shipping for transportation, is supply led versus demand led. In most shipping, demand grows and ship owners build new ships to meet that demand. In cruise shipping, the owners build new and innovative ships and then market them to create demand. Wood [2] writes "Definitions of globalization are legion and reflect the particular orientations and interests of researchers, as well as the complex and multidimensional nature of the phenomenon itself (p. 397)." He views the cruise industry from the perspective of deterritorialization in which "culture, social life and economic activity is no longer rooted primarily in the immediate physical geography of place (p. 398)." He sees cruise ships representing "a unique level of deterritorialization. Huge floating chunks of capital, they are intrinsically mobile and capable of being repositioned at a moment's notice. Unlike land resorts, cruise ships can change their locations to escape bad weather, political instability, or other things their owners may not like. Major events like September 11 can elicit massive redeployments of whole fleets (p. 398)." His article concentrates on the legal and regulatory aspects of this deterritorialization. Marti [3] also discusses globalization in the cruise industry. He writes, "Globalization is occurring due to a rising acceptance of the cruise product around the world as a tourism option. Cruise line strategies that promote globalization include: organic expansion, operating alliances, and mergers/takeovers. Organic expansion results when an established line places a vessel in a new regional market (other than North America) on a seasonal or permanent basis, while supporting the venture with its existing infrastructure. Operating alliances happen when two or more operators combine elements (usually marketing and sales) of their business with the joint aim of expanding into new regional markets. Mergers/takeovers occur when one company either takes a stake in another or assumes control, sometimes in stages and sometimes in one go [4]. According to Wood (2000), further evidence of globalization includes the following: an increasing internationalization of cruise company ownership, the use of flags of convenience (FOCs), registries that have no genuine link to the nationality of ownership, to circumvent home country labor laws, taxes, and maritime regulations and extremely heavy reliance on a global crew population, coming from 100 countries or more (p. 25)." Luthans and Doh [5] write "Globalization can be defined as the process of social, political, economic, cultural, and technological integration among countries around the world. Globalization is distinct from internationalization in that internationalization is the process of a business crossing national and cultural borders, while globalization is the vision of creating one world unit, a single market entity (p. 6)." "The vision of creating one world unit, a single market entity" is reflected in Cruise Lines International Association's (CLIA) [6] mission to "foster their members' success by advocating, educating and promoting the common interests of the cruise community." The community comprises cruise lines with over 95% of global capacity, key suppliers, ports, destinations, travel agencies, and travel agents. Initially focused on North America, CLIA has absorbed the regional cruise community organizations over the past

10 years. CLIA's regions are Australasia, Brazil, Europe, North America, the UK, Ireland, Asia, and Canada. Working together with the Seatrade Organisation out of the UK, CLIA has been spreading the gospel of cruising as a vacation form since 1975.

The Cruise Industry can be likened to a three-legged stool. One leg is hospitality, another is shipping, and the third is tourism. According to Cruise Industry News (2017–2018) [1], the industry had estimated sales of $37.8 billion US in 2017 and capacity for 25.2 million passengers on 365 ships. In comparison, the UNWTO [7] estimated that tourism represents 5% of global GDP, approximately $3.2 trillion US in 2010. According to Stopford [8], there were 74,000+ ships in 20,007 including 3600+ ferries. Thus, while large in absolute terms, the cruise industry is relatively small.

The industry is dominated by 5 international corporations, Carnival Corporation with 10 brands, Royal Caribbean Cruises Limited with 6 brands, Norwegian Cruise Line with 3 brands, MSC Cruises with 1 brand, and Genting Hong Kong with 3 brands. The relationship between the five companies, based on CIN (2017–2018) (p. 6) [1], is shown in **Table 1**.

The geographical extent of the current cruise industry is illustrated in **Figure 1.**

According to *Cruise Industry News Annual Report 2017–2018* [1], p. 8 there were 365 cruise ships with a capacity of 25.2 million passengers and an estimated sales revenue of $37.8 billion US worldwide. **Figures 2–5** show the distribution in 2017 in comparison with 2004 and 1998. 1998 is chosen for comparison since it is the first year that CIN Annual recognized the importance of the Asian market by including Asia in their statistics.

The trend has been a substantial growth in the European and Asian market shares and a corresponding decline in the North American market share. Coggins [9] chronicled the development of the modern cruise industry from a secondhand fleet in a tertiary port into a global industry centered in North America and the growth of Europe into the industry's second global center.

Company	Ships	Berths	Capacity	Market Share
Carnival Corporation	106	234,208	11,104,117	44.1%
Royal Caribbean Cruises Limited	50	123,792	6,021,020	23.9%
Norwegian Cruise Line	25	50,646	2,213,796	8.8%
MSC Cruises	14	40,500	1,759,140	7.0%
Genting Hong Kong	9	15,409	1,022,419	4.1%
Total 5 Companies	204	464,555	22,120,492	87.9%

Table 1.
Top five cruise companies.

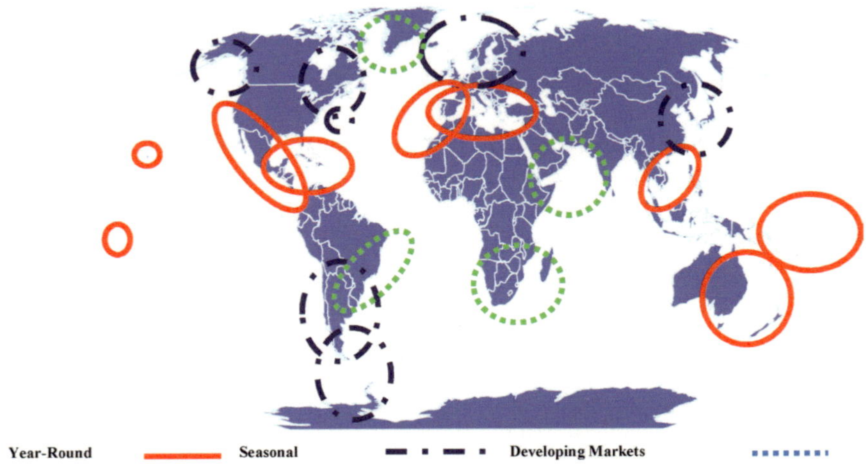

Figure 1.
World cruising regions 2017.

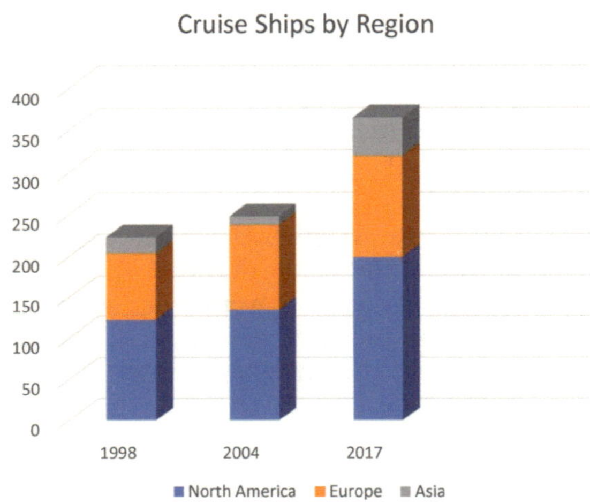

Figure 2.
Cruise ships by region 1998, 2004, and 2017.

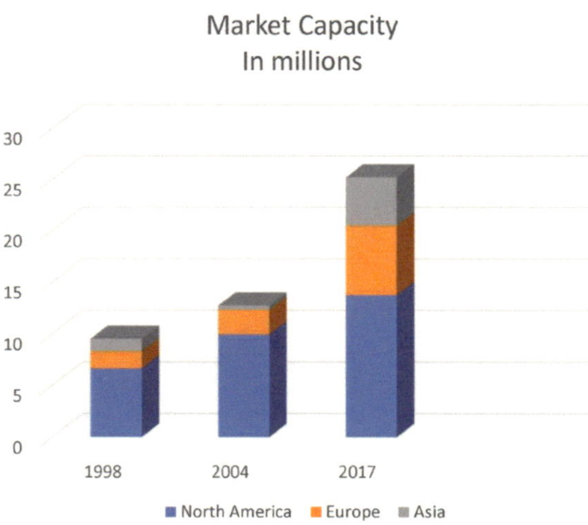

Figure 3.
Market capacity by region 1998, 2004, and 2017.

Figure 4.
Sales revenue by region 1998, 2004, and 2017.

Figure 5.
Market share by region 1998, 2004, and 2017.

2. Development of the North American and European cruise industries

The modern cruise industry can be said to have begun with the sailing of the *Sunward* in 1966. Seeing her alongside the quay in Nassau late December 1966, her crisp modern lines and large windows accented with potted plants stood in sharp contrast to the aged former coastal liners that were characteristic of the Miami cruise trade. The modern cruise industry was concentrated in North America though the early 1990s. The geographical distribution of the industry in 1966 is illustrated in **Figure 6**.

Most of North America's growth followed Marti's [3] definition of organic expansion throughout the Caribbean and then to Alaska and the Mexican Riviera and eventually to Europe. The major exception was Princess Cruises. Their 1974 acquisition by London-based P&O Lines provided an infusion of capital leading

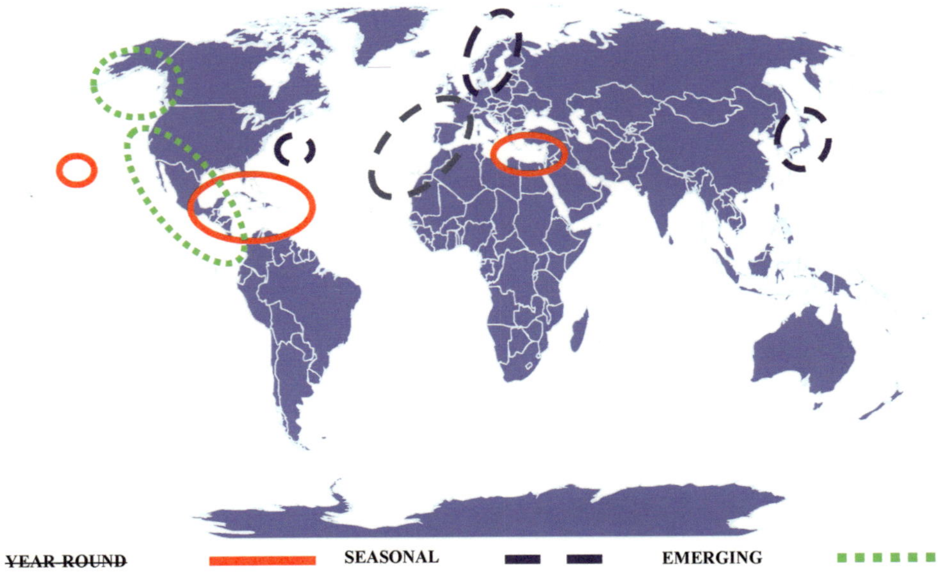

Figure 6.
Major world cruise areas 1966.

to a major upgrade of their fleet by the year's end. This pattern would be repeated between North America and Europe in the 1990s and between Asia and North America in 2000. In 1970, the industry carried 500,000 passengers. The major lines were Home Lines, Sitmar Cruises, Norwegian Caribbean Line (NCL), Cunard Line, Holland America Line (HAL), and Princess Cruises. In 1975, the TV series "Love Boat" started a 10+ year run that brought cruising into the living rooms of millions of Americans who had never seen the ocean. Royal Caribbean Cruises Limited started in 1971 with two new ships. Royal Viking Line (RVL) started with three new ships in the luxury segment and Carnival Cruise Line with the 1960-built ex-*Empress of Canada* as *Mardi Gras*. By 1980, the industry carried 1.4 million passengers, Carnival had three secondhand ships, Royal Viking and Royal Caribbean lengthen their ships to meet demand, and NCL proved the concept that a 2000-passenger ship could be successful in 1-week cruises with the converted ex-*France* operating in *Norway*. The early 1980s saw the advent of second-generation cruise ships with Carnival, Royal Caribbean, and HAL newbuilds. These were followed in quick succession by third-generation newbuilds from Carnival, Sitmar, and Princess in the mid-1980s. Ward [10] described the industry with this inflection point, "The first edition of this book, reviewing, testing, and evaluating 120 ships was published in 1985, when cruising was viewed as an expensive, rarefied experience." At the same time boutique cruise ships the size of large yachts appeared. In 1984, Seatrade held their first cruise shipping conference in New York City. In 1985, the industry carried 2.2 million passengers. In 1988, 3.2 million passengers were carried and the industry began to consolidate. HAL brought Home Lines and Carnival brought HAL. Princess brought Sitmar and Admiral Cruises was acquired by Royal Caribbean. NCL had brought RVL in 1984 but continued to operate it as a separate brand. That same year, fourth-generation cruise ships made their debut with Royal Caribbean's *Sovereign of the Seas*. Sporting multi-deck atriums and broadway-sized show theaters, these were the largest ships built since the 1930s. In 1990, there was a boutique ship proliferation and the industry carried 3.6 million passengers. By 1992, this was 4.1 and by 1994 the numbers were 4.5 million. Up to this point, the focus of statistics was North America. However, in 1995, North American passenger numbers declined to 4.1 million, the first decline since the start of record keeping.

A key factor in this growth was cruising's high customer satisfaction resulting in repeat cruisers. The industry continues to attract new cruisers but repeat passengers are important. Miller and Grazer [11] write, "Cruise lines have long recognized the importance of repeat passengers. According to ship personnel, many sailings have at least forty percent repeat customers. Cruise lines often sail with passengers who have 700 or more days with that particular line (p. 78)." In order to retain these passengers, cruise lines need to offer new experiences in terms of ships and ports. Gibson [12] writes "The success of a cruise business, in terms of securing repeat customers and capturing new business, is directly related to reputation. In turn, past and present customers and their perception of service and product quality directly inform that reputation (p. 169)." As mentioned earlier the cruise industry is supply led. A new ship rewards repeaters something different and entices new-to-cruising passengers with, what Richard Fain, Chairman of Royal Caribbean, calls the latest "Wow!" factor. According to the 1998 CLIA Industry report [13], 24% of perspective cruise passengers were repeat passengers. In surveys taken between 1990 and 1996, 59–70% of these passengers intended to definitely/probably take another cruise. This makes these passengers particularly important to a cruise line's profitability. In spite of all the bells and whistles added over the past 30 years, executives at cruise conferences often remark that passengers pick their cruise because of the destination. Newness in both destinations and hardware remains important in attracting and retaining passengers. Josiam et al. [14] discuss the pull factors in attracting passengers. They write "Prior research identifies five pull factors with respect to cruise travel motivation (Lu, 2001). These five pull factors are national environment and safety, entertainment and sports recreation, nature and wilderness, learning opportunity, and modernity and facilities. Lu also points out that 'nature & wilderness' is the main reason pulling travelers to take cruise ship tours (85)." These factors are all inherent characteristics of a destination. The need to offer new destinations in order to retain repeat passengers is another factor driving fleet expansion.

The stagnation of 1994/1995 led to an attention shift outside of North America to Europe and Asia. Globalization in Europe would be led by newbuildings in the UK and German markets, followed by an attempt at pan-European cruising by Festival Cruises. Festival was eventually forced into bankruptcy by the owner's financial problems with his tanker fleet. This globalization was characterized initially by Marti's [3] organic expansion which was followed by mergers and acquisitions as North America-based lines brought or merged with Europe-based lines. The major exception was MSC Cruises. Backed by the world's second largest container shipping company MSC, MSC Cruises was able to take advantage of Festival's demise and modernize their fleet overnight. Since then they have expanded into the Caribbean, South America, and Asia as well as being a dominant player in Europe. They are well along the way to overtaking Norwegian Cruise Line as the third largest cruise company.

3. Literature review

Josiam et al. [14] write, "There are only a few research studies on travelers' motivation to experience a cruise vacation and their subsequent satisfaction with that experience. Because Asian travelers are an emerging segment of the cruise industry, there is need for cruise operators to better understand the needs of the ethnic Chinese segment and the Taiwanese traveler in particular. The purpose of this article is to address this gap in the literature (p. 77)." In the years since this was written, Carnival, Royal Caribbean, and NCL have put major ships in Asia targeting the Chinese market. They've overcome cultural issues by recruiting their management teams from Asian hospitality, consumer goods, and marketing industries.

The cruise industry in general has not been the subject of many academic articles. A search of the topics cruise industry and repeat passengers, cruise industry and globalization, and cruise industry and repeat purchase behavior of the Academic Search Premier, Business Source Premier, and ABI Inform databases resulted in only 18 academic articles since 1997. Of these only four were relevant to this chapter. This is probably due to cruising's relative position in the hospitality, tourism, and shipping industries. There are two good resources from the textbook perspective. Mancini [15] approaches the industry from the view of the travel agency professional and is excellent for achieving CLIA certification. Gibson [12] gives a detailed comprehensive analysis of the industry from the operational perspective. In 2011 the Shanghai International Cruise Economy Research Center was established. Located in Shanghai's Baoshan District, the center has produced a body of work on the Chinese cruise industry. Since 2014, they have published an annual report on China's cruise industry. Titled The Green Book of the Cruise Industry, Annual Report on China's Cruise Industry [16], the collection of academic articles is published in both Chinese and English.

4. Methodology

Using a grounded theory approach, this chapter looks at changes in the quality, not necessarily the quantity of the supply (ships) as a leading indicator of an inflection point in demand and the emergence of a port or region as a major cruise center serving a largely indigenous market. This chapter covers the development of Asia into a global cruise center. The purpose of the research, initially conducted in 2013, was to examine the growth of the modern cruise industry from the viewpoint of the quality of the hardware, the ships, and to identify any patterns that could be applied to the rapidly evolving Asian market. Specifically, Asia had reached the inflection point similar to the late 1980s and early 1990s in North America when the industry moved rapidly through several generations and the late 1990s and early 2000s in Europe when the industry jumped from first- and second-generation ships to fifth and sixth generation and beyond. This development is described in depth in Coggins [9]. Data from *Cruise Industry News Annual* 1995–2017 [1, 17, 18] and *Berlitz Guides to Cruising* 1983–2017 [19–23] was examined to develop a chronicle of the industry's growth. Daymon and Holloway [24] quoting Pettigrew (1997) (p. 338) wrote "A grounded theory approach enables you to undertake processual research, that is, research that focuses on 'a sequence of individual and collective events, actions and activities unfolding over time in context.' For example, grounded theory studies have the potential to offer original insights into how things happen,..." (p. 118). In summary, they conclude, "Grounded theory is an under-utilized but potentially important research approach for public relations and marketing communications. It holds great potential for tracing social processes in their context. It begins without hypothesis and allows both the data and theoretical sampling to guide the choice of conceptual framework and emerging theory. Researchers follow a systematic, structured process of data collection and analysis" (p. 128).

5. Asia through 1995: green shoots

In regard to early growth in Asia, Coggins [9] writes:

> *"The mid-1990s were times of surprise developments in the Asian market. Through Western eyes this region is often seen as a homogeneous market. However, it is*

DOI: http://dx.doi.org/10.5772/intechopen.88157

diverse, both geographically and market-wise. Stretching from Tasmania in the south to the Kamchatka Peninsula in the north and the International Dateline in the east to the Irrawaddy River in the west, the Greater Asian cruise region can be divided along the Sunda Straight Line into the Asia and South Pacific regions. Both of which followed different paths of development. The Asia region can be further divided into Southeast Asia with Singapore as the dominant homeport and hub of developments in the early 1990s. Destinations in this region are in Thailand, Malaysia, Vietnam, Cambodia, and Indonesia. Hong Kong serves as the major homeport for the Central Asia region. Destinations are Northern and Central Vietnam; Coastal China, north to Shanghai and south to Hainan Island; Taiwan; and the Philippines. Shanghai and the Beijing port cities serve as hubs for the China region. Destination ports are found in Southern Japan, South Korea, and Vladivostok in Far Eastern Russia. The final region, Japan, consists mainly of the Japanese Islands and their many ports.

Market-wise the region is multi-tiered. The South Pacific region's growth has been driven by locally sourced passengers in Australia and New Zealand. Markets for the other regions can be divided into Western sourced and local sourced passengers. Traditionally, Western sourced passengers usually visited the region between January and early May as part of World and Circle-the-Pacific Grand cruises. These passengers trended to be affluent and travelled on premium and luxury lines such as Princess, HAL, Cunard, SilverSea, Seabourn, HAPAG, and P&O Cruises. However, all Western cruise lines now operating year-round in Asia also market those cruises to Western audiences. Prior to globalization of the industry in the Asian region, the local sourced cruise market was concentrated in Japan. Many of these passengers were part of corporate charters. The rest were those wanting to travel in a Japanese culture cocoon provided by the market's ships. Geography and ships spending more than 4 months a year in the region are the determinants for which ships are included in this study.

Fueled by an increase in Japanese cruisers, industry expectations prior to 1994 were that Japan would lead Asia's breakout as the third global cruise region. This was encouraged by the 1989 maiden voyages of the boutique sized Oceanic Grace and the medium sized Fuji Maru. These were joined by similarly sized Orient Venus and Nippon Maru the following year. The world class Asuka debuted in 1991. The excitement generated by these five ships in a market known for its older and smaller ships convinced The Seatrade organisation to hold Cruise Forums in Yokohama in 1990 and 1993. In 1992, the Asian fleet consisted of 24 ships over 20 lines. These ships sailed out of Japan, Tahiti, Australia, and a number of Asian ports for both local and Western sourced markets. That year the 1961-built Shangri-La World and 1965-built Royal Pacific inaugurated short cruises out of Singapore. In 1994 short cruises started out of Bali. Details on ships' age, size, and passenger capacity can be found in Appendix A. **Table 2** *contains the ship and company distribution across various Asian cruising regions 1990 through 1996. The volatility of the Asian Market 1990 through 1995 is shown in* **Figures** *7–9.*

By 1995 Singapore had become the epicenter of the growth in Southeast Asia. Walking onboard Star Cruises Langkapuri Star Aquarius in late 1994 as part of Seatrade's Asia Pacific 94 Cruise Shipping Convention's ship visit program, I instantly felt that cruising in Asia had changed forever. The result of this impression was a May 1995 presentation on the Asian Cruise Market at Cruise and Ferry 95 [25]. Aquarius was the equivalent of any contemporary North American cruise ship of equal size. Star's competitiveness was reconfirmed by a one-night cruise out

Homeport/Source Market	Year	Lines	Ships	Berths
Tahiti	1990	1	1	160
	1991	1	1	160
	1992	1	1	160
	1993	2	2	585
	1994	1	1	160
	1995	2	2	310
Australia	1990	2	2	1,600
	1991	3	5	3,694
	1992	2	3	2,150
	1993	2	2	1,500
	1994	5	5	3,084
	1995	4	9	4,940
Japan	1990	6	9	3,982
	1991	7	9	5,536
	1992	7	10	5,536
	1993	6	9	4,930
	1994	6	9	4,930
	1995	9	9	4,940
China, Philippines. Thailand Local Market	1990	5	5	2,148
	1991	5	5	2,148
	1992	6	7	3,663
	1993	6	6	3,048
	1994	6	6	3,048
	1995	8	13	8,815
Western/Worldwide	1990	5	5	1,758
	1991	5	6	1,942
	1992	3	3	1,808
	1993	8	9	1,797
	1994	8	8	2.303
	1995	9	11	3,655
Total by Year	1990	18	22	9,648
	1991	20	27	13,480
	1992	20	24	13,317
	1993	22	28	11,860
	1994	25	29	13,525
	1995	30	39	20,245

Table 2.
Cruise lines and ships operating in Asian cruise regions 1990–1995.

of Singapore on SuperStar Gemini in 1995. Star Cruises was founded in 1993. In 1994 they started operations with two 1989 and 1990-built state of the art Baltic Sea ferries, Athena and Kalypso. Employed on the highly competitive Sweden-Finland run these ships were the equivalent of the latest cruise ships. An unexpected devaluation of the Swedish Krone created a financial crisis for their original owner, Rederi AB Slite. Unable to pay for new ships under construction in Germany, the line was forced into bankruptcy and their ships became available at an attractive price. Converted for cruise service in Asia they were renamed Langkapuri Star Aquarius and Langkapuri Star Pisces. Star Aquarius was assigned to Singapore and Star Pisces to Hong Kong. They signaled a marked departure from the obsolete ferries and aging ocean liners usually deployed in emerging markets. Star operated short 2–3 day cruises that appealed to the Asian cruise passenger. The ships were equipped with multiple dining venues, a large casino, and top local entertainment. The cruises were priced so that they could be enjoyed by the average citizen, even taxi drivers. This was made possible by unbundling the cruise offering into a basic fare based on accommodations that included a basic dining package, Other

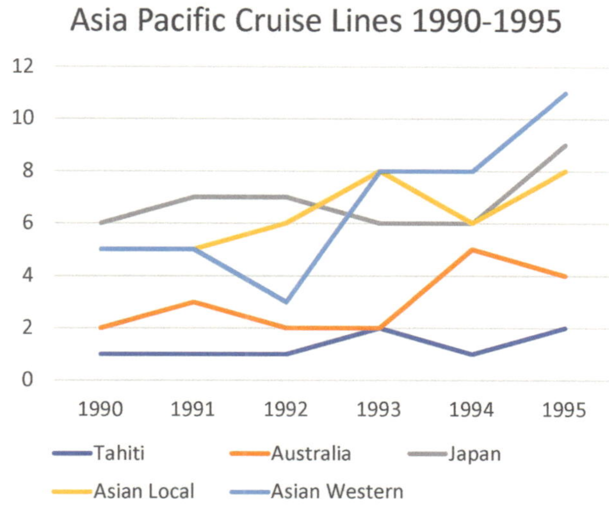

Figure 7.
Asia/Pacific cruise lines by region 1990–1995.

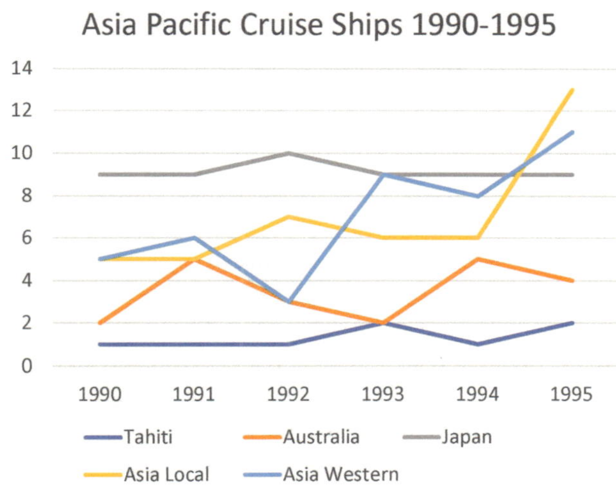

Figure 8.
Asia/Pacific cruise ships by region 1990–1995.

dining venues required extra payment. The Langkapuri prefix was later dropped. Star Aquarius was joined by competitors, cruise ships the 1990-built Nautican, ex-Crown Monarch, and the 1969-built Leisure World, ex-Skyward. By 1996 Star Cruises was leading the expansion in Asia adding 1988-built cruise yacht sisters MegaStar Aries and MegaStar Taurus and the 1992-built SuperStar Gemini ex-Crown Jewel. U.S.-based Renaissance Cruises was also operating 1989-built boutique sisters Renaissance I and Renaissance II. These cruise yachts targeted a North American and worldwide fly-cruise passenger base. The same year P&O Spice Island Cruises started with 3–5 day cruises out of Bali with the 1962-built Bali Sea Dancer, ex-Illiria, and Klub Awani started short cruises out of Jarkarta with the 1966-built Awani Dream-I ex-World Renaissance. Two ships under Malaysian ownership, Empress Cruise Lines' 1966-built The Empress ex-Sunward, and Berjaya Holiday Cruise's 1962-built Coral Princess also entered service. By 1996 Star was fully established with a fleet of 5 ships."

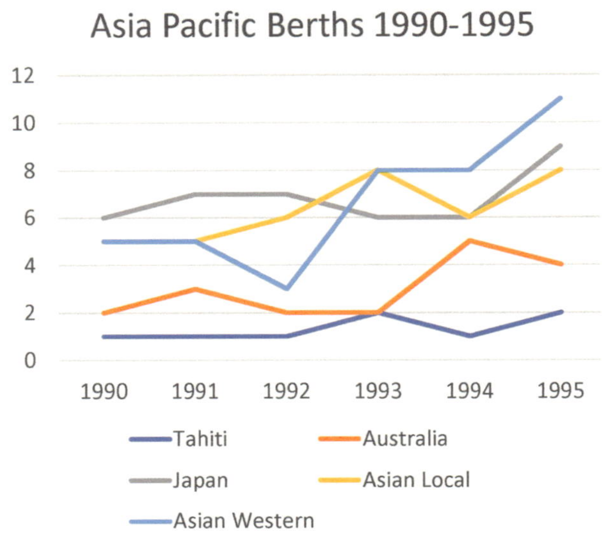

Figure 9.
Asia/Pacific cruise berths by region 1990–1995.

6. Asia: post 1995—blossoms and an early winter

In 1996, the principal indigenous Asia fleet consisted of 26 ships with 16,204 berths. The Japan-based fleet included seven ships in four lines. Two of these were built in the early to mid-1970s, the rest between 1989 and 1991. These ships were Japan Cruise Line's 1975-built *New Utopia* and 1990-built *Orient Venus*, Mitsui OSK's 1972-built *Shin Sakura Maru* and 1989-built *Nippon Maru*, NYK Cruises' 1991-built *Asuka*, and Showa Lines' 1989-built *Oceanic Grace*. K-Line's 1974-built *Song of Flower* is not included since she was marketed and deployed worldwide. In 1997 she was transferred to Radisson Seven Seas Cruises. The fleet stayed stable until 1998. That year Showa sold *Oceanic Grace* to P&O Spice Island Cruises and left the cruise business, and *New Utopia* was retired. Meanwhile, Japan Cruise Line's *Pacific Venus* entered service. In September of the following year, *Shin Sakura Maru* left service leaving the fleet at five ships over three lines with 3056 berths. The fleet remained unchanged until 2002 when *Orient Venus* was withdrawn along with *Fuji Maru*. The fleet stabilized at three ships, three lines, and 1904 berths until 2006. That year *Asuka* was sold and *Asuka II*, NYK's subsidiary Crystal Cruises' 1990-built *Crystal Harmony*, replaced her. This raised the number of berths to 2280. As of mid-2013 the Japan-based and -oriented fleet remained at three lines with three ships and 2280 berths. In a March 2012 press release, Princess Cruises announced the deployment of the 1995-built *Sun Princess* to Japan from April to July 2013. The deployment and itineraries were specifically targeted at the local market. This marked the largest deployment by a Western brand since the *Queen Elizabeth* 2 operated out of Japan in the late 1980s. This will be discussed further under the pan-Pacific category.

In 1996, Windstar Cruises' 1987-built *Wind Song* and Club Mediterranee's 1992-built *Club Med II* sail-assisted cruise yachts operated out of Papeete, Tahiti. In 1998 these were redeployed and the luxury cruise ship 1998-built *Paul Gauguin* took up residence. *Paul Gauguin* was designed and built for Tahiti service and was still there in 2017. The passenger cargo ship *Aranu* began service between Tahiti and the Marquesas in 2000. *Aranu* is not included in the statistics since her primary purpose is transportation. In 2013 Windstar's 1988-built *Wind Spirit* resumed their Tahiti service.

Indonesia saw a number of cruise ventures in the late 1990s. P&O Spice Island Cruises operated the 1962-built former Mediterranean cruise liner *Illiria* as *Bali Sea Dancer* from 1995 to 1997. In 1998 she was replaced by the *Oceanic Grace* operating as *Oceanic Odyssey*. In 1999 P&O Spice Island Cruises fell victim to the Asian financial crisis and was shut down. There was another start-up attempt out of Jarkarta in 1996 and 1997. Klub Awani started short cruises with the 1966-built *Awani Dream I*, the former *World Renaissance*. She was joined a year later by the former 1976-built *Cunard Countess* as *Awani Dream II*. In 1998 Klub Awani succumbed to the Asian financial crisis and left the industry.

There was a brief attempt at cruising out of the Philippines by Mabuhay Holiday Cruises. They operated the converted 1983-built Japanese ferry, *Fuji Sunshine*, as *Mabuhay Sunshine* on short cruises out of Manila. Operations ceased after 1 year, another victim of the financial crisis.

Siam Cruise Company operated the converted Stockholm-Helsinki ferry, 1962-built *Svea Jarl*, as *Andaman Princess* out of Pattaya, Thailand, since the early 1980s. The December 2004 Indian Ocean Earthquake and Tsunami was disastrous for the company as many of its ports were severely impacted. Even though *Andaman Princess* was unscathed, the company went out of business in 2005.

The atmosphere in Asia 1996–1998 was one of optimism and expansion. Royal Caribbean operated *Sun Viking* out of Singapore for North American cruisers. Carnival was in discussions with Hyundai regarding a cruise joint venture, and Star was busy buying up high-quality secondhand cruise ships and introducing cruising throughout the region. All this changed as the Asian financial crisis, which began in 1997, caused a shakeout in the market. In 1997, Royal Caribbean sold *Sun Viking* to Star Cruises and left the market. Carnival's brief joint venture with Hyundai also ended that year before a ship could be put in operation. By 1998, *Nautican* had moved to one-night gaming cruises, and Renaissance had ceased Singapore operations. However, Metro Holdings Ltd. Sun Cruises started up with 1963-built *Sun Vista*, Celebrity Cruises' ex-*Meridian*, and *Sun Viva* 1, a former Renaissance cruise yacht. Another former Renaissance cruise yacht, *Sun Viva* 2, was added the following year. Unfortunately, *Sun Vista* was lost to an engine room fire that May. Sun Cruises ceased operations in 2000. New Century Cruise Line added converted ferry, *Amusement World*, in 1998. They would cease operations by 2001. In 1998 two Malaysian-owned lines were in operation. The following year Berjaya Holiday Cruise would withdraw their 1962-built *Coral Princess* to concentrate on their core resort business. Empress Cruise Lines would continue to operate *The Empress* for 4 more years before leaving the market in 2004. In 1998, Star Cruises' fleet consisted of *Star Aquarius*, *MegaStar Aries*, *MegaStar Taurus*, *SuperStar Gemini* in Singapore, *Star Pisces* in Hong Kong, and *SuperStar Capricorn* deployed to New York and Australia. Later that year, Star introduced the brand-new *SuperStar Leo*. Designed by Tillberg Design, *Leo* raised the bar for the Asian market as the first newbuild, aside from the Japanese market, on a par with the industry's state-of-the-art ships. In 1999 *Leo* was joined by *SuperStar Virgo* who took over the Singapore cruises as *Leo* joined *Pisces* in Hong Kong.

The year 1999 also saw the start-up of Hyundai Cruises. Operating three ships, 1973-built *Kumgang* ex-*Capricorn*, 1972-built *Pongnae* ex-*Sagittarius*, and 1972-built *Pungnar-Ho* ex-*Island Princess* on short cruises to North Korea, the company lasted 3 years until 2001 before withdrawing as a result of changes in the political situation. As 1999 progressed Star sold *Capricorn* and *Sagittarius* to Hyundai, while *Aries* and *Taurus* were assigned to the charter market. In 2000, Star acquired the 1980-built *SuperStar Taurus* ex-*Leeward* and 1982-built *SuperStar Aries* ex-*Europa*. The industry was anticipating the arrival of Star's Libra class newbuilds. The first was due in 2001 and the second in 2002. Late in 1999 Star acquired Norwegian Cruise Line and the Libra class ships debuted as NCL's *Norwegian Star* and *Norwegian Dawn* in 2001 and 2002, respectively. In 2001, Star sold *SuperStar Taurus* and *SuperStar Aries*. By 2002 Star's Asian fleet had settled into its basic configuration for the next 5 years as the company's attention was focused on growing its NCL fleet. *Virgo* and *Gemini* were in Singapore, and *Pisces* and *Leo* were in Hong Kong. *Gemini*'s size also made her an excellent market opener as Star tried various new markets around Asia. In 2003, the SARS epidemic struck Hong Kong and effectively shut down the tourism industry throughout Asia for the next several months. *Leo* was sent to Australia in early spring to ride out the downturn. Her southbound transit was used to thoroughly disinfect the ship and effectively quarantine the crew.

7. The Australian market: a long growing season

The development of the Australia/New Zealand/South Pacific cruise market goes back a long time. P&O Cruises and Sitmar Cruises had been sailing out of Sydney since the 1970s. In the 1980s, P&O Cruises operated the 1959-built *Oriana* and the smaller 1966-built *Sea Princess* out of Sydney. Sitmar competed with the 1957-built converted troopship *Fairstar*. In 1986 *Oriana* was retired, leaving *Sea Princess* to maintain the P&O presence. In 1988, Princess Cruises purchased Sitmar Cruises. *Fairstar* continued to sail under the P&O banner; however, the name was not changed in deference to *Fairstar*'s many years of Australian service and reputation as "The Fun Ship." The following year, *Sea Princess* returned to Princess Cruises. In 1998 Australia relaxed its cabotage regulations, and Cruising Down Under, a port cooperative marketing association, was more than 2 years into its concerted effort to attract more cruise lines to the region. Given Australia's long coastline, this relaxation allowed non-Australian cruise lines to offer shorter cruises calling at Australian ports. That same year *Fairstar* was replaced by the 1956-built *Fair Princess*, Sitmar's former *Fairsea*. In the mid-1990s P&O Cruises had occasional competition for the lower end of the market from CTC Cruise Lines' 1976-built *Karellya* with seasonal augmentation from their 1972-built *Southern Cross*, ex-*Spirit of London*. Star Cruises based their 1973-built *Norwegian Capricorn*, ex-*Royal Viking Sea*, in the region in 1999 and 2000. In 2000, the 1984-built *Pacific Sky*, ex-*Fair Sky*, replaced *Fair Princess*. In 2003, she was joined by the 1998-built *Pacific Princess*, ex-*R Three*, which brought year-round big ship total berths to 1888. Adding the 1986-built *Pacific Sun*, ex-*Jubilee*, increased this to 3274 in 2004. Two years later the three ships were joined by 1982-built *Pacific Star*, ex-*Tropicale*, bringing the total to 4396 berths. This number dropped to 4098 in 2007 as *Pacific Sky* and *Pacific Princess* withdrew and the 1991-built *Pacific Dawn*, ex-*Regal Princess*, was added. In 2008 *Pacific Star* left Australia bringing the total down to 3076 berths. In 2010, the two ships were joined by the 1990-built *Pacific Jewel*, ex-*Ocean Village* 2, raising the total to 4666 berths. The following year they were joined by the 1989-built *Pacific Pearl* for a total of 6136 berths. The addition of the 2001-built *Carnival Spirit* in 2012 added a new brand and brought the total to 8236 year-round berths. In 2013 *Pacific Sun* was sold which brought the total down to 6750. Between 2002 and 2013, P&O Cruises went from one ship with 1200 berths to three ships with 4650 berths plus one state-of-the-art ship with 2100 berths from sister-brand, Carnival Cruise Line. Since 1998, Captain Cook Cruises has operated small, 1800–3100 grt, 120–175 passenger cruise ships along the Great Barrier Reef and out of Fiji. Captain Cook also operates two river boats on the Murray River but the river numbers are not included in the statistics. Orion Expedition Cruises sailed the 2003-built *Orion* from 2005 through 2013 on expedition cruises out of Australia. From 2011 to 2012, they chartered the former 1991-built *Renaissance Four* as *Orion II*. These numbers are included in the statistics. In 2013 Orion Expedition Cruises was acquired by

Lindblad Expeditions National Geographic, and *Orion* was renamed *National Geographic Orion*.

8. The Asian market post-2005: rejuvenation and growth

In 2004 *Leo* returned to Hong Kong for a short period of time before being transferred to NCL as *Norwegian Legend*. Star's fleet remained steady until 2006 when NCL's 1988-built *Norwegian Sea* arrived in Asia as *SuperStar Libra*. At the same time, Costa Crociere positioned the mid-sized 1992-built *Costa Allegra* in Shanghai and Hong Kong on a year-round basis. Their target market was Mainland China. This was in contrast to *Sun Viking* who targeted Royal Caribbean's traditional customers. In 2007 Star introduced NCL's 1993-built *Norwegian Wind* as *SuperStar Aquarius* on short multi-night cruises out of Hong Kong. *Pisces* was primarily used in one-night cruises to nowhere. *Libra* was used to test new markets in Asia and the Mediterranean. The next change was the lay-up of *Gemini* in 2009. *Costa Allegra* operated through 2010; however, after her first season she was also marketed in Europe. In 2011 she was replaced by the larger 1992-built *Costa Classica*. *Classica* remained in Asia through 2012. That year she was joined by the still larger 1996-built *Costa Victoria*. In 2013 *Classica* returned to Europe and was replaced by the 2000-built *Costa Atlantica*. In 2012 Star added NCL's 1992-built *Norwegian Dream* as *SuperStar Gemini*. *Libra*, *Aquarius*, and *Gemini* were deployed throughout Asia in 2013.

As previously mentioned Costa upped the ante by increasing their ship numbers and size 2010 through 2013. Having seasonally deployed the 1995-built *Legend of the Seas* in Asia since 2008, Royal Caribbean International (RCI) assigned her to Asia year-round in 2010. Post-Panamax[1] 1999-built *Voyager of the Seas* joined *Legend of the Seas* in 2012. This was a bold move and a strong statement of RCI's confidence in the Asian market as she was the largest ship in Asia. In 2013, *Legend of the Seas* was replaced by *Voyager*'s larger near-sister the 2004-built *Mariner of the Seas*. RCI deployed their ships out of Shanghai spring through fall and out of Hong Kong and Singapore in the winter. However, they advertised that worldwide RCI's primary target market was the local Asian population. With these two ships, RCI had the newest and largest ships in the Asian market, a generation ahead of the competition. Historically, this has been a winning combination in passenger shipping. Star's response was refurbishment and opening new homeports and markets by deploying their ships throughout Asia. They homeported a ship in Kota Kinabalu, Malaysia, and Xiamen, China, and made maiden calls in Yangon, Myanmar. Indigenous cruise lines also started in China and Korea in 2012, though they would be gone in several years. China Cruise started operations out of Hong Kong with the 1992-built ex-*Radisson Diamond* as *China Star*. As the first SWATH[2] cruise ship, *China Star* holds a special place in cruise ship history. HNA Tourism brought the 1986-built ex-*Jubilee* and is operating her as *Henna* out of Hainan Island. In Korea, Harmony Cruise started operations with the 1990-built ex-*Costa Marina* as *Harmony Princess*. In 2013, Oriental Dragon entered the cruise field with the 1982-built ex-*Sun Viking* as *Oriental Dragon*.

After 2008, a new category of Asian Market ships has been developed, ships that seasonally migrated throughout the Pacific. Spending the northern winter in Australia or Asia and the summer in Alaska, US West Coast, or Northern Asia, these ships can be called pan-Pacific ships. They include some of the lines' most modern and cutting-edge ships. Examples are: Princess Cruises' 1995-built *Sun Princess*, 2004-built *Diamond Princess* and *Sapphire Princess* rotating between Australia

---

[1] Post-Panamax: A ship too large to fit through the Panama Canal, generally a ship exceeding 100,000 grt.

[2] SWATH: Small water plane area twin hull.

and Japan; RCI's 1997-built *Rhapsody of the Seas* and 2001-built *Radiance of the Seas* rotating between Alaska and Asia and Australia, respectively; and Celebrity Cruises' 1995-built *Celebrity Century* and 2008-built *Celebrity Solstice* following a similar pattern as the RCI ships. The migration patterns are shown in **Figure 10**.

2013 was an important year for the question, "Is Asia the next global cruise center?" What was different from the mid to late 1990s, the last period of rapid growth? In the mid to late 1990s, Star Cruises was the only company introducing relatively new ships on a regular basis. Seasonal deployments by major cruise ships were pass-throughs as part of world or circle Pacific long cruises. The major cruise terminals were Singapore's Cruise Centre, Yokohama Cruise terminal, Hong Kong's Ocean Terminal, and Langkawi, Malaysia. While both Singapore and Hong Kong promoted their cruise facilities and location as cruise hubs, there were no regional cruise port organizations. Cruising Down Under was just getting started and writing the book on regional cruise port promotion. The Seatrade Organisation held a cruise tourism forum in Yokohama in 1993; cruise conferences in Singapore in 1994, 1996, and 1998; and cruise conferences in Cairns, Australia, in 1995 and 1997. These conferences/conventions provided an opportunity for cruise industry executives, tourism officials, and port authorities to get together. They also served to raise the industry's awareness as a vacation option through accompanying travel agent training sessions. The budding industry was hard hit by the Asian financial crisis toward the end of the decade and then again by the SARS epidemic in 2003. Star Cruises, with parent company Genting, was able to rationalize their fleet and persist.

While most of Asian tourism was suffering from the impact of the SARS crisis, Chinese tourism made a quick rebound in the second half of 2003 and into 2004.

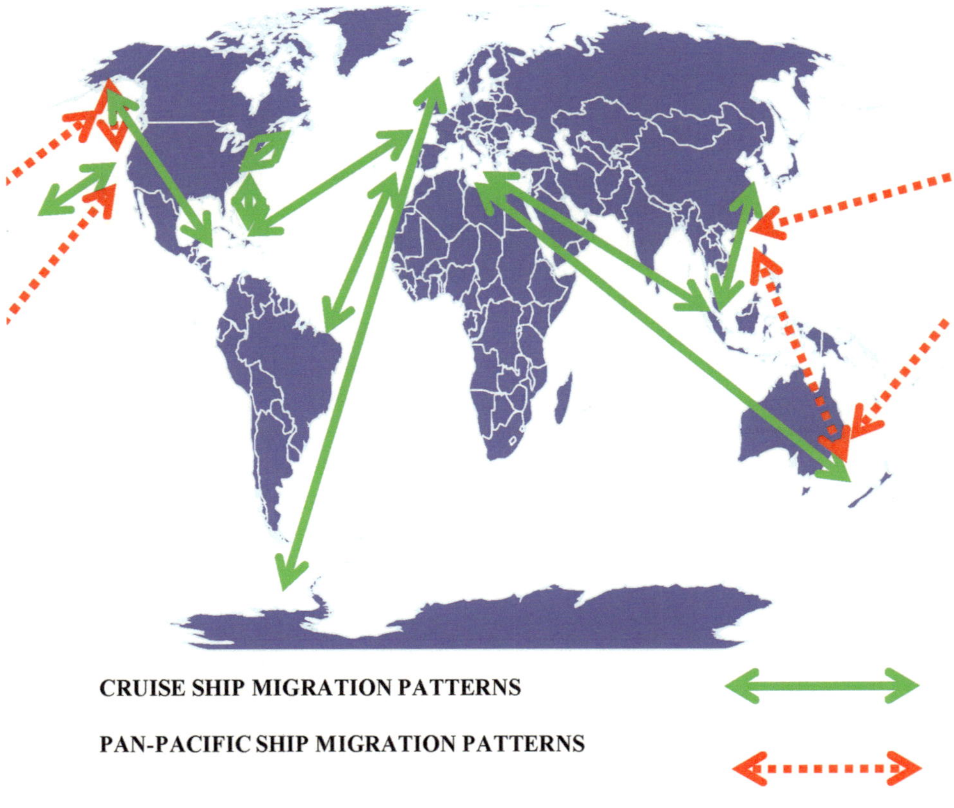

Figure 10.
Cruise ship migration patterns 2017.

China Today [26] wrote "The 'Analysis of Functioning Characteristics of the 2003 Consumer Products Market and Prices and 2004 Development Trends' published by the China National Commercial information Center isolates five characteristics. The first is the rapid growth in commodity housing and tourism that kept the retail volume of consumer products at a stable rate of increase as hot consumer products like cars and IT electronic products continued to increase. The second is unbalanced development of urban and rural areas and of different regions. Third is the contribution of hot consumer products to the increase in the total retail volume of social consumer products. Fourth is substantial growth in the catering industry, and fifth, that the middle class is a main force in hiking up consumption growth." This was the same year that Costa Crociere opened its office in Hong Kong to prepare for *Costa Allegra*'s China Debut in 2006. As the world's economies slipped into the Great Recession, China's continued with relatively robust growth. By 2008, Royal Caribbean was back in Asia on a seasonal basis. Saporito and Ramzy wrote "The world's largest multinational companies, many of them headquartered in the U.S., have been betting on the rise of the Chinese consumer for many years now. But as the economies in the U.S. and Europe have struggled to revive in the past few years, firms in nearly every sector, from automobiles to consumer goods to telecommunications, have placed a larger share of their chips on the Middle Kingdom. It is simply a matter of numbers: China's economy grew 9.1% in the last quarter, compared with <2% in most of the West. While incomes in the West are stagnant, individual Chinese are expected to get a lot richer [27]."

The situation in 2013 was much different from in 1998. Instead of Star being the only major year-round cruise line, Costa Crociere and RCI were also operating frontline ships on a year-round basis. Seeking to take advantage of what Saporito and Ramzy (2011) termed China's shift toward consumerism "As for China, the numbers behind any big shift toward consumerism there are potentially world altering. China's 2011 GDP is roughly $6 trillion. If consumer spending goes up from the current 36% to reach 45% of GDP-the government's stated goal-$540 billion in spending would flow into consumer goods and services...." With regard to travel potential, they wrote "Boston consulting Group estimates there are 1 million millionaire households in China, When those folks start hitting the road, Bridle (Hong Kong-based luxury-hotel company New World Hospitality's Chief Operating Officer) wants to be ready, and so New World recently spent $230 million to acquire Rosewood hotels and resorts, to lure travelers...The exodus is already under way. There are an estimated 54 million outbound trips from China, a number that quadrupled in the past 10 years. By the end of the decade, the figure could easily reach 100 million... [27]".

By 2013, there were also a number of pan-Pacific ships seasonally rotating through the region. The world cruise and circle Pacific ships still passed through, but the pan-Pacific ships made concerted efforts to target the local source passenger. More importantly, the infrastructure for growth was in place. New dedicated cruise terminals had been constructed or were under construction in Singapore, Hong Kong, Shanghai, Xiamen, Sanya, Qingdao, Dalian, Tianjin, Busan, Keelung, and Kaohsiung, to name a few. Ports had formed alliances to promote cruise calls such as Japan-Korea Strait Coastal Region Tourism Promotion Network, Kyushu District Transport Bureau, Taiwan Strait Tourism Association, and Micronesian Cruise Association. In 2008, the Hong Kong Tourism Board (HKTB), in cooperation with CLIA, set up a program to train travel agents in selling cruises. The Chinese Government included cruise industry development in its Fifth Five-Year Plan (2011–2015) and declared 2013 as marine tourism year [28]. Among measures to increase cruise tourism, China's Ministry of Transport and Communications has streamlined customs' procedures, permitted Chinese companies to form cruise lines, and eased cabotage[3] regulations so that foreign flag cruise ships can call at multiple Chinese ports on a single itinerary [29]. The cabotage issue was critical in the development of the China source market. China's long coastline makes short cruises, 3–5 days popular in the Asian market, difficult to operate without calls at Chinese ports. For example, Shanghai to Hong Kong is 824 nautical miles.[4] In addition, there's the political situation which can change itineraries overnight as in 2017 with South Korea. The other major factor was the relaxation of restrictions on overseas travel in the early 2000s. In side conversations with China Overseas Shipping Company (OSCO) executives at Seatrade's 1998 Asia/Pacific Cruise Conference, they mentioned the issue with cruise development in China wasn't money/affordability but travel restrictions. In 2006, the China Cruise and Yacht Industry Association (CCYIA) was formed. CCYIA is a nonprofit organization dedicated to the development of the cruise industry in China. It conducts research and serves as a forum for discussions between key stakeholders. The Asia Cruise Association was formed in 2009 and serves as the cruise industry's association in Asia. It recently joined CLIA's global organization and performs the same functions but in Asia. The Asia Cruise Terminal Association (ACTA) was formed in 2010. Led by the Singapore Cruise Centre, it is mandated to promote cooperation among terminal developers and operators, increase awareness of existing facilities, and promote the region's development as a primary cruise destination. UBM's Seatrade returned to the region with a "House Party" conference to promote cruising in 2005 in Singapore. In 2008 they held their first All Asia Cruise Convention at the North Bund Cruise Terminal in Shanghai. The second convention was held in Suzhou in 2010. For the third they returned to Shanghai in 2012. Cruise Shipping held their first Cruise Shipping Asia/ Pacific conference in Singapore in 2011. The second was held in 2012 and the third in 2013. Like the conferences in the 1990s, these five were accompanied by travel agent training sessions. In 2014 Cruise Shipping and UBM combined efforts under the Seatrade Asia/Pacific brand. Cruise Shipping Conferences were held in Hong Kong in 2014, Busan Korea in 2016, and Baoshan Shanghai in 2016 and 2017. One can conclude that the hardware is in place, but the modern cruise operations are extremely complicated. With the average cruise ship carrying close to or more than 2000 passengers, and newbuildings (new ships) carrying 4000 plus, the software has become increasingly more important. Rapid clearance of customs, quarantine, and immigration (CQI) is important, as are sufficient tour options and language capable guides. Yap [30] questions the return on investment from the new terminals. It's very difficult for a cruise terminal to make money unless it's a mixed-use facility with multiple revenue generators. The value of a cruise terminal is its ability to increase the number of cruise calls. Using a conservative estimate of $100.00 US spent per passenger or crewmember, each call can be worth between $200,000 and $300,000 US. If the terminal can take yearly calls from 10 to 50, it may well be worth the cost. The number of ships trading in Asian waters has been rising steadily over the last few years.

When the bulk of this chapter was written, the question was "Is Asia the next global cruise hot spot?" By 2017 the answer was a firm "Yes!" From 2013 through 2017, major developments had taken place in the Asian operations of Star Cruises/ Genting Hong Kong, Costa Crociere, Royal Caribbean International (RCI), and Princess Cruises. Post 2017 these are being joined by global brands Norwegian Cruise Line, MSC Cruises, AIDA Cruises, and Carnival Cruise Line. Corben wrote

[3] Cabotage: The right to transport passengers and goods directly between two ports in the same country. Usually restricted to national/domestic flag carriers and can be a detriment to foreign flag cruise operations.

[4] 1 nautical mile = 2000 yards.

> *"Asia's tourism industry is booming, buoyed by rising incomes, low-cost air transport, and China's growing outbound market….The World Travel and Tourism Council said dependence on tourism has been growing, especially with the 'spectacular growth' in China's outbound market.*
>
> *'China expanded its 'approved destination status' scheme from 14 countries to 113 by 2012, leading to a 700 per cent increase in outward visits by Chinese tourists, from 10 million in 2000 to 78 million by 2015,' the Council said." Corben goes on to quote Oliver Lamb, of Sydney-based Pacific Aviation Consulting, "regional economic progress has driven tourism growth. The middle class is forecast to grow from 190 million to 400 million in the coming decade."*
>
> *"The growth of the middle class-the strength of the Asian middle class, the emergence of [air] carriers that are specifically targeted in wealth and well within the Asian middle classes' needs and low fuel prices-you are getting a perfect storm of positive dynamics for leisure travel in the Asia Pacific," Lamb told VOA [31].*

The growth of the low-cost carriers has been a boon to the pan-Asia ships by greatly reducing the cost of the air portion of a cruise.

In 2015, RCI placed their lead ship of the *Quantum* Class, *Quantum of the Seas*, into service in Shanghai. She was the first newbuilding since *SuperStar Virgo* to enter the Asian Market. The same year, RCI started a joint venture, SeaSky Cruises, with Ctrip.com, exclusively for the Chinese market. Celebrity Cruises 1995-built *Celebrity Century* was renamed *Golden Era* and modified for the Chinese passenger. Costa also augmented their Asian fleet with the 2003-built *Costa Fortuna* and the 2007-built *Costa Serena*. Meanwhile, Princess Cruises made a concerted effort to develop their Japan market and establish a strong presence in China by deploying their 2015 Mitsubishi Heavy Industries-built sisters, *Sapphire Princess* and *Diamond Princess*.

In 2016, Genting Hong Kong, parent company of Star Cruises and Crystal Cruises, introduced the first ship of their Chinese market luxury brand, Dream Cruises. *Genting Dream* rotates between Guangzhou (Nansha Port), Hong Kong, and Sanya. In 2017 she was joined by sister ship *Genting World*.

In 2017, Princess Cruises introduced their purpose-built *Majestic Princess* into the Chinese market. She was joined by another purpose-built ship, Norwegian Cruise Line's *Norwegian Joy*. AIDA Cruises joined the list of Western cruise lines operating year-round in Asia with the 2008-built *AIDAbella*. Not to be outdone, Costa added the extensively rejuvenated 1993-built *neoRomantica* to their Asian fleet. In 2019, Costa will add the purpose-built *Costa Venezia*. In 2020, she will be joined by a yet unnamed sister. 2017 was a landmark year as *Cruise Industry News Annual 2017–2018* [1] designated Asia/Pacific as the number 2 cruise region with a 15.7% market share, 59 ships, and a capacity of 3,972,701 passengers. In 2018, MSC Cruises will dedicate the 2009-built *MSC Splendida* to Asia and China. While seemingly late to the game, MSC Cruises had maintained a sales office in Hong Kong targeting the Asian and Chinese source markets since 2004.

Of the 84 cruise ships on order as *Cruise Industry News Annual 2017–2018* [1] went to press, seven were dedicated to the Asian (1) and Chinese (6) markets. Maybe more important than the number of ships being dedicated to the Asian market was the 2017 agreement, announced by Carnival Corporation press release on February 22, 2017 [32], between Carnival Corporation, Fincantieri S.p.A., and the China State Shipbuilding Corporation (CSSC). This brings together the world's largest cruise corporation, one of the world's most prolific cruise ship building yards and China's major shipbuilding corporation. The binding agreement called for the building of two 135,000 grt/4200-passenger cruise ships, with an option for 4 more, for the new Carnival China brand. The first ship is to be delivered in 2023. These will be the first major cruise ships constructed in China and may mark the emergence of China as a major player in cruise ship construction. Mitsubishi Heavy Industries is the only other Asian shipyard with major cruise ship construction experience. Their ships include Crystal Cruises' 1990-built *Crystal Harmony*, NYK Cruises' 1991-built *Asuka*, and Princess Cruises' 2004-built sisters, *Diamond Princess* and *Sapphire Princess*. However, they have been unsuccessful in obtaining continuous orders. The Carnival China ships may mark the emergence of China as a major player in cruise ship construction. Given the size of China's coastal middle class, the growth of cruising as a vacation option, and the low market penetration, the potential exists for China for China to be not just a major source of cruise passengers but a new major center for cruise ship construction. True globalization will be achieved when these yards are constructing ships for non-Asian brands for non-Asian deployment.

Meanwhile, the Australian-South Pacific market continued to grow. By 2017, P&O Australia's fleet consisted of 5 secondhand ships: ex-Holland America ships, 1993-built ex-*Ryndam*, *Pacific Aria*, and 1994-built ex-*Statendam*, *Pacific Eden* and ex-Princess' ships, 1991-built ex-*Regal Princess Pacific Dawn*; 1997-built ex-*Dawn Princess*, *Pacific Explorer*; and 1990-built ex-*Crown Princess*, *Pacific Jewel*. In 2019, they'll be joined by the rebranded 2008-built ex-*Carnival Splendor*. P&O Australia is augmented by Carnival Corporation sister brands, Princess Cruises and Carnival Cruise Lines. Princess is represented by formerly North America, and Europe deployed 1998-built *Sea Princess*, 1995-built *Sun Princess*, and 2001-built *Golden Princess*. Carnival is represented by the 2001-built *Carnival Spirit*.

Royal Caribbean International (RCI) and Celebrity Cruises represent Royal Caribbean Cruises Limited. RCI's fleet includes 2000-built *Explorer of the Seas*, 2001-built *Radiance of the Seas*, and 2016-built *Ovation of the Seas*. *Ovation of the*

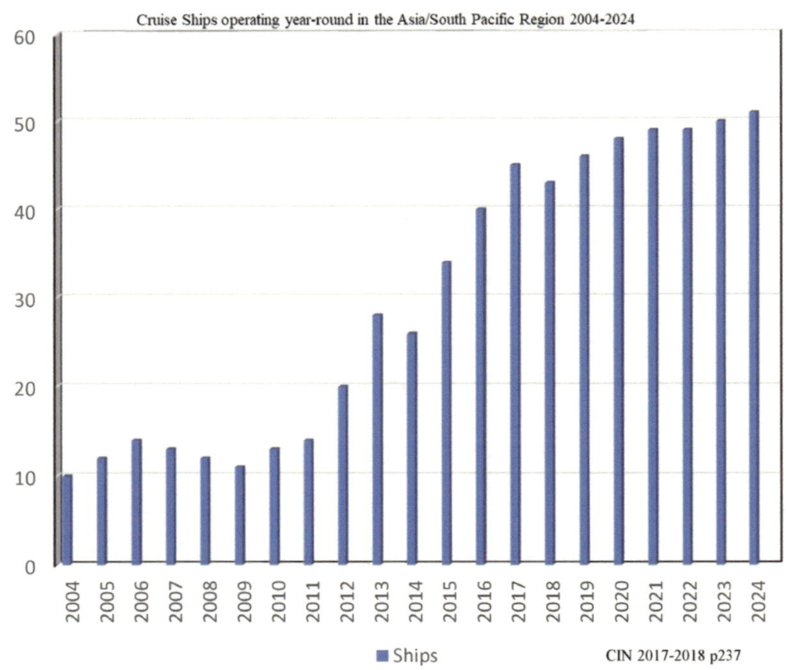

Figure 11.
Cruise ships operating year-round in the Asia/South Pacific region 2004–2024.

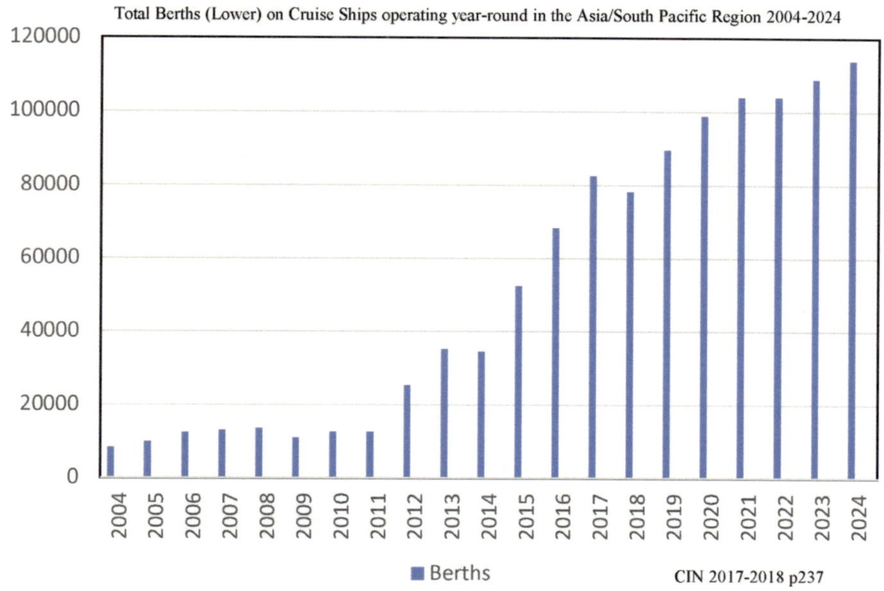

Figure 12.
Total berths (lower) on cruise ships operating year-round in the Asia/South Pacific region 2004–2024.

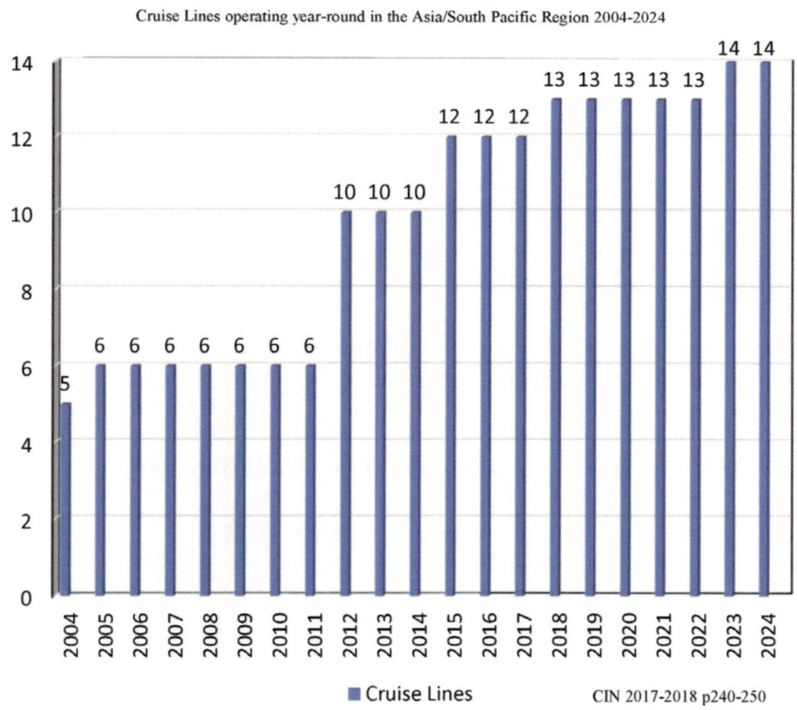

Figure 13.
Cruise lines operating year-round in the Asia/South Pacific region 2004–2024.

Seas rotates between seasonal homeports of Sydney and Shanghai. 2010-built *Celebrity Solstice* flies the flag for Celebrity.

Figures 11–13 show the growth in Asia/South Pacific cruise ships, berths, and number of cruise lines operating year-round, respectively.

9. Conclusions

Asia has long played a role in worldwide passenger shipping. Prior to the 1980s, Asia was part of international line voyages and seasonal world cruises and circles Asia/Pacific cruises for mostly North American and European sourced passengers. The cruises within the Japanese Islands were mostly corporate charters or targeted to national passengers. International cruise operations can be said to have begun in 1982 when the converted cruise ship ex-*Finnstar* began operations as *Pearl of Scandinavia* (12,456 grt/515 pax). Taking advantage of improvements in the US/China relations, the ship offered a way for Americans to visit several ports in China in comfort during the ship's 4-week round trip itinerary from Japan to Singapore. In 1988, following extensive renovations at Singapore's Sembawang Shipyard, she was renamed *Ocean Pearl*. Sold to Croisieres Paquet in 1994, she ceased Asian operations in 1995.

However, globalization, in terms of the modern cruise industry and transformation of Asia into the industry's third global center, reached Asia in 1993/1994 with the start of Star Cruises. A Malaysian leisure/gaming company, Genting Group, took a North American business model and adapted it to Asian tastes. This was the first indigenous cruise line in Asia with state-of-the-art ships. Marketing itself to the local population in Singapore and Hong Kong with short 2–4-day cruises, Star provided numerous dining venues with a pricing model that unbundled the cruise fare into included and extra-cost specialty dining. As chronicled in this chapter, Star Cruises rapidly expanded through the mid-1990s until the 1998 Asia financial crisis. Star persevered through the downturn maintaining a presence in Hong Kong and Singapore. With the Chinese Government's attention to the cruise industry in the mid-2000s, the industry resumed growth. Meanwhile, to the south, the Australia-South Pacific market continued slow but steady growth. In 2004, Italian cruise company, Costa Crociere, establish an office in Hong Kong and in 2006 began operations out of Hong Kong and Shanghai targeting the mainland China market. Growth continued with both Star and Costa increasing their fleets and Royal Caribbean International returning to Asia. The period from 2013 through 2015 marked a turning point in the rate of growth. With the development of cruise ship construction capabilities in China, Asia is poised to move from the cruise industry's third global center to a possible rival for second place or even eventually first place!

A. Asia cruise ship age, size, and capacity data 1990–2020

Ship	Year built	Entry	GRT	PAX	Market
AIDAbella	2008	2017	68,203	2050	Asia
Amusement World ex-ferry Patricia	1967	1998	16,254	1200	Singapore
Andaman Princess ex-ferry Svea Jarl	1962	1989	4898	276	Thailand
Aruna	2000	2000	3800 dwt*	200	Tahiti/local passenger & freight
Asuka	1990	1990	28,717	390	Japan
Awani Dream 1 ex-Renaissance	1966	1996	8630	587	Indonesia
Awani Dream II ex-Cunard Countess	1976	1997	17,593	750	Indonesia

Ship	Year built	Entry	GRT	PAX	Market
Bali Sea Dancer ex-Illiria	1962	1996	3852	143	Indonesia ex-UK/EU/AU
Carnival Spirit	2001	2012	84,000	2100	Australia
Carnival Splendor	2008	2019	113,323	2974	Australia
Celebrity century *Golden Era*	1995 2015	2008	71,545	1814	Asia, Alaska, Australia China
Celebrity Solstice	2008	2008	121,878	2852	Asia, Alaska, Australia
China Star ex-Radisson Diamond	1992	2012	19,800	354	China
Club Med II	1992	1992	10,000	450	Tahiti/Western sourced
Coral Princess ex-Princesa Leopoldina	1962	1996	9842	399	Malaysia
Costa Allegra	1992	2006	28,430	820	Hong Kong/China
Costa Atlantica	2000	2013	85,700	2112	
Costa Classica	1992	2011	52,950	1928	Asia
Costa Fortuna	2003	2015	102,587	2716	Asia, China
Costa NeoRomantica	1993	2017	57,150	1578	Asia
Costa Serena	2007	2015	114,147	3000	Asia, China
Costa Venezia	2019	2019	132,500	3700	China
Costa Venezia sister	2020	2020	132,500	3700	China
Crystal Harmony *Asuka II*	1990 2006	2006	49,900	960	Worldwide Japan
Diamond Princess	2004	2008	115,875	2674	Japan
Explorer of the Seas	2000	2015	137,308	3114	Australia
Fair Princess ex-Fairsea	1956	1989	24,724	890	Australia
Fairstar	1957	1986	23,764	976	Australia
Fuji Maru	1989	1989	23,340	328	Japan
Genting Dream	2016	2016	151,300	3360	China
Genting World	2017	2017	151,300	3360	China
Golden Princess	2001	2016	108,865	2624	Australia
Harmony Princess ex-Costa Marina	1990	2012	25,441	772	Korea
Henna ex-Jubilee	1986	2012	47,262	1486	China
Karellya	1976	1994	15,065	472	Australia
Legend of the Seas	1995	2008	69,130	1800	Asia
Leisure World ex-Skyward	1969	1994	16,254	1071	Singapore
Mabuhay Sunshine ex- Fuji Sunshine	1983	1997	7200	400	Philippines
Majestic Princess	2017	2017	141,000	3600	China
Mariner of the Seas	2004	2013	137,276	3114	Asia, China
MegaStar Aries	1988	1996	2928	100	Singapore
MegaStar Taurus	1988	1996	2928	100	Singapore
MSC Splendida	2009	2018	137,936	3274	Asia, China

Ship	Year built	Entry	GRT	PAX	Market
Nautican ex-Crown Monarch	1990	1994	15,271	560	Singapore
New Utopia	1975	1975	13,789	650	Japan
Nippon Maru	1990	1990	21,903	408	Japan
Norwegian Joy	2017	2017	164,600	4200	China
Oceanic Grace *Oceanic Odyssey*	1989 1998	1989	5218	120	Japan Indonesia ex-Au, NZ, UK, US
Oriana	1959	1981	41,910	1750	Australia
Orient Venus	1990	1990	21,884	390	Japan
Oriental Dragon ex-Sun Viking	1982	2013	18,556	714	China
Orion National Geographic Orion 2013	2003	2005	4000	106	Australia Worldwide
Orion II ex-Renaissance Four	1991	2011	3990	120	Australia
Ovation of the Seas	2016	2016	168,666	4180	China, Australia
Pacific Aria ex-Ryndam	1993	2015	55,819	1260	Australia
Pacific Dawn ex-Regal Princess	1991	2006	69,845	1590	Australia
Pacific Eden ex-Statendam	1994	2015	55,819	1260	Australia
Pacific Explorer ex-Dawn Princess	1997	2017	77,499	1950	Australia
Pacific Jewel ex-Ocean Village 2	1990	2010	70,000	1590	Australia
Pacific Pearl ex-Ocean Village	1989	2011	63,564	1470	Australia
Pacific Princess ex-R Three	1998	2003	30,277	688	Australia
Pacific Sky	1984	2000	46,392	1200	Australia
Pacific Star ex-Tropicale	1982	2005	36,674	1022	Australia
Pacific Sun ex-Jubilee	1986	2003	47,262	1486	Australia
Pacific Venus	1998	1998	26,000	720	Japan
Paul Gauguin	1998	1998	18,800	320	Tahiti/Western sourced
Pearl of Scandinavia ex-Finnstar		1982	12,456	515	Asia
Quantum of the Seas	2015	2015	168,166	4180	China
Radiance of the Seas	2001	2008	90,090	2146	Asia, Alaska, Australia
Renaissance I	1989	1996	3990	110	North America ex-SIN
Renaissance II	1989	1996	3990	110	North America ex-SIN
Rhapsody of the Seas	1997	2008	78,491	2000	Asia, Alaska, Australia
Royal Pacific	1965	1992	13,176	615	Singapore
Sapphire Princess	2004	2008	115,875	2674	Japan
Sea Princess ex-Kungsholm	1966	1981	27,670	714	Australia
Sea Princess	1998	2012	77,690	2016	Australia

Ship	Year built	Entry	GRT	PAX	Market
Shangri-La World	1961	1992	16,254	900	Singapore
Shin Sakura Maru	1972	1972	19,811	552	Japan
Song of Flower	1974	1990	8282	214	Japan/Western
Southern Cross ex-Spirit of London	1972	1994	17,042	798	Australia
Star Aquarius ex-Athena	1989	1994	40,000	1900	Singapore
Star Pisces ex-Kalypso	1990	1994	40,012	2192	Hong Kong
Sun Princess	1995	2013	77,499	2100	Japan
Sun Viking	1972	1994	18,556	714	Asia/Western sourced
Sun Vista ex-Meridian	1963	1998	30,440	1106	Singapore
Sun Viva I ex-Renaissance V	1990	1997	4077	100	Singapore
Sun Viva II ex-Renaissance VI	1990	1997	4077	100	Singapore
SuperStar Aquarius ex-Norwegian Wind	1993	2007	50,760	1529	Hong Kong
SuperStar Aries ex-Europa	1980	2000	37,301	678	Asia
SuperStar Capricorn ex-Royal Viking Sea Kumgang 1999	1973	1997	28,078	850	Asia Korea
SuperStar Gemini ex-Crown Jewel	1992	1995	19,046	820	Singapore
SuperStar Gemini ex-Norwegian Dream	1992	2012	50,760	1732	Asia
SuperStar Leo Norwegian Legend 2004	1998	1998	75,000	1974	Hong Kong North America
SuperStar Libra ex-Norwegian Sea	1988	2005	42,276	1472	Asia
SuperStar Sagittarius *Pungnar-Ho*	1972	1998	25,000	610	Asia Korea
SuperStar Taurus ex-Leeward	1980	2000	25,000	950	Asia
SuperStar Virgo	1999	1999	75,338	1974	Singapore
The Empress ex-Sunward	1966	1994	10,558	410	Malaysia
Voyager of the Seas	1999	2012	137,280	3114	Asia/China
Wind Song	1987	1990	5307	160	Tahiti/Western sourced
Wind Spirit	1988	1990s	5350	148	Tahiti/Western sourced

PAX: number of passengers in lower beds. Space is sold by cabins. Once the lower beds are sold, the cabin is essentially sold. When all lower beds are filled, the ship is at 100% occupancy.
**DWT: measure of amount of cargo a ship may carry. Aruna is a passenger/cargo vessel. Therefore, her size is measured in DWT.*

Author details

Andrew O. Coggins
Lubin School of Business, Pace University, USA

*Address all correspondence to: acoggins@pace.edu

References

[1] Mathisen O, editor. Cruise Industry News Annual Report 2017-2018 State of the Industry and Future Forecast. 30th ed. New York: Cruise Industry News; 2017. 400 p

[2] Wood RE. Cruise Tourism: A paradigmatic case of globalization? In: Dowling R, editor. Cruise Ship Tourism. Wallingsford, UK: CABI Publishing; 2006. Retrieved from: Created from pace on 15 03 2018 10:47:25

[3] Marti B. Cruise line logo recognition. Journal of Travel & Tourism Marketing. 2005;**18**(1):25-31. DOI: 10.1300/J073v18n01_03

[4] McVicar M. The globalization of the cruise industry. In Cruise Shipping Convention. Princeton, NJ: Miller Freeman; 1996:24-26

[5] Luthans F, Doh JP. International Management: Culture, Strategy, and Behavior. 8th ed. New York: McGraw-Hill; 2012. p. 646

[6] Cruise Lines International Association. Available from: http://www.cruising.org

[7] World Tourism Organization. UNWTO Tourism Highlights: 2013 edition. Geneva: World Tourism Organization; 2013. Retrieved from: http://www.unwto.org

[8] Stopford M. Maritime Economics. 2nd ed. New York: Taylor and Francis; 2009. 815 p

[9] Coggins AO Jr. The globalization of the cruise industry: A tale of ships. Worldwide Hospitality and Tourism Themes. 2014;**6**(2):138-151

[10] Ward D. Berlitz Cruising and Cruise Ships 2018. London, UK: APA Publications; 2017. 736 p

[11] Miller AR, Grazer WF. Complaint behavior as a factor in cruise line losses. Journal of Travel and Tourism Marketing. 2003;**15**(1):77-91. DOI: 10.1300/J073v15n01_05

[12] Gibson P. Cruise Operations Management: Hospitality Perspectives. 2nd ed. London: Routledge; 2012. 312 p

[13] CLIA. The Cruise Industry—An Overview: Marketing edition 1998. New York: Cruise Lines International Association; 1998. 46 p

[14] Josiam BM, Huang T, Spears DL, Kennon L, Bahulkar GA. Understanding ethnic Chinese travelers on North American cruise tours: Motivations, perceptions, and satisfaction of cruisers. Journal of China Tourism Research. 2009;**5**(1):77-101

[15] Mancini M. Cruising: A Guide to the Cruise Industry. 2nd ed. New York: Delmar Learning; 2004. 212 p

[16] Wang H, editor. Report on China's Cruise Industry. Shanghai: Shanghai International Cruise Business Institute; 2018

[17] Mathisen O, editor. Cruise Industry News Annual. New York: Cruise Industry News Nissen-Lie Communications; 1995-2006

[18] Mathisen O, editor. Cruise Industry News Annual Report State of the Industry and Future Forecast. New York: Cruise Industry News; 2007-2016

[19] Ward D. Berlitz Complete Handbook to Cruising. Berlitz Guides: Lausanne; 1989-1995

[20] Ward D. Berlitz Complete Guide to Cruising and Cruise Ships. Oxford: Berlitz Publishing Company, Ltd.; 1996-2002

[21] Ward D. Berlitz Ocean Cruising & Cruise Ships. Singapore: APA Publications GmbH & Co. Verlag KG; 2003, 2003-2005

[22] Ward D. Berlitz Complete Guide to Cruising & Cruise Ships. Singapore: Apa Publications GmbH & Co. Verlag KG; 2006-2014

[23] Ward D. Berlitz Cruising and Cruise Ships. London, UK: APA Publications; 2015-2017

[24] Daymon C, Holloway I. Qualitative Research Methods in Public Relations and Marketing Communications. London: Routledge; 2002. p. 2002

[25] Coggins AO Jr. Asian cruise market: A candidate for multi-tier development? In: Cruise and Ferry 95 Conference Proceedings; May 1995; Vol. 1 Session 3. Rickmansworth, UK: Cruise and Ferry Secretariat; 1995

[26] China's middle class hikes up consumption growth in 2003. China Today. 2004. Retrieved from: http://search.proquest.com/docview/235786470?accountid=13044

[27] Saporito B, Ramzy A. A Great Leap Forward. 2011;**178**(17). Retrieved from: http://web.b.ebscohost.com.rlib.pace.edu [Accessed from: 31 October 2011]

[28] Waldmeir P. On board China's first luxury cruise liner. 2013. Financial Times Ltd. Retrieved from: http: //www.ft.com/cms/s/2/9/a491018-e9cl-11e2-bf03-00144feabdc0.html [Accessed from: 12 July 2013]

[29] Steinmetz T. China announces series of measures to increase cruise tourism. 2010. eTurboNews; 18 January 2010; eTurboNews Inc; Retrieved from: http://www.eturbonews.com/13902/china-announces-series-measures-increase-cruise-tourism [Accessed: 23 August 2013]

[30] Yap B. Rough seas forecast for China's fast-growing cruise industry. 2013. Business and Financial News, Breaking US and International News Reuters.com, Thomson Reuters. Retrieved from: http://www.reuters.com/assets/print?aid=USBRE97E05820130815

[31] Corben R. Asian tourism: Tourism boom for ASEAN economies, buoyed by rising middle class. Chinese American Forum. 2017. XXXIII, 4. Retrieved from: http://www.voanews.com/a/tourism-boom-asean-economies-rising-middle-class/3751172.html?trk1&utm_medium=email&utm_campaign=20'703-08&utm_source=newsletter

[32] Carnival Corporation & PLC. Carnival Corporation Cruise Joint Venture in China to Order Firstever Cruise Ships Built in China. 2017. Retrieved from: http://www,carnivalcorp.com/phoenix.zhtml?c=200767&p=irol-newsArticle&ID=2248174 [Press release: 22 February 2017]

Section 3

Peace

Chapter 14

Treating the Enemy: Victims of the Syrian Civil War in Israel

Anthony Luder

Abstract

Between February 2013 and December 2018, many thousands of victims of the Syrian civil war crossed the closed border between the two warring states and received, at no cost, high-level and extensive medical and humanitarian care in Israel. Overall mortality rates were very low, and more than 40 Syrian babies were born in Israel. All the patients returned to Syria after their treatment which extended in some cases into many months. Severe medical disease, surgical conditions and the major traumas of war injuries.were treated in in-patient and ambulatory settings. The story of this unique campaign contains many themes: military, legal, medical, social, humanitarian, ethical, media, personal and political. There have been very few, if any, precedents for a campaign of this nature involving two bitter enemies, over whose mutual border real and potential threats are constantly being played out.

Keywords: Israel, humanitarian medical treatment, Syrian civil war, Ziv Medical Centre

1. Research methods

This chapter is based on research conducted by the following means:

a. Field work observation including visits to border areas, field hospital and other relevant sites

b. Direct contact with staff, patients and members of civilian and military authorities

c. Participation in staff questionnaire studies regarding the impact of the programme on civilian health workers and establishments

d. Interviews with journalists, diplomats and foreign aid workers

Relevant references to background material and theoretical literature are included.

2. Introduction

One of the principal characteristics of *Homo sapiens* is that he is competitive and assertive. This has had no doubt a major influence on his evolution as a dominating and intelligent species, but there have been huge costs. Principle among these is man's tendency to cruelty, violence and warfare. Indeed, it has been estimated that in the last two millennia, there have been very few years in which war has not been recorded somewhere on the globe. However, in parallel with this are the positive aspects of man's nature, and among these are charity, sympathy, empathy, compassion and generosity. In relation to conflict, these have been expressed in many ways including emergency and ongoing welfare campaigns, sustainable development initiatives, peace-making and preserving, refugee care and the provision of medical services. In particular the norms regarding the treatment of civilians and respecting their rights as non-combatants or casualties of war have been codified in numerous treaties and conventions since 1864 until the present day. These are jointly now referred to as "The Hague Conventions on Humanitarian Law and the Geneva Conventions" [1].

In time of war, the victims are frequently caught in a double bind of bad fortune. On the one hand, they are often the casualties of fighting, suffering both physical trauma and psychological damage; but equally times of conflict are often marked by outbreaks of disease and famine, and indeed pre-existing routine medical conditions, which are neglected, may lead to irreversible consequences and complications. On the other hand, available medical treatment and services may typically be very limited and of poor quality, especially for the civilian population.

3. Syria and Israel

The State of Israel was officially declared on May 14,1948, following the partition resolution 181 passed in the United Nations on November 29, 1947. This was the legal and political basis for the establishment of two states "for two peoples", and it was accepted by the Jewish state but rejected by the entire Arab world and most Moslem states then and until this day. Immediately Israel was invaded by five regular Arab armies with the intent of strangling the new Jewish state at birth, and among these was the Syrian army. An armistice with Syria was signed on July 29, 1949, notably being the last agreement to be signed and illustrative of the fact that Syria has traditionally been the most ferocious and inflexible of Israel's enemy neighbours. This reputation was reinforced after the 6-day war of 1967 and the Yom Kippur War of 1973. Israel prisoners of war were particularly badly treated by Syria including illegal denial of Red Cross rights, torture and other criminal acts. Syrian hostility and hatred for Israel has been a constant feature of its Middle East posture, and this has included gross anti-Semitic statements by Assad himself and other members of the regime. In addition, Syria has rejected various peace feelers sent out over the years even after Egypt, and later Jordan signed peace agreements with Israel in 1979 and 1994. On the Israeli side, attitudes towards Syria have similarly been marked by disdain and disgust. This intransigence and immovable hostility form the background for the state of relations between the two states and help inform the reader as to the mentality and attitude of the Syrian population which has been exposed throughout its life to the monopoly of hatred and fear provided by the Assad regimes. In the light of these facts, the campaign of humanitarian and medical aid for Syrians that took place in Israel between 2013 and 2018 is even more remarkable than the facts themselves.

4. The Syrian civil war and its effect on medical services

In 2011, within what has ludicrously been called "the Arab Spring", one of most destructive and vicious wars recorded since the Second World War broke out in

Syria. Although its scope and extent has subsided considerably in the last year, even now in 2019, foci of fighting continue to be active in different parts of the wrecked country. The numbers of dead have been estimated as above 500,000, and the numbers of severely wounded and injured well over 2 million. Between 2 and 5% of the pre-war population have become medical victims, but the true numbers are unknown, and estimating these has been made very complicated by the existence of millions of internal and external refugees, within Syria, in massive camps on the borders of Turkey, Iraq, Kurdistan, Lebanon, Jordan and many more thousands who have risked life and limb to reach more distant havens. It is noteworthy that the Assad government regime has made a special target of the medical system in Syria [2–7]. More than half of all doctors in Syria have fled the country, and many hundreds have been deliberately murdered, mostly by Assad forces. Entire provinces and cities have been left bereft of even basic medical services. Of special note are the brutal tactics employed by Assad and his Russian allies in this respect; it was learnt from the Nazis in the Second World War that the elimination of medical care was a cheap and efficient way of forcing people to leave their homes and cleansing an area ethnically, and the Nazis indeed made special efforts to target medical facilities, being so clearly marked. The Russian government used this criminal method in many places, for example, in Chechenia and Afghanistan. In Syria the tactic has been extensively employed. Especially cynical is the "second-wave" tactic in which after an initial assault and after numerous casualties have been concentrated in care areas; these areas are then subjected to secondary attack, thus completing the initial lethal intent. The repeated use of banned chemical weapons has exacerbated the results of these barbaric actions.

The northern border of Israel in the Golan Heights adjoins the Syrian province of Daraa, home to about 200,000 people in normal times, but estimates put the number of additional refugees anywhere between 1 and 3 million. The city of Daraa and the surrounding areas became known as the cradle of the revolution in 2011 after 15 boys from prominent families were arrested after writing antigovernment graffiti, thus sparking mass demonstrations. It is estimated that about 5–7% of the pre-war population has been killed in the war. The entire area has been essentially without organised health services since the war broke out; this has naturally placed an enormous strain on the civilian population and placed in jeopardy the stability of continued civil life.

The border area with Israel is a zone of especial sensitivity. Since 1974 the frontier has been patrolled by a special UN force (United Nations Disengagement Observer Force (UNDOF)) and for the most part was quiet and stable. In the years leading up to the civil war, the Assad regime began to adopt new tactics designed to disturb this equilibrium, mainly through the establishment of terrorist groups primarily the so-called Front for the Liberation of the Golan. This was actually a front for the Lebanese terrorist organisation Hezbollah, which later became a prime Iran-sponsored ally of Assad in the war. During the war years, the border area itself came under the control of various groups, primarily the Druze in the north around the village of Hader, Syrian Democratic Forces in the centre and a small ISIS-Daish enclave in the south. Israel for its part declared an official policy of neutrality in the Syrian war, clearly holding Assad to account for his own numerous war crimes and responsibilities but officially favouring no group; Israel restricted its own actions in Syria to surgical strikes only whenever and wherever its own interests were threatened. While none of the rebel or unofficial groups were in anyway connected with Israel, nevertheless tacit areas of mutual interests became defined. Among these from the Israel perspective were the humanitarian imperative to aid a population in severe distress, the need for stability and continued quiet along the border, the prevention of massive waves of refugees congregating in the area and on the other side the urgent need for humanitarian assistance for the local and refugee population including the provision of medical assistance for civilians and combatants alike. Thus a remarkable and in some ways unique programme of medical assistance was born, provided at no charge by Israel, for the citizens of its enemy neighbour Syria. There has never been a precedent for a campaign similar in scope and duration between two hostile neighbours, and therefore the nature of this event and its effects on Israelis and Syrians are of considerable interest and importance.

5. Israeli humanitarian assistance and medical aid to Syrians

At the end of February 2013 on a Saturday night much like any other, a routine Israeli Defense Forces (IDF) military patrol along the border with Syria came across a group of seven badly wounded Syrian combatants located close to the border fence. They were mostly unconscious and clearly in need of urgent medical care. A local operational decision was made, based on their medical condition alone, to take in these individuals and transfer them by military ambulance to the nearest hospital capable of caring for severe trauma, the Ziv Medical Centre (ZMC) in Safed, Northern Israel. No high-level command or political considerations were involved. Upon the arrival at the emergency room, which came as a surprise to the staff, the wounded were transferred to the trauma department, and all seven began complicated and prolonged investigations, surgeries and other treatments. All seven survived and were eventually returned to Syria by the military authorities. At the beginning this episode was considered to be an isolated exception, but in the subsequent weeks, repeated transfers of wounded Syrians were made, and it became apparent quickly that this trickle of wounded Syrians was becoming a flood. A public debate opened in the media and political echelons. The questions were difficult. Who were these combatants? Why should Israel get involved, and what would be the risks and costs? Should civilians also be offered medical aid? What was the legal framework? Would all the patients return to Syria, and could they return for follow-up? How would continued care be guaranteed in Syria? The Israeli government decided on a two-pronged policy:

1. Syrians who required medical assistance and who reached the border between the two states would be offered whatever aid they required on a humanitarian basis.

2. No Israeli soldiers or civilians would enter Syria.

These have remained the publically defined limitations of the medical assistance programme since then.

Israel has had a long record of offering high-quality humanitarian aid to victims of disasters all over the world. In the last decade alone, Israel has sent fully equipped medical missions to Africa, Turkey, Haiti, Nepal and other countries, often being the first and quickest among international efforts. The IDF has a full rescue system ready to deploy at short notice and on stand-by at all times. Although this arrangement had never been utilised within Israel's own borders, the equipment and procedures were prepared and were able to be put in place within a short time. It was decided to open a fully equipped field hospital near the border in the Northern Golan, close to the Druze village of Majdal Shams, as a first step. This facility had X-ray, laboratory, intensive care capabilities as well as a fully functional operating room and admission ward. Patients were initially treated there after undergoing triage and following stabilisation either returned to Syria or were transferred onwards to one of the civilian hospitals in Northern Israel. During the years 2013–2018, the two hospitals mainly involved were ZMC as already mentioned and the hospital at Nahariya, although the hospital at Poriah and the Rambam hospital in Haifa also treated some individuals. The medical staff were mainly drawn from the reserve forces of the IDF and were in practice physicians and surgeons working in routine civilian practice all over the country. Thus the burden of this project fell indirectly on all the Israeli health system. The field hospital operated for various periods of time, depending on the flow of patients and the available resources. At one point the Assad regime forces began shelling the hospital (in line with their policy of targeting medical facilities as explained above), and this required determined countermeasures by the IDF to silence this. After a period however, it was decided that the optimal procedure was the direct transfer of patients to civilian hospitals, and the field hospital became inactive most of the time.

The transfer of patients in both directions across the border was at all times the sole responsibility of the IDF, with each transfer taking on the character of a fully fledged military operation. This was especially true after terrorist organisations launched sporadic attacks along the lines in an attempt to harm IDF forces in the course of their activities. Initial triage was carried out at the crossing points by regular IDF paramedical staff. Thereafter the patients remained under the responsibility of the military until they returned home, even when they were being treated in civilian facilities. The contacts and arrangements made by the IDF with groups on the Syrian side, for the purposes of coordination and logistics, are beyond the scope of this chapter. Nevertheless, it is clear that some form of communication existed and enabled fairly smooth operations to take place throughout this period.

Many thousands of Syrians were transferred to Israel for medical treatment in the years 2013–2018. At the beginning all patients were treated as in-patients; however as time went on, it became apparent that the health needs of the entire population of the Daraa region required a significant expansion of the scope and nature of the programme. In late 2017 the head of the IDF announced that a major shift of policy had been decided upon. Henceforth not only severely injured or sick patients would be treated as in-patients but that a complete ambulatory system would be set up for the day care of patients suffering from all manner of routine medical problems. This initiative was coined the "Good Neighbours Initiative", echoing an earlier and similar policy vis-à-vis Lebanon in the 1980s, called "The Good Fence". A further feature of this remarkable initiative was to provide medical supplies and drugs to patients in Syria for up to 3 months after treatment in Israel. It was also widely rumoured that international medical aid agencies were also provided with security guarantees for their personnel working inside Syria. Following its promulgation, regular groups of Syrian civilians including women and children were brought by chartered buses to out-patients' clinics at ZMC and Nahariya for clinic and day hospital treatment. Many additional thousands of patients thus benefited from the medical assistance programme, and all of this should be stressed at the highest professional level at no cost to the patients. This stands out in stark contrast to the situation in neighbouring Arab and Moslem countries where Syrian patients often had to pay dearly for medical care even when available, which more often than not was sporadic and often limited or sub-standard.

6. The nature of the Israeli medical assistance programme for Syrians

For readers interested in reading further about the medical details of the injuries, diseases and suffering of the Syrian patients and the treatment that was given, they can do so in the book *Complicated War Trauma and Care of the Wounded: The*

Israeli Experience in Medical Care and Humanitarian Support of Syrian Refugees [8], written and edited by the staff of ZMC. A general summary will be given here. Approximately 80% of the in-patients treated were male, and about 20% were under the age of 18. Patients were treated in almost every department of the hospital but especially in intensive care, surgery, orthopaedics, paediatrics and obstetrics. Of note, 24 babies were born to Syrian mothers in ZMC during the duration of the programme. Many of the patients suffered from injuries during combat either directly or collaterally. Among these were severe limb injuries, head and neck, abdominal and chest injuries, and those requiring and plastic surgery. Often these patients required very prolonged treatment including repeated surgery, treatment for severe infections, pain relief and nutritional resuscitation. Almost all patients came with no medical records or documentation, making assessment doubly difficult. Patients who had received medical care in often from severe complications such as botched procedures, multiple resistant bacterial infections, and severe pathogens (such as polio which broke out in various places in Syria). In addition, increasingly patients arrived in Israel with medical problems such as congenital malformations, genetic disease, cancer as well as "routine" disorders such as cardiovascular disease, diabetes and neurodegenerative disease.

Mortality was surprisingly low among in-patients, <5%. Considering the severe condition in which many arrived, the complications and lack of medical documentation, this was an impressive achievement. The work of the orthopaedics department in limb salvage and rehabilitation was especially noteworthy with its chief being invited to lecture worldwide and the author of many books and articles. However, the medical and nursing staffs of all departments worked with commendable skill and efficiency for their patients. Nor were the psychological and social aspects neglected. Psychologists and medical clowns ("dream doctors") working in Arabic provided invaluable support for these unfortunate people, who found themselves in a strange country, a country which all their lives they had been taught to hate, fear and despise, suffering severe pain and disability and above all being completely dependent on the goodwill and skill of caretakers with whom they had almost nothing in common. Social workers also worked hard to provide relief both as facilitators and educators, contact providers between the medical and military authorities and also provide the basics which the patients completely lacked such as clothes, toiletries, reading material and for the children toys and even tablet computers. Arabic-speaking teachers also provided educational materials and teaching programmes.

7. Media exposure and social and financial support for the Israeli Syrian medical assistance programme

From the beginning the medical assistance programme was initiated according to local and operational requirements rather than as a result of a considered national strategy. This was reflected by the fact that no agreed budgetary arrangement existed. The costs were considerable, not the least of which was the provision of expensive re-usable medical devices that in many cases were lost to the hospital after the discharge of the patients. The former head of ZMC in a television interview stated that he was proud of the opportunity to express universal humanitarian values but that no one was footing the bill, which ran into hundreds of millions of shekels. Hospitals began to run up considerable deficits. This affected their ability to continue everyday operations. In 2017 this came to a head with the outbreak of industrial action at the Nahariya hospital. At a governmental level, there was a predictable interdepartmental dispute with the ministries of defence, health and the treasury all trying to shift financial responsibility on another department. On the other hand, local communities in the Galilee, both Arab and Jewish, opened their hearts and pockets with a constant stream of philanthropic donations both of money and articles. Yet while this surprising response reflected the quality of Israeli society, it was insufficient to bridge the budgetary deficiencies. In addition, hundreds of foreign delegations of journalists, diplomats, politicians and public organisations visited the hospital and the patients (while being careful not to photograph faces), and these sometimes also resulted in valuable donations and support, but still not sufficient to cover the huge costs incurred. It is important to stress that while for the most part the existence and nature of the humanitarian programme were never a secret, no major publicity initiatives were undertaken by the government. The publicity that occurred was mostly restricted to occasional reports by news agencies and written and video reports in online sites [9]. Surprisingly, this meant that large parts of the Israeli public itself were not aware of the programme and its nature, and this was even truer abroad. It could be argued that this low-profile publicity policy was a mistake, yet the whole issue was highly sensitive from Israel's standpoint, and there were arguments for limiting exposure. Interestingly, the head of ZMC has been invited to light a flaming torch at the national independence celebrations in 2019 as a tribute to the people who worked in the programme and its results, yet this is taking place only after the programme has ceased. This no doubt reflects the dilemma that Israel faced and faces with respect to the public face of this programme.

8. Legal and ethical aspects of the Israeli medical assistance programme for Syrians

One of the important points to study with regard to this programme was the legal and ethical framework in which it took place. The patients who came to Israel came for different reasons. At the start many were unconscious when they crossed the border so that one could not talk about voluntary or consensual transfer. Once in Israel, the individuals were the legal responsibility of the IDF and military law, yet their status was ill-defined. Unlike prisoners of war or refugees, groups that are covered by clear frameworks of international convention and law, the Syrian patients were not defined as either nor were they tourists. They came or were brought usually without documentation of any kind. This meant that these patients had no defined legal standing nor, therefore, defined protection. It is certainly my belief backed by extensive experience and exposure that the human and medical rights of these patients were rigorously safeguarded at all times by the dedicated medical and hospital staff that treated them, yet nevertheless the theoretical possibility of a breach of rights existed, and if this had occurred in practice, the patients would have had little legal or other recourse beyond the unsure solution of military law. This must certainly be a source of concern for any similar scenario whether in Israel or in any other country faced with a similar situation. An example of this nonoptimal situation was the restriction on transferring patients to other medical facilities in Israel in the case of need. The limitation on this was enforced and backed by a decision of the Israel Supreme Court. In one prime example, a paediatric patient requiring a bone marrow transplant could not be treated in Israel (for medical and social reasons) and needed transfer to an academic centre in an Arab country. This could not be done via the safe and direct route through Israel but rather via a return to Syria. Although in this case the transfer was completed without incident, it was certainly arguable that the patient's best interests could have been better served.

Another area of ethical concern relates to the area of research. There is no doubt that the huge amount of experience gained and the complexity of the medical challenges faced required documentation and reporting. In many cases clinical protocols and techniques required modification and alteration, and the results of the study of these constitute a form of clinical research as defined by the Israel Ministry of Health. Clinical research in Israel is governed by the principles of the World Health Association's Declarations of Helsinki and other international standards, as given expression by the regulations and laws extant in Israel. Principal among the tenets of ethical clinical research is the requirement for for full explanation to be given to the participant and also for his or her voluntarily given free, informed consent to be recorded on a signed, approved consent form (or in the case of minors or others unable to give legal consent, the agreement of their legal custodian). Putting aside the legal complexities of compliance with these requirements in the case of non-citizens with undefined status, there is the ethical issue of consent from someone who is completely dependent on the medical institution in which he finds himself or herself. Even assuming that the participant can be fully informed, how free can his/her decision be? On the public stage, it is also highly problematic to what extent these dependent noncitizens can be included in clinical research. The settlement of these weighty issues required a high degree of professional and ethical wisdom yet remained in the last resort a kind of ad hoc approach.

9. The effects on society and the region of the Israeli Syrian medical assistance programme

The medical assistance programme in Israel for Syrian patients certainly had important effects on everyone involved. These will be discussed by category:

9.1 Hospital staff

Many staff members either have fought on the Syrian or Lebanese front themselves in various wars or have or had close family members, friends, colleagues, neighbours or acquaintances who were involved in or wounded, hurt or killed in such fighting. Possibly worse are those who suffered the egregious cruelties and tortures of imprisonment in Syria. These experiences certainly made it very difficult sometimes for those involved to relate to Syrian patients as any other patient. At times the Syrians added significantly to the burdens of an already overworked and understaffed hospital. There were occasions during which there were insufficient resources available for regular Israeli patients because of the large numbers of Syrians. No doubt these facts, combined with the medical complexities of these patients and the resulting extra burdens of work placed upon the staff, led to a degree of dilemma, resentment and even resistance among staff members. I am not aware that these feelings ever rose above the level of occasional grumbling and discontent, yet the hospital certainly had to devote resources to the psychological well-being of staff members, via individual and group discussions and focus groups. On the other hand, when the new hospital director took over his post in 2015, one of the first things he did was to organise hospital-wide consultations about whether to continue or cease the programme of humanitarian assistance, and the conclusions were loud and clear to continue. On a simple human level, when one is faced with suffering and distress, one feels an inner compulsion to help, and this is augmented by one's professional obligations. As Churchill plainly stated regarding a moral obligation, "one can do no other". But dealing with these feelings and dilemmas engenders a cost. In 2016 these issues became the subject of detailed study, and the results of this have been published [10]. This study concluded that the ability of staff to function was influenced by hindering and facilitating factors and that it was important to identify these in order to minimise the former and strengthen the latter.

9.2 Society in Israel

The support by gifts and actions that was forthcoming from all aspects of society has been referred to already. To some extent this was the result of identification with civilians caught up in the maelstrom of war and by events beyond their control. There was a widespread hope and belief that good deeds speak from themselves and that inevitably the provision of medical aid would contribute in some way to changing attitudes and opinions on both sides of the border. On a more general level, the national media gave scope to the expression of pride in the altruism and selflessness of a country surrounded by hatred and ferocious aggression responding with kindness and (expensive) humanitarian action. This speaks to the basic Jewish value of "healing the world" ("tikkun olam"), in which every individual is enjoined to help making the world a better place. There is also the strong associated memory of the holocaust during which Jews were the defenceless victims of merciless cruelty, murder and oppression. There is a national consensus that Jews, of all people, cannot therefore stand idly by while similar suffering falls on others.

9.3 Syrians

This is the most difficult category to understand, partly because of the natural reticence, suspicion and fear they had in talking freely (something they are not used to in their home country) and partly because of the confusion engendered by the circumstances of their stay in Israel. Given the limited evidence available, one can say that some patients expressed gratitude for the kindness shown to them, and one would like to hope that this and the reactions of their friends and neighbours may lead to positive changes among some Syrians. This hope was reinforced when some Syrian refugees in Europe published blogs stating that the real enemy of the Syrian people was Assad and that Israel was their friend [11]. On the other hand, the Assad regime and its Iranian-Hezbollah allies are exploiting the humanitarian programme to make conspiracy and other mendacious claims against Israel. The last word on this certainly has not been written, and it is still too early to know whether and what the long-term outcomes will be.

10. Conclusions

The Israeli and Syrian programme of humanitarian and medical assistance between 2013 and 2018, devoted to the victims one of the bloodiest wars since World War II, has many unique characteristics, and among these are the setting of one state affording aid to citizens (combatant and non-combatant citizens of an enemy state), the nature and treatment of the medical issues involved, the ethical and legal problems associated and the short- and long-term effects on people on both sides. It has been stressed that the provision of medical treatment is a humanitarian imperative even for (perhaps especially for) the enemy, but this also impacts political and strategic interests and may create serious dilemmas for the people involved. This chapter has summarised the events and posed more questions than for which there are available answers. It is the author's hope that the reader's interest will be stimulated and that the various issues raised will lead him to constructive reflection. Medical treatment is a professional imperative, but it may often lead to unexpected and wider results. Whether this will happen and to what extent, time will be needed to judge. In the meantime it is the author's hope that decision-makers and ordinary citizens will strengthen their determination to help those in need even in the most difficult and extraordinary of circumstances.

Conflict of interest

The author was a staff member of Ziv Medical Centre during the period described in the chapter.

Author details

Anthony Luder[1,2]

1 Ziv Medical Centre, Safed, Israel

2 Azrieli Faculty of Medicine, Bar Ilan University, Safed, Israel

*Address all correspondence to: luder.a@ziv.health.gov.il

References

[1] Fleck D. The Handbook of International Humanitarian Law. Second ed. USA: Oxford University Press; 2008. ISBN 0-19-923250-4

[2] Elise B, Widney B. Doctors in the crosshairs: Four years of attacks on health care in Syria (PDF) (Report). Physicians for Human Rights. Available from: https://s3.amazonaws.com/PHR_Reports/doctors-in-the-crosshairs.pdf [Accessed: 04 May 2019]

[3] Syrian medical voices from the ground: The ordeal of Syria's healthcare professionals (PDF) (Report). The Center for Public Health and Human Rights of the Johns Hopkins Bloomberg School of Public Health and the Syrian American Medical Society; February 2015. Available from: https://www.sams-usa.net/wp-content/uploads/2016/09/Syrian-Medical-Voices-from-the-Ground_F.pdf [Accessed: 04 May 2019]

[4] Spagat M. Attacks on medical workers in Syria: Implications for conflict research. PLoS Medicine. 2018;**15**(4):e1002560

[5] Tammy L, Lisa C. Chicago doctors risk arrest, torture to aid dire medical care void in Syria. NBC Chicago. Available from: https://www.nbcchicago.com/investigations/Chicago-Doctors-Syrian-War-Hospital-295954681.html [Accessed: 04 May 2019]

[6] Physicians for Human Rights. The Syrian conflict: Eight years of devastation and destruction of the health system. Available from: https://phr.org/resources/the-syrian-conflict-eight-years-of-devastation-and-destruction-of-the-health-system/ [Accessed: 04 May 2019]

[7] Hall R. Syrian and Russian forces 'weaponised healthcare' by deliberately targeting ambulances in civil war. Available from: https://www.independent.co.uk/news/world/middle-east/syria-war-russia-healthcare-ambulances-civil-weapons-army-government-a8654841.html [Accessed: 04 May 2019]

[8] Zarka S, Lerner A. Complicated War Trauma and Care of the Wounded: The Israeli Experience in Medical Care and Humanitarian Support of Syrian Refugees. New York: Springer; 2018

[9] Ziv Medical Center treats Syrian casualties. Available from: https://youtu.be/RBXZx3A79Tg [Accessed: 09 June 2019]

[10] Young SS, Denise C, Lewis DC, Gilbey P, Eisenman A, et al. Conflict and care: Israeli healthcare; providers and Syrian patients and caregivers in Israel. Global Qualitative Nursing Research. 2016;**3**:1-15

[11] Osmo L. For Syrian refugees in Greece, Israel is no longer the enemy. Available from: https://www.ynetnews.com/articles/0,7340,L-5473381,00.html [Accessed: 04 May 2019]

Chapter 15

Peace Revolution as a Three-Dimensional Process: The Israeli-Palestinian Case

Sapir Handelman

Abstract

The Israeli-Palestinian struggle is a classic case of intractable conflict. Establishing a long-lasting change requires a revolutionary peace process. The paper describes peace revolution as a three-dimensional process—peacemaking, peacebuilding, and peacekeeping. Each of these three components is itself a three-level process. Peacemaking means involving different societal elements (leaders, elites, and people) in the struggle to reach a negotiated peace deal by using political-elite diplomacy, public diplomacy, and people-to-people diplomacy. Peacebuilding means constructing international, bilateral, and domestic frameworks for a stable peace. Peacekeeping means building political, militaristic, and civilian devices to maintain a stable social order.

Keywords: intractable conflict, peacemaking, peacebuilding, peacekeeping, Israeli-Palestinian conflict

1. Introduction

The Israeli-Palestinian is a classic case of intractable conflict where ordinary citizens are at the middle of the struggle. It is a lengthy fight where generation after generation is born into the reality of violence, despair, and suffering. The conflict seems to operate as a destructive evolutionary system that has a life of its own. Almost any substantial attempt to generate the conditions for a positive change in the Israeli-Palestinian case, so far, has failed and complicated the situation beyond imagination. The main argument of this essay is that a revolutionary peace process is required in order to break the evolutionary progression of violence and despair.

A revolutionary change-building program requires applying peacemaking, peacebuilding, and peacekeeping measures simultaneously.[1] However, peacemaking, peacebuilding, and peacekeeping are controversial concepts that should have different interpretations in different situations. For example, following the Second World War, the UN was established as a major peacekeeping institution. The aim was to create an institution that would be able to manage, stop, and prevent clashes between armies.[2] The Israeli-Palestinian case—an intractable conflict where ordinary civilians are at the center of the confrontation—is a different type of conflict. It requires the establishment of different mechanisms to build, keep, and maintain order and stability.

---

[1] Cf. Galtung [1] and Kelman [2].

[2] See Snow [3].

Category	Meaning	Means
Peacemaking	Consensus building	Diplomacy in three dimensions: political-elite diplomacy, public diplomacy, and people-to-people diplomacy
Peacebuilding	Building a framework for a peaceful social order	International support, peaceful relationship-building between the parties and domestic reforms within each one of them
Peacekeeping	Building mechanisms to keep law, order, and stability	Political, civilian, and militaristic mechanisms to cope with tensions, disputes, and crises

Table 1.
Peace revolution as a three-dimensional process.

The struggle to build a peaceful social order has to cope with different types of conflicts and crises. The three elements of a peace revolution—peacemaking, peacebuilding, and peacekeeping—should be formulated according to the logic of the situation.[3] This paper suggests a multidimensional process, which might be appropriate for crises similar to the Israeli-Palestinian case. Peacemaking is a consensus-building process that involves different societal elements (leaders, political elites, and ordinary citizens) in efforts to conclude a negotiated peace deal.[4] Peacebuilding means constructing international, bilateral, and domestic frameworks for a peaceful social order that copes with the needs and concerns of the conflicting parties.[5] Peacekeeping suggests creating political, civilian, and militaristic means to maintain order and stability (**Table 1**).[6]

The structure of the paper follows the logic of the central argument—peace needs to be made, built, and kept. It is divided into sections: peacemaking, peacebuilding, and peacekeeping. Each section focuses on different aspects of the challenge of change in the Israeli-Palestinian situation. However, each of the sections concretizes that the distinction between peacemaking, peacebuilding, and peacekeeping is more of a theoretical outline that helps us to understand the complexity of the situation, shed light on the challenge of peace, and assist in developing new creative ideas.[7]

The paper combines theoretical research, comparative case studies, and experimental practice. It grows out of the literature on peacemaking, peacebuilding, and peacekeeping. It draws lessons from peace processes in different situations of intractable conflict, such as the struggle for change in Northern Ireland during the "troubles" and the struggle to dismantle the Apartheid system in South Africa. It offers practical insights from the Minds of Peace Experiment (MOPE)—a short-term Israeli-Palestinian public negotiating assembly—which has been taking place in different forms, variations, and places. This multifaceted methodology intends to tackle the study of peace revolution from different points of view.

2. Peacemaking

There is an agreement among peace researchers that peacemaking means negotiating a peace contract that can put an end to a conflict. This paper suggests a

3 Cf. Popper [4].

4 See Fisher [5] and Handelman [6].

5 Cf. Fisher [5].

6 Cf. Handelman, ([6], 9–10). The three elements of peace revolution—peacemaking, peacebuilding, and peacekeeping—are intertwined. Moreover, often enough, it is hard to, clearly, distinguish between peacebuilding and peacekeeping. See Lakhdar, Brahimi. "Report of the Panel on United Nations Operations," United Nations document A/55/305 – S/200/809, 21 (August 2000): 5.

7 Cf. Ratner [7] and James [8].

Level of operation	Mechanisms	Description
Top	Political-elite diplomacy	Peacemaking engagement between political elites
Middle	Public diplomacy	Interactions between political elites and ordinary people
Bottom	People-to-people diplomacy	Peacemaking engagement between ordinary people

Table 2.
Peacemaking diplomacy in three dimensions.

revolutionary peacemaking approach that attacks the challenge of reaching a negotiated contract from different angles and viewpoints. It offers a look at a peacemaking revolution as a consensus-building process, which involves key elements of the conflicting parties—leaders, elites, and people—in a multidimensional negotiating process. It is a more conclusive strategy than the dominant peacemaking experience in the Middle East, which, often enough, involves only leaders and elites.[8]

A revolutionary peacemaking approach, according to this paper, is a consensus-building process that operates on three levels: political elite, "ordinary" people, and the interactions between the two. It suggests a three-level structure of peacemaking diplomacy: political-elite diplomacy, public diplomacy, and people-to-people diplomacy (**Table 2**).

Political-elite diplomacy offers various channels of communication between official and unofficial elites of the opposing sides, who are interested in reaching a peaceful settlement to the conflict. In general, political-elite diplomacy comprises three main channels of interaction: track II diplomacy (unofficial dialog between elites who do not have official positions in the government), secret diplomacy (secret negotiations between officials), and track I diplomacy (formal negotiations between officials).[9]

Classical examples, such as the Oslo Accords of the 1990s, demonstrate that political-elite diplomacy offers efficient operative channels for helping leaders and elites reach innovative agreements in stalemate situations. Its main disadvantage is that it does not offer effective methods to involve the publics in the peacemaking efforts, prepare the people for a change, and help them deal with ongoing crises along the peace road. As a result, political-elite diplomacy is vulnerable to violent acts of spoilers, radicals, and extremists, who are determined to use aggressive means to crush any effort to reach a negotiated peace contract. Indeed, violent events made a major contribution to the collapse of the Oslo Accords of the 1990s. The cumulative effect of the ongoing violence has led to a loss of public belief in the possibility of creating a constructive change. The decrease of public support of the peacemaking gives the momentum to the opposition of the peace process, who makes sure that the conflict will continue.[10]

People-to-people diplomacy offers various modes of interaction linking the opposing sides at the grassroots level, such as different dialog groups, multinational workshops, educational projects, scientific collaborations, and partnership in peacemaking grassroots organizations. More focused on peace dialog than other collaborative projects, classical examples such as The Parents Circle-Families Forum[11] and Seeds of Peace[12] indicate that people-to-people diplomacy can be

[8] Cf. Handelman and Chowddhury [9].

[9] I labeled these three modes of communication "the political-elite model." See, for example, Handelman [10] and Handelman [11]. For a further discussion, see also Agha et al. [12].

[10] For a further discussion, see Handelman [11] and Kelman [13, 14].

[11] https://theparentscircle.org/en/pcff-home-page-en/

[12] https://www.seedsofpeace.org/about/

effective in building peace coalitions, showing that there are peace supporters on both sides,[13] and preparing ordinary citizens for change. The main disadvantage of people-to-people diplomacy is that it, often enough, is disconnected from the leadership level. It hardly involves political leaders in the grassroots peacemaking channels and can barely motivate and influence them to reach innovative negotiating agreements. The result is that people-to-people diplomacy, which usually does not operate on a mass scale, faces many difficulties in transferring the spirit of change to the operational political level.[14]

Public diplomacy, in our multidimensional configuration, is designed to close the gaps of the two previous diplomatic modes (political-elite and people-to-people) by using different methods of marketing, public relations, and social protest. It operates in two opposite directions. In one direction, public diplomacy provides instruments for leaders to prepare the public for a substantial peacemaking process, get their feedback on new ideas, receive their input on the limits of possible compromises, and generate public support in negotiating groundbreaking agreements (top-down). In the other direction, public diplomacy offers tools for people to motivate political leaders to initiate a peacemaking process (bottom-up).[15]

This paper suggests creating a (peacemaking) public diplomacy institution—an Israeli-Palestinian Public Negotiating Congress. A public negotiating congress (PNC) is a democratic peacemaking institution that invites representatives of the conflicting people to negotiate different solutions to their conflict. All congress participants, who reflect the political spectrum in the conflicting societies, would have to commit to principles of non-violent discourse.[16]

The congress is built to involve the conflicting publics in the peacemaking efforts, prepare the people for change, and motivate the leaderships to reach agreements. The idea to establish an Israeli-Palestinian Public Negotiating Congress is inspired by the multiparty negotiations that enabled a revolutionary change in the struggle against Apartheid in South Africa and in Northern Ireland during the "troubles."[17]

In South Africa and Northern Ireland, leaders came to the conclusion that they need a public diplomacy device to involve the public in the peace process. These leaders used diplomatic interactions to create the multiparty congresses. In the Israeli-Palestinian situation, so far, leaders do not even consider creating a similar public diplomacy device. They mainly focus on political-elite diplomacy in the effort to stabilize the situation. As an alternative choice, it is worth examining the possibility that an Israeli-Palestinian Public Negotiating Congress—which can be regarded as an Israeli-Palestinian version of the multiparty negotiations in South Africa and Northern Ireland—will emerge from people-to-people interactions. One people-to-people project that is designed to reach this goal is the Minds of Peace Experiment.

The Minds of Peace Experiment (MOPE) is a short-term Israeli-Palestinian public negotiating assembly. The MOPE invites teams of Israelis and Palestinians to negotiate a peace deal, generally over a 2-day period of five sessions. The assembly is

---

[13] A well-known characteristic of protracted conflict is the mirror image: each side believes that the rival is not a partner for peace and is not even capable to peruse it, to say the very least. The American psychologist Urie Bronfenbrenner [15] discovered the "mirror image" during the Cold War.

[14] Cf. Kelman [16].

[15] The modern version of public diplomacy was developed during the Cold War. It was defined as "direct communication with foreign peoples, with the aim of affecting their thinking and, ultimately, that of their governments" Gifford ([17], 199). This version of public diplomacy is hardly relevant to cases like the Israeli-Palestinian struggle. For a further discussion, see Handelman [18].

[16] For a further discussion, see Handelman [11].

[17] For a further discussion on conflict and peacemaking in South Africa, see Sparks [19]. For a further discussion on the peace process in Northern Ireland, see Mitchell [20].

co-moderated by Israelis and Palestinians, who lead the interaction in a framework of general rules. The dialog is open to the public and invites its participation.

The Minds of Peace Experiment was conducted in various sizes and formats and in different locations. It has been demonstrated as a powerful instrument for people-to-people diplomacy. The various rounds of the MOPE indicate that the initiative is effective in involving ordinary people in the struggle for peace, preparing them for painful compromises, and creating peacemaking coalitions. However, without extensive use of public diplomacy, the influence of the MOPE is doomed to remain marginal. There is a necessity to create domestic and international pressure to institutionalize the initiative. The MOPE needs to grow, develop, and transform into a major revolutionary institution—an Israeli-Palestinian Public Negotiating Congress with substantial political influence.[18]

2.1 Concluding remarks

This paper suggests looking at a peacemaking revolution as a consensus-building development that involves the different societal elements—leaders, elite, and people—in the struggle for peace and stability. To reach this goal, it is necessary to create a balance between political-elite diplomacy and public diplomacy. Political-elite diplomacy provides diplomatic channels for leaders to reach agreements. Public diplomacy intends to involve the public in the peacemaking efforts, prepare the people for a change, and motivate the leaderships to accomplish a settlement. A major public negotiating congress is a public diplomacy instrument that has the potential to create the equilibrium.[19] On the one hand, it can serve as a political tool for leaders to create public support in a negotiating process that can produce a peace contract (top-down). On the other hand, it can serve as political instrument for people to influence leaders and demand that they initiate an effective peacemaking policy (bottom-up).[20] Moreover, a public negotiating congress can be discovered as a revolutionary device that could invite new political groups and leaders to the political arena.[21]

The multiparty negotiations in Northern Ireland and South Africa taught us that an Israeli-Palestinian Public Negotiating Congress can be an effective peacemaking institution that could open new political opportunities and push the train of change in unimagined directions. In both cases, political leaders established the multiparty talks in order to generate public support in the peacemaking. In the Israeli-Palestinian case, political-elite diplomacy is the main peacemaking setting. There are no signs of leadership interest and motivation to establish a public diplomacy device for involving the publics in the change-making efforts. As a desperate choice, this paper suggests considering the option of a public negotiating congress growing from people-to-people interactions.

The Minds of Peace Experiment is a grassroots initiative that intends to demonstrate the peacemaking potential of a major public negotiating congress, to help evaluate its possible outcomes, and to generate support for its creation. However, I did not find any example where a major public negotiating congress emerged of people-to-people

---

[18] For a further discussion, see, for example, Handelman [21, 22] and Handelman [23].

[19] Creation of a major public negotiating congress, our proposal for a public diplomacy institution, is designed to connect three components: influencing the leaderships, preparing the public for change, and utilizing the media to create a peacemaking atmosphere in these two dimensions (leadership and people). For a further discussion on the concept of public diplomacy, see Gilboa [24] and Soroka [25].

[20] For a further discussion, see Handelman [23].

[21] Compare to Huntington [26], who suggests a model of sociopolitical revolution.

activities.[22] Perhaps, the Minds of Peace initiative is doomed to fail like almost all other peacemaking initiatives so far. Nevertheless, it is impossible to predict the future.[23]

3. Peacebuilding

Peacebuilding, in this paper, means building the conditions for a peaceful social order that can cope with the fears, needs, and concerns of the opposing factions. It is a multidimensional configuration, which needs to cope with challenges in three main dimensions: international, generating international support for a peaceful social order and marginalizing the impact of international spoilers; interparty, building peaceful relationships between the conflicting parties; and intraparty, domestic reforms within the opposing parties in order to cope with internal obstacles for peace and stability (**Table 3**).

International. In this paper, we suggest looking at the Israeli-Palestinian struggle as a communal conflict. It is a struggle between two communities—Israeli and Palestinian—who were destined to live side by side. We believe that this approach has the best chances to cope with the conflict constructively and help the conflicting parties to reach a negotiated resolution. Any attempt at "globalizing" the conflict—for example, analyzing it in Huntington's terms of clash of civilizations—marginalizes the ability to resolve the conflict or, even, to transform it.[24] However, there are certain problems that Israelis and Palestinians cannot solve by themselves. They need international assistance in coping with essential problems standing in the way of peace and stability.

Coping with the problem of the Palestinian refugees, which will, probably, need to relocate in different locations,[25] and the urgent need to marginalize the impact of an international spoiler, such as Iran, are two examples of major problems for which Israelis and Palestinians will need international assistance and intervention. This means that any realistic peace initiative needs to establish working relationships with the international community in order to guarantee its commitment and support.

Diplomacy, as a key instrument of foreign affairs, is the tool to reach international support. Naturally, there are major disagreements between Israelis and Palestinians upon the very essence of the desired international intervention in the peace process. For example, who are the international players that should take part in the peace process? What will be their role? Where is the line between legitimate and illegitimate intervention?[26]

According to the methodology suggested in this paper, Israelis and Palestinians need to reach a peace agreement in bilateral negotiations (peacemaking), while the international community should support it, marginalize the influence of spoilers, and assist in implementing the agreements. The boundaries of international intervention should be negotiated and determined early in the peacemaking stage.

Interparty. There is a broad consensus that the only feasible settlement to the Israeli-Palestinian conflict is a "two-state solution"—the establishment of a

[22] The multiparty negotiations in South Africa and Northern Ireland established by political leaders. See, for example, Mandela [27].

[23] See, for example, Popper [28].

[24] Cf. Hassner [29].

[25] See, for example, the Geneva Initiative: http://www.geneva-accord.org/.

[26] No doubt that Israelis and Palestinians see any American intervention in the peace process in different lights.

Level of operation	Goal	Means
International	Generating international support for peace and stability	Diplomacy
Interparty	Building peaceful relationships between adversaries	Sociopolitical initiatives, such as economic collaboration, education for peace, and reconciliation projects
Intraparty	Building the foundations for order and stability in the opposing parties	Domestic reforms within the opposing parties

Table 3.
Peacebuilding as a three-dimensional configuration.

Palestinian state beside Israel. Nevertheless, it seems impossible to completely separate between the two national units. Interaction between Israelis and Palestinians is inevitable. For example, there is no continuity of land between the West Bank and Gaza. It looks that the holy places in Jerusalem require a special arrangement in a framework of two-state solution. Arab residents of Israel are relatives of Palestinians in the West Bank and Gaza.[27]

Israelis and Palestinians will need to create mechanisms for building peaceful relationships, which are critical for maintaining peace, order, and stability. The challenge necessitates multidimensional peacebuilding measures, including joint economic projects, education for peace and tolerance, and reconciliation. Let me demonstrate the challenge by focusing on certain aspects of these three dimensions:

1. Economic cooperation: Ordinary Palestinians and Israelis are struggling in their daily life. Palestinians are struggling to make a decent living and support their families in a difficult situation of developing their society, while Israelis are struggling under the burden of the high cost of living in Israel. Economic cooperation can benefit the two sides. For example, Israelis are interested in buying quality low-price goods, which Palestinians know how to manufacture and sell.

Creating Israeli-Palestinian free-trade zones can benefit the two sides.[28] Israelis, who are interested in buying quality goods at reasonable prices, can create a market for Palestinians who can manufacture quality goods at a low cost. The economic interests of the two sides can be a vehicle for peaceful relation building. For example, it can demonstrate to the people the interdependence of the two societies; it can assist in developing friendly relationships between adversaries (or more precisely former adversaries); and it has the potential of reducing hostility and the impact of prejudice on the attitude of people of the opposing sides toward each other.

2. Education: Hostile relationships between neighbors, which are destined to live side by side, are a proven recipe for clash. To live in a peaceful social order, the two sides—Israelis and Palestinians—will need to overcome classical symptoms of intractable conflict, such as chronic mistrust, prejudice, and dehumanization of the other. Education, in general, and peace education, in particular, can play an important role in coping with the challenge.

[27] See, for example, Handelman [11].

[28] Compare to https://truman.huji.ac.il/sites/default/files/truman/files/aix_group-summaries_lessons_learnt-final-24-9-2016-covertext.pdf p.10.

Education has a critical influence on worldview and the sociopolitical attitude of human beings, especially of the young generation. Israelis and Palestinians will need to do major reforms in their educational curriculum—such as stopping the incitement, teaching the very essence of tolerance and pluralism, and even teaching the other's culture and traditions. However, changing educational programs is not easy. The old system has its own dynamic evolution and protective mechanisms.

Observations show that in transition periods, between war and peace, educational systems, often enough, are transformed or more precisely revolutionized, by force. For example, after the Second World War, the Allied Forces forced major domestic reforms in the educational systems of Japan and Germany. They insisted that the new educational system be based on liberal values.[29] These paradoxical cases, where peace and liberal education were forced by coercive means, have a general lesson. They demonstrate that building the conditions for peace and stability, by establishing a new framework of rules and institutions, cannot be free from elements of force, power, and manipulation.[30] Good intentions are not enough.

3. Reconciliation: In the middle of the twentieth century, after the Second World War, it was almost impossible to imagine peace and reconciliation in Europe. About 50 years later, former entrenched enemies, such as Germany and France, established a confederation, the European Union. Today, it is almost impossible to imagine a violent conflict between members of the EU. It looks that there is a reconciliation in Europe. Is reconciliation possible in the Middle East? Is reconciliation possible between two national communities, Israelis and Palestinians, whose ethnic, religious, and cultural identities seem to be so different? Is reconciliation possible after about 120 years of intractable conflict that seems to have a life, dynamic, and evolution of its own?

Analyzing the situation in the light of Huntington's theory—the clash of civilization—leads to pessimism.[31] In this framework, the Israeli-Palestinian conflict is a point of clash between different cultural units (civilizations). Therefore, it is impossible to solve the conflict and reconcile between the parties. The old city of Jerusalem, which is extremely important to believers of different religions, demonstrates the problem.

In contrast to Huntington's theory, this paper suggests analyzing the situation from a different perspective. Huntington's theory globalizes the problem and calls it a symptom of "clash of civilizations," while our approach examines the conflict as a communal struggle—a conflict between two national communities. Our approach holds better chances of coping with a difficult situation. Huntington's theory offers despair in advance. Israelis and Palestinians cannot afford to be engaged in a cold peace. For peace and stability, it is mandatory to develop tools for reconciliation.

From a practical perspective, there are good reasons for optimism in this direction. Palestinians, who believe that the Arab states have part of the blame in their situation, see the deteriorating situation of the Arab world in contrast to the prosperity of the West and Israel. It is reasonable to assume that they have a desire (or, at least, a secret desire) to be part of the success. Israelis have aspired, for a long time, to become part of the new Middle East and stop being a fortified isolated castle. Peace and reconciliation between Israelis and Palestinians may open a gate to fulfill these aspirations.

---

[29] See, for example, Schaller [30] and Shillony [31].

[30] Cf. Handelman [11].

[31] Huntington [32].

There are grassroots initiatives that focus on reconciliation between the two parties.[32] These successful programs operate on a very minor scale. They need to expand, integrate into educational systems, and operate on a mass-scale level.

Intraparty. The focus on the internal situation within the opposing parties adds another important dimension to the struggle for building a momentum for a peace revolution. It suggests domestic reforms within the opposing societies, within the Israeli and the Palestinian societies, in order to create opportunities to resolve the struggle and to form a framework for a long-lasting stable peace. The idea of suggesting domestic reforms within each party draws on insights of constitutional economists, like James Buchanan [33], and political scientists, like Samuel Huntington [26]. These thinkers emphasized that an adequate framework of rules and institutions is a necessary condition for the evolutionary transition from social chaos to a peaceful social order.

In our context, domestic reforms that improve the internal cohesion of each society, the rule of law, and the accountability of political leaders may help the opposing populations to discover the value of peace, to start believing that it can be achieved, and to explore possibilities for reaching it. These necessary measures could potentially create an effective framework for a substantial peace process and reduce the impact of radicals, extremists, and spoilers. The "paradox of violence" can demonstrate the importance of reforming major elements within each of the opposing societies.[33]

A classical characteristic of intractable conflict is the paradox of violence—almost any progression toward a positive change is likely to cause a growth in the level of violence. It is possible to identify two main reasons for this observation. The first is spoilers—radical elements increase efforts to sabotage almost any kind of peace process by violent means. The second is internal tensions—any progress toward peace between opposing societies tends to increase tensions within each one of them. This symptom characterizes developing societies that lack sufficient instruments to cope with domestic tensions and disagreements by peaceful means. Let me elaborate on the second reason, which is more related to the focus of this section (domestic reforms in the conflicting societies).

A society is built of various elements, such as individuals, ethnic groups, economic corporations, religious congregations, and political associations. These different social elements do not necessarily hold similar priorities, preferences, and sociopolitical agenda. Intractable conflict is a unifying force. Opponents may collaborate in order to fight a joint enemy. However, as soon as there is progress toward peace, tensions within each of the conflicting parties appear and become a dominant factor. For example, the struggle against the Apartheid system in South Africa had unified the nonwhite people. This "unification" made the impression that the struggle is between the "black" population and the "white" one. However, the progress toward a new governmental system exposed the diversity within the "black" people and led to violent clashes within the nonwhite camp.[34]

Israeli academics have emphasized that the Palestinian authority is a developing entity.[35] It lacks instruments to cope with social crises that can follow transition from one sociopolitical order to another. The unilateral withdrawal of the Israeli forces from the Gaza Strip, led by the former Israeli Prime Minister Ariel Sharon in 2005, demonstrates the difficulties and the obstacles.

---

[32] For example, visit http://www.musalaha.org/.

[33] See Handelman [11].

[34] See, for example, Ottaway [34, 35].

[35] See, for example, Inbar [36].

Sharon's plan to withdraw Israeli troops, and about 8000 Jewish settlers, from Gaza and 4 small areas in the West Bank had a dramatic effect on the situation. Following the unilateral withdrawal, Israel—a modern country with established democratic institutions—survived the shock, but the Palestinian authority collapsed. The events that followed were a coup by Hamas in Gaza and a bloody civil war within the Palestinian society. Since then the Palestinian society is politically divided. The radical Islamic movement, Hamas, which is committed to radical Islamism, controls Gaza, while the secular nationalist movement Fatah, whose official agenda is building an independent Palestinian civil society based on the 1967 cease-fire line (two-state solution), administers the major parts of the West Bank.

Israeli scholars point out that the tragic situation in the Gaza case enfolds a general lesson—any intention to divide the land endangers the security of Israel. The Palestinian authority in the West Bank is a developing entity that lacks instruments to cope with social crises that can follow a transition from one sociopolitical order to another. There is a grave danger that any Israeli withdrawal from the West bank will lead to a repeat of the Gaza scenario—collapse of the Palestinian authority, radical elements, such as Hamas and the Islamic State of Iraq and Syria (ISIS), taking control and launching missiles at the center of Israel.[36]

In any framework of partition of the land between the two peoples, domestic reforms in the Palestinian society are a precondition to a successful peace process. For the sake of peace and stability, it is necessary for the Palestinians to establish the foundations of a modern independent state: building public institutions; creating a stable, efficient, and transparent administration; disarming violent groups; and developing all other mechanisms of a decent civil society.

The difficult task of creating the conditions for peace and stability requires preparing the opposing societies, Palestinians and Israelis, for coexistence in any possible framework. This means that domestic reforms in the Palestinian society are not enough to create a long-lasting change. There is a need for domestic reforms within the state of Israel, especially, in regard to the sensitive issue of "national identity" and its practical implications.

Israel is a multicultural society. The Israeli population includes a majority of Jewish citizens who came from different parts of the world and a large minority of non-Jewish citizens (about 20% Arabs). Nevertheless, Israel is considered a Jewish state. It is true that a major part of Arab-Israelis' integration in the Israeli society is expressed through participation of the Arab population in the democratic processes of Israel.[37] Nevertheless, the fact that a non-Jewish population belongs to a Jewish state holds many elements of exclusion. The politics of exclusion is expressed in many dimensions of Israeli social life. For example, in the psychological dimension, many Arab-Israelis see themselves as second-class citizens, and in the symbolic sphere, the national symbols of the country are taken from Jewish tradition.

According to pluralist perception, having a national home is a basic need. Human beings need a place that will accept them simply because they belong.[38] The non-Jewish citizens of Israel have a problem seeing the Jewish state as their national home. As Professor Joseph Agassi [38] noted, this problem has direct and indirect implications on the Israeli-Palestinian conflict.

---

36 Cf. Inbar [36].

37 See, for example, Landau [37].

38 In Robert Frost's words, "Home is the place where, when you go there, they have to take you in."

According to Agassi, establishing a stable decent Palestinian state will necessarily lead to tensions within Israel. The reason is that Arab-Israelis, who live in different parts of the country and have difficulties seeing the Jewish state as their national home, can see the new Palestinian state as their natural national homeland. The inevitable result, according to Agassi, is that they will aspire to live (on their land in Israel) under a Palestinian rule. Jewish Israelis are likely to object and reject such a drastic political motivation. The different motivations can lead to a dangerous clash.

Due to the situation of the Arab world, in general, and the Palestinian society in particular, the establishment of a decent and stable Palestinian state looks like a dream at this stage. However, Agassi's analysis enfolds a lesson—Israelis will have to think seriously about how to better integrate ethnic minorities in Israel. The existence of Arab citizens of Israel has many important effects upon the conduct of the country in general and its relations with Palestinians in the territories in particular.[39] Improved relationships between the Arab minority and the Jewish majority in Israel might pave the way for better relations with a future Palestinian polity and create direct and indirect opportunities for peacemaking. It can help the Jewish population in Israel to overcome the obsessive fear of losing the Jewish character of the state. The implications can be substantial and dramatic. For example, the people in Israel might overcome prejudice against Arabs, be more receptive to examine seriously creative solutions to the conflict, and even consider including Arab representatives in Israeli delegations for future negotiations.

3.1 Concluding remarks

Transition from one social order to another is difficult for almost any society. A transitional period for developing entities, which have hardly developed political and social mechanisms to cope with new challenges, can end in disaster. Huntington [26] pointed out that the lack of an effective framework of rules and institutions in changing societies can be used and abused by a new sociopolitical force to take control. The new political player who comes to power is not necessarily able to, interested to, or knowledgeable about how to establish a new sociopolitical order that can benefit the members of society.

The collapse of Gaza to the hand of the radical movement Hamas demonstrates the danger of drastic unilateral moves in the West Bank situation. Moreover, it shows that the three elements of peacebuilding (international support, relationship building, and domestic reforms) are intertwined. For example, it is quite clear that Palestinian domestic difficulties are not the only internal Palestinian problems. They are also an Israeli problem and a regional problem. It is in the best interests of Israelis, Egyptians, and Jordanians to help the Palestinians establish a viable stable polity that could fight the expansion of religious fanaticism.

The analysis of the peacebuilding challenge in the Israeli-Palestinian situation also demonstrates that peace revolution is a composite of peacemaking, peacebuilding, and peacekeeping. These elements are intertwined and need to be applied simultaneously. Peacebuilding measures (international support, relationship building, and domestic reforms) can help in providing a safety net for stability during a peacemaking process. It helps to guarantee that if the negotiation fails, the outcomes will not be disastrous as they have been in the past.

[39] Cf. Landau [37], who notes that many Arab-Israelis have family relatives among the Palestinians in the territories.

4. Peacekeeping

After the Second World War, peacekeeping was understood as division between entrenched enemies.[40] The guiding principle was "Good fences create good neighbors." The end of the Cold War and the growing numbers of intrastate struggles have led to alteration in this view of peacekeeping. The concept of peacekeeping was extended to cases where it is impossible to hermetically separate enemies.[41]

The unavoidable contact between Israelis and Palestinians shows that it is mandatory to design and implement a nontraditional peacekeeping strategy. A nontraditional strategy involves different societal elements—such as citizens, political leaders, and special security forces—in the efforts to maintain peace, order, and stability.

The challenge of peacekeeping is multidimensional. To simplify and demonstrate the need to design a multidimensional strategy to keep peace and stability, the paper suggests focusing on three levels of peacekeeping: political, military, and civilian: An Israeli-Palestinian Congress for Peace and Security can be a political institution for monitoring joint activities and coping with tensions, disputes, and ad hoc sociopolitical problems between the two sides. A joint border security force can be established to protect the east border of a new Palestinian state in the West Bank (the border between the new Palestine and Jordan in a framework of two-state solution). A joint civil guard can be established to help in keeping order and stability in places where Israeli and Palestinian civilians are in direct contact (**Table 4**).

Let me elaborate.

Politics. Peace revolution is a dynamic process, which has an evolutionary dynamic. Political instruments that were created to lead a change in the peacemaking phase need to be modified and changed in the peacekeeping stage. This evolutionary progression needs to be considered at the beginning of the process.

The peacemaking section of this paper proposes establishing a powerful instrument for the peacemaking part of a peace revolution—a major Israeli-Palestinian Public Negotiating Congress. The congress is a consensus-building institution that is planned to involve different societal elements of the conflicting societies (leaders, elites, and people) in the peace efforts. Its main tasks are to offer political alternatives to the violent struggle, prepare the publics for a change, and motivate the leaderships to reach agreements. However, once a peace agreement has been achieved, this peacemaking institution needs to be transformed, or it will become useless. The logic of the evolutionary progression of a peacemaking revolution proposes that a pubic negotiating congress—a major peacemaking institution—should be transformed into a major peacekeeping institution, which could be labeled as congress for peace and security.[42]

The inevitable friction between Israelis and Palestinians will require political instruments to cope with inevitable tensions, disagreements, and joint problems. In the post-conflict phase, a joint peacekeeping congress could deal with tensions, disputes, and ad hoc problems, initiate and coordinate joint projects in various fields (such as education, economics, and politics), and establish mechanisms for reconciliation.

Similar to the UN, which is the global peacekeeping institution, the main actual power of the peacekeeping congress (Israeli-Palestinian Congress for Peace and Security) is its very existence. In the peacemaking stage, a public negotiating congress involves the publics in the struggle for peace and generates public pressure

---

[40] See, for example, Snow [3].

[41] Ibid., 102–103.

[42] See, for example, Handelman [8, 11, 26, 36].

Level of operation	Goals	Mechanisms
Political	Coping with sociopolitical problems, coordinating joint activities, and monitoring shared mechanisms	Israeli-Palestinian Congress for Peace and Security
Military	Protecting the border between a new Palestinian state and Jordan	A joint border guard
Civilian and police	Coping with civilian problems and keeping law and order in friction points	Security cooperation and a joint civil guard

Table 4.
Peacekeeping in three dimensions.

to reach a settlement. In the post-conflict phase, the peacekeeping congress should remind everyone of the high cost of conflict and the precious value of peace.

A difficult question is how to start and build this institutional evolution (from peacemaking congress to a peacekeeping congress), which is so necessary for a peace revolution. Unfortunately, this critical discussion is not in scope of this paper.[43]

Military. In a framework of a "two-state solution," Israel demands that the new Palestinian state will be demilitarized. However, it is a joint interest of Israelis and Palestinians that the eastern border—the border between the new state of Palestine and Jordan—be protected from invasion of hostile forces (such as ISIS). Who will protect the border between Palestine and Jordan after Israel pulls back its military forces from the area?

In different rounds of the Minds of Peace Experiment (MOPE)—a small-scale Israeli-Palestinian public negotiating assembly, which was conducted in different locations with different delegations of Israelis and Palestinians—the delegations agreed on the creation of a joint Israeli-Palestinian security force that will operate in a security zone near the border.[44] This idea has different versions with different implications. For example, in some of the assemblies, the delegations agreed that the joint security force would become part of the IDF. In other assemblies, Palestinians were concerned that soldiers, with IDF uniforms, in Palestinian areas would remind the people of the occupation and the consequences could be harmful. To prevent such complications, the delegations in these assemblies agreed that the border guard unit would have their own special uniforms. In addition, it is worth considering that the border guard unit will be linked to Israel, Palestine, and the Israeli-Palestinian Congress for Peace and Security (which was, previously, proposed as a political peacekeeping institution). Of course, the details need to be discussed and negotiated by the two sides.

Another option which was raised by some scholars is that, eventually, the Palestinians will need to be in charge of protecting their border. They propose a two-stage process. In the first stage, an international force will protect the border and train a Palestinian border guard unit. In the second stage, the international force will leave, and the Palestinian force will take responsibility.[45]

---

43 The goal of the Minds of Peace project, which was briefly presented at the peacemaking section, is to begin such an evolutionary process. A detailed analysis of the initiative and other options to reach the same goal is beyond the focus of this paper.

44 For sample agreements that ordinary people have reached, visit http://mindsofpeace.org/category/agreements/ and http://mopdocuments.blogspot.com/.

45 Compare to https://www.fpa.org/usr_doc/Israel_and_Palestine_Two_States_for_Two_Peoples_2010.pdf pp./48–49.

It seems that the first proposal has better chances of being accepted by Israelis and Palestinians. It is hard to imagine Israelis and Palestinians agreeing that an international force, and later a new Palestinian security unit, will be in charge of their security. A joint Israeli-Palestinian border guard unit, as in the first proposal, can indirectly serve also as a peacebuilding instrument. Its cooperative feature can help to explore possibilities of improving the relations between Israelis and Palestinians.

Civilian and police. The security challenges in the making of a new social order are multidimensional. The interdependence between Israelis and Palestinians, which makes the security problem so difficult to handle, nevertheless holds peacebuilding opportunities. Let me demonstrate by focusing on the three main problems: order and stability within Palestinian territories, settlements, and holy places.

1. Order and stability within Palestine: As already mentioned, the Palestinian society is suffering from symptoms of a developing entity. Israelis, who object to the "two-state solution," claim that any attempt to implement this type of solution is doomed to fail and would endanger the security of Israel.[46] The fear is that a new Palestinian state in the West Bank will collapse into civil war similar to the Gaza crisis in 2008. Since civil wars usually end in the victory of one party and not power sharing,[47] the results can be a hostile regime (such as Hamas and ISIS) in the West Bank. That would be a serious security threat near Israeli towns.

Building a strong and efficient Palestinian police force is necessary to prevent this dangerous scenario. Israel can help in training the Palestinian police. The cooperation between security forces of the two sides, which works quite well in the West Bank, could be modified, tailored, and expanded for the new situation. In addition, a joint civil guard can be established in order to help in stabilizing a new social order.

2. Jewish settlements in the West Bank: Any form of solution, which is based on the establishment of a Palestinian state, has to cope with the presence of Jewish settlements (about 400,000 settlers) in the West Bank. The "optimal" solution to the problem is probably a mix of three options: (1) border modifications and land exchange: annexation of Jewish settlements to Israel and compensation to Palestinians in return; (2) evacuation of Jewish settlements; and (3) Jewish settlements in the West Bank will remain under Palestinian sovereignty.[48]

The settlements in the West Bank that cannot be annexed to Israel (option 1) and cannot be evacuated (option 2) will need to remain under Palestinian sovereignty (option 3). This will create major security problems. For example, who will solve disputes between Jewish neighbors? Should religious Jewish settlers call Palestinian police in such matters? Can a Palestinian police officer serve as a moderator in a dispute between religious Jews?

A joint Israeli-Palestinian civil guard can be helpful in such situations. It could assist in coping with such sensitive problems that are beyond the capacity of a

---

[46] Cf. Inbar [36].

[47] Cf. Toft [39].

[48] For different peace plans, see Golan [40].

regular police force. Of course, the two sides will need to discuss and negotiate the very essence of any joint civil guard. This project—the creation of a joint civil guard—has also peacebuilding implications. It can contribute to the transformation of hostile relationships between entrenched enemies who fight one another into cooperative relationships between neighbors who are trying to cope with joint problems.

3. The holy places in Jerusalem: The holy city of Jerusalem, the walled area, which is so important to believers of different religions, needs to be administered with much care, sophistication, and creativity. A joint civil guard, which will be subject to a joint municipality, can take into consideration the needs of those who care about the city. It can become a symbol of pluralism, tolerance, and peace.

4.1 Concluding remarks

This section suggests three peacekeeping mechanisms that operate in three intertwined dimensions: congress for peace and security (politics), a joint border guard (military), and a joint civil guard (civilian). It would be important, efficient, and beneficial that Israelis and Palestinians discuss and negotiate the structure, authority, and operation of any peacekeeping mechanism beginning as early as the peacemaking step. It could help avoid future complications when implementing any negotiated peace contract. Moreover, it could be a trust-building move that demonstrates to the people that any peace agreement would be signed and implemented only when mechanisms to keep security, order, and stability are established.[49]

5. Summary

Intractable conflict is a severe crisis. It is a longtime struggle where generations in turn are born into the reality of aggression, despair, and violence. The conflict seems to have a life of its own. It is like a disease that controls the body. A revolutionary process is needed to create a sustainable change.

Revolution is an "overthrow of an established social order" Friedrich ([41], 5). Peace revolution is a conclusive attack on the foundations and structure of the conflict and the sociopolitical destructive mechanisms that constantly feed it. Peace revolution is planned to involve, at least, three key elements of the opposing parties (leaders, elites, and people) in a change-building process that tackles the conflict from different levels, sides, and directions.

A revolutionary peace process needs to take into consideration that peace needs to be made, built, and kept. Peacemaking suggests diplomatic instruments to involve key social elements of the conflicting parties (leaders, elites, and people) in a multidimensional negotiation of a peace contract. Peacebuilding offers a program to construct a negotiated framework for a new social order, which copes with the needs, fears, and concerns of the conflicting factions. Peacekeeping advocates the creation of a multidimensional system of different operating mechanisms (political, militaristic. and civilian) to maintain law and order.

Distinguishing between the three elements of a peace revolution (peacemaking, peacebuilding and peacekeeping) is not always clear. Moreover, as this paper shows,

[49] Anwar Sadat, the former president of Egypt, in his historical speech in the Israeli Knesset, addressed, quite effectively, the pathological Israeli fear. To read the speech, visit https://ecf.org.il/media_items/833.

these elements are intertwined. It will be a mistake to concentrate on one element of the challenge of peace (such as peacemaking) without taking into account the others. It can lead to the same old familiar failures.

Intractable conflict, similar to almost all phenomena in the social sciences, is a complex phenomenon.[50] It is a composite of components, factors, and variables of different dimensions, such as psychology, economics, and religion. Peace revolutionaries need to take into account, as much as possible, the complexity of the situation and, accordingly, construct an innovative multidimensional approach to change. This is the main message of this paper.

Notes on contributor

Sapir Handelman is the co-laureate of the 2010 Peter Becker Award for Peace and Conflict Research. He is an associate professor (senior lecturer) and the head of the conflict studies division at Achva Academic College, Israel. Dr. Handelman founded and leads the Minds of Peace NGO, which is based on his concepts of conflict resolution in intractable conflicts.

[50] For a thoughtful discussion on the very essence of complex phenomena, see Hayek [42].

Author details

Sapir Handelman
Minds of Peace and Achva Academic College, Israel

*Address all correspondence to: sapir.handelman@gmail.com

References

[1] Galtung J. Peace, War and Defense: Essays in Peace Research I1. Copenhagen: Christian Ejlers; 1976

[2] Kelman H. Conflict resolution and reconciliation: A social-psychological perspective on ending violent conflict between identity groups. Landscapes of Violence. 2010;**1**(1):5. Available from: http://scholarworks.umass.edu/lov/vol1/iss

[3] Snow D. Cases in International Relation. 4th ed. New York: Pearson—Longman; 2010

[4] Popper K. Models, instruments and truth. In: Notturno M, editor. The Myth of the Framework: In Defense of Science and Rationality. London and New York: Routledge; 1994. pp. 154-185

[5] Fisher R. The potential for Peacebuilding: Forging a bridge from peacekeeping to Peacemaking. Peace & Change. 1993;**18**(3):247-266

[6] Handelman S. Peacemaking Contractualism: A Peacemaking approach to cope with difficult situations of intractable conflict. Global Change, Peace & Security. 2016;**28**(1):123-144

[7] Ratner S. The New UN Peacekeeping: Building Peace in Lands of Conflicts after the Cold War. New York: St. Martin's Press; 1996

[8] James A. Peacekeeping in International Politics. New York: St. Martin's Press; 1990

[9] Handelman S, Chowdhury J. The limits of political-elite diplomacy: Leaders, people and social conflicts. Israel Affairs. 2017;**23**(3):465-495

[10] Handelman S. Two complementary views of Peacemaking: The Palestinian-Israeli case. Middle East Policy. 2008;**15**(3):57-66

[11] Handelman S. Conflict and Peacemaking in Israel-Palestine: Theory and Application. London and New York: Routledge; 2011

[12] Agassi J. Liberal Nationalism for Israel: Towards an Israeli National Identity. Jerusalem and New York: Gefen Pub. House; 1999

[13] Kelman H. Social-psychological dimensions of international conflict. In: Zartman W, editor. Peacemaking in International Conflict: Methods & Techniques (Rev. Ed.). Washington, DC: U.S. Institute of Peace; 2007a

[14] Kelman H. The Israeli-Palestinian peace process and its vicissitudes: Insights from attitude theory. American Psychologist. 2007b;**63**(4):287-303

[15] Bronfenbrenner U. The Mirror image in soviet-American relations: A social Psychologist's report. Journal of Social Issues. 1961;**17**:45-56

[16] Kelman H. Negotiation as interactive problem solving. International Negotiation: A Journal of Theory and Practice. 1996;**1**(1):99-123

[17] Gifford M. Managing Public Diplomacy. The Washington Quarterly. 1985;**8**(3):199-213

[18] Handelman S. Two complementary settings of Peacemaking diplomacy: Political-elite diplomacy and public diplomacy. Diplomacy & Statecraft. 2012c;**23**(1):162-178

[19] Sparks A. Tomorrow Is another Country: The Inside Story of South Africa's Negotiated Revolution. Sandton, South Africa: Struik Book Distributors; 1994

[20] Mitchell G. Making Peace. New York, NY: Alfred A. Knopf; 1999

[21] Handelman S, Pearson F. Peacemaking in intractable conflict – A Contractualist approach. International Negotiation. 2014;**19**:1-34

[22] Handelman S. People-to-People Diplomacy in Israel and Palestine: The Minds of Peace Experiment. London and New York: Routledge; 2014

[23] Handelman S. The minds of peace experiment: A laboratory for people-to-people diplomacy. Israel Affairs. 2012a;**18**(1):1-11

[24] Gilboa E. Searching for a theory of public diplomacy. The Annals of the American Academy of Political and Social Science. 2008;**616**(March): 55-77

[25] Soroka S. Media, public opinion and foreign policy. Harvard International Journal of Press and Politics. 2003;**8**(1):27-48

[26] Huntington S. Political Order in Changing Societies. New Haven, CT: Yale University Press; 1968

[27] Mandela N. Long Walk to Freedom: The Autobiography of Nelson Mandela. Boston: Little, Brown and Company; 1994

[28] Popper K. The Poverty of Historicism. London: Routledge; 2002

[29] Hassner RE. "To halve and to hold": Conflicts over sacred space and the problem of indivisibility. Security Studies. 2003;**12**(4):1-33

[30] Schaller M. The American Occupation of Japan: The Origins of the Cold War in Asia. New York: Oxford University Press; 1985

[31] Shillony B-A. Politics and Culture in Wartime Japan. Oxford: Oxford Clarendon Press; 1981

[32] Huntington S. The clash of civilizations? Foreign Affairs. 1993;**72**(3):22-49

[33] Buchanan J. Moral Science and Moral Order. Vol. 17 of the Collected Works of James M. Buchanan. Indianapolis: Liberty Fund; 2001

[34] Ottaway M. South Africa: The Struggle for a New Order. Washington D.C.: The Brookings Institution; 1993

[35] Pearson F. Cultural factors in Peacemaking: The Israeli-Palestinian context. Israel Affairs. 2017;**23**(3): 525-544

[36] Inbar E. Israel's Palestinian challenge. Israel Affairs. 2006;**12**(4):823-842

[37] Landau S. Settings, factors and phenomena of conflict in Israeli society. In: Albrecht HJ, Simon JM, Rezaei H, Rohne HC, Kiza E, editors. Conflicts and Conflict Resolution in Middle Eastern Societies – Between Tradition and Modernity. Berlin: Duncker & Humbolt; 2006. pp. 257-274

[38] Agha H et al. Trach-II Diplomacy: Lesson from the Middle East. Cambridge, MA: MIT Press; 2004

[39] Toft M. Ending civil wars: A case for rebel victory? International Security. 2010;**34**(4):7-36

[40] Golan G. Israel and Palestine: Peace Plans and Proposals from Oslo to Disengagement. Princeton: Markus Wiener Publishers; 2006

[41] Friedrich C, editor. Revolution. New York: Atherton Press; 1966

[42] Hayek F. Studies in Philosophy, Politics and Economics. Chicago: The University of Chicago Press; 1967

Chapter 16

Approaches to Analysis of Interstate Cooperation

Alexander Rozanov, Maria Ivanchenko, Alexandra Baranova, Elena N. Antonova, Mikhail Smirnov, Olga Belyaeva, Maria Ilicheva, Ludmila Ilicheva, Maria Krotovskaya, Tatiana Grabovich, Zaru Utekova, Dmitry Medvedev, Natalya Ogneva, Furat Al-Mutairi, Elvira Shishlo, Amina Surpkelova, Irina Kopachevskaya, Irina Sokurova, Yulia Borisova, Fernando Joao, Artyom Pakulskikh, Polina Chernova, Alexandra Khramova, Oksana Gryuk, Jesus Yaniz Gonzalez, Valentina Komleva, Alina Papsheva and Arkadi Bessonov

Abstract

At the present day cultural diplomacy plays a rather important role in the development of international relations and world politics. This concept is receiving increasing attention from various countries, international and non-governmental organizations and other actors. This trend exists due to a number of reasons, such as the desire of states to create a positive image of their country, the expansion of international cooperation, changes in the global and domestic political situation, the protection of national interests, the prevention of conflicts between states, etc. Cultural diplomacy, beyond historical precedents, consists of a relatively new practice of a country's foreign policy, which has traditionally focused on trade and security and defense issues. It is true that in European countries there are institutions of cultural foreign relations since the beginning of the century, but in the last decade the issues, related to the projection of the international image of countries, have become more important.

Keywords: cultural diplomacy, soft power, peace

1. Introduction

Currently, in the international system, cooperation as a form of interstate relations is implemented more often than conflict. However, their practical aspects have been little conceptualized in international relations, especially in the context of the fact that these forms are categories of dialectics. In this regard, in order to determine the role of inter-state cooperation in international relations, it is necessary to correlate cooperation with its paired category.

D. Shevchuk notes that "conflicts and cooperation are among the most significant characteristics of international relations, considered as a process, and are inextricably linked sides of interaction between their participants [1]. In the language of Friedrich Hegel and Karl Marx [2–4], they are a "dialectical pair" - that is, mutually presupposing and mutually determining opposites that can "change places".

In the theory of interstate cooperation and conflict, there are two directions: "liberalism" and "realism". The development of the liberalist concept took place until the mid-30s of the last century, after this concept was replaced by the concept of realism, which operated until the 70s.

Prior to this period, the problems of cooperation were secondary to the problems of conflict. Thus, the theory of cooperation was based on the theory of conflict. In accordance with this, starting from the 50s, such a direction of the theory of inter-state relations as conflictology began to be formed, bringing the theory of inter-state conflict into an independent direction.

But the same could not be said about the theory of interstate cooperation, which for a long time remained unnoticed by researchers in the field of international relations. The main focus of research in this area was the study of military-political unions as a form of interstate cooperation.

However, since the 60s, the need to study the problems of interstate cooperation has gradually come to the fore. During this period, issues of integration processes, which were considered as a form of interstate cooperation, become relevant. Already in the 80's, cooperation became an independent direction in the theory of international relations, as well as the direction of conflictology.

The prerequisites for studying interstate cooperation are the need for answers to such questions as internal reasons for the formation of cooperation, obstacles to the development of cooperation in the international environment, types and forms of cooperation, and many others.

At the same time, translation as a fundamental component of collaboration becomes an important issue for researchers. As a result, a fairly large amount of material has been generated for the study of problems and models of interstate cooperation.

The classical dialectic between realistic and liberal theories of international politics, expressed by R. Keohane and R. Rosecrance, can be overcome [5]. Neither paradigm explains the only correct international behavior. While realism is the dominant approach, liberal theories of transnationalism and interdependence help illuminate how national interests are being studied and changed.

Cohen and his fellow critics argue that neorealism, formulated definitively in the" Theory of international politics " by K. Waltz, systematizes the concepts of realism, but focuses on the structure of the international system at the expense of systemic processes. Focused on the concept of bipolarity, Waltz's theory tends to be consistent [6].

At the same time, it is important to note that realism and neorealism deny the very possibility of cooperation in interstate interaction. K. Waltz notes that "States, when planning or implementing their foreign policy, strive to maximize relative benefits, i.e., seek to acquire more opportunities than their partners."

Classical realists also focus more on human nature. They believe that people are generally selfish and aggressive. The main actors in the international system, States, are guided by these principles, which leads to the inevitability of conflicts.

In turn, neorealists are more focused on the distribution of power in the international system. The theory is based on the claim that the international system does not have a sovereign power that could conclude and enforce binding agreements. Without such power, States are given the opportunity to do what they like, which ultimately prevents States from trusting each other and, as a result, effectively cooperating.

This situation is further reinforced by the realistic assumption that the main goal of the state is to maximize power and security. Therefore, without a global center of power and influence that would keep States aspiring to power, it is difficult to prevent international conflicts.

This is why realists view international relations as a constant battle and struggle for survival. Even if some States do not try to increase their power and are happy with the way things are going, they cannot trust other States to think the same way. If another state suddenly decides to stop cooperation, the security of the first state will be under serious threat. Because all States know this, they all try to protect themselves by seeking control, building up their military capabilities, and forming alliances with other States. This, in turn, leads to another realistic concept-the security dilemma.

The security dilemma is that under conditions of uncertainty and limited rationality, perceived external threats (real or imagined) create a sense of insecurity in those States that consider themselves the targets of such threats, which encourages these States to take measures to increase their strength and ability to counter these threats (creating alliances, building up weapons, etc.).

Therefore, if one state registers that another state is suddenly increasing its military power, it will assume that it is going to attack, even if it is not. A state that believes it is under threat will also have to increase its military strength, which in turn will cause alarm to the primary state, and this spiral may continue for a long time.

This is an infinite situation, and that is why realists believe that cooperation is not only difficult, but at the very least impossible. The security dilemma arises from fear between States. Many of these States lack contact with each other, which ultimately leads to a lack of trust.

In order to move to interstate cooperation, the security dilemma between the two countries must not only stop growing, but also "turn around" in the opposite direction, the result of which will be that States can trust each other. However, even if States agree to certain international agreements on armaments, nothing will prevent one of them from violating the agreement, which still does not exclude a security threat.

Nevertheless, there is some disagreement among realists about this. While "offensive" realism asserts that States must always act aggressively to survive, because the international system encourages conflict and the inevitability of war, "defensive" realism is less negative. Its representatives believe that cooperation or conflict depends on the situation. For example, if two States have the same mindset and share the same views, they are more likely to cooperate.

The reason for this may be a better understanding between countries such as Germany and France, which share the same views and thus trust each other more. Therefore, the international system does not necessarily generate conflict.

Thus, first of all, realism ignores the importance of different concepts of identity and culture in different States. For example, districts with the same religion and culture are more likely to cooperate with each other. Realism has been sharply criticized for exaggerating the importance of States and for not taking into account other actors, such as various non-governmental organizations.

The opponents of realism are the theory of liberalism or institutionalism. Liberalism began to take shape immediately after the end of the First world war. Europe was so shaken by what had happened that politicians wanted to find a way to prevent any future wars.

The reason why liberal views have become more popular since the cold war is that States have begun to adopt international laws, arms control has increased significantly, as well as the role of international organizations has increased, and the movement towards democratic principles has begun in many States.

Unlike classical realists, liberals believe that human nature is such that people are able to restrain aggression. Their main assumption is that war is not inevitable, and there is much more scope for inter-state cooperation if anarchic factors are neutralized. This will lead to global changes.

The main obstacle to cooperation is the lack of a sufficient number of international institutions. According to liberalists, if the world created international organizations that promoted peaceful change, disarmament and the implementation of international laws, cooperation would be much easier to achieve.

If necessary, these international organizations can use law enforcement against States. States that are bound by rules and regulations created by institutions will have no choice but to cooperate. In the globalized world in which the international system now finds itself, new actors, such as transnational corporations and non-governmental organizations, will promote interdependence and integration among States, which in turn will lead to a peaceful international environment.

Another obstacle to cooperation is the huge deficit of democracy at the global level. Liberals believe that democratic States act peacefully towards each other, and most of the conflicts and threats in the world come from non-democratic States.

Another explanation may be that democratic States are aware that cooperation with other countries is beneficial to them. This is particularly valuable from an economic point of view, especially in a globalized world and in a free trade system. Organizations such as the WTO promote free markets, and States use this to improve their economic efficiency.

Neoliberalism became an extension of liberalism. In turn, the argument of R. Rosecrans, a proponent of neoliberalism, consists in the statement that an open trading system offers States maneuverability due to economic growth, and not military intervention. He softens his argument with realistic considerations of blasphemy, but cannot clarify the realist-liberal connections in his theory or fully explore the connections between power and non-power incentives that influence the behavior of States.

The synthesis of neorealism and neoliberalism is justified: the system theory uses the former for analysis at the level of structure, and the latter for analysis at the level of process. In the study of international relations, neoliberalism refers to a school of thought that believes that States should strive to extract absolute, rather than relative, gains in relation to other States.

At the same time, neoliberal thinkers of international relations often use game theory to explain why States cooperate or do not cooperate. Since their approach emphasizes the possibility of mutual benefits, they are interested in institutions that can negotiate mutually beneficial agreements and compromises.

As a result, neoliberalism is a response to neorealism, while not denying the anarchic nature of the international system, neoliberals claim that its importance and effect have been exaggerated. The neoliberal argument focuses on the alleged underestimation by neorealists of the varieties of cooperative behavior possible in a decentralized system.

Neoliberalism asserts that even in an anarchic system of Autonomous rational States, cooperation can arise through the cultivation of mutual trust and the creation of norms, rules and institutions.

From the point of view of the field of international relations theory and foreign interventionism, the debate between neoliberalism and neorealism is intra-paradigm, since both theories are positivist and focus mainly on the state system as the main unit of analysis.

In addition, neoliberalists note that with the development of democracy in countries, the concept of neorealism is increasingly losing relevance. Thus, Y. V. Borovsky and P. A. Gvozdev note that "the democratic world" completely removes "military and political restrictions for the expansion of diverse interstate cooperation, integration and the formation of international institutions" ([7], p. 127).

Thus, neorealism denies the very need for inter-state cooperation, and neoliberalism finds more and more grounds for developing cooperation.

Considering the dialectical relationship between conflict and cooperation, it is also important to introduce concepts such as the concept of "hard power" and the concept of "soft power", which determine the very possibility of cooperation.

"Hard power" includes military interventions, coercive diplomacy, and economic sanctions, and relies on such material resources as the armed forces and economic resources." Accordingly, when implementing the "hard power" policy, it is impossible to talk about the possibility of interstate cooperation.

On the contrary, the implementation of the "soft power" policy creates a space for interstate cooperation. The concept of "soft power ""implies complete subordination of the object, but not out of fear, but out of the confidence that the subject is completely right and his attitudes are a good alternative, or the only correct ones" [8, 9].

J. Nye emphasized that soft power is based on the attractiveness of certain States to other participants in international relations [10].

Thus, the implementation of the policy of "soft power" allows the state to dominate, while not destroying the possibility of forming interstate cooperation.

In general, the theory of international relations has various definitions of interstate cooperation, which come down to the general formulation that inter-state cooperation is considered as a situation "when some actors regulate their behavior in accordance with the actual or expected preferences of others through a process of [mutual] policy coordination" [11].

Thus, according to this definition, inter-state cooperation involves the interaction of States within the framework of coordinating their policies in accordance with the goal that unites them. At the same time, an important parameter in their interaction is the possibility of obtaining mutual benefits from the cooperation process. Similarly, the inability of one of the partner States to obtain benefits calls into question the possibility of implementing the cooperation process itself.

In contrast to conflict, when the parties seek to reduce the benefits of the opposite side, cooperation involves the search for mutually reinforcing benefits, as a solid basis for partnership on any issues important to both sides. In this regard, it is important to note that cooperation is always, at least, bilateral, in which the parties try to take into account the interests of the other party and avoid negative consequences for any of the parties.

Thus, cooperation is based on cooperation, in which the parties try to reach an optimal consensus that provides benefits for the parties to cooperation. At the same time, R. G. Mumladze notes that "interstate regulation of international relations is a set of obligations voluntarily assumed by various countries and General rules of action in the sphere of world economic relations" [12].

Accordingly, inter-state cooperation is described in the categories of obligations assumed by States within the established General rules of action. An international Treaty is a form of General rules and specification of States 'obligations in the framework of cooperation. According to V. Vezhnovets and A. Borodich, the international Treaty "as the main source of international law, plays a key role in the development of interstate cooperation across the entire spectrum of international relations, both in bilateral and multilateral formats" [13].

In order to reveal the concepts of interstate cooperation, it is important to consider the conditions under which it can be implemented. Within this framework, E. Milner introduces a number of hypothetical conditions for the implementation of interstate cooperation.

It is useful to classify the conditions for interstate cooperation:

1. the "reciprocity hypothesis". This hypothesis is based on the possibility of implementing equal opportunities for partner States, both in obtaining benefits from cooperation, and in incurring losses or receiving penalties for failure to fulfill their obligations under concluded international treaties.

2. "Hypothesis about the number of actors". This hypothesis is related to the statement that the more actors involved in the cooperation process, the less benefits each of the partner States can receive from this cooperation. And, accordingly, on the contrary, reducing the number of actors expands the prospects for cooperation for the interacting parties in cooperation.

3. "the hypothesis of the iteration". This hypothesis is based on the statement that the longer the relationship exists between States, the more likely they are to enter the stage of cooperation. Due to the fact that iteration involves repeating something many times, in this case we mean the repeated repetition of successful experiences of cooperation between specific States. If there is not enough experience, the probability of successful inter-state cooperation is sharply reduced.

4. hypothesis of international regimes". This hypothesis presupposes the expectation that partner States have similar principles and rules for decision-making. The regime presupposes a set of norms, principles, and rules of decision-making in the field of establishing international relations. It is the international regime is a regulatory basis for the solution of international conflicts and the implementation of inter-state cooperation.

Central to regime theory is the thesis of" hegemonic stability", according to which regimes were created and protected by the dominant powers.

5. "Hypothesis of epistemic communities". This hypothesis suggests the development of self-organizing expert communities, which are based on collective values, are able to influence the adoption of economic and political decisions.

6. "the hypothesis of power asymmetry". This hypothesis assumes that States are unequal in relation to power and cooperation is most likely if one of the States has a strong influence in international politics, which will eventually contribute to achieving stability.

In revealing the power asymmetry hypothesis, it is necessary to affirm that States are extremely unequal in terms of the power they wield and their influence in world Affairs, but they are equal before the law and in terms of their rights and obligations. In particular, the principle of "one country, one vote" should theoretically equalize all members of international organizations.

Another important aspect of inter-state cooperation is the need to ensure collective security. "Collective security refers to an order of inter-state cooperation in which any act of aggression against any of the participants in such a system is regarded as aggression against all other participants."

Another important aspect is the need to ensure mutually beneficial economic interaction between States. At the same time, "a country's foreign economic relations are a whole area that includes various forms of international cooperation with other countries and international organizations."

The specifics of interstate cooperation at the current stage of development of international relations is the active participation of international and transnational organizations that determine the rules for forming and conducting cooperation within the framework of international law.

Thus, "in modern international relations, an important role belongs to international organizations as one of the organizational and legal forms of international (interstate) cooperation".

At the same time, the role of intergovernmental organizations is being strengthened. Thus, "the infrastructure of the modern international system is also formed by intergovernmental organizations and other formats of multilateral interaction of States" [14].

2. Results

The current state and dynamics of development of interstate cooperation processes are determined by international and domestic processes that have transformed the spheres of international politics and economy over the past 50 years.

Firstly, with the collapse of the international order that emerged after World War II, the need to develop new agreements on cooperation between states has significantly increased. Although cooperation is not always mutually beneficial, attempts by states to reduce the negative impact of their political decisions on each other can lead to an overall increase in their well-being.

Secondly, from the concepts of "transnationalism" and "interdependence", in the context of which neorealist propositions became widespread in the 1970s and 80s, scientists came to the concept of globalization, which implies not only the traditional consideration of the international system as anarchic, but also the transformation of the principle of political territoriality, on which international relations were traditionally based on.

Thirdly, it is necessary to recognize the general decline of the traditional system of diplomacy. On the one hand, professional diplomacy is giving way to political support, 'loud' diplomacy and diplomacy of insults. On the other hand, professional diplomacy is being transformed into international technical management.

The development and existence of a state as a subject of international relations and international law cannot take place without external relations with other subjects of international law. The need for external relations requires the organization of an apparatus for the implementation of such relations and the regulation of these relations by means of international law.

3. Discussion of results

The problems of world politics, international relations, and everything that happens in the international arena have always been at the center of attention of journalists, politicians, analysts, and society as a whole. Aspects that are directly related to the search for means that will allow us to approach the implementation of foreign policy decisions or how to do it-in other words, aspects of diplomacy – were of interest, rather, to a narrower circle. The reasons for this attitude to diplomacy are understandable and partly justified. First of all, it is necessary to understand what is happening, outline the main foreign policy priorities and approaches, and then only look for ways to implement them.

Today, diplomacy is largely multi-party in nature and simultaneously involves the participation of more than two parties in solving and discussing problematic issues. This is due to the fact that the globalization of the modern world affects the interests of many parties at once.

Multilateral negotiation and multilateral diplomacy give rise to new opportunities but at the same time and difficulties in the bilateral environment. For example, an increase in the number of parties when discussing a problem situation leads to a more complex overall structure of interests, the formation of coalitions, and the appearance of leading States in negotiating forums. In addition, a large number of procedural, organizational and technical problems arise in multilateral negotiations, namely: the need to agree on the venue; the agenda, decision-making and decision-making; and the chairmanship of forums; accommodation of delegations, etc. All this, in turn, contributes to the bureaucratization of negotiation processes.

It is also necessary to note other features of modern diplomacy, which are due to current trends in global political progress. The interdependence of the world and globalization have increased the importance of diplomacy, which is carried out at the highest and highest levels, as it provides an opportunity for "broad linkages" between different aspects. It is also necessary to take into account the fact that agreements signed by top officials of countries provide additional guarantees for their implementation. In addition, at these meetings, heads of state have the opportunity to quickly get the necessary information "first-hand" and exchange views.

In addition, diplomacy at the highest and highest levels has a downside. First of all, the scale of decisions made dramatically increases the degree of responsibility for them, and, accordingly, the price of a possible error. This problem is particularly acute in crisis situations. In addition, it should be borne in mind that if agreements that were reached at the highest or high levels are suddenly considered erroneous after they are signed, it is much more difficult to abandon them than those signed similarly at a lower level, because in this situation, the country's officials are discredited.

Another limitation of diplomacy at the highest and highest levels is that it is largely determined by personal antipathies and sympathies, and this has an impact on foreign policy decisions. In addition, it should be borne in mind that diplomacy at the highest and highest levels can only be effective if it is well prepared. In other words, the participants of these meetings may be "hostages" of the public's hopes for a quick solution to the problem situation and take unjustified steps. It is for this reason that G. Nickolson was quite reserved about top-level and high-level diplomacy [13]. He believed that there were situations when the foreign Minister or the head of the Cabinet should be present at important conferences, but their private mutual visits should not be too encouraged. These visits, he wrote, raise hopes, lead to misunderstandings, and often create confusion.

In modern diplomacy, the emphasis is not just on refusing outright deception. The informative and communicative function of diplomacy is primarily aimed at forming a dialog.

A bilateral dialog is a recognition that the other side has its own goals and interests. This is not only natural and natural, but also a productive factor in terms of the progress of relations. It follows that the main function of communication and information is not the Directive imposition of one's own point of view, but the desire to seek a mutually acceptable solution to problems through dialog.

The ideas of progress in the inter-state dialog are also reflected in theoretical works on negotiations. The concept of hard bargaining, when each participant was concerned only with their own interests and presents their position as extremely closed, is replaced by the concept of joint analysis of the problem with the partner. It implies a focus on mutual satisfaction of interests and an open nature of negotiation processes.

The focus on dialog in the modern world is conditioned by the need to seek solutions to emerging problems related to the fight against terrorism, the environment, the development of integration processes, conflict resolution, etc. through joint efforts. As a result, solving international problems objectively becomes the main function of diplomacy.

Author details

Alexander Rozanov[1*], Maria Ivanchenko[1], Alexandra Baranova[2], Elena N. Antonova[3], Mikhail Smirnov[2], Olga Belyaeva[2], Maria Ilicheva[4], Ludmila Ilicheva[2], Maria Krotovskaya[2], Tatiana Grabovich[3], Zaru Utekova[5], Dmitry Medvedev[6], Natalya Ogneva[7], Furat Al-Mutairi[1], Elvira Shishlo[2], Amina Surpkelova[2], Irina Kopachevskaya[2], Irina Sokurova[2], Yulia Borisova[2], Fernando Joao[1], Artyom Pakulskikh[1], Polina Chernova[1], Alexandra Khramova[8], Oksana Gryuk[9], Jesus Yaniz Gonzalez[2], Valentina Komleva[2], Alina Papsheva[2] and Arkadi Bessonov[2]

1 NUST MISIS, Moscow, Russian Federation

2 Russian Academy of National Economy and Public Administration, Moscow, Russian Federation

3 MGIMO University, Moscow, Russian Federation

4 All-Russian Academy of Foreign Trade, Moscow, Russian Federation

5 Lomonosov Moscow State University, Moscow, Russian Federation

6 Gubkin Russian State University of Oil and Gas, Moscow, Russian Federation

7 Immanuel Kant Baltic Federal University, Kaliningrad, Russian Federation

8 MSU, Moscow, Russian Federation

9 Technical School of The Ministry of Labor and Social Protection, Russian Federation

*Address all correspondence to: rozanov-88@list.ru

References

[1] Shevchuk D. World Economics. – Litres, Moscow, 2017. – 982 p.

[2] Eliküçük Yıldırım, N., & Aslan, M. (2020). China's Charm Defensive: Image Protection by Acquiring Mass Entertainment. Pacific Focus, 35(1), 141-171.

[3] Hegel, Georg Wilhelm Friedrich (1895). Vorlesungen über die Philosophie der Religion. London: Kegan Paul, Trench, Trübner & Co. Eng. tr. E.B. Speirs and J. Burdon Sanderson as Lectures on the Philosophy of Religion, New York: Humanities Press, 1974. pp. 56-58.

[4] Karl Marx (1997). 'Capital II: The Process of Circulation of Capital' embodying the whole volume of the *Collected Works of Karl Marx and Frederick Engels: Volume 36*. - International Publishers: New York. – P. 867

[5] Keohane, Robert O. (2020) Understanding Multilateral Institutions in Easy and Hard Times". *Annual Review of Political Science*. 23: 1-18.

[6] Waltz Kenneth N. Theory of International Politics - Addison-Wesley Publishing, 1979. — 256 p.

[7] Borovsky Yu. V., Gvozdev P. A. Realism in polemics with neoliberalism: the main points of discussion at the turn of the century/Yu. V. Borovsky, p. A. Gvozdev//Bulletin of MGIMO University, 2015, Pp. 126-135.

[8] Hegel, Georg Wilhelm Friedrich (2010). The science of logic. Ed. by Di Giovanni George. - Cambridge: Cambridge University Press. p. 751.

[9] Soft Power and US Foreign Policy: Theoretical, Historical and Contemporary Perspectives, ed. Inderjeet Parmar and Michael Cox, Routledge, 2010.

[10] Nye, Joseph S. (2011). The Future of Power. New York: Public-Affairs. p. 84.

[11] Bakhmetev, A. R. Cultural diplomacy as a phenomenon of modern politics (on the example of the European Union)/A. R. Bakhmetev. - Young scientist. — 2019. — № 17 (255).

[12] Mumladze R. G. World economy. Regional trend. Investment processes: textbook-Moscow: Rusains, 2016. - P. 272

[13] Vezhnovets V., Borodich A. An international negotiation process. - Moscow: Liters Publishing House, 2016. - P. 339

[14] Hunter Alan. Soft Power: China on the Global Stage//Chinese Journal of International Politics. — 2009. —Vol. 2. — P. 378—389.